The South Carolina historical and genealogical magazine

South Carolina Historical Society

THE
SOUTH CAROLINA
HISTORICAL AND GENEALOGICAL
MAGAZINE

PUBLISHED QUARTERLY BY THE
SOUTH CAROLINA HISTORICAL SOCIETY

EDITED BY
MABEL LOUISE WEBBER

VOLUME XIII.

PRINTED FOR THE SOCIETY BY
WALKER, EVANS & COGSWELL CO.
CHARLESTON, S. C.
1912

OFFICERS

OF THE

SOUTH CAROLINA HISTORICAL SOCIETY,

MAY 19, 1911—MAY 19, 1912

President,

HON. JOSEPH W. BARNWELL.

1st Vice-President,

HENRY A M SMITH, ESQ

2nd Vice-President,

HON THEODORE D JERVEY

3d Vice-President

HON F H WESTON

4th Vice-President,

HON JOHN B CLEVELAND

Secretary and Treasurer and Librarian,

MISS MABEL LOUISE WEBBER

Curators

LANGDON CHEVES, ESQ ,   D E HUGER SMITH, ESQ ,

CHARLES W KOLLOCK, M D ,

PROF YATES SNOWDEN,   CAPT THOMAS PINCKNEY,

PROF C J COLCOCK,   HON. C A WOODS,

A. S SALLEY, JR , ESQ ,   G M. PINCKNEY, ESQ.

Board of Managers,

ALL OF THE FOREGOING OFFICERS

Publication Committee,

HENRY A. M. SMITH,   JOSEPH W BARNWELL,

A S SALLEY, JR

THE

SOUTH CAROLINA

HISTORICAL AND GENEALOGICAL

MAGAZINE

PUBLISHED QUARTERLY BY THE

SOUTH CAROLINA HISTORICAL SOCIETY

CHARLESTON, S. C.

VOLUME XIII., NO. 1.   JANUARY 1912.

Entered at the Post-office at Charleston, S. C., as
Second-Class Matter.

PRINTED FOR THE SOCIETY BY
WALKER, EVANS & COGSWELL CO.
CHARLESTON, S. C.
1912

PUBLICATION COMMITTEE.

JOSEPH W. BARNWELL,   HENRY A. M. SMITH,
                A. S. SALLEY, JR.

EDITOR OF THE MAGAZINE
MABEL L WEBBER

CONTENTS.

PUBLICATION COMMITTEE.

JOSEPH W. BARNWELL,   HENRY A. M. SMITH,
          A. S. SALLEY, JR.

EDITOR OF THE MAGAZINE
MABEL L WEBBER

CONTENTS.

N. B.—These Magazines, with the exception of No. 1 of Vol. I and No. 4 of Vol XI, are $1.25 each to any one other than a member of the South Carolina Historical Society. Members of the Society receive them free. The Membership fee is $4 00 per annum (the fiscal year being from May 19th to May 19th), and members can buy back numbers or duplicates at $1 00 each In addition to receiving the Magazines, members are allowed a discount of 25 per cent on all other publications of the Society, and have the free use of the Society's library.

Any member who has not received the last number will please notify the Secretary and Treasurer,

Miss Mabel L. Webber,
South Carolina Historical Society,
Charleston, S C

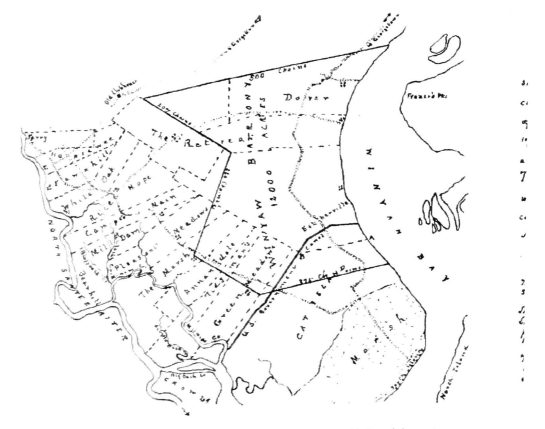

Reduced to one-third less than orig

Charleston, S. C

The South Carolina Historical and Genealogical Magazine.

VOL XIII   JANUARY 1912   No 1

THE BARONIES OF SOUTH CAROLINA.

By Henry A M Smith

VI

WINYAH BARONY

The Winyah Barony derives its name from its situation on the shore of the large bay of that name which lies between the Town of Georgetown and the sea   The name. Winyah—variously spelled Winyaw, Win-e-au. Wee-nee-a, Wyneah—was the Indian name given to that body of water, and it would appear also to the locality.   There was also a tribe or sub-tribe of Indians, called "Winyahs" The barony was originally laid out to Landgrave Robert Daniell as part of his patent, entitling him to 48,000 acres

Robert Daniell first appears on the record on 3ᵈ June, 1678. when a warrant was issued to survey out a lot in Charles Town for him[1] On 4ᵗʰ April, 1679, he appears as sailing from Barbados for Carolina,[2] and on the same boat there also sailed to Carolina Thomas Drayton, Jʳ and Stephen Fox On 15ᵗʰ December, 1680,[3] and on 10ᵗʰ May, 1682,[4] he is mentioned under the title of "Capt ," as owning lands

---

[1] Printed Warrant Book. p 167
[2] Hotten, p 362
[3] Historical and Genealogical Magazine of S C, vol 11, p 126.
[4] Ibid, p 51

in South Carolina   On 7th May, 1682,[5] he is granted lot
34 in Charles Town, and he is again referred to by that
rank in a deed dated 1693[6] and in a will, making him an
executor, in 1695[7]   In May and August, 1692, we find
him styled "Major,"[8] and on 24th November, 1693,[9] he is
styled "Major," and commander of the ship "Daniel of Carolina," and on 12th September, 1696,[9] 10th March 1696/7,[10]
and 10th January, 1697,[11] he is also styled "Major" in records
on file.   In 1698 he is also styled "Major" in the communi-
cations from the Lords Proprietors to the Governor and
Council at Charles Town[12]   In 1702 he is styled "Col,"[13]
and so again in 1710, 1712 and 1716   In what service or
how he obtained his successive promotions the record does
not disclose

He was an active opponent of Landgrave James Colleton when the latter was governor, and an active adherent
of Seth Sothel during the latter's stormy administration,
and was, in 1692, together with James Moore, excepted
by the Lords Proprietors from the general pardon they
extended to all who had been concerned in the expulsion
of Governor Colleton   This notwithstanding, he assisted
the Lords Proprietors in 1698 in the preparation of the
final set of "fundamental" Constitutions they submitted
for the government of the Colony, and which they sent
over to Carolina by Major Daniell, at the same time en-
trusting him with several blank patents for Landgrave
to be filled out by himself,[14] and another   He himself was
created a Landgrave by patent dated 12th August, 1698[15]

In the expedition against St Augustine, in 1702, he was
second in command to Governor James Moore and acquitted
himself well   He was Deputy Governor under Sir

[5]Ibid vol 9, p 17
[6]Ibid vol 11, p 128
[7]Ibid vol 10, p 83
[8]Printed Journal Grand Council, pp 19, 55, 61
[9]Ibid, vol 8, p 210
[9]Ibid vol 10, p 236
[10]Ibid vol 10 p 24
[11]Collections Historical Society, vol 1, p 144
[12]Collections Historical Society S C, vol 1, pp 145, 146
[13]Rivers Sketch, p 201
[14]Collections Historical Society of S C, vol 1 pp 145, 146
Collec Hist Soc Committee S C   1 1701 1714 p 111

Nathaniel Johnson, who, in 1706, appointed him Deputy Governor of North Carolina[16] He was again appointed Deputy Governor of the Province of South Carolina in 1715, during the Yemassee war, and after the departure of Governor Craven acted as governor and held his post until the arrival, in 1717, of Governor Robert Johnson[17] He was a member of the Commons House of Assembly in 1706 and also in 1712 and 1713 In the year 1712 it was suggested that he should have the command of the expedition against the Tuscaroras, but an agreement between himself and the committee of the Commons House having the matter in charge could not be reached[18] He died in May, 1718, aged 72 His tombstone was fortunately discovered in 1908, and was, by the Society of the Colonial Dames of America, placed against the wall of the south porch of St Philip's Church His stone states that he was "a brave man who had long served King William in his "Wars both by Land and Sea," but the record shows only his apparent continued residence and service in the Province There he was undoubtedly a brave, capable, active and prominent man[19]

His ownership of the Winyah Barony did not continue long—one day It was granted to him with other lands aggregating 24,000 acres on the 18th June, 1711,[20] and the next day, 19th June, 1711, he conveyed the whole 24,000 acres so granted, including this Barony, to Landgrave Thomas Smith. the second Landgrave of the name[21]

The Barony from its long ownership in the Smith family was afterwards called the "Smith" Barony and was the only barony in South Carolina distinctively known as "Smith's" Barony; but it was properly "Daniell's"

[16]McCrady. vol 1, p 461
[17]Rivers Sketch p 268
[18]S C Hist and Genealogical Magazine, vol 10. p 43
[19]For an account of the finding of this tombstone see The News & Courier for 23d June. 1908 and "Days of Yore" part I, p 29 A Robert Daniell was commissioned 2d June 1714. Chief Justice during the absence of Chief Justice Trott Off Hist Com Bk Q Q 1685-1712, p ——
[20]Off Hist Com Memorial Bk 5 p 147.
[21]Ibid

Barony, or more properly, as it was styled at first, the "Winyah Barony"

Of Thomas Smith, the second Landgrave, the record shows that he came to the Province with his father in 1684, and accumulated before his death a very considerable property in land and slaves   The record does not show what consideration he paid to Landgrave Robert Daniell for the 24,000 acres, including the Winyah Barony purchased in 1711, nor what step he took to settle up and utilize the Barony prior to 1732

In October, 1732, he advertises in the *South Carolina Gazette* that he has for sale "14,000 acres of Land on "Winyaw River fronting the same, most of it not above "6 miles from the Town on *Sampit* River"   He did not sell, and the growth of Georgetown, which was laid off in 1734,[2] seems to have encouraged the Landgrave in founding a competitive town, for in the *South Carolina Gazette*, for the week 16th to 23d July, 1737, we find the following advertisement

"*South Carolina, July primo, 1737*

"Whereas at the request of several of the In-"habitants of the Province as well as Strangers I "Landgrave *Thomas Smith* have laid out a Township "on a Bluff of my *Winyaw* Barony containing 690 "half acre Lotts fronting *Winyaw*-River, it being "about 6 Miles from George Town, nearer the River's "Mouth, the River before the Town is about a Mile "and half wide, and generally fresh Water, whereon "500 Sail of Vessels may ride before the said Town, "it being about a Mile front on the River, and con-"tains on the Bay front 30 Lotts, 100 Feet front and "200 & odd Feet deep, every 2 Lotts deep is a cross "Street, there runs from High-water Mark 11 Streets "through the Heart of the Town, and 12 Cross Streets, "the broad Streets from the front in the Center of "the Town is 100 Feet wide and the rest 60 ditto "And whereas several Persons are desirous to rent or

"purchase 50 Acre Lotts 2 or 3 Miles from the back
"of the said Town for Country Seats, be it known
"that I the said *Thomas Smith* will rent for 10 or 12
"Years, each 50 Acre tracts for 5 l *per* Year *Pro-*
"*clamation Money,* or to sell that Quantity for 40 l
"in the same Specie, to the Quantity of 150 Acre
"Tracts, and I the said *Thomas Smith* propose to give
"*gratis* for the Use of the said Town, 100
"acres for a Common of Wood—Land on the back of
"the Town, and the Timber that grows on that 100
"Acres the Inhabitants of the Town are welcome to
"make use of it *gratis* for building, I will also give to
" any Church of England Minister that may settle and
"preach there, 2 Lotts about the Center of the Town
"for a Dwelling-house, Church and burial Place, and
"the same to any Presbyterian Minister, as also to any
"Baptists, and in case any Body of our Friends called
"Quackers that comes to settle in the said Town with
"their Teachers, the same Donation which shall be
"employ'd by all them and their Successors for ever,
"besides 10 Acres for each, about 3 Miles from the
"said Town, and if such a School-Master as I and my
"Heirs shall approve of him, and his Successors shall
"have a Town-Lott and 10 Acres to him also, as
"Witness my Hand the Day and Year before written

Thomas Smith

"N B I shall sell each half Acre Lott clear of all
"Charges for 40 s *Proclamation Money* or 10 l. this
"Currency I have also Right of 2360 Acres of Land
"to dispose of, together or in small Parcels, And will
"sell or Rent 2000 Acres of Land on *Black-River*
"joining on Mr *Commander's,* great part of which
"is good Rice *Swamp,* that the Spring Tide flows on,
"some Corn Land and a Quantity of it good Light-
"wood Land never work on Also 6000 Acres on
"*Charlestown* Neck some of it 9 or 10 and some 20
"or 30 Miles from the said Town, Rice, Corn and
"Lightwood Land never work'd on At my *Goose*
"*Creek* Plantation is a Quantity of Red Oak Hogs-
"head and Barrel Staves to be sold "

There is no map or plan in existence that the writer of this article has been able to discover of this projected town on the Barony, and there is no evidence on the record that the several inhabitants of the Province and the strangers who urged the Landgrave to lay out the town ever testified to their opinion of its desirability by purchasing lots and settling on them   The advertisement has its value to the student of the "origins" of rice planting in South Carolina by showing that as early as 1732 the value for purposes of rice culture of swamp-land irrigated by the flow of the tide had become known

The sale of lots could not have progressed satisfactorily—if at all—for eighteen months later in the *Gazette* for the week 29th December to 5th January, 1737, we find the following advertisement

"These are to give Notice to all poor Protestants of "any Nation whatsoever, that are willing to come and "settle on a Township, laid out by Landgrave *Thomas* "*Smith* of *South Carolina* about Six Miles from the "Mouth of *Winyaw*-River & about 50 Miles to the "North ward of *Charles town*, that the Said *Smith* "to the first 150 Families that will claim this Dona- "tion and come to settle that Town within 5 Years "after the Date hereof, will give to each Family, on "their Arrival at *South Carolina*, a Town Lott, con- "taining half an Acre English Measure, as also 6 acres "back of the said Town, to them and their Heirs for- "ever, clear of all Charges for 10 Years, the said "*Smith* obliges himself to pay the Kings Quit-Rent "for that Time, upon Condition, that the Possessors "of the said Lotts within 4 or 5 Years at most after "Possession, do build a wooden House 25 Feet long "and 16 wide with a brick Chimney, and after the Ex- "piration of *Ten* Years after Possession to pay the "Kings Quit-Rent   There is also a Common of 100 "Acres of Wood Land on the back of the said Town "where all the Inhabitants of the said Town are well- "come to get Timber *gratis*, and those that settle "on the 6 Acres of Land back of the Town, may keep

"Cattle and Hogs, sufficient to maintain a Small
"Family, there being many thousand Acres of Land
"to graze on. And in case such a Body of People that
"comes to settle on the Land according to my Pro-
"posals, will bring on a Minister, I will give unto
"such Minister a Town-Lott and 10 Acres of Land
"back, as also Land sufficient for a Church, all of
"which I confirm
"*Given under my Hand this 18th Day of October 1737*
Thomas Smith

The second Landgrave, Thomas Smith, died 9th May,
1738 [23] Before his death he seems to have given away a
portion of the barony to his eldest son, Thomas, for in the
latter's will dated 3d December, 1729, probated 15th January,
1729/30, he devises to his sister, Justinah Moore, 1,000
acres out of 3,000 acres given him by his father in the
upper part of his barony on "Wineaw" river.[24] After her
brother's death, Justinah Moore advertises in the Gazette
that she possessed and was prepared to sell this 1,000 acres.
The second Landgrave Thomas Smith survived his eldest
son, Thomas, and had by a second wife a younger son also
named Thomas By his will dated 3d May, 1738, the
second Landgrave made the following disposition of the
remainder

"And whereas I have laid out a Township on my
" Wynyaw Barony and have advertised to sell Part of
"it and to give Part of it to Strangers according to
"my Printed Advertisement as also to rent out Part,
"I do Authorize and Empower my Loving Wife
"Mary Smith to sign such Writings that either the
"Purchasers or Renters may be sure of a good Title
"According to agreement made with her During her
"Widowhood * * * And whereas I have reserved
"for myself twenty Lotts on the front of the said
"Township which runs back to the first Cross Street "
he disposes of the lots viz to "son Henry Smith" lots

[23] S C Hist and Genealogical Magazine, vol 11, p 140
[24] Probate Court Charleston Bk 1671-1727, p 228

16 and 46 "as appears in the Model of the said Town";
to "son Thomas Smith" lots 13 and 43; to "son George
Smith" lots 10 and 40, to "son Benjamin Smith" lots
19 and 49, to "loving Wife Mary Smith" lots 22 and
52, to "Daughter Anne Waring" lots 25 and 55; to
"Daughter Moore" lots 28 and 58; to "Daughter Sarah
Bowen" lots 7 and 37, to "Daughter Mary Scriven"
lots 4 and 34, to "Daughter Elizabeth Smith" lots 1
and 31, to "Dorothy Bassett daughr of my good
Friend the Reverend Nathan Bassett" lot 106

"And Whereas I have thirty one Grand Children &
"Great Grand Children I give unto each a Town Lott
"which amounts to thirty-one Lotts beginning at
"Numbr Three hundred and one Fronting Church
"street to Number Three hundred and fifteen joyning
"Broad Street and from Number three hundred and
"thirty-one to three hundred forty-five on Broad Street
"and three hundred Sixty one being the Corner lott of
"the first Cross Street from Church Street   *   *   *
"to be drawn by Lotts   I also give unto my aforesaid
"Grand children and Great Grand Children Two thou-
"sand acres of Land to make each of them a small
"Retireing Country Seat which Two thousand acres of
"Land is to begin from the back Part of my Barony
"that is near Santee River and to Run towards Winyaw
"River to Joyn that land which I have by my Printed
"Advertisement given away to Ministers and Poor
"People and a free School Churches Meeting houses
"&c   *   *   *   As to the Remainder of my Winyaw
"Barony that extends to the Northward and South-
"ward of the sd Town   Item I give & bequeath unto
"my Sons Henry Smith Thomas Smith George Smith
"and Benjamin Smith one thousand acres each which
"is to be run out in Proportion to the North & South
"side of the Barony   *   *   *   Now what is still
"more remaining of my Barony Land I do Empower
"my Loving wife to sell to any Purchaser that will
"buy it "25

The name of the proposed Town was Smith-Town or "Smiths-Town".[26] The effort to create a town however failed. Whether from its more advantageous position or from its earlier start, Georgetown which lay some six or seven miles to the Westward maintained its place as the Port-Town and after the death of the second Landgrave, Thomas Smith, apparently all attempt to build up the town on the Barony ended.

The Landgrave's son George mentioned in his will died under age and unmarried[27] and his 1,000 acres of the barony devised under his father's will was by the others interested transferred to his three brothers, Henry, Thomas and Benjamin, who partitioned the 4,000 acres among them; 1,333¾ acres falling to Henry Smith who advertises in the Gazette on 18th May, 1752, for sale

"2 or 3000 Acres of land at *Winyaw* joining Smith-"Town either in thousand acre tracts or 500 or as the "purchaser chuses."

On 25th March, 1756, Henry Smith sold his 1,333¾ acres to Elias Horry, and in the deed of conveyance it is described as bounding Southeast on "Smiths-Town".[28]

The rest of the barony (with the exception of the share of Benjamin Smith) seems to have been gradually disposed of by the children and grandchildren of the Landgrave and passed into the hands of strangers.

Out of the share going to him, Benjamin Smith, on 2nd March, 1757, sold 346 acres to Elias Horry,[29] but the remainder continued in his family for many years. From Benjamin his part of the Barony apparently passed to his eldest son, Thomas, from whom it next passed to his eldest son, Thomas John, who died in 1834, and some time after whose death the remaining part owned by him, which constituted the "Retreat" plantation, was sold away

[26] M C O Charleston Bk Q Q, p 366
[27] Mes Con Offi Charleston Bk Q Q, p. 368 There was an elder son by his first wife also named George who predeceased his father The George named in the will was by the second wife and apparently born after his brother's death
[28] Ibid
[29] Mes Con Off Charleston Bk R R p 362

On 28th August, 1733, Mr Thomas Lynch had obtained a grant for 4,500 acres, lying mainly to the South of the Barony It included however the valuable tidal rice swamps on Santee river which had been omitted from the barony grant At the date the barony was run out the value of the tidal swamps for rice cultivation was not yet known. The lines of the new grant overlapped or interfered with the lines of the barony, and the result was litigation between Thomas Smith and Thomas Lynch The exact result of this litigation the available remaining records do not disclose, but apparently by some settlement the title of the various purchasers from Thomas Lynch to so much of their land as was included in this "overlap" was confirmed

Possibly by exchange, as part of the "Retreat" plantation as owned by Thomas John Smith lay to the west of the barony line and included part of a grant to Thomas Lynch

The map of the barony published with this is from an old copy of the map made in the litigation between Thomas Smith and Thomas Lynch over the conflicting lines of the two grants

The location of the Town called Smiths-Town apparently from the map accompanying the deed to Elias Horry from Henry Smith, fronted on Winyah Bay just west of Estherville plantation and east of the east line of the Retreat plantation, where the high land comes to the beach or water's edge, without intervening marsh or mud flats

---

VII

WISKINBOO BARONY .

The Wiskinboo Barony derived its name from the locality in which it lay, viz at Wiskinboo or on Wiskinboo Swamp which is in what is now Berkeley County, one of the leads of Wadboo or Fairforest Swamp, between the Cooper and the Santee rivers

It was granted under the patent as Landgrave of the first Landgrave, Thomas Smith, and was apparently the only

Barony in South Carolina granted as such under his patent. There were other large grants of land made to the first and the second Landgrave under this patent which entitled him to four baronies of twelve thousand acres each, or forty-eight thousand acres in all   But none of these other grants were distinctively for twelve thousand acres of land in one body as a Barony.   They were all for lesser and varying areas and although taken out as part of the total 48,000 acres, yet were not laid out as Baronies   There were certainly two Thomas Smiths who preceded Landgrave Thomas Smith in their advent to the Province.[1]   The first was the Thomas Smith who came over with the very first fleet,[2] with Paul Smith[3]   They seem to have come over together, but their exact relationship is not stated on the record   Paul Smith died prior to June, 1672[4]   Thomas Smith appears to have been joined by James Smith, for a number of warrants for land are issued to them jointly, between 21st May, 1672 and 16th April, 1675.[5]   But there is no apparent connection between this Thomas Smith and the Thomas Smith who arrived in the Province in July, 1684, with his wife Barbara, and with Thomas and George Smith, Mathew Crosse, Philip Adams, Joan Atkins, Johanah Atkins, Elizabeth Adams, Aron Atkins, Ellen and Mary Atkins, and Michael Peirce[6]

Thomas and George Smith were evidently his sons Thomas, subsequently the second Landgrave, and George, subsequently Dr George Smith   For no reason apparent save the identity of name, the Landgrave has been supposed to be the same with the first Thomas Smith who came over in 1670, and it has been stated that James Smith was his brother who later established himself in Boston and founded a family of Smiths there

The record in South Carolina would not seem to indicate that the Thomas Smith who arrived in 1670 in the first fleet with Paul Smith was the same as the Thomas Smith

[1] Printed Warrant Bk, pp 4, 95
[2] Ibid
[3] Collections Historical Society of S C, vol 5, p 134
[4] Printed Warrant Bk p 17
[5] Ibid, pp 9, 16 96
[6] Printed Warrant Bk 1680-1692, p 166

14   SO CA HISTORICAL AND GENEALOGICAL MAGAZINE

who arrived in 1684 and was subsequently created a Landgrave and was Governor of the Province. Under the offer
of the Lords Proprietors to induce and encourage the settlement of the Province, each intending settler was entitled
on landing to a grant of so many acres for himself and to
so many acres additional for each person (including servants) he brought with him   The Thomas Smith who arrived in 1670 received on 12th April, 1675, a warrant for
150 acres to which he was entitled for his personal arrival
in the first fleet as an intending settler' On 12th April,
1675, Thomas Smith and James Smith received a warrant
for 550 acres, to which they were entitled for servants
brought over by Thomas Smith in the first fleet in 1670'
On 20th January, 1684-5, the Thomas Smith who arrived
in 1684 received a warrant for 650 acres, which included
the acres to which he was entitled for his personal arrival
in 1684, as an intending settler.' It does not seem plausible
that the same Thomas Smith should have received twice
over the bonus in acres given to an intending settler for
his personal arrival, and until some other connection is
shown it must be assumed that these two Thomas Smiths
were different persons

It has been stated that Landgrave Thomas Smith was
the son of Cassique John Smith   Not only is there nothing
on the record to support this surmise, but there is an entire
absence of anything on the record to indicate any sort of
connection with Cassique John Smith, who appears to have
died without any children

Landgrave Thomas Smith appears to have been a "Chirurgeon," inferred from the clause in his will which be-
queaths to his son George "all my instruments that belong
"to chirurgevy and one-half of all my medicines * * *
"alsoe my large brass mortar and pestle '"[10]

His wife Barbara died sometime prior to March, 1687
(1688 new style) for on 22nd March 1687/8 he was in the
presence of Bernard Schenckingh, Esq, high Sheriffe of

'Printed Warrant Book, 1677-1679, p 95
'Ibid p 96
'Printed Warrant Book 1680-1692 p 166
'T ile i   .t   i   i   .   i i Pk 1671 1727 i 33

Berkeley County William Smith, Thomas Smith, Junior, James Barbott, gentleman, and divers others, including Anna Cornelia Van Myddagh married by the Rev William Dunlop to "Sabina de Vignon Dowager Van Wernhaut ""[11]

She was the widow of M' John d'Arsens, Seignieur de Wernhaut (often erroneously referred to as "Lord" Wernhaut) who was apparently a Dutch or Flemish gentleman of some means He arrived in the Province sometime in 1686, for on 29ᵗʰ Sept' 1686 the Proprietors directed that as he was the first of his nation to settle in the Province he should have measured out to him such a quantity of land as he might desire, not exceeding 12,000 acres,[12] and on 29ᵗʰ Oct', 1686, a warrant was issued by the Proprietors for the grant to 'Mons John d'Arsens, Seigneur of Wernhaut" of 12,000 acres."[13] Thomas Smith having married the widow made application that the 12,000 acres be transferred to him, and there being apparently no children of the Wernhaut marriage, the Proprietors on 9ᵗʰ Dec', 1689, granted his request and directed that the 12,000 should be granted to Smith."[14]

Smith does not appear before this marriage to have acquired much landed property beyond the 650 acres at his arrival, but on the 10ᵗʰ Nov', 1688, a warrant was issued to him for "that poynt of land in Charles Towne wᶜʰ is "comonly called and knowne by the name of the Oyster poynt,'"[15] and on 16ᵗʰ Dec', 1688, a grant was issued to him for 6 acres being the "poynt "'"[16]

The new wife did not long survive the marriage She died in December, 1689, and was buried from "the house formerly belonging to the aforesaid John van Arsem. Lord Wernhoudt" according to a certificate duly made by the "Hon'ble Collonell Andrew Percivall Lieut Coll Robert "Quary Chief Judge of the Court of Pleas Ralph Izard and

[11]S C Hist and Genealogical Magazine, vol 6, p 179
[12]Transactions Historical Society S C, vol 1, p 117
[13]Calendar of State Papers America and West Indies, vol 1685-1688, p 270
[14]Transactions Historical Society S C, vol 1, p 123
[15]Printed Warrant Bk. 1680-1692. p 20
[16]Off Sec State Grant Bk 38 p 74

"James Moore Esq "*" who were by Thomas Smith requested to attend the funeral"

She does not appear to have left any children by either d'Arsens or Smith

It is not known where was the house referred to   It may have been the brick house on the Back river or Medway plantation or the house devised by Landgrave Smith to his son George as "all my brick house in Charles Town con-"taining four roomes one above another with convenient "passage to and from it"

On 6th Oct, 1690, a commission was made out by the Proprietors to Thomas Smith "one of the Cassiques of "Carolina" appointing him Governor of the Province," but he seems never to have acted under this Commission, as Sothell was then in possession of the post   On 13th May, 1691, he was one of the grand council of the Province, and on 19th April, 1692, was appointed deputy for Thomas Amy, one of the Proprietors   On 12th April, 1693, he was commissioned as Sheriff for Berkeley County, with instructions that the power given to the Governor (Col Philip Ludwell) to remove a sheriff should not apply to him[18] On 29th November, 1693, he was appointed Governor and Commander in Chief of the Province[20]   He died in November, 1694, in the 46th year of his age and was buried on his Medway plantation, on Back river, where his tombstone still exists

Archdale describes him as "a wise sober and moderate "and well living Man" and the Proprietors writing to Gov' Archdale on 10th Jan', 1695, say   "We forward copies "of letters written by Colonel Smith not long before his "death, that you may enjoy with us his satisfactory account "of the growing condition of the province and of the peace "and union to which he had brought it   He appears to us "to have been a man not only of great parts, integrity and "honesty but of a generous temper and a nobleness of

[17]"Off Hist Com" Bk, 1672-1692, p ——
[18]"Transactions Historical Society, vol 1, p 124
[19]"Transactions Historical Society S C, vol 1, p 131
[20]"I. t.l 1 174

"spirit as to the public good as is scarcely to be met withal
"in this age'"[1]

On the 13th May, 1691, he was created a Landgrave by
a patent of that date which entitled him to grants of land
to the aggregate of four baronies or 48,000 acres, but he
seems during his lifetime to have taken out grants for but
a comparatively small amount   His total grants outside of
the "oyster point" and some six other lots in Charles Town
appear on the record to have been 2,850 acres on Medway
or Back river, 500 acres on Ashley river and 350 acres
elsewhere in Berkeley County   He had in Charles Town
a house of some size for on 20th Sept', 1692, the Commons
House of Assembly met there [2]

The initiation of the cultivation of rice in South Carolina has been attributed to him, but upon no contemporary
testimony, and the cultivation of rice in the province seems
to have preceded by years his alleged introduction of it [22]
The "gloss" or statement of "first rice patch" as marked
on Landgrave Smith's lot in Charles Town in the copy of
Crisps map of Charles Town, published with Ramsay's
history of South Carolina, has been established to be a
later interpolation   No such statement is on the original
map

By his will, dated 26th June, 1692 the first Landgrave
devised all his lands (but does not mention his Landgrave-
ship) to his eldest son, Thomas, about that time styled
"Capt " Thomas Smith, and who was a member of the
Commons House in 1694. By a codicil to his will, dated
15th July, 1693, the Landgrave bequeathed and assigned to
Landgrave Joseph Blake his patent as Landgrave with all
the baronies and rights thereto appertaining [23]

This, made at that date, is a little singular, as by the
Fundamental Constitution the dignity conferred by a patent as Landgrave was intended to descend to the eldest son
and continue in the male line, and was incapable of aliena-
tion after 1701   It was possibly intended as a temporary

[1]Cal St Papers Am & West Ind Vol 1693-1696, p 425
[2]Printed Council Journal for 1692, p ——
[22]Sunday News for 9th Decr, 1900
[23]Probate Court Charleston Will Bk, 1671-1727 p 33

transfer as security for debt   At any rate we afterwards find the second Landgrave procuring grants of land to be credited to the 48,000 acres to which this patent entitled him[23]

The second Landgrave procured large grants of land in varying amounts under his patent, and on 20th Sept[r], 1716, procured a warrant under which there was laid out to him a barony of 12,000 acres in one body   This was the only grant of a barony granted distinctively as such in South Carolina for 12,000 acres under Landgrave Thomas Smith's patent as Landgrave, dated 13th May, 1691

It was laid out near Wiskinboo Swamp in Berkeley County   The grant was dated 8th June, 1717[24]   In his description of the boundaries of the barony in his memorial, dated 23rd May, 1733, the second Landgrave describes it as bounding on M[r] Gough and company's Barony, also on M[r] John Allston's land, M[rs] Ann Harrison, M[r] William Waties, M[r]. Creaque, M[r]. Henry Tazeyell and Elias Ball. Out of this barony at that date, viz, 23rd May, 1733, he states he had only 3,000 acres left, the rest having been sold or given away

The barony referred to as M[r] Gough and Company's was the Cypress Barony described in the number of this Magazine for January, 1911

Wiskinboo Swamp is one of the branches of Fair Forest Swamp, which is a head of Wadboo creek and traverses part of Wadboo Barony   The Wiskinboo Barony therefore lay probably west or northwest of the Cypress Barony and east or northeast of the Wadboo Barony and on the waters of Wiskinboo Swamp

There is on record a deed of gift from Landgrave Thomas Smith to his son George Smith, J[r], dated 1st Sept[r], 1718, for 1,000 acres, which according to the plat is "per Watboo Barony" and lies between lands of Capt Ed[rd] Hyrne and of Capt Warrien (Waring)   Both Edward Hyrne and Benjamin Waring were sons-in-law of the second Landgrave, and the author of "The Olden Time of Carolina" p 66, states that on 1st Dec[r], 1724, "Col Edward

[23]"Off Hist Com" Bk 1714-1717 p 79
[24]Ibid

Hyrne and Barbary his wife" received a conveyance of
584 acres near the head of a branch of Cooper river, known
by the name of Watboo branch and being part of a Land-
graveship formerly granted to Landgrave Thomas Smith,
and that Benjamin Waring and Anne his wife had also
part of that Barony.

In his will, dated 3rd May, 1738[25] the second Landgrave
makes the following reference to the Barony

> "I give and bequeath unto my daughter Mary
> "Scriven one thousand acres of Pine Land Joyning on
> "Whiskimbo and a thousand acres joyning that to my
> "daughter Elizabeth Smith "

The writer of this article has never been able to find any
map of the Barony nor any deeds or maps of parts of it,
which by collection together might indicate the lines and
location of the Barony, and can only give its general
location as above

As a distinctive "Barony" its duration was very short.

The second Landgrave to whom the grant of the Barony
was issued seems to have arrived in the Province with his
father in July, 1684   He died 9th May, 1738, and was
buried at his plantation at Goose Creek[26]   He had a large
number of children and has left innumerable descendants.
He was twice married   The name of his first wife the
writer of this article has never been able to satisfactorily
determine   It was certainly not Sarah Blake, daughter of
Col Joseph Blake, as stated by Landgrave Smith's descendant the "Octogenarian Lady"[27] (Mrs Poyas), for the
simple reason that there was no such person   Col Blake
(who was also a Landgrave and Proprietor and twice
Governor of the Province) had one daughter, but her
name was Rebecca, she was born in 1699; too young to
have been the mother of the second Landgrave's children,
born, as stated by Mrs Poyas, Thomas in 1691, George in
1693, Anne in 1695, Barbara in 1697, Sabina in 1699, etc

[25]Probate Court Charleston Bk   1736-1740, p   292
[26]S C Hist and Genealogical Magazine, vol 12, p 140
[27]Olden Time of Carolina, p 62

Besides she married in 1717 George Smith the second son of the second Landgrave Smith [*] There was no Sarah Blake to whom Thomas Smith could be married. For his second wife he married in 1713, Mary Hyrne

At the time of his death he was a very large landed proprietor, retained his title of Landgrave to the last, and was still the owner of the Winyah Barony (purchased by him from Landgrave Robert Daniell) intact, altho' he had disposed of the greater part of the Wiskinboo Barony

Many of the facts concerning the two Landgraves Thomas Smith, stated in this article are at variance with the statements of the Octogenarian Lady, whose account has been generally accepted and followed, as well as with those contained in a genealogical publication entitled "Some account of the Smiths of Exeter and their descendants, by one of them" (Arthur M. Smith) printed for private circulation, Exeter, 1896, which contains a chapter on Landgrave Thomas Smith of South Carolina and his descendants

The writer can only say that for what he has stated he has endeavoured to rely only on record contemporaneous evidence, while for a period in time so remote, M[rs] Poyas (having no sufficient access to the records) was naturally repeating in many instances that which came to her by that most fallacious channel for the transmission of facts, family tradition, and her account has been hitherto generally accepted and followed

[*] S. C. Hist. and Genealogical Magazine, vol 1, p 157

Copied and Edited by MABEL L. WEBBER

(Continued from the October Number)

CHRISTNINGS P' THE REV' M' GUY

Mary-Anne y' Daught' of Emanuel Smith bap' Dec'
y' 27 1721

Francis the Son of Stephen & Alice Todd ⎱
Joseph the Son of Ibid   ⎰ bap' Dec' y'
Mary y' Daught' of Ibid   29 1721

Elizabeth the Daught' of John & Eliz Tankard bap' Dec'
y' 29, 1721

Mary y' Daught' of Edward & Abigale White bap' Dec'
y' 29, 1721

Mary y' Daught' of Martha Gibbon bap' Dec' y' 29
1721

Moses the Son of ——— Butler bap' Jan' y' 7—1721/22

John the Son of Tho & Reb· Holman bap' Jan' y' 19
1721/22

Lois-Frances the Daught' of ——— Galloway bap'.
March y' 4 1721/22

Jane y' Daughter of Tho & Jane Headon bap' March y'
4 1721 22

Elizabeth y' Daught' of Isaac & *Fran' Stewart bap'
March y' 9 1721 22

Francis the Son of Tho & Eliz Rose bap' March y' 23
1721/22

Mary y' Daughter of W'' & Mary Cattell & ⎱ April y'
Benjamin═Godfrey y' Son of ibid bap' ⎰ 2, 1722

Christopher y' Son of W'' & Rebecca Guy bap' April y'
4 1722

*Franc' erased

W^m. the Son of W^m & Mary Miles bap^d April y^e 4 1722.

Margaret the Daught^r of Tho & Mary Miles April y^e 4 1722.

Anne y^e Daught^r of John & Mary Bull bap^d April y^e 24 1722.

Benjamin the Son of W^m. & Anne Parrott bap^d. May y^e 6 1722

Joseph==Elicot y^e Son of Rowland & ———— Storey bap^d June y^e 10 1722

Sarah y^e. Daught^r. of Edwd & Bridgett Brailsford bap^d July y^e 6 1722

Hannah y^e Daught^r of Joseph & Leah Clair Bap^d July y^e 22, 1722

Jonathan y^e Son of Edwd. & Abigale White bap^d p^r the Revd Mr Hesketh

Edward the Son of Ed^wd & Mary Butler &

Joseph the Son of Joseph & Sarah Steant

                                    July ye 26 1722

Thomas the Son of — — Siminett bap^d Augt ye 5 1722

Benjamin ye Son of Benj & Eliz Perrey Bap^d Augt ye 12 1722

Joseph Stent an adult bap^d Sept ye 2 1722

Anne y^e. Daught^r of W^m & Mary Chapman bap^d Septr 2 1722.

Richard the Son of Rich^d & Sarah Woodward bap^d Sepr 2 1722.

Charles ye Son of Charles & Eliz Brewer bap^d Sept ye 22 1722

John ye Son of Rich^d & Susannah Godfrey bap^d Oct ye 7, 1722

Peter ye Son of W^m & Mary Cattell bap^d Octr ye 13 1722

Thomas the Son of John & Eliz Woodward

Charles the Son of Charles & Mary Armstrong

Mary the Daught^r of Charles & Mary Armstrong

Mary the Daught^r of Edwd & Elizabeth Wormsley

Hannah ye Daught^r of Tho & Jane Headon

Wm Eyres the Son of Tho & Abigail Lancaster

Elizabeth the Daughter of Stephen & Jane Russell

} bap^d Oct ye 21 1722

MARRIAGES Pᵉ THE REVᵈ Mᵉ GUY

Francis Stokes & Sarah Popwell mard March yᵉ 8. 1721/22

Thomas Williams & Mary Wade mard May yᵉ 4 1722
Henry Parsons & Martha Vincent mard May 29, 1722
David Mᶜquin & Catherine Samways mard June 11 1722
Francis Ladson & Sarah Clark mard Augᵗ. yᵉ 7 1722
Wᵐ Kenneday & Elizabeth Turner mard Augᵗ 7 1722.
Wᵐ Spencer & Sarah Hill mard Novʳ. yᵉ 20. 1722
Thomas Croskeys & Eliz Gantlett mard Novʳ yᵉ 29, 1722
Samuel Fairead [?] & Mary Ayre marᵈ pʳ Revᵈ Mʳ Garden March yᵉ 3. 1722/23.
Tho Elliott & Isabella West mard April yᵉ. 18 1723
George Boddington & Willoughby Wells mard May yᵉ 16 1723
Andrew Deveaux & Hannah Girerdeau mard June yᵉ 18 1723
George Pope & Sarah Humphreys mard June yᵉ 19 1723
James Canty & Eliz Stevens mard July yᵉ 24. 1723
Robt Kendal & Eliz Creek mard July yᵉ 24 1723
Arthur Middleton & Sarah Morton mard Augᵗ yᵉ 3ᵈ 1723
Robᵗ Mackewn & Susannah Hackett mard Augᵗ. yᵉ 3 1723
Robᵗ Yonge & Hannah Eve mard Augᵗ yᵉ 15 1723
Abramh Neale & Catherine Atkins mard Sepᵗ yᵉ 2 1723.
Wᵐ Elliott Senʳ & Hester Butler Senʳ mard Sept yᵉ 19 1723
Tho Hext & Judith═Ester Torquet mard Sept yᵉ 26, 1723.
Richᵈ Timmons & Mary Stanyarne mard Oct yᵉ 6. 1723.
Tho Bartlett & Elizabeth Lewis mard Novʳ yᵉ 13 1723
Edwᵈ Perry & Rosamond Miles mard Decʳ yᵉ 11 1723
Joseph Barnart & Eliz Styring mard Decʳ yᵉ 15. 1723
Richᵈ Baker & Mary Bohun mard Decʳ yᵉ 19 1723
John Smith of Charlestown & Margaret Williamson marᵈ Jany yᵉ 23 1723/4

Joseph Elliot & Mary Chapman mard Jany ye 23 1723/4.

Isaac Emanuel & Priscilla Jones mard Febry y 6 1723/4

John Freeman & Eliz Arnold mard Febry ye 27 1723/4

Wm Simmons & Anne Tanner mard March ye 21 1723/4

Joseph Turner & Tabitha Nichols mard y 26 March 1724

Wm Emms & Anne Skipper mard ye 26 April 1724

Wm Atkinson & Hannah Adams mard Augt ye 6 1724

Peter Perry & Eliz Holman mard Augt ye 13 1724

Henry Wood & Anne Grady mard Augt. y^e. 18. 1724

Joseph Elliot & Edith Whitmarsh mard Sepr y^r 2 1724

John Hewson & Dorothy Stocks mard Sepr 22^d 1724

John Delonay & Mary Tucker Spinster mard Novr. ye 26 1724

Saml Williams & Leda Andru of St Betheole^ms mard Dec^m ye 23 1724

Thomas far & amarichah Ellett mard Jan ye 21 1724/5

Abram Morsheo & Elesabeth Clay mard Octo ye 13. 1725

Charles Wallis & Mary Armsetrong mard Jan. ye 12 1725/6

Bengemen Childs & hanna Ellett mard Jan ye 13. 1725/6

Robord Ellett & Elizabeth harford [?] mar^d Jan ye 25 1725/6

Thomas Holeman & Leah Clare mar^d feb ye 1 1725/6

Thomas Rose & Elesebeth Coppin mar^d March ye 6. 1725/6

Miles Reuers & Mary Warde mard Mar ye 15 1725/6

Benjamin Atwell & Mary Knight of Jam^s Isl^d mard Decr 23 1724/5 [sic]

Charles Wallace & Mary Armstrong wid mard Jany 12 1725/6

Peter Hoskins & Rebecca Boswood mard April 14. 1726

Benjamin Godfrey als Garnie^r & Martha Williams mard June y^e 9 1726

Thomas Drummond & Mary Clogy Spinst^r mard July y^e 25 1726

John Dart & Hannah Livingston Widdow mard Augt 19. 1726

William Bellinger Widdow'. & Mary Dunavan Spinst'
marrd Octob' 14 1726

William Fuller Jun'. & Martha Whitmarsh Spins'=mard.
p' the Rev⁴ M' Dyson Chaplin of Fort S' George
Jan' 11 : 1726/7

Joseph Williams & Eliz Stanting mard March 9 1726/7
John Rivers & Martha Smallwood mard April 27 1727
John Gwin & Mary Ramsay mard May 17, 1727
Thomas Witter & Elizabeth Hearn mard June 19 1727
David Mᶜquin & Martha Bodet mard July 9ᵗʰ 1727
Rice Edwards & Jael Deer mard July 9ᵗʰ 1727
Daniel Cartwright & Sarah Butler mard Sept' 7ᵗʰ 1727
Samuel Rivers & Eizabeth Tankard mar⁴ p' M' Dyson
May 9ᵗʰ 1727

Joseph Mackintosh & Mary Perryman wid mard Oct' 5
1727

Wᵐ Holman & Ruth Bodet mard Nov' 14, 1727
Aylift Weedon & Johanna Johnson widd 3 times pub⁴
mard Dec' 8ᵗʰ 1727

George Mugford & Mary Dickens 3 times publish⁴. mard
Dec' 21 1727

John Edmundson & Mary Smith Spinster mard Jany 14,
1727/8

Wᵐ Carr & Mary Ayres widdow mard Jany yᵉ. 24, 1727/8
John Anger & Hannah Perry mard March the 20. 1727/8
John Cattell & Sarah Hall Spinster mard April 24 1728
John Heydon & Mary Pastong (a Molattoe belonging to
Coll. Wᵐ. Bull) being 3 Lᵈˢ Days publish'd) mard April
26 1728

John Williams & Mary Rivers Widd mard May 14 1728
Wᵐ Emms of S' Pauls & Eliz Elliott widd mard. June
27 1728

John Russ & Mary Wood Spinster mard. July 12 1728
Thoˢ Brown & Anne Harris Spinster mard July 14, 1728
Henry Perrineau & Elizabeth Hall Spinster mard July
30ᵗʰ 1728.

John Daniel & Martha Wells Spinst' mard. Sept'. 12
1728

W^m. Newball & Rebecca Butler wid mard Octob^r 30.
  1728

Saml Bowman & Sarah Ladson Spins^r mard Decr. 19
  1728

James Manning & Sarah Folkinham (3 Ld^s D pub^d) mard
  Decr. 29 1728

John Farr & Constance Reynolds of St Pauls mard Jany
  30 1728/9

Saml Urwin & Catherine Neal Widdow mard Febry 29th
  [?] 1728/9

Zachariah Story & Mary Ellis of James's Isl^d mard March
  10 1729

Richd Wright & Elizabeth Woodward mard March 20
  1729

——[torn] & Mary two free negroes 3 times pub were
  mard April 13 1729

CHRISTNINGS P^r REV^d M^r GUY

Anne=Booth y^e Daughter of Richard & Mary Fuller Bap^d.
  Jan^s y^e 25 1722/23

Nathaniel y^e Son of Dr Duncan bap^d Feb^ry y^e. 4 1722/23

Ann y^e. Daught^r of James & Ann Palmer bap^d Feb^ry. y^e.
  16 1722/23

Andrew y^e Son of Peter & Cath Cattell bap^d March y^e
  17 1722/23

Elizabeth y^e Daught^r of Joseph & Eliz Heap bap^d.
  March ye 22 1722 23

John & Mary an adult negro man & negro woman bap^d
  April ye 12 1723 both belonging to Mr John Godfrey

Mary the Daughter of W^m. & Deborah Webb bap^d May
  16 1723

Anna ye Daugt^r of Mary Thomas bap^d ⎫ bap^d
W^m the Son of Philip & Mary Evans   ⎪ May ye 19
James the Son of Robt & Anne Ladson   ⎬ 1723
Margaret y^e. Daught^r of W^m & Martha Ladson ⎭

Sarah ye Daught^r of Robt & Johanna-Drayton Johnson
  bap^d May 26 1723

Mary ye Daught^r of John & Mary Gibbs bap^d July y^e

Mary ye Daught^r. of Charles & Eliz Hill bap^d Augt ye 5 1723

Mary ye Daught^r of Benjamin & ———— Godfrey als Garn^t bap^d Augt 5, 1723

W^m. ye Son of W^m & Allice Gibbs bap^d Augt ye 30, 1723

Tho ye Son of Tho & Mary Mells bap^d Sept. 15 1723

John ye Son of &

Elizabeth ye Daught^r of } John & Eliz Mells bap^d. Sept. 15 1723

Tho· ye Son of W^m & Mary Miles bap^d Novr ye 10 1723

Anne ye Daught^r of Arthur & Martha Hall bap^d Novr. ye 22 1723

Sarah ye Daught^r of W^m & ———— Allen bap^d. Novr ye 22 1723

Eliz ye Daught^r of James & Eliz Samways bap^d Decr ye 8 1723

Mary-Henrietta ye Daught^r of W^m & Mary Bull bap^d. Decr y^e. 29 1723

Mary-Lucy ye Daugh^t of Burnaby & Lucy Bull bap^d Decr 29. 1723

Susannah y^e. Daught^r of Edwd & Mary Rawlins bap^d May ye 13 1724

Henry Wood an Adult bap^d. June ye 21 1724

Benjamin the Son of Benj & ———— Godfrey als Garn^r bap^d Augt 3, 1724

Sarah ye Daughter of John & Eliz Tankard &
Mary ye Daughter of Joseph & Eliz Dill } bap^d Augt 30 1724

Benjamin the Son of Rich^d & Susanna Godfrey bap^d Sept y^e. 20 1724.

Sarah ye Daught of Francis & Sarah Ladson &
Rachel-Ladson ye Daught of Benj & Eliz Perry } bap^d Sep^t ye 27, 1724

Hannah ye wife of Tho Booth bap^d October ye 2 1724

Mary ye Daughter of Henry & Eliz Wood an Adult bap^d. Oct ye 2 1724

John ye Son of Isaac & Frances Stewart bap^d Oct ye 2^d 1724

W^m the Son of Robert & Sarah Wood bap^d. Oct y^e. 2^d. 1724

Benjamin the Son of Robert & Sarah Wood bap^d Oct. ye 2^d 1724

Sarah ye Daught^r of Robt & Sarah Wood bap^d ye 2^d. 1724

Susannah Daught^r of Robt & Sarah Wood bap^d Oct. ye 2^d 1724

Elizabeth ye Daught^r of Tho & Hannah Booth bap^d Oct ye 2^d 1724

Anne y^e. Daught^r of Joseph & Mary Barton bap^d Oct ye 2^d 1724

John ye Son of Joseph & Mary Barton bap^d Oct ye 2^d 1724

Rebecca ye Daughter of Robt & Sarah Wood bap^d Oc^t ye 16 1724

Stephen the Son of Robt & Sarah Wood bap^d Oct ye 16 1724

John ye Son of John & Eliz Lupton bap^d Oct ye 16 1724

Lucretia ye Daughter of John & Eliz Lupton bap^d Oct ye 16. 1724

Anne ye Daughter of John & Eliza· Lupton bap^d. Oct ye 16 1724

Hannah y^e. Daughter of John & Eliza Lupton bap^d Oct ye 16 1724

John ye Son David & Catherine M'quin bap^d Oct ye 18 1724

Peter Wood an Adult bap^d Oct ye 25 1724

Jacob ye Son of Jacob & Eliz Ladson Bap^d Oct ye 25. 1724

Charles ye Son of W^m & Mary Cattel bap^d December ye 26. 1724

Pirscilla ye Daughter of Isaac & Pirscilla Emanuel bap^d Jan ye 14 1724/5

Mathew y^e. Son of Mathew & Mary Smallwood bap^d Jan ye 24 1724/5

Anne ye Daughter of Mathew & Mary Smallwood bap^d. Jan ye 24 1724/5

Mary ye Daughter of Thos & Abigal Langester bap^d Jan ye 31, 1724/5

Edward ye Son of Edward & Rosemond Peary bap^d feb. ye 21 1724/5

Joseph ye Son of Joseph & Elizabeth Dell bap^d. feb ye 28 1724/5

George ye Son of W^m & Mary Chapman bap^d feb ye 28 1724/5

Charles ye Son of Willm & Rebeckah Guy bap^d March 2. 1724/5

Mary Anne ye daugh^r of Jeremiah & belinda Burrows bap^d Mar ye 7 1724. 5

Mary ye Wife of John Williams bap^d Mar 18 1724 5

John ye Son of John & Mary Williams bap^d Mar ye 18 1724 5

Thomas Son of Thomas & Jane haydon bap^d Mar ye 21 1724/5.

Elis ye daught^r of Rich^d & Mary Beaker bap^d May ye 23 1725

Martha ye daught^r of W^m & Martha Ladson bap^d. Aug ye 29 1725

Elizabeth ye daugh^r of Isaac & Sarah Battoon bap^d Sep^tr ye 5. 1725

Debbora ye daught^r of W^m debbero Webb bap^d. Octo ye 24 1725

hanah rebeckah ye dartr of Joseph & Eleseth heape, bap^d Oct ye 24. 1725

Mary ye Wife of Mathew Smallwood bap^d. Octo ye 31 1725

Anne y^e. daugh^r of henary & anne Wood Bap^d Novem ye 28 1725

Benj & Eliz Son & Daugh^r of W^m & Mary Cattell bap^d Febry 8 1725/6

Jeremiah ye Son of W^m & Mary Miles Bap^d feb ye 13 1725/6

Peter ye Son of Peter & Cath^n Cattell Bap^d. Mar ye 11 1725/6

Jeudith ye daugh^r of Joseph & Martha hull   ⎫   Bap^d
Elesebeth ye daugh^r of Joseph & Martha hull ⎬   April 1
                                                           ⎭   1726

Elesebeth y⁵ daughtᵣ of philop & Mary Euens Bapᵈ Aprl
    y⁵ 1 1726
Elesᵇ y⁵ daughᵣ of Wm & Anne Branford Bapᵈ April y⁵
    1 1726
Margret y⁵ daughᵣ of Thomas & ——— Whaly Bap". y⁵
    April 3 1726
Anne y⁵ daughᵣ of James & Elesebeth Samwis [Sam-
    ways?] Bapᵈ Aprl y⁵ 10 1726
Wᵐ y⁵ᵉ Son of Wᵐ & Debearo Weeb Bapᵈ April y⁵ 11
    1726
Sary Mary y⁵ Daughᵗ of Isaac & priscilla Emanuel Bapᵈ
    April y⁵ 11. 1726
James y⁵ Con of David & Catarne Macquin bapᵈ Aprᵗ y⁵
    17 1726
Robᵗ the Son of Charles & Eliz Hill bapᵈ April 17 1726
Mary y⁵ Daughᵣ of Robt & Anne Ladson bapᵈ April y⁵
    30 1726
Sarah y⁵ Daughᵣ of Peter & Eliz Perry bapᵈ May
    y⁵ 15 1726
Anne the wife of Roger Saunders (formerly Jon Fitch)
    bapᵈ May 15 1726
Thomas the Son of Jon & Anne Fitch bapᵈ May 15
    1726
Stephen the Son of Jon & Anne Fitch bapᵈ May 15
    1726
Susannah y⁵ Daught of Joseph & Constant Fitch bapᵈ
    May 15 1726
Mary y⁵ Daughᵣ of Joseph & Eliz Barnart bapᵈ. May
    15 1726

FUNERALS Pᵣ Y⁵ REVᵈ Mᵣ GUY.

Capt Richᵈ. Godfrey bur'd October 27 1725
James Samuaes Beurd January y⁵ 13 1725/26
Cattarn y⁵ wife of David Macquen Beurᵈ Jan y⁵ 13
    1725/6
Anne y⁵ Daughᵗ. of Robᵈ Jones Beuᵈ. Jan y⁵ 14 1725/6
Charles Armstrong Beurd Aug y⁵ 26 1725 [sic]
Mᵣ Laᵣ. ponge [?] a Young Gentleman belonging to the
    Scarborough man of war buᵈ feb ᵣ 1 ᵣ⁵ ᵣ

Mary y' daught' of W^m & Deborah Webb beur March
    y' 16 1725/6

Benj & Elizabeth Son & Daug' of W^m & Mary Cattell
    burd Feb^ry 10 1725/6

Charles Jones Sen' burd Sep' 14 1726

Miles Rivers burd February 15 1726/7

Joseph Hull burd February 15, 1726/7

Joseph the Son of Joseph & Eliz Heap burd Febry 21,
    1726/7

Thomas Gibson burd March y' 2^d 1726/7

Samuel Jones burd March 7th 1726/7

Robt the Son of Charles & Eliz Hill burd May 16 1727

Susannah Fitch burd July 11 1727

Leah the wife of Thomas Holman bur'd October 23, 1727

W^m the Son of John & Mary Heydon (Serv^ts of Coll
    Wm Bull) bur'd May 20, 1728

Anne the Daughter of Th^s & Jane Heydon burd. May 27,
    1728

Catherine the Daughter of Arthur & Martha Hall bur'd
    June 26, 1728

George the Son of Thomas & Elizabeth Rose burd June
    26, 1728

William Townelly Clark to the Honble the Gov' & Council
    &c burd July 29 1728

One Crofts, An apprentice of Mr Wells (bound out by
    Coll. Bull) burd Sept. 8, 1728.

Mr Ludlam of Goosecreek burd Sept' 29 1728

The Rev^d M' Ludlam Rect' of S' James Goosecreek burd
    Oct 12th 1728

John the Son of Benjn & Marg' Godfrey burd Sept 30
    1728

Deborah the Daughter of W^m & Deborah Webb burd
    Octo' 25 1728

Jane the daughter of W^m & Rebecca Guy bur'd Nov' 17
    1728

Old M^r. Ferguson bur'd. Dec 11, 1728

Martha wife of David M^c quin bur'd Dec' 25 1728

Anne* daught' of Mrs Smith of Goosecreek bur'd Dec 27,
    1728

*Justi~ ~~~~~~ ~~~ ~~~~ ~~~~~ ~ ~~

Mary daughter of Hannah Conyers bur'd January 16 1728/9

Mary the wife of Wm Cattell bur'd Janry 24 1728/9.

Mary the wife of Th^s Pritchard burd Febry 17 1728/9

Peter Cattell Senr bur'd Febry 21, 1728/9

Edwd. the Son of Wm Cattell bur'd April 25. 1729

————the Son of Rich^d. Capers of Stono burd May the 1st. 1729

Mary the wife of Wm Carr on James Island bur'd May 16 1729

Elizabeth the daughter of W^m & Martha Fuller Junr Bur'd June 1, 1729

————the Daughter of Justina Moore of Goose Creek widd bur'd June 6, 1729

Mrs Ayres widdow on James's Isl^d bur'd Augt 23^d 1729

George Lee Servt of Francis Yonge Esq burd the 5th Septr 1729

W^m the Son of W^m & Ruth Holman burd Septr 28—1729

Thos the Son of Edm^d & Eliz Bellinger bur'd Sept 29 1729

One Mr Howard on Jam^s Isl^d burd Oct 4th 1729

Katherine Vincent Sp^r Buried Octo^br ye 22^d 1729 in St Pauls Parish

Godfrey the son of Charles & Eliz Hill bur'd Nov 20 1729

Thos the son of Thos & Jane Heydon bur'd Novr 23^d 1729

Mary the wife of Thos. Dymes burd Novr 30 1729

Richard the Son of Thos Dymes bur'd Decr 2^d 1729

Bridget the wife of M^r. Ed^d Brailsford burd Dec 22 1729

CHRISTNINGS PER THE REV^d. M^r GUY

Jane ye Daught^r of W^m & Mary Chapman bap^d June ye 12th 1726

James ye Son of James & Mary Sutherland bap^d Augt ye 1st 1726   (At Johnson's Fort)

John ye Son of Capt Hatton an Indian Trader bap^d Augt 1st 1726

Martha ye Daught^r of Francis & Sarah Ladson bap^d Aug^t
   ye 14 1726

Mary y^e. Daught^r of Edward & Rosamond Perry bap^d
   Augt ye 14 1726.

Anne ye Daught^r. of the widdow Stocks, als Hewson, bap^d.
   Augt 14 1726.

John Sullivant an Adult bap^d Augt 14 1726

Thomas ye Son of Thomas & Esther Haward bap^d Sept^r
   4 1726

John ye son of Ibid bap^d Sep^t 4 1726.

Samuel Langley an Adult of Johnsons Fort bap^d Sep^t 4
   1726

Mary ye Daughter of Xtopher Jenkins* bap^d Sep^t 4 1726
Anne ye Daughter of ——— Sullivant a Widdow bap^d
   Sepr 4 1726.

Josiah Sullivant an Adult bap^d Sepr. 11 1726
Elisha Sullivant bap^d Sep^t 11 1726
Mary ye Daught^r of Charles & Mary Wallace bap^d Nov^r
   21 1726

Rebecca the Daught^r of W^m & Rebecca Guy priv Bap^d
   Decr. 9th. 1726.

Joseph the Son of Tho & Mary Dymes bap^d. ⎫
N B Robt the Son of Ibid, was rec'd into ⎬ Decr 30th.
   the Congregation &c being bap^d before ⎭   1726

Elizabeth the daughter of Abraham & Eliz Musheau bap^d.
   Decr 30 1726

Henry the Son of Joseph & Eliz Heap bap^d pr Feb 21.
   1726/7

John the Son of Thos & Jane Heydon bap^d Febry 26
   1726/7

Mary Anne the Daughter of John Drayton bap^d. March 2^d
   1726/7

Catherine the Daughter of Arthur & Martha Hall bap^d.
   March 5 1726/7

Mary the Daught^r of Lieutenant Stevens on Edistow Isl^d.
   bap^d March 17 1726/7

---

*This name is 'Jinks", as the last letters in the entry
are blotted, and the name "jjuks" on page 185 of the Oct 1911
issue, may also possibly be read Jinks.

Susannah ye Daughter of Tho & Eliz Rose bap^d p^r y^e
Rev^d M^r. Dyson May ye 6 1727

Susannah ye Daught^r of John & Mary Delony bap^d May
21 1727

Mary the Daughter of Thos & Mary Mell bap^d July 19
1727

Eliz the Daughter of Peter & Rebecca Hoskins bap^d July
19 1727

Miles the Son of Mary Rivers Widd bap^d July 21 1727

Isaac the Son of Tho & Leah Holman bap^d July 21 1727

Peter the Son of Peter & Elizabeth Perrey bap^d July 21
1727

Thomas the Son of Rich^d & Mary Fuller bap^d Augt 25
1727

Thomas the Son of Isaac & Francis Stewart bap^d Sepr 2
1727

Martha the Daughter of W^m & Martha Ladson bap^d Sep^t
3 1727

Elizabeth the Daughter of Sam^{el} Williams of St Barthol ·
Par bap^d Sep^t 10 1727

John the Son of Joseph & Eliz Dell [Dill] bap^d Sep^t 24
1727

Thomas the Son of Roger & Anne Saunders bap^d Novr. 12
1727

James the Son of James Streater (overseer to M^{rs} Ca-
wood) bap^d Decr 3 1727

Thomas the Son of Jeremiah & Belinda Burrows bap^d
Febry 18 1727/8

Margaret the Daughter of Joseph & Elizth Baley bap^d
Febry 25 1727/8

Mary an Adult Molatto belong^g to Coll Wm Bull bap^d
Febry 25 1727/8.

Joseph the Son of Joseph & Martha Hull bap^d March y^e
24 1727/8

George the Son of Thos & Elizabeth Rose bap^d April the
21 1728

Anne the Daughter of Rich^d & Mary Stevens of Edisto
bap^d May 5, 1728

W^m the Son of John & Mary Heydon (Servts of Coll
Bull) bap^d May 10 1728

Anne the Daughter of Tho' & Jane Heydon bap' May y' 24 1728

Catherine the Daught' of Arthur & Martha Hall recd into the Congregation (being privately bap" before) June 2" 1728

George the Son of Stephen & Jane Russell bap⁴ June 2 1728

Nathaniel the Son of } Charles & Eliz Brewer
Mary the Daughter of } bap⁴ June 29 1728

Mary the Daughter of Cap' Sutherland bap⁴ June 30ᵗʰ 1728

Mary the Daughter of Henry Wood Jun' bap⁴ July 12ᵗʰ 1728

W'" the Son of W" & Ruth Holman bap⁴ July 14, 1728

Godfrey the Son of Charles & Eliz Hill bap⁴ July 15, 1728

Edward the Son of W'". & Mary Cattell bap' July 15 1728

Abraham the Son of Francis & Mary Ladson bap⁴ July 21 1728

Mary the Daughter of Robt & Anne Ladson bap⁴ July 22, 1728

Obadiah the Son of John & Province Wood bap⁴ Aug' 18 1728

Joseph the Son of Thos & Mary Mell bap⁴ Sept' 12 1728

William the Son of Ayloff & Joanna Drayton-Weedon bap" Sept 28 1728

Jane the Daughter of W'" & Rebecca Guy bap⁴ Sept 29 1728

John the Son of Benjamin & Marg' Godfrey bap⁴ Sept 29 1728

Mary the daughter of ——— Hannah Conyers bap⁴ October 7 1728

John Samways bap⁴ October 14 1728

Elizabeth the Daughter of Mʳ Bryan bap⁴ October 26 1728

Thos' the Son of Th' & Prischilla Oldham bap⁴ Nov 2 1728

Sarah the Daughter of Edw⁴ & Rosamond Perry bap⁴ Dec' 25 1728

Catherine the Daughter of Mr Ralph Izard bap^d Jany 27
1728/9

Martha the Daughter of John & Sarah Cattell bap^d Febry
9 1728/9

John the Son of Peter & Catherine Cattell bap^d Febry 21
1728/9

————the Daughter of Thomas & Martha Whaley bap^d.
March 9 1728/9.

Elizabeth the Daughter of W^m. Fuller Junr ⎰bap^d March
Mary the Daughter Ibid   ⎱21 1728/9

Anne the Daughter of David M'quin bap^d March 21
1728/9

Kezia the Daughter of Jacob & Eliz Ladson bapd March
30 1729

Elizabeth the Daughter of ———— Mackintosh bap^d
March 30 1729

Catherine the Daughter of W^m & Mary Chapman bap^e
April 13, 1729

Mary the Daughter of Coll & ———— Herbert of Goosecreek bap^d May 18 1729

Elizabeth the Daughter of Peter & Elizabeth Perry &

Elizabeth the daughter of John & Martha Rivers bap^d May
25 1729

John the Son of Benj. & Martha Godfrey (als Garnier)
P^rs bap^d July 3^d 1729

Samuel Atwood the Son of Samuel & ———— Williams
bap^d Augt 17 1729

Elizabeth the Daughter of Charles & Eliz Crubin bap^d.
Augt. 31 1729

Margaret the Daughter of Francis & Lydia Yonge bap^d
p^r Sep^t 18 1729

Thomas the Son of Edmund & Elizabeth Bellinger bap^d
pr Sept 25 1725

Joseph the son of Joseph & Eliz· Heap bap^d pri October
3^d 1729

John the Son of Christopher & ———— Jinks bap^d Nov^r
30 1729

Richard the Son of Thos & Mary Dymes bap^d Novr 30
1729

Elizabeth y'. Daughter of James & Sarah Manning } bap^d Dec^r

Henry the Son of Abraham & Eliz Musheau } 21. 1729

James the Son of Peter & Reb Hoskins bap^d Decr. 26. 1729

Catherine the Daughter of Henry & ——— Wood bap^d Decr. 28 1729

Eliz the Daughter of Jeremiah & Belinda Burrows bap^d Janry 11th 1729/30

Sarah the daughter of Peter & Amarynshia Taylor of Goosecreek bap^d Feb 22^d 1729, 30

Anne the Daughter of John & Mary Heydon at Coll Bulls' bap^d March 18 1729/30

Sarah the Daughter of W^m & Rebecca Guy bap^d March the 19th 1729/30

Martha Wood an Adult bap^d April 29th 1730—

Sarah the wife of Alex^r. Long bap^d. May 3^d 1730

Rebecca the Daughter of W^m & Ruth Holman bap^d May 10th 1730

Rich^d the Son of Edmund & Elizabeth Bellinger bap^d May 14 1730

Moses the Son of W^m & Mary Miles bap^d May 18 1730

Sarah the Daughter of Benjn & ——— Waring of Goosecreek bap^d May 24 1730

MARRIAGES.

James Smith & Mary Cockran Spinst^r of St Pauls parish mar^d April 27 1729

Francis Wilkinson. & Margaret Arden Sp^r mar^d May 8th 1729

William Harris, & Mary Ladson Sp^r. mard July 3^d. 1729

Samuel Stocks & Eliz Samways Widd mard July 3^d 1729

Thomas Pritchard & Susannah Elliott Widd mard Sep^t 2^d. 1729

Joshua Snowden & Elizabeth Evans Widdow mard Septr 20 1729

James Taylor & Hester Wood Sp' mard October 23ᵈ 1729.

William Snow of Goosecreek & Sarah Herbert Sp' mard
  Oct' 30 1729

Nathaniel Starling & Anne Ayers Sp' mard Dec' 11
  1729

Charles Jones & Rachel Edghill Sp' mard Dec' 16, 1729

John Andrew Deha & Margaret Caroll of Goosecreek pᵗʰ
  mard Dec' 18 1729

William Flood & Mary McElvey Spinst' mard Febry 4
  1729/30.

Charles Bret & Rebecca Worden Spins' mard Febry 15
  1729/30

Jonathan Daniel & Catherine Croomy Spr mard April 5ᵗʰ
  1730

Wᵐ Middleton & Mary Izard Sp' of Goosecreek mard
  April 21, 1730

Richard Glandal & Hannah Gibson widdow mard April
  29 1730

Peter Girerdeau & Elizabeth Bohun Spins' mard Dec'
  19ᵗʰ 1730

Thomas Drayton & Eliz. Bull Spr mard Dec'. 26ᵗʰ 1730

Zebulon Guy & Anne Allein mar'd January 13 1730/31

William Cheatham & Sarah Fuller mar'd February 22ᵈ
  1730/31

Thoˢ Stocks & Rachel Holman Sp' mard May 20ᵗʰ 1731

Stephen Bull & Martha Godin Sp' mard p' the Revᵈ
  M' Commissary Garden April 27, 1731

Thoˢ Barlow & Susannah Godfrey Widd mard July 29
  1731.

Benjᵐ Savage & Elizabeth Smith widd Aug' 19 1731

John Champneys & Mary Musgrove Sp' mard Aug' 31
  1731

Thoˢ Goreing & Jane Heydon Wⁱdˣ Mard Septembᵣ 9ᵗʰ
  1731—

Josiah Cantey & Elizabeth Boswood Sp' Mar'd October
  3ᵈ 1731

William Stocks & Rachel Ladson Sp' mard Dec' 9 1731

Stephen Hartley & Eliz Newton Sp' being 3 Lᵈˢ Day
  Pub January 13 1731/2

Jacob Bonneau & Eliz Webb Sp' were mard January 16 1731, 2

James Ker & Hester Gibbons mard January 26 1731, 2

Rich^d. Webb & Priscilla Emanuel widd mard February 13 1731 2

Peter Furcher & Catherine Daniel Widd mard February 22 1731 2

James Osmond & Mary Hall Spin' mard April 13th 1732

Peter Tomplet & Isabella Black Sp' mard April 17, 1732

Wm Cattell Jun' & Anne Cattell Sp' mard May 17 1732

Thos Butler & Elizabeth Ladson Sp'. mard June 13, 1732

Samuel Marcus & Priscilla Burnly Sp' mard June 18 1732

Robt Ladson & Sabina Rose Sp' mard Aug'. 3^d 1732

Edward Simpson & Sarah Cheatham Wid mard Aug' 6 1732

Edward Hill & Jane Clare Sp' Mard Nov' 3^d 1732

John Man & Anne Vincent Sp', mard Nov' 16 1732

Elding King & Eleanor Norman Sp' mard January 4 1732/3

John Purkis & Elizabeth Ayers widd mard February 4th 1732 3

Josiah Baker & Rebecca Butler Sp'. mard March 12 1732 3

Samuel Witter & Loveridge Wilkie Widd mard March 14 1732/3

FUNERALS.

Belinda Burrows burd Jany — 1729 30

One Griffith an Overseer of Mr J^o Cattell's burd January 12th 1729 30.

Mr Thos Dymes bur'd January 14 1729/30

Mrs Deveaux burd Jany 24 1729 30

- ———— Son of Jeremiah Burrows bur'd January 26 1729 30

Sarah the Daughter of Samuel Crawford burd April 15th 1730

Mary the Daughter of Benjn & Marg^t Godfrey bur'd June 8, 1730

Mary the Wife of John Stanyarne of S' Pauls bur'd July
  12, 1730
George the son of W^m & Anne Brandford bur'd July 12
  1730
Mary the Daughter of W^m & Martha Fuller Jun' burd
  Aug'. 7 1730
Mary the Daughter of John & Mary Delony bur'd Aug'.
  26 1730
Richard the Son of Rich^d & Mary Fuller bur'd Sept' 8th
  1730
William the Son of Ahft & Johanna Wedon bur^d. Sep'.
  12th 1730
Anne Daughter of David & Martha M'quin bur'd Sep' 12
  1730
Tho* Holman Sen' Bur'd October 7th 1730
George Smith burd October 12th. 1730
Moses the Son of W^m & Mary Miles bur'd Octob' 16
  1730.
Sarah the Daught' of W^m & Rebecca Guy bur'd Oct 24
  1730
Anne the Daught' of Wm Fuller Sen' bur'd Oct'. 25
  1730
Francis the Son of Francis & Lydia Yonge bur'd Oct' 26
  1730.
Anne y' Wife of Nathaniel Starling bur'd Dec' 21, 1730
M'' Forguson the mother of M'' Jones bur'd February 6th.
  1730/1
M' Samuel West bur'^d February 20 1730/1
M' James Boswood Sen'. bur'd February 25, 1730/1
M' Tho* Haydon bur'd February 28, 1730/1
M' Edward Byrch bur'd March 29th 1731
Tho* the Son of Charles & Eliz Crubin bur'd April 15
  1731
M' Wm Cheatham bur'd July 10th 1731
M' Samuel Frith bur'd July 19 1731
M' James Walford bur'd Aug' 25, 1731
M' Sam' Crawford bur'd October y' 25th 1731
Tho* the Son of Tho* & Eliz Drayton bur'd Nov'. 10
  1731

Anne Smallwood bur'd Nov' 11ᵗʰ 1731

Mr Wᵐ Fuller Senʳ. Bur'd Novʳ 14, 1731

Mʳˢ Ruth Holman bur'd Novʳ 20ᵗʰ 1731

Mʳ John Godfrey Junʳ Bur'd Decʳ 7ᵗʰ 1731

Wᵐ Son of Stephen Bull burd February 27ᵗʰ. 1731/2

Richard Edgell, Burd April 30ᵗʰ 1732

Judith the Daughtʳ of Charles Hill bur'd May 25 1732

Hester the Daughter of Edmund Bellinger bur'd July 2ᵈ 1732

James the Son of Thoˢ Rose burd Augˢ 9ᵗʰ 1732

Mary the Daughʳ of John Hayden burd Augˢ 14 1732

Jonathan Stocks bur'd Augˢ. 14 1732

Henry Hodgkins burd Augˢ 24 1732

John Durson burd Septʳ 4 1732.

Arthur Hall bur'd at Stono Church October 7, 1732

Sarah Perry the Mother of Benjamin Perry burd Octʳ 1732

Joseph Falkinham bur'd November 21, 1732

John Riggs bur'd Novʳ. 29 1732

(To be continued)

ORDER BOOK

of

John Faucheraud Grimke

August 1778 to May 1780

The Order Book of John F Grimké, Lt Col of S. C. Artillery, is to be found in the same parchment bound volume which contains his *Journal of the Campaign to the Southward*, printed in Vol XII, 1911, of this magazine

John F Grimke, the son of John Paul Grimké and Mary Faucheraud his second wife, was born Dec 16, 1752, and died at Long Branch, N J, 9th August, 1819 [1] He studied law in London and was one of the American students who petitioned George III against the measures that infringed on Colonial Rights He returned to South Carolina at the beginning of hostilities, and entered the Continental Army, being commissioned captain in the Artillery, 16th Sept, 1776, and was promoted major 25th Oct, 1778 [2]

Lt Col° Barnard Elliott of Artillery Corps died 25th Oct 1778; Major Beckman was promoted to his place and Capt John F Grimke succeeded him as major On Aug 24, 1778, he was appointed Deputy Adj General with rank of Colonel This information is given in the Order Book, as is seen below, but varies from the statement in the *Journals of Continental Congress*, Nov 1778 (p 1137) that, "Mr Ed Hyrne and John Grimké were nominated by the delegates of South Carolina for Adjutants general" "Captain Edmund Hyrne was elected deputy adjutant general in the Southern department." Col. Grimké certainly served as Dep Adj. Gen· until he was taken prisoner at the seige of Charlestown, 12th May, 1780

---

[1] Died, at Long Branch, State of New Jersey on the 9th August, the Hon John F Grimke Senior Associate Judge of the Court of Sessions and Common Pleas of this State, in the 67th year of his age, after an illness of more than a year, which he bore with the fortitude and resignation of a Christian He lived and died a Soldier Patriot and Christian—(*The Courier*, Aug 21, 1819)

[2] O'Neall *Bench and Bar of S C*

In March, 1781[1] Lt Col Grimké and Major Habersham were arrested and placed in close confinement upon the very slim pretext of having written a personal letter which was construed to be a breach of parole, this imprisonment in the City Guard lasted for five weeks, and then they were released upon orders received from Lord Cornwallis

Col Grimké considered that his imprisonment rendered his parole null and void, and as no other parole was given him after his release, he considered himself at liberty to return to duty, joined General Green's Army,[1] and served to the end of the war

He was elected Judge of the Court of Law, 20th March, 1783[2] Was Speaker of the House of Representatives from March 1785 to March 1786, and a member of the Convention of 1788 which adopted the Federal Constitution[3]

Princeton gave him the degree of L. L. D in 1789[4] In 1799, when Judge Burke was elected Chancellor, Judge Grimké became Senior Associate, and thus virtually Chief Justice of South Carolina

He married, Oct 12, 1784, Mary Smith, daughter of Thomas Smith, Esq and Sarah Moore his wife The ancestry of his wife, and a list of his children will be found in the *Rhett* and *William Smith* genealogies, printed in Vol IV of this magazine

Judge Grimké published several volumes and addresses, among which are the following *Revised Edition of the Laws of South Carolina to 1789, Public Laws of South Carolina.* (Phila, 1790); *Duty of Executors and Administrators,* (N Y, 1797), this was published anonymously, and *Duty of the Justice of the Peace*

[1] *Moultrie's Memoirs,* v 2 p 173 et seq
[2] O'Neall's *Bench and Bar of S C,* v 1, p 39
[3] O'Neall's, *Bench and Bar*
[4] Appleton's *Dict Am Biog*

August 24: 1778.

Head Quarters.

24:    General Orders by Major General Howe.

Parole, Louis Le Grand.

Tomorrow being the birthday of Our great Ally the King of France, Fort Moultrie, & Fort Johnson are in Honor of the day to fire 21 Guns each: the firing at Fort Moultrie to begin precisely at one O'Clock & five minutes after it finishes it is to be taken up by Fort Johnson.

Col°. Nicholas Eveleigh having resigned his commission as Dep: Adj: Gen: for the State of South Carolina & Georgia & is no longer to be considered and Obeyed as a Continental Officer.

Major John F. Grimké is appointed to act as Dep: Adj: Gen: for the States of South Carolina & Georgia with the rank of Colonel in the room of Colonel Eveleigh resigned 'till the pleasure of Congress be known.

25:    Parole. Howe.

26:    Parole, Hancock.

The Troops are to be divided into two Brigades: The 1st. 2 & 6th Regiments will form the first Brigade, under the command of Brig: Gen: Moultrie; the 3d: & 5th Regiments will be commanded by Col°: Isaac Huger as Col°: Commandant & will form the second Brigade, the Artillery will receive their Orders from the Commander in Chief

---

August 1778

Head Quarters Charles Town.

27:

Parole, Congress

The Honble: Continental Congress having passed several Resolutions respecting the future government of the Army, the D: Adj: Gen: will transmit Copies to the Com^g: officers & Brigades & the Com^g: Officers of Artillery who are to publish them to their respective Commands that the Commanding officers of Regiments may govern themselves accordingly.

A Return of the N°. of Officers in the different Corps, with their Rank, date of Commission or Brevett is to be immediately made to the D: A: G:

Head Quarters Charles Town

28: Parole, Monmouth.

Head Quarters Ch. Town

29: Parole Moultrie.

30:
Head Quarters Ch. Town
Parole, Grimké.

31:
Head Quarters Charles Town
Parole, Pinckney

SEPTEMBER.

1:
Head Quarters Charles Town
Parole, Rutledge.

2.
Head Quarters Charles Town
Parole, Elliott.

3:
Head Quarters Ch. Town
Parole, Taarling

Cap Benjamin Cattell of the 1st Continental Regiment & Capt James Coil & Capt: Harthorn of the Sixth Continental Battalion in the State of South Carolina having resigned their Commissions are no longer to be respected or obeyed as Continental Officers.

4:
Head Quarters Charles Town
Parole, Nelson.

5:
Head Quarters Charles Town
Parole, Page.

In future all Regimental Returns are to be made to the Commanding officer of the Brigades to which the Regiments respectively belong, who will make Brigade Returns to the Commander in Chief.

The Returns for this Month are to be made immediately in the manner above directed that a General Return may be transmitted to the Board of War by the next Post.

The General in the future expects the Returns will be punctually made the first day of every month.

Head Quarters Charles Town

6:    Parole, Mifflin.

Head Quarters, Charles Town.

7:    Parole, Fayette.

The Readiness with which the troops turned out last night upon the alarm was truly pleasing to the General and the conduct of the officers has his entire approbation.

After orders.

The Main Guard is immediately to be reinforced with 1 Sergeant 1 Corporal & 11 Privates, which reinforcement is to enable the officer of the Main Guard to Relieve the Militia Guard upon Burns Wharf: Orders for this purpose will be given by the Dep: Adj: Gen: to the Officer of the Guard.

Head Quarters Charles Town

8:    Parole M'Laine

Capt George Cogdell of Col: Huger's Regiment having resigned his commission, is no longer to be respected or Obeyed as a Continental officer

September, 1778, Head

8:    After Orders

Capt. Thomas Shubrick of the 5 South Carolina Regiment is appointed Brigade Major to Isaac Huger Esq: Col: Commandant of the Second Brigade, & is to be Obeyed & Respected accordingly.

9:    Parole, Parker.

10.   Parole, Fenwicke.

11:    Parole, Barton.

The General having been informed that some of the Officers commanding the Magazine Guard at Dorchester, have frequently absented themselves from their Command, is therefore under the necessity of strictly forbidding any officers in future from quitting the town during their command.

The Adj: Gen: will furnish the next relieving officer

12: Parole, Starke.

The Main Guard is to be reduced to-morrow to 1 Capt,. 2 Subs, 2 Sergts. & 30 Rank & File.

The Magazine Guard to be reinforced with 6 Privates.

The Brigade Returns some time since ordered are expected at the Head Quarters, the General being desirous of transmitting them to the Board of War.

Detail

1st. Brigade	Captains	Lieut	Sergts	R & File
	1	2	2	15
2d Brigade	1	1	3	30
	2	3	5	45

13: Parole, Galphin.

Col Thompsons Battallion to be in readiness for Command immediately the Offr Comdg of that Brigade to which it belongs will give the necessary orders respecting Waggons, Provisions, & Ammunition & will attend Head Quarters tomorrow Morning to Receive further orders.

Detail for Town Duty

	Captains	Lieut	Sergts	R & F.
1st. Brigade	1	1	-	17
2d Brigade	1	2	3	32
for Command				
1st. Brigade		1	1	11
2d. Brigade		1	1	19
		2:	2:	30

September 1778.   Head Quarters Charles Town

14: Parole Philadelphia

The Guard at Dorchester to be relieved tomorrw by a Detachment from the third Regiment

The main Guard tomorrow is to be relieved by 1 Lieut, 1 Sergt: & 20 Rank & File

The magazine Guard to be relieved by 1 Sub 1 Sergt: & Ten R... ...

The Sixth Regiment is to Return to Town on Wednesday Morning the D: Q: M: General is to provide boats for that Purpose.

The General having been informed that some officers express a doubt whether the officers who are Members of assembly are exempt from Duty during the Sessions of the assembly by an order some time since issued: the General intended that Order as a standing Order to Exempt all officers who are Members of Assembly from Duty during their attendance upon the assembly unless the necessity of service should make their Presence absolutely requisite at their Posts or with their Detachments or Corps

Detail.

	Cap:	Lieut:	Serg⁵:	R. & F.
1ˢᵗ Brig:		1	2	12
2 Brig:	1	1	2	22

15: Morning Orders

The Guard at Hobcaw to be relieved very early tomorrow Morning by a Detachment from the Second Regiment consisting of the usual number.

Parole Holzendorf.

A General Court of Enquiry to sit this afternoon at some Convenient place in Charles Town to enquire into the Conduct of L⁺: Mayson of the third Regiment towards Lieut⁺. Taggart of the same Corps & to Report whether the Officers of the Third Regiment have reason to refuse doing Duty with L⁺. Mayson.

This Court to Consist of one Field officer as President & four other Members taken according to Detail

Major Huger President

Officers

1ˢᵗ Brig.	2
2 Brig	2

September 1778   Head Quarters Charles Town

A General Court Martial to sit at some convenient Place in Charles Town on Friday at 10 oClock in the Morning for the tryal of L⁺. Roux of Col⁺: Mottes Battallion put in arrest by Capt Motte of the same Corps for disrespect to his Commanding Officer

This Court to Consist of one Field officer as President 12 other members taken according to Detail

Major Horry President

Officers

1ˢᵗ. Brig.	5
2ᵈ Brig	7

Detail for Duty

	Cap	Lieuts	Sergᵗˢ	R & F
1ˢᵗ Brig		1	1	12
2ᵈ Brig	1	1	3	22

An officer from the Third Regᵗ is immediately to be appointed in the room of Lᵗ Mayson to take command of the Detachment marching to Dorchester & who is to proceed immediately

After Orders

A Sergeant Corporal & Six Privates to be warned for immediate Duty & are to Parade at the Main Guard where they will receive orders

	Detail	
	Sergᵗ	R & F
1ˢᵗ Brigade	0	3
2ᵈ Brigade	1	4

16   Parole Manly

The Court of Enquiry ordered to Enquire into the Conduct of Lieutᵗ Mayson of the Third Regiment have Reported as follows that Lieutᵗ Maysons making an apology upon the Field to Lieutᵗ Taggart proceeded from a Consciousness of his having used Lᵗ Taggart ill & not thro' Cowardice   They therefore think that the officers of the third Regiment may with propriety do duty with him The General approves of the Determination of the Court orders Lieutᵗ Mayson to Return to Duty & that the officers of his Corps Receive & Respect him as usual

The Court of Enquiry is disolved

Detail as Yesterday

17   Parole. Laurens

Cap' Oliver Towles of the 3ᵈ Regiment having never been exchanged with the Enemy is therefore to be considered as amenable to no Military Duty until his is released from his Parole by a proper & equal exchange

The necessity of Service requires that the order exempting officers who are Members of assembly from all duty during their attendance thereupon should in some degree be superceded. The Dep Adj Gen. will if occasion requires warn some Field officer as President of the Court Martial which is to sit tomorrow tho' such officer should be Member of Assembly

	Detail			
	Cap	Lieut	Sergt	R & F
1ˢᵗ Brig	1	2	2	23
2ᵈ Brig	0	0	0	17

Major Beckman is appointed President of the Court Marshal to sit tomorrow

Detail	
	Officers
1ˢᵗ Brigade	11
2ᵈ Brigade	1

Roster for

Field-officer of the Day   President of Courts Martial *
    Names

C Huger Promoted

L · C M'Intosh

Ma Huger   Sep 15

Co Motte   Resigned September 19 1778

L C Mayson   Under orders to March

M . Horry Absent

C Thompson   Under Orders to March

L C Elliott Sick   Died Oct 25 1778

M Wise In the Country

C Roberts

L C Marion   Evidence [?]

M Beckman   Sept 17   Promoted to be Lᵗ Colᵒ Oct 25
    1778

L C Henderson
Maj Brown Sept 26   Resigned
C Sumpter   Resigned Sept 19 1778
L C Scott
M Pinckney

18   Parole United States

The General has thought it proper to publish the following resolutions of Congress

In Congress   May 29. 1778

Resolved—That all Military officers & Soldiers in the Service of the United States are & of right ought to be amenable to the laws of the State in which they reside in Common with other Citizens

But as to the Propriety of undertaking distant expeditions & Enterprizes or other Military operations & the mode of Conducting them, the General or Commanding officer must finally Judge & Determine at his Peril

Detail

	Cap	Lieuts	Serg	R & F
1" Brig	1	1	2	23
2 Brig	0	1	3	17

Charles Town Sep 18 1778

Sir

I am ordered by the General to Signify to you that it is his Pleasure the remainder of Col°· Thompsons Reg' (deducting the 74 to have marched yesterday) should Continue to do duty in Town until They are ready to March or that Col° Sumpters Reg Should arrive in Town to Relieve them   I am also commanded to inform you that the General desires you would apply to that Commanding officer of the Detachment from Col° Thompsons Corps which marched to the Southward to account for the Stores delivered him during the Expedition

I am, Sir
with Respect
Your very ob' Hum Serv'
J F Grimke \ D \ G

Col° _ Huger

*Tabular

10:   Parole, Abingdon.

Col: Motte of the 2d Regt: & Col: Sumpter of the 6th Regt. having resigned their Commissions are no longer to be Considered as Continental officers

A Detachment of the Third Regt: in proportion to the Waggons now ready are to march for Orangeburgh with all possible Expedition

the 6 Reg: arrived in town.

20:   Parole, Drayton

		Detail			
		Cap:	Lieut:	Serj:	R: & F:
Brig	1	1	1	2	23
	2	0	1	3	17

September. 1778   Head Quarters Charles Town

21:   Parole Maryland.

The Court Martial now setting is to try Charles Trouble-field, a Private in the Second Continental Battalion in this State for Desertion   Lt. Col: Marion will produce the Evidences.

Lieut Cato West of the Third Continental Battalion in this State having resigned his Commission on the 14 Inst.. is no longer to be respected or Obeyed as a Continental officer.

The Guard at Dorchester to be relieved tomorrow Morning by a Detachment from the 1st. Brigade consisting of 1 Lieut. 1 Sergt. 2 Corpl: & 15 Privates

22:   Parole, General Howe.

The detachment from the First Brigade ordered to Relieve the Guard at Dorchester, yesterday, is countermanded until further orders.

*A Return of the Number of Officers, Supernumerary officers, Vacancies etc: in the Cont: Regiments in South Carolina; Sepr. 22, 1778.

1st. Regiment. Field officers 3: Supernumerarys 1, Col. C: C: Pinckney Supernumerary Captains 7. Su-

*The tabular form of the original omitted owing to the diffi-
nlty in reproducing.

pernumerary 1, Cap' Theus Supernumerary.
Brevet Cap' 2. Supernumeraries Capt' Elliott &
Hext. Cap' Lieutenant, none, one vacancy
Lieutenants 7, Brevet Lieutenants 3 Supernumer-
ary, Lieut. Fishburn 2^d Lieutenants or Ensigns 4,
vacancies, 5

2^d. Regiment. Field Officers 2, Captains 8, Supernumerary
Captains, Dunbar & Hall Capt Lieutenant, none,
1 vacancy Lieutenants 9, 2^d Lieut' or Ensigns
3, 6 vacancies.

3^d Regiment Field officers 3, Supernumerary field officer
Col Thompson Captains 11; Supernumerary cap-
tains, Jos Warley, Goodwin, Caldwell, Towles &
Hart Captain Lieut, none, 1 vacancy. Lieutenants
9 2^d Lieuts or Ensigns 10, Supernumerary Henry
Ramsey, no commission

[4th] Regiment * Field officers 3 Captains 6, & 6 vacancies Cap' Lieut' 6 & 6 vacancies Lieutenants 4,
& 8 vacancies 2^d Lieutenants none, 36 vacancies

5th Regiment Field officers 2 Supernumerary Col" Isaac
Huger Captains 4, 2 vacancies Cap'" Lieutenants
1 vacancy Lieutenants 1, 8 vacancies 2^d Liepten-
ants or Ensigns 3, vacancies 6

6th Regiment Field officers 2 Captains 3, & 3 vacancies
Cap' Lieut 1 vacancy Lieutenants 6 & 3 vacancies
2^d Lieutenants or Ensigns, 1, & 8 vacancies.

Names of Officers to be promoted & of those who have no
Commissions

5th Regiment Capt' Blamyer & Martin Capt Lieut.
Keith Lieutenants Guerry, Kenny, Hogan, Fotheringham, Warren & Ogier

6th Regiment Capt' Bowie, Armstrong & Lacie Capt
Lieut Hampton L'' Pollard, Brown & Redmond
2^d Lieu' Joel Doggett, no Commission

23 Parole, Bowen

Lieu' Richard Muncreef of the Fifth Continental Battalion in this State having resigned his Commission on

—

*Not numbered in original

the 21st Instant is no longer to be respected or obeyed as a Continental officer.

24:   Morning orders.

An Officer to be immediately warned to attend the General Court Martial now sitting as a Member, in the room of Capt. Dunbar who is too ill to attend.

Parole, Moultrie.

The Court Martial ordered to sit for the tryal of L^t. Roux of the Second Continental Battalion in this State have reported as follows—The Court is of opinion that L^t. Roux is not Guilty of the Charge under wheih he was arraigned & do therefore acquit.   The General therefore discharges L^t. Roux from arrest & orders him to Return to Duty.

September 1778   Head Quarters Charles Town

25:   Morning orders.

An officer to be warned for & immediately to attend the General Court martial now setting as a Member in the room of Capt. Charnock who is Sick

Parole, Huger.

Capt. Harleston of the Second Continental Battalion in this State is appointed a Member of the General Court Martial now sitting, in the room of Capt. Charnock taken ill.

26:   Morning orders.

A Field Officer to be summoned to immediately attend the General Court Martial as President in the room of Major Beckman taken ill; an officer member of of assembly may be warned if there are no other Field Officers in Town.

Major Brown is appointed President of the General Court Martial now setting in the room of Major Beckman.

Parole, Sullivan.

27:   Parole, Burke.

28:   Morning Orders.

An officer to be immediately warned as a member of the

General Court Martial now sitting in the room of L': Prevost.

An officer to be immediately warned to attend the General Court Martial now sitting as a Member in the room of Cap'. Bowie taken ill.

The General Court now sitting are to try J: B: Taylor of the Second Regiment, confined by L'. Prevost, for desertion, also John Pinker of the fifth Battalion confined by—Bennett a Private in the same Corps for Desertion.

Parole—Thompson

29: Morning Orders.

An officer is to be immediately warned to attend the Gen: Court Martial as a Member in the room of Cap'. Turner taken ill.

Cap'. Roberts of the Corps of artillery is appointed a Member of the General Cort Martial now sitting in the room of Cap'. Turner taken ill.

Parole, Monmouth.

Sir

In Obedience to the General Commands I am to inform you that you must still Continue with your Detachment the Guard you keep at Dorchester over the Magazine until you receive further Orders from Head Quarters. I am extremely Sorry that the absolute necessity of Service should be the occasion of your not having been relieved in proper time to join your Regiment. Should it be requisite for your Regiment to advance higher up the Country than Orangeburg I shall use my Endeavours to have you immediately in order that you may march with your Corps.

I am Sir
Your Ob'. Hum'. Serv'.
John F. Grimke D. A. G.

To Lien'. Mayson
or the Officer
Com' at Dorchester

30: Parole. Sullivan

ABSTRACTS FROM THE RECORDS OF THE COURT OF ORDINARY OF THE PROVINCE OF SOUTH CAROLINA, 1700-1710[1]

By A S Salley, Jr

(Continued from the October number)

August 2, 1706, Mary Davis, widow, and Elizabeth Godfrey, widow, executed a bond to Governor Johnson for Mrs. Davis's proper administration of the estate of Col William Davis, late of the province, deceased Witness John Barnwell, D. S (Page 108)

August 2, 1706, Lewis Pasquereau and Benjamin Godin executed a bond to Governor Johnson for Pasquereau's proper administration of the estate of Thomas Tomson Witness: John Barnwell, D S (Page 109)

November 20, 1706, John Whilden, Robert Murrill and John Huggins executed a bond to Governor Johnson for John Whilden's proper administration of the estate of John Whilden, late of Seewee, deceased (Page 110)

November 26, 1706, Marie DuBosc, widow, and Dr John Thomas, chirurgeon, executed a bond to Governor Johnson for Mrs DuBosc's proper administration of the estate of James DuBosc, late of Charles Town, deceased (Page 111.)

December 18, 1706, John Lawrence and Gunning Bedford executed a bond to Governor Johnson for Lawrence's proper administration of the estate of James Braxton, late of Charles Town, deceased (Page 113)

December 14, 1706, "Madam Elizabeth Blake and Coll George Logan" executed a bond to Governor Johnson for Mrs Blake's proper administration of the estate of John Milward, late of the Province, deceased (Page 114)

December 31, 1706, Jonathan Drake, Thomas Summers and John Raven executed a bond to Governor Johnson for

---

[1] The second volume of wills and bonds of the Court of Ordinary (now Probate Court, Charleston County) is erroneously labelled "1687-1710" The records therein begin in 1700 and end in 1711

Drake and Raven's proper administration of the estate of Joseph Ellicott. (Page 115.)

February 6, 1706-7, William Wells and Evan MacPherson executed a bond to Governor Johnson for Wells's proper administration of the estate of William Adams (Page 116.)

February 12, 1706-7, John Woodward and Richard Woodward executed a bond to Governor Johnson for John Woodward's proper guardianship of James Stanyarne, minor, son of James Stanyarne, late of the province, deceased. (Page 117.)

March 12, 1706-7, Joseph Ellicott, Edward Loughton and William Gibbon executed a bond to Governor Johnson for Ellicott's proper administration of the estate of Joseph Ellicott, deceased Witness John Barnwell (Page 118)

March 6, 1706-7, Mary King, widow, executed a bond to Governor Johnson for her proper administration of the estate of Thomas King (Page 119)

March 26, 1707, Henry LeNoble, Lewis Pasquereau and Peter de St Julien executed a bond to Governor Johnson for their proper administration of the estate of Alexander Thesée Chastaigner (Page 120)

February 10, 1706-7, John Fripp, William Whippey and John Jenkins executed a bond to Governor Johnson for Fripp's proper guardianship of Ralph Bailey, minor, son of Henry Bailey, late of Colleton County deceased (Page 121)

In 1707, Margaret Ladson, and Richard Cartright executed a bond to Governor Johnson for the proper administration of the estate of Thomas Cuby by "Margarett Ladson late widdow and relict of Thomas Cuby late of this province deced and administratrix with the will anexed of ye sd deced " (Page 122)

May 23, 1707 Robert Lewis, William Murrill and John Murrill executed a bond to Governor Johnson for their proper administration of the estate of John Murrill Witness John Barnwell (Page 123)

August 19, 1907, Andrew Allen, William Gibbon and Elisha Prioleau executed a bond to Governor Johnson for

Allen's proper administration of the estate of Evan Mac-Pherson late of Charles Town, deceased   (Page 125)

September 17, 1707, Samuel Eveleigh and David Ferguson executed a bond to Governor Johnson for Eveleigh's proper administration of the estate of Thomas Martin Witness George Evans   (Page 126.)

October 16, 1707, Samuel Pugson and Susannah, his wife, John Wright and Henry Bullock executed a bond to Governor Johnson for Mr and Mrs Pugson's proper administration of the estate of John Wilkinson, late of Curacoa, deceased Witness George Evans   (Page 127.)

November 6, 1707, Dorothy Hamilton, widow, William Gibbon and Henry Bower executed a bond to Governor Johnson for Mrs Hamilton's proper administration of the estate of John Hamilton Witness George Evans (Page 128)

January 30, 1707-8, Thomas Elliott, George Evans and Thomas Booth executed a bond to Governor Johnson for Elliott's proper administration of the estate of John Elliott. (Page 129)

February 21, 1707-8 Elizabeth Hilliard, John Lawes and Peter Mailhet executed a bond to Governor Johnson for Elizabeth Hilliard's proper administration of the estate of Thomas Hilliard   (Page 130)

May 25, 1708, Mrs Mary Hatchman, Nathaniel Laws and John Fidling executed a bond to Governor Johnson for Mrs Hatchman's proper administration of the estate of her late husband, Joseph Hatchman   (Page 131)

August 24, 1708, Rachel Duggall, Nathaniel Snow and Michael Boss executed a bond to Governor Johnson for Rachel Duggall's proper administration of the estate of John Duggall, late of Berkeley County, deceased   (Page 132)

Will of William Adams, glover, of Charles Town, South Carolina, made June 1, 1707, gave children, William, John, Jane and Lydia Adams, all of his estate real and personal, after deducting all charges for their bringing up, to be equally divided between them, appointed Peter Guerard and William Elliott, executors, directed that his son, William be bound as an apprentice until twenty-one to the said William Elliott, directed that his daughter, Jane, live with her sister, Eliza Grimball, wife of Thomas Grimball, until she should reach the age of eighteen and that she should be "brought up to her needle"; directed that his daughter, Lydia, be brought up until she reach the age of eighteen and be "put to school to learn" by Mrs Elizabeth Wetherick and that the executors agree with Mrs Wetherick for the same   Witnesses   William Sadler, John Child, Timothy Bellamy, Thomas Hepworth. Recorded July 22, 1707 (Page 133)

Will of Christopher Smith, of Carolina, gentleman, made July 9, 1706, and proved before Governor Johnson, May 3, 1709, directed his funeral expenses to be first paid out of his estate, desiring that they amount to not more than £5 current money of the province; gave granddaughter, Mary Beresford, a tract of seventy acres of land which he had purchased of Philip Dobridge and which had formerly belonged to James Hutton and situated in Berkeley County on Mawan, or Thomas, or Col Daniell's Island, but in case of her death without issue it was to go to his said grandson, Christopher Smith; gave grandson, "Christopher Smyth the son of John Smyth", deceased, when he should attain the age of twenty, a plantation in Berkeley County, known as Cowpens, Upper Fork, and containing one thousand acres, also one half of his negroes, horses, mares, cattle, plate, household stuff and personal estate; gave his wife the use of said plantation, slaves, cattle, hogs and premises in consideration of her furnishing said grandson meat, drink, washing, lodging and apparel necessary and convenient and of her "educating of him at school & buying of him books & all things requisite for his learning until he be twenty years of age", gave granddaughters, Mary and Elizabeth, children of his said son, "John Smyth deceased", a negro apiece as they attain the age of eighteen, and in the event of the death of either the other was to get both negroes unless the one so dying should leave issue; gave "wife Dorothy Smith" the tract of land upon which she then lived, called Stock Prior, in Berkeley County, up

Charles Town Neck, containing five or six hundred acres, houses, out-houses, barns, stables, etc, for life, in lieu of dower, also all the remainder of his personal estate for life, all the white servants during their "times", horses, mares, hogs, cattle, household goods, plate, goods, wares, grain and merchandise upon condition that she constantly employ the negroes on the plantation so as to keep the same in good repair, gave all of said property to grandson, Christopher Smyth, after the death of testator's wife, and in the event of his death without issue the bequest was to go to his grandchildren, Mary Beresford and Mary and Elizabeth Smyth, or such of them as should be living; appointed wife, Dorothy Smith, guardian of grandson, Christopher, and sole executrix, but in case of her death William Elliott, planter, of Berkeley County, was to act as executor and guardian. Witnesses Thomas Broughton, William Smith, George Logan and Henry Wigington (Pages 134-135.)

November 12, 1708, John Moore and Richard Wigg executed a bond to Governor Johnson for Moore's proper administration of the estate of Simon Merrick, late of Berkeley County, deceased (Page 136)

December 23, 1708, John Barnwell, Esq, and Capt Joseph Page, executed a bond to Governor Johnson for Barnwell's proper administration of the estate of Charles Morgan, late of Granville County, deceased Witness Job Rothmahler (Page 137)

January 14, 1708-9, Sarah Freer and William Gibbon executed a bond to Governor Johnson for Sarah Freer's proper administration of the estate of John Freer late of Colleton County, deceased Witness Job Rothmahler (Page 138)

May 5, 1709 Sarah Rhett, Thomas Broughton and Ralph Izard executed a bond to Governor Johnson for Mrs Rhett's proper administration of the estate of John Kimber Witness: Job Rothmahler (Page 139)

May 12, 1709, Mary Bulline, Dominick Arthur and John Gough executed a bond to Governor Johnson for Mary Bulline's proper administration of the estate of Roger Weeks (Page 140)

May 12, 1709, Elizabeth Shand and Richard Park executed a bond to Governor Johnson for Elizabeth Shand's proper administration of the estate of James Shand, late of Berkeley County, deceased (Page 141)

In May, 1709, Mrs Page and John Barnwell executed a bond to Governor Johnson for Page's faithful administration of the estate of Joseph Page of this province, deceased Witness Job Rothmahler. (Page 142)

May 25, 1709, William Smith, Samuel Eveleigh and Dove Williamson executed a bond to Governor Johnson for Smith and Eveleigh's faithful administration of the estate of Richard Nixon, deceased, late of the Province Witness. James Goold. (Page 144 "Trott Secretary Ends " Page 143 contains a blank bond)

Sept 9, 1709, Daniel Quintard and Capt Jonathan Drake executed a bond to Governor Johnson for Quintard's faithful administration of the estate of Jaques Marseau, deceased, late of the province Witness. James Mazyck (Page 145)

August 5, 1709, John Holland, Sr , gentleman, and Dr John Hutchinson executed a bond to Governor Johnson for Holland's faithful administration of the estate of John Holland, Jr , deceased, late of the province Witness Thomas Hepworth, Dep Sec (Page 146)

August 25, 1709, William Nash, Jr , and Charles Armstrong executed a bond to Governor Johnson for Nash's faithful administration of the estate of Daniel Nash, deceased, late of the province Witness Henry Wigington, Secretary (Page 147)

Letters of administration on the estate of Daniel Nash, deceased, were granted to William Nash, Jr , August 25, 1709 (Page 148.)

The warrant of appraisement on the estate of Daniel Nash was directed to John Jarvis, Samuel Shaddock, James Green, Thomas Stanyarne and William Green (Page 148)

August 31, 1709, Mary Neud and Philip Gendron executed a bond to Governor Johnson for Mrs Neud's faithful administration of the estate of Nicholas Neud, deceased, late of the province Witness. Henry Wigington Secretary Letters of administration were granted to Mary

Neud, "widd of S^a Nicholas Neud," August 31, 1709, and a warrant of appraisement was directed to Peter Gaillard, Peter Robert, Jr, Henry Bruneau, Daniel Huger, Sr, and Charles de Creux   (Page 149)

August 31, 1709, Prudence Mary Bonin, widow, and Henry Bruneau, gentleman, executed a bond to Governor Johnson for Mrs Bonin's faithful administration of the estate of Aman Bonin, deceased, late of the province   Witness   H Wigington, Secretary.   Letters of administration were granted to Mrs Bonin on the same day, and a warrant of appraisement was directed to Peter Le Chevalier, Elisha Prioleau, Charles Franchome, Isaac Porcher, Jr, and Peter Manigault on the same day   (Pages 149-150)

August 30, 1709, William Beard and Thomas Dalton executed a bond to Governor Johnson for Baird's proper guardianship of Anne Dearsley, an infant   Witness   T Hepworth   (Page 151)

October 20, 1709, Matthew Beard, James Moore and James Beard executed a bond to Governor Johnson for Matthew Beard's proper guardianship of Margaret, Edward, Nicholas and Ann, orphan children of Nicholas Mahum, deceased   Witness T Hepworth   (Page 153 Page 152 is blank)

October 25, 1710, Roger Saunders, John Bourne and John Fulham executed a bond to Governor Gibbes for the said Saunders's faithful administration of the estate of William Saunders, deceased late of the province   (Page 154)

John Collins, of Charles Town, by his will, made August 13, 1707, and proved before Governor Johnson, February 9, 1709, gave wife, Elizabeth, a town lot in Charles Town, a negro woman, a pacing horse and all of his furniture, gave son, Jonah Collins, his lands at Carnadey (1,300 acres), Primatt's and Washhoe plantations; gave son, Alexander Collins, Tibwen and Bull's Island plantations, gave daughter, Elizabeth Collins, a feather bed and furniture, a negro girl and £150 currency when eighteen or married, gave daughter, Jane Collins, a like legacy on like terms; directed his executors to sell his "Plantation on ye Neck of the Town on Cooper River" and the stock on the same and divide the proceeds of sale equally between his said daughters, and reckoned a part of the £150 currency already bequeathed to them, the remainder thereof being paid to each of the brothers from their shares, gave wife a third of his whole estate real and personal, and the remainder to his children to be equally divided among them, appointed wife executrix and son, Jonah, executor   Witnesses George Bedon, Mary Floyd, Peter Mailhet, Mary Parris and Jacob Satur   (Pages 155-157)

January 20, 1710 (1711), John Bollard, Andrew Allen and Thomas Hawley executed a bond to Governor Gibbes for Bollard's faithful administration of the estate of William Bollard, deceased, late of the province   (Page 158)

May 25, 1711, Manly Williamson, John Williamson and Andrew Allen executed a bond to Governor Gibbes for the Williamsons's faithful administration of the estate of John Maitland, deceased, late of the province   (Page 159)

(To be continued)

AN EARLY REVOLUTIONARY INCIDENT—This Day arrived here, in the Sloop Commerce Capt Richardson from New York, the Remains of the Hon Edward Fenwicke, Esq a Gentleman not less distinguished by his Goodness of Heart, than his ample Fortune   He had resided several Years in England on Account of the Education of his numerous Family, which having in a great Measure accomplished, he returned last Year to this his native Country   Being attacked with a violent Disorder, he was advised to avoid our Summer Heats, and accordingly, about six Weeks ago, sailed for New York, where after suffering much with a becoming Fortitude, he died on the 7th of this Month   As he lived beloved and respected so he died sincerely regretted by all who had the Happiness of being acquainted with so good and worthy a Man

In the same Vessel returned here Mrs Fenwicke, Widow and Messrs Edward & Thomas Fenwicke Sons of the above-mentioned Gentleman

(*South Carolina and American General Gazette* 21 July, 1775)

When the Hon Edward Fenwicke, a member of the King's Council in South Carolina died in New York on 7th July, 1775, his widow and sons chartered the sloop Commerce for the voyage to Charles Town, whither they carried his remains for interment   (See *So Ca and Am Gen. Gazette* of 21st July, 1775, for the obituary notice)

The war had but just begun for it was only on 19th April of the same year that the first gun had been fired at Lexington, and on 3rd July Washington had taken command of the American forces gathered around Boston

In Charles Town Lord William Campbell, the Royal Governor, was still living on Meeting Stdeet, but the powers of government had been since 14th June exercised by a Council of Safety, appointed by, the Provincial Congress, who were busily engaged in levying troops and otherwise preparing for the struggle.   The misfortunes that then befell the sloop Commerce are to be gathered from the "Case of Peter Berton, late of New York" as presented by him to the Royal Commissioners—(See Ontario Archives, Vol II, page 864)   Captain Richardson of the Commerce had been instructed to return as promptly as possible to New York, bringing passengers but no goods   When ready to return she had been "taken possession of by orders of a Rebel Committee and employed by them 27 or 28 days "   When released she sailed for New York, and was seized in October, 1775, at Sandy Hook, by his Majesty's ship, King Fisher

She was sent into Halifax, where she was condemned as a prize, and brought into New York in 1776 by Capt" Mountague [sic] The claimant "thinks this was the Pretence of Capt Mountague's seizing it " We get in this a glimpse of the disregard of private rights when war is flagrant—a disregard finely pictured in Cooper s novel "Miles Wallingford," where he tells of the treatment of the American ship "Dawn" by the belligerants, France and England

The names of two sons of M' Fenwick are to be found in the Confiscation Acts of 1782; first, Edward Fenwick, who had married a daughter of John Stuart, the Commissioner of Indian Affairs, and who had signed the address to Lord Cornwallis upon his success at Camden, and, secondly, John Fenwick, who held a commission in the Royal militia The latter was almost certainly the Col Fenwick who was taken by Col Harden, just previous to his capture of Fort Balfour in 1781 (*Contributed by D E Huger Smith, Esq*)

WITHERSPOON TOMB-STONE INSCRIPTIONS—The following inscriptions, copied by Mr S A Graham, a member of this Society, are from a Witherspoon burying-ground in Williamsburg County, about two and a half miles south of Lower Bridge, on the Broomstraw Road There are a number of other graves, with stones, but the inscriptions are obliterated

Esther Dubose Witherspoon
Daughter of Robert & Catherine D Witherspoon
b Apl 15, 1816, d Aug 12, 1820

Langon Cheves Witherspoon
Son of Robt & Catherin M
Born Apl 1 1818 D Aug 5 1820

Robert Sidney Witherspoon
Born 18th Sep 1704 d Aug 26 1849

Mary A A Witherspoon
Daughter of Thos & Janet Witherspoon Died June 15 1808

Robert Witherspoon
Son of James & Grandson of John Witherspoon
who was borne in Aug 1728 Died 15 Apl 1783

Elizabeth Witherspoon
Consort of Robert Witherspoon & Daughter of William
& Mary Heathly
who was born June 5th 1740 & died July 5 1820
aged 80 years & one month

Joseph M'Kee
who departed this life the 31st March 1760
aged 77 years
also of
Ann M'Kee his second wife
who died the 29th Dec 1778 aged 57 years
& also of
Elizabeth M'Kee his third wife
who died the 6 of July 1810 aged 66 years

Mrs Ann Witherspoon
Wife of Gavin Witherspoon
Died February 27, 1816, aged 47 years   She was a
devoted Christian
This monument is erected to her memory by her daughter
E W Montgomery

INSCRIPTIONS FROM THE "CHAPEL OF EASE" OF ST JAMES
CHURCH GOOSE CREEK, SITUATED NEAR MOUNT HOLLY, S C
(*Contributed by Mr Jos I Waring*)

(Headstone)

In Memory of
Dr Robert Broun
who departed this Life
25th Nov 1757
Aged 43 years

_____

(Slab on brick foundation)

Long may this marble remain
to testify to the filial affection
of Mrs Mary Loocock who caused it
to be erected—
Sacred to the Memory
of her beloved Brother Robert Broun M. D
who departed this life
6th of June 1766
Aged 44

_____

(Slab on brick foundation)

Long may this marble
as a testimony of filial affection
of Robert Broun
who caused it to be erected
Sacred to the Memory of
his beloved Brother
Archibald Brown
who departed this Life
the 1st day of Dec 1797
Aged 16 years

(Slab)

Sacred to the Memory of
Aaron Loocock Esq
who departed this Life
10ᵗʰ Feby 1794
Aged 61 years

———————

(Slab)

Sacred to the Memory of
Mrs Caroline Deas
who departed this Life
on the Evening of 21ˢᵗ Dec 1816
Aged 35 years 7 ms 3 days

- - - -

(Headstone)

Sacred to the Memory of
Richard Couch Esq
who died 2ⁿᵈ Feby 1786
Aged 45 years

(Headstone)

Mr John Reidheimer
who departed this Life on May 10ᵗʰ 1826
Aged 72 years
Actively patriotic in the War of the
Revolution, he sustained the charactor
of firm love for his Country
As a Christian he was devout
As a man honest
As a friend sincere
And he now reaps the reward,
of his toils in the Bosom
of his God

(Headstone)

Sacred to the Memory of
Peter Reidheimer
who departed this Life
July 17ᵗʰ 1812
Aged 57 years
"Come hither mortal cast an eye
Then go thy way prepared to die
Here read thy doom for die thou must
Some day like me be turned to dust"

TWO EARLY TRADERS IN CAROLINA—The following abstract of articles of agreement, is taken from the *Collections of the N Y Hist Soc , Abstracts of Wills*, Vol 2, p 440

Articles of Agreement made in Charlestowne Berkeley County. Carolina April 20, 1685, between Richard Codner, master of the ketch "Adventure" 16 tons burden and Humphrey Ashley mariner   The said Codner has let 1/3 of the vessel to said Ashley for a trading voyage along the shore as they shall agree And said Ashley is to pay £4 10s per month, while on the voyage, and is to put in 1/3 of the trading stock, and 1/3 of the provisions, and to pay 1/3 of the Port charges, the voyage not to exceed 4 months, to begin April 17, last   The said Ashley is to find one man besides himself, and a negro boy, and he is to pay their wages   The said Codner is to pay the wages of himself & 3 men   Each are bound in the sum of £50 to keep the agreement

LIST OF PUBLICATIONS

OF THE

SOUTH CAROLINA HISTORICAL SOCIETY.

COLLECTIONS.

Vol. I., 1857, $3.00; Vol. II., 1858, $3.00; Vol. III. 1859, out of print. Vol IV., 1887, unbound, $3.00, bound $4.00; Vol. V., 1897, paper, $3.00.

PAMPHLETS.

Journal of a Voyage to Charlestown in So. Carolina by Pelatiah Webster in 1765. Edited by Prof. T. P. Harrison, 1898.
                                                    75c.
The History of the Santee Canal. By Prof. F. A. Porcher. With an Appendix by A. S. Salley, Jr., 1903.
                                                    75c.

THE SOUTH CAROLINA HISTORICAL AND GENEALOGICAL MAGAZINE.

Volume I, 1900, Edited by A. S. Salley, Jr. Complete Volume.
                                                    $10.00
    Single copies of Nos. 2-4, $1.25 each.
Volume II to IX, 1901-1908, Edited by A. S. Salley, Jr.
                                        Unbound $5.00 each.
    Volume X to XII, 1909-1911. Edited by Mabel L. Webber.   Unbound $5.00 each.
Single copies of No. 4, Vol. XI, $2.50 each. Members get a discount of 25 per cent. on the above prices.
    Address: South Carolina Historical Society,
                                        Charleston, S. C.

THE

SOUTH CAROLINA

HISTORICAL AND GENEALOGICAL

MAGAZINE

PUBLISHED QUARTERLY BY THE

SOUTH CAROLINA HISTORICAL SOCIETY

CHARLESTON, S. C.

VOLUME XIII., NO. 2.   APRIL 1912.

Entered at the Post-office at Charleston, S. C., as
Second-Class Matter.

PRINTED FOR THE SOCIETY BY
WALKER, EVANS & COGSWELL CO.
CHARLESTON, S. C.
1912

PUBLICATION COMMITTEE.

Joseph W. Barnwell,   Henry A. M. Smith,
        A. S. Salley, Jr.

EDITOR OF THE MAGAZINE
Mabel L. Webber.

CONTENTS.

CONTENTS.

N. B.—These Magazines, with the exception of No. 1 of Vol. I and No. 4 of Vol. XI, are $1.25 each to any one other than a member of the South Carolina Historical Society. Members of the Society receive them free. The Membership fee is $4.00 per annum (the fiscal year being from May 19th to May 19th), and members can buy back numbers or duplicates at $1.00 each. In addition to receiving the Magazines, members are allowed a discount of 25 per cent. on all other publications of the Society, and have the free use of the Society's library.

Any member who has not received the last number will please notify the Secretary and Treasurer,

Miss Mabel L. Webber,
South Carolina Historical Society,
Charleston, S. C

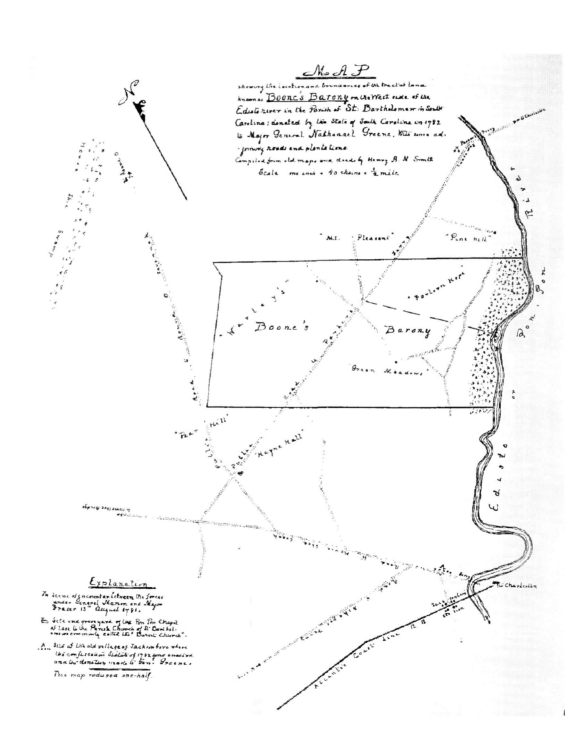

The South Carolina Historical and Genealogical Magazine.

| VOL. XIII | APRIL, 1912 | No 2 |

THE BARONIES OF SOUTH CAROLINA
By Henry A. M. Smith

VIII

BOONE'S BARONY

This barony, popularly denominated such, was one in so far as it was laid out to a Cassique who was entitled under the Fundamental Constitutions to hold a barony, but was not one under the true definition of a barony in South Carolina as given in the first article of this series on the baronies of South Carolina, because it did not contain the requisite number of acres, viz 12,000 It is also not at all clear that it was laid out specifically as a barony to which the grantee was entitled under his patent as a Cassique It rather appears to have been a direct purchase from the Lords Proprietors It has been included in this series, first, because it was generally known as a barony, but mainly by reason of the special interest attaching to its ownership successively by three persons who played prominent parts in the history of South Carolina

The first grantee was John Smith As to the identity of this particular John Smith with the Cassique of that name there has been some confusion In 1675 there came to the Province a John Smith (or Smyth) who was recommended by the Earl of Shaftsbury to the Governor and Council, in a letter dated 14 June, 1675, "as my particular "friend" The letter further instructed that a Manor should be set out to him "to any Number of Acres prescribed for "Man" in our Fundamentall Constitutions"[1]

The number of acres prescribed in those Constitutions for a Manor was not less than 3,000[2]

This John Smith arrived in 1675 with his wife and a number of servants, and received warrants in that year for land to be laid out to him aggregating 1,800 acres[3]

The land actually laid out and granted to him on 20th November, 1676, was a tract of 1,800 acres on the Ashley River, opposite the barony of the Earl of Shaftsbury and at a place called by the Indian name of Booshoo, Boochaw or Boochawee. It included the site of the later town of Dorchester and was subsequently transferred or regranted to the settlers of that Town[4]

The name of the wife of this John Smith was certainly Mary This John Smith certainly died prior to 28th April, 1682, for on that day letters of administration on his estate were applied for by his widow Mary Smith (or Smyth)[5] Previous to his death, from 1680 to 1681, he acted as deputy to one of the Proprietors His widow, Mary Smith, subsequently, viz December, 1682, married Arthur Middleton, and after his death for a third (so far as the record shows) husband, Ralph Izard[6] So far as the record shows this John Smith left no children, and his widow, when the wife of Ralph Izard, made a will devising to him her interest in the Boochaw property[7] This John Smith, whose wife was Mary, was, by the editor of the Shaftsbury papers (vol V of the Transactions of the S C Historical Society) and also by the present writer, assumed to have been the Cassique, but this as-

---

[1] Collecⁿˢ Hist Soc of S C, vol 5, p 470
[2] Ibid, p 98
[3] Printed Warrant Book 1672-1679, pp 105, 106, 110
[4] S C Hist and Genealogical Magazine, vol 6, p 63
[5] Off Hist Comⁿ S C, vol 1672-1692, p 6
[6] S C Hist and Genealogical Magazine, vol 6, p 64
[7] Ibid, vol 5, p 220

sumption seems to have been an erroneous one, from the following :

In May, 1682, the Lords Proprietors write to the Governor and Council that Mr John Smith had agreed for 10,000 acres of land, but that the conveyances could not be prepared so as to be forwarded by the same ship as their letter, but that his agents could select the 10,000 acres, but no grants should be made until further instructions[8]

On 21st November, 1682, the Lords Proprietors write to the Governor and Council that they had granted patents for Cassiques to six persons, one of whom was "Mr Jno "Smith "[9] On 13th November, 1682, a warrant was issued to lay out 6,000 acres of land to "Mr John Smyth & Anne "his wife" to be laid out pursuant to the instructions of the Lords Proprietors dated 10th May, 1682[10] On 27th January, 1682/3 a formal grant with the usual plat attached was issued to "John Smith and Anne his wife" for 5,800 acres[11] Later, viz on 9th March 1682/3, warrants were issued to lay out to "John Smyth & Anne his wife" 140 acres, due for two servants brought to the Province in September, 1682, and a "Towne lott in Colleton County"[12] (Presumably at Wiltown or New London)

It would appear more plausible that the dignity of a Cassique conferred on 21st November, 1682, was conferred on the John Smith whose wife was Anne, and who had in May, 1682, agreed for 10,000 acres and had actually in November, 1682, procured a warrant for 6,000 acres, than on the John Smith whose wife was Mary, who had several years before received a grant for but 1,800 acres and who had died prior to 28th April, 1682, seven months before the patent was issued

---

[8]"Collec" Hist Soc of S C vol 1, p 106
Calendar State Papers America and West Indies, vol 1681-1685, p 234
[9]Rivers Hist Sketch of S C, p 397
Calendar State Papers America and West Indies vol 1681-1685, p 339
[10]Printed Warrant Book, 1680-1692, p 73
[11]Off Hist Com" Memo Bk, vol 1, p 500
[12]Printed Warrant Book, 1680-1692 pp 78 79

The John Smith to whom the warrant for 6,000 acres was issued would appear from the record to have been in the Province when the land was granted, arriving with his servants in September, 1682   He does not further appear on the record, which likewise fails to show to what extent he settled up and improved his grant of 5,800 acres

We next find the barony in the possession of Joseph Boone, who gives the following statement in the Memorial, stating his ownership made in 1733 concerning its acquisition by him

> "Five thousand eight hundred acres granted to John
> "Smith and Ann his wife the 13 March 1682 in Col-
> "leton County butting & bounding Easterly on the
> "Fresh River of Edisto and Westerly on land not yet
> "run out and Northerly and Southerly on land not
> "yet laid out the said Five thousand eight hundred
> "acres being in joint tenancy to said John Smith and
> "Ann his wife the aforesaid John Smith being the
> "first that dyed the sole right was then vested in his
> "wife Ann and by certain conveyances from her the
> "said Ann (then widow) to her Nephew John Smith
> "and Frances his wife and from them by a certain
> "deed of Lease & Release from said John Smith and
> "Frances his wife bearing date the 18th February 1711
> "conveyed to Joseph Boone & is now in his occupa-
> "tion "[3]

Of Joseph Boone, it appears from the record that he was the son of Thomas Boone of London, Merchant, and Sarah his wife, and apparently came to South Carolina about 1694   He was a merchant engaged in trading between England and the Province, and in 1704 was sent to England to represent the party in the Province that was in opposition to Governor Johnson and those in favor of the Church Act   He took an active part in the political life of the Province, and in 1715 was sent with Richard Beresford to England to obtain if possible from the Pro-

[3] Off Hist Comm S C Memo Bk vol 3 p 46

prietors some abatement of the measures complained of by the Province, and it need be to invoke the assistance of the Crown against the Proprietors. In this, as in the other measures taken by the popular party which culminated in the revolution of 1720 Boone was conspicuous and active against the Proprietary government." He had a house in Charles Town as well as his place in the country", and in 1715 during the Yemasse war an irruption of Appalachee Indians plundered and burned his settlement on the barony on the Edisto and destroyed a ship he was then building."

He married Anne Alexander, one of the daughters of Landgrave Daniel Axtell and the widow of John Alexander." He died in 1734 without children, and by his will devised certain of his property, including this barony, to his widow for life, and after her death to the sons of his brother, Charles Boone, by his second marriage."

He directed in his will that he be buried at Mt. Boone. Mt. Boone was a property of some 1,200 acres that had been given to his wife by her mother, Dame Rebecca Axtell, and is situate about 2 to 2½ miles Southwest of the present village of Summerville. M". Poyas, the "Octogenarian Lady" the author of "Carolina in the Olden Time" states inaccurately

> "M" Boone his" (i e the second Landgrave Smith)
> "friend was about his own age and married to his
> "wife's sister Anne the daughter of Col Blake who
> "tells us in her will that her mother survived her
> "father and gave her the plantation near Dorchester
> "which she named Mount Boone; she willed the same
> "to her nephew the Hon: Joseph Blake, who changed
> "the name to Newington"

This statement of hers has been accepted and followed by others. It is wholly incorrect. Anne Boone was not

"M'Crady S C under the Proprietary Government
"Ibid, p 469
"Ibid, p 570
"Off Hist Com" Memo Bk 3, p 46
"Probate Court Charleston Book 1732-37, p 197

a daughter of Col. Blake, who had no daughter named Anne,[19] nor was she the sister of the wife of the second Landgrave, Thomas Smith, who did not himself marry a daughter of Col Blake, and the Newington place and the Mt Boone place were entirely distinct [20] The Newington place received its name apparently from Dame Rebecca Axtell coeval with her settlement there and years before her daughter married Joseph Boone   The Newington place was by M[rs] Axtell given to her daughter Elizabeth, who married Colonel Joseph Blake, the son of the immigrant, Admiral Benjamin Blake, and under M[rs] Blake's will Newington passed to her son Joseph Blake, commonly called the Honorable Joseph Blake   To M[rs] Boone her mother gave an adjoining tract which (presumably, after M[rs] Boone's second marriage) was called Mt. Boone   The name still survives in "Boone Hill Church" the name given to a Methodist Church now on a part of the old Boone Hill tract, about one mile Southwest of Summerville   The old residences of Newington and Mt Boone were about half a mile apart, separated by what was then rice fields and is now thick swamp   The road called the Orangeburg or Cypress road runs within 100 yards of the ruins of the old Mt Boone mansion which now consists only of the brick foundations of an old brick house of considerable size

---

[19]S C Hist and Genealogical Magazine, vol 13, p 19

[20]The writer of this article has had occasion before this to call attention to grave inaccuracies on the part of M[rs] Poyas in her publications and desires to say in explanation, that M[rs] Poyas for her zeal and labor in the perpetuation of the history of her family and of her people deserves the thanks and gratitude of all   Having little opportunity to refer to contemporary records she relied upon family traditions, a most unsafe thing to do when it comes from a period so remote as a century and a half   The consequence is that for the earlier periods she is very inaccurate and even for her own family descent is not to be relied upon unless her statements can be verified and corroborated by some record

Close by the old house is the following stone, now broken in half

"Here Lyeth the Body of
"Mr Joseph Boone
"Who departed this Life the 24th
"day of February 1734
"Aged 57 years"

During his lifetime Joseph Boone added to his Edisto barony by a number of grants of adjoining land (5 grants in number) aggregating 1886 acres, which added to the 5,800 acres granted to John Smith swelled the record acreage to 7,686

Anne Boone, the widow of Joseph Boone died in 1751 By her will she makes certain devises to Charles and Thomas Boone, the children of her brother-in-law, Charles Boone, by Mary, his second wife[a] She also devised her Mt Boone place to her nephew, the Honorable Joseph Blake, but for some reason (perhaps because the devise lapsed, he having apparently predeceased his aunt) the property seems to have been sold by her executors as going under the residuary clause of her will to her granddaughter, Ann Slan

Under the terms of the will of Joseph Boone, upon the death of his widow the barony and other property went to his nephews, and in 1752 Thomas Boone, who had been born in England in 1729, came to Carolina and took possession. In 1759 he was appointed Governor of New Jersey, where he continued until 1762, when he was appointed Governor of South Carolina and held the post there until 1764 He purchased from Sir John Colleton the latter's residence near Charles Town, formerly known as Exmouth It lay on the Cooper River, south of Magnolia Cemetery, at a place afterwards occupied by the Oaks Club and now by the tanks of the Standard Oil Co The name was changed (possibly by the last Sir John Colleton) to that of "Bachelors Hall" The administration of Governor Boone in South Carolina was not a successful

[a] Prob... C... Ch... B... 1747-52 ... 459

one   He quarreled with the General Assembly and seems to have received a good deal of adverse comment   He left in 1764, and if he afterwards returned to look after his estates in the Province the writer has not discovered any evidence of it on the record   He seems to have remained in England during the revolutionary war and the Legislature which met at Jacksonborough in 1782 included him among those subjects of the Crown in list No 1 whose estates were confiscated as being subjects of his Britannic Majesty [22]   He presented to the British Royal Commission of Enquiry into the losses and services of the American Loyalists a Memorial from which many of the facts here stated have been taken [23]   In this he states that the value of his property lost by confiscation was £41,207. 4^s 4^d Sterling, say $200,700   This, however, includes his negro slaves on the barony, which, according to John Tunno, one of his witnesses, "were the best negroes he ever knew in "that part of the country."

The same General Assembly which passed this confiscation Act, passed an ordinance by which in recognition of the services of Major General Nathanael Greene three commissioners named in the ordinance were directed to invest ten thousand guineas in the purchase of an estate to be presented to him by the State of South Carolina [24]

The Hon William Johnson of South Carolina (one of the Associate Justices of the U S Supreme Court) the official biographer of General Greene, in that he was selected by the family to act as such and had all General Greene's papers turned over to him for the purpose, writes of this presentation as follows [25]

"In South Carolina, Boones Barony, a very valuable "body of land to the south of the Edisto, with a pro-"portion of the slaves attached to the land as the "property of one of the confiscated estates, were or-

[22] Stats of S C vol 4 p 516, vol 6 p ——
[23] Lenox Library, N Y Transcripts Schedule of Losses of So Ca Claimants, vol 2, pp 437-475
[24] Stats of S C, vol 4, p. 515.
[25] Ibid, vol 2 p 401

"dered by the Legislature to be conveyed to General
"Greene   As there were a number of other slaves
"constituting a part of the same gang, he made ap-
"plication to the Legislature, to have a value set upon
"them, and give him credit for a few years, that he
"may be enabled to purchase them   This also was
"immediately acquiesced in   The slaves were valued
"and transferred to him, and thus he became not only
"a slave owner, but a slave purchaser, a characteristic
"which gave no little umbrage to his quondam friends
"the Quakers, and which has been often dwelt on with
"some surprise, by those who were acquainted with
"his early enthusiasm in the cause of human freedom "

The barony lay between Parker's Ferry on the Edisto
River and Jacksonboro, and it was in this region that
Greene was encamped for months in 1781 and 1782   He
had ample opportunity to inspect the lands and observe the
negro slaves and their health and capability, and there can
be but little doubt but that the selection by the Commissioners of this estate to be presented to him was approved
of, if not suggested, by him

The journal of the Senate for the session in 1782 shows
that it was reported to that body that upon surveying
Boone's Barony it was found to contain much more land
than at first reported and that the ten thousand guineas
was not enough to pay for it all   Thereupon it was resolved to give him the whole tract

The record shows, that by a deed dated 16th May, 1782,[20]
the Commissioners of Forfeited Estates under the Act of
1782, conveyed to Major General Nathanael Greene for
£14,865 12' 10ᵈ Sterling the plantation late the property
of Thomas Boone, on the west side of Edisto River, containing 6,640 acres

The acreage stated in the deed is only 6,640 acres, but
as appeared by the later survey made in 1796 the actual
acreage was 7,420 acres, substantially the original grant
to John and Ann Smith, with the additions made by

[20] M C O Charleston Bk M 5, p 448

Joseph Boone   The value stated, £14,865 12^s 10^d Sterling, presumably represents the total value exceeding the 10,000 guineas which the Legislature originally agreed to donate, and it would appear therefore that General Greene received an estate which was supposed to contain 6,640 acres, worth £14,865 12^s 10^d, but which in reality contained 7,420 acres and was worth correspondingly more This value, say about $72,395 75 in U S currency, was a prodigious one for the times, especially in the impoverished condition of a war devasted people, and shows that the property, when conveyed to General Greene, must have been in very excellent condition, both with regard to the extent and title of the arable acreage and to the buildings and plantation equipment   It certainly appears that no considerations of petty limitation restricted the generosity of the people of South Carolina, either in the original donation or its enlargement at the suggestion of the recipient

Criticism of a considerable and invidious character was directed at General Greene because notwithstanding his Quaker antecedents and early atmosphere he became a large slave owner, and as a large landed proprietor in the South was one of that class subsequently execrated as being mercenary traders in human flesh and heartless slave drivers   He seems to have removed his slaves from their homes in South Carolina to Georgia, but there is nothing in the record to show that like some others who changed principles for profit and joined the same class, he ever abused by any ill treatment those in his power as their owner and master

He no doubt possessed that large mindedness that enabled him to recognize that if he was to utilize the estates donated to him by the gratitude of the Southern States he could do so only by resorting to the sole supply of labor that the region and the times permitted, viz · negro slaves

Exactly what General Greene did in the way of utilization of the barony it is impossible now to say

The State of Georgia followed the example set by South

Carolina in recognizing in a most concrete way the services of General Greene."

> "The beautiful and highly improved place of the "late Governor Graham in Georgia" (also confiscated) "called Mulberry Grove (the *la plus belle* of the con-"quered lands) was ordered to be conveyed to him; "and with a most delicate attention to the comfort and "known personal attachment to himself and Wayne, "the adjoining plantation was conveyed to the latter "

In 1785 General Greene established his residence in Georgia at Mulberry Grove and seems to have removed his slaves there from South Carolina. He died not long afterwards, on 19th June, 1786

He died considerably involved financially, mainly to creditors at the North who were pressing for settlement, and his widow had great difficulties in her attempts to extricate his estate. What use she made of the property on the Edisto River in South Carolina does not appear, but judgments were recovered against the estate and in 1801 the South Carolina property was sold by the Sheriff. The estate was sold in the subdivisions designated on a plat from a resurvey made in 1796, which found the contents to be 7,420 acres, and was disposed of in two tracts

To Andrew Burnet was sold on 3[d] Nov'r, 1801, four of these subdivisions, viz No 1, called the Old Ground, No 4, called Turkey hill, No. 6 and No. 7, aggregating 4,517 acres and covering all the barony lying between the public road to Ashepoo and the Edisto River.[*] To Felix Warley on the same day was sold tract No 2, called the Savannah, No 3, called the New Ground and No 5, aggregating 2,903 acres, comprising the remainder of the barony lying south or west of the public road[*]

The part purchased by Andrew Burnet was afterwards divided into two plantations, the Northern containing 1,505

---

[*]Johnsons Greene *Ibid*
[*]M C O Charleston Bk J 8, p 200
[*]Ibid, Bk A 8, p 446

acres. called "Forlorn Hope" and the Southern called
"Green Meadows" containing 3,015 acres   The destruction of the records of Colleton County during the invasion
of the State by Sherman's army makes it impossible to
further trace with much accuracy the devolution of these
properties

A D' Joseph Glover seems to have owned "Forlorn
Hope" in 1838   He devised it to his daughter. M" Elizabeth S Postell and by the latter's children it was sold
away subsequent to 1865   The tract purchased by Felix
Warley continued in his family until about 1904. when it
was also sold away   The map published with this article
is taken from a copy of the map made in 1796   Adjoining
the barony to the south and southwest were the two plantations called "Hayne Hall" and "Pear Hill" which belonged to Col Isaac Hayne the revolutionary officer who
was executed on the gibbet by the British in August. 1781,
and whose plantation entries with regard to the two places
have been published in previous numbers of this Magazine
"Hayne Hall" seems to have been his home and residence
and it was in the garden at this residence that he was
buried after his execution   This is stated on the authority
of Col Stephen Jarvis. then a British officer. a Lieutenant
in Major Fraser's command. who states that he saw his
grave the day after he was buried.[30]   In his will Col Hayne
directs that he be buried by the side of his wife[31]   Hayne
had been captured about a month before. not far from
his home   Exactly where the writer has not been able to
locate   Johnson in his Traditions of the Revolution (not
a very safe authority) says at the plantation of a M" Ford
about four miles beyond Parker's ferry   The Royal Gazette
of the date says in general terms at the Horse Shoe, which
referring to the Horse Shoe Creek or Swamp might mean
anywhere within five or ten miles from Parker's ferry and
about the same from Hayne's own home   Some revenge
for Hayne came soon, for the very next day Major Fraser's command encountered General Marion's on the cause-

[30]Journal of American History vol 1 No 4 p 728
[31]Probate Court Charleston Will Bk A p 41

way leading to Parker's ferry and suffered a "sad disaster." According to Jarvis, "We lost one hundred and twenty-"five killed and a great many wounded, and the enemy "retired without the loss of a man All our artillery were "killed or wounded before they could bring their guns to "bear upon the enemy"[42] This incident is no part of the history of the barony, but is referred to here to draw attention to this account of Jarvis, whose MSS. published in the Journal of American History, is a most valuable contribution to the history of the revolutionary war in lower Carolina This severe disaster inflicted by Marion on the enemy on the Parker's ferry causeway has never been given its proper position and credit, although one may be permitted to doubt if the number in dead alone could, as appears in the printed statement of Jarvis', have been 125 Considering the number engaged and giving due proportion to the wounded that number seems impossible According to McCrady, citing James Life of Marion, the Americans next day counted twenty-seven dead *horses* on the field; the British had already buried their dead

[42] Ibid

ABSTRACTS FROM THE RECORDS OF THE COURT OF ORDINARY OF THE PROVINCE OF SOUTH CAROLINA, 1700-1711

By A S Salley, Jr

(Continued from the January Number)

Will of George Fullerton, of Charles Town, province of South Carolina, merchant, made October 8, 1708, and proved before Governor Johnson, January 3, 1709, gave William Rhett, Jr, son of William Rhett, of Charles Town, merchant, £200 currency of Carolina; gave Sarah Rhett, daughter of said William Rhett, a like sum; gave Catherine Rhett, daughter of said William Rhett, a like sum; gave William Rhett, Sr, and Sarah, his wife, a like sum and £100 "Sterling money of England", which he had then lying in the hands of Robert South, of London, merchant; gave the said Sarah, wife of the said William, a negro boy called Snow Hill, gave the poor of St Philip's Parish, Charles Town, £20 currency of Carolina, gave the rector of St Philip's for the time being £10 currency of Carolina; gave remainder of his estate to brother, "William Fullerton", of "the Shire of Ayre in the west of Scotland", appointed friends, William and Sarah Rhett, and wife as executors Witnesses Bentley Cooke, Mary Pearce and Sarah Cooke (Pages 160-161)

Will of Thomas Hubbard, of Berkeley County, made August 26, 1709 and proved before Governor Gibbes, August 19, 1710 gave wife, Hester Hubbard, all of his real and personal estate for life, gave John Lawes, after the decease of said wife, a negro man, provided the said John Lawes should make over the land on which he lived, adjoining testator, to one of his daughters, Ann or Dorothy Lawes, but if he should refuse to give the land to either of the aforesaid daughters, then the negroes were to be sold and the money divided between testator's two sons, William Waties and Henry Furwell; gave his granddaughters, Ann and Dorothy Lawes, after the death of his wife, two Indian girls, Inolly and Nanney; gave daughter,

Elizabeth, £100 currency of Carolina, to be paid by
William Waties after said wife's death, gave son, Henry
Furwell, one half of his goods, chattels, slaves, horses and
cattle, excepting such as had already been bequeathed; gave
son, William Waties, the house and land where testator
then resided and the other half of his personal estate not
otherwise bequeathed, provided that he pay testator's daughter, Elizabeth Hubbard, £100 in five payments of £20
per annum after the death of testator's wife, but it was
stipulated that if the said Elizabeth should marry Thomas
Martin that she should not receive anything, and the £100
should be divided between Henry Furwell and William
Waties, gave Hugh Fling all of his wearing apparel and
twenty shillings in money, appointed "Capt Peter
Guerard & Percival Pawley" executors and bequeathed
them twenty shillings each   Witnesses   William Waties,
Jr, Katherine Waties and Capt Percival Pawley   (Pages
162-163)

Will of John Thomas, of Charles Town, St Philip's
Parish, and province of South Carolina, surgeon, made
July 22, 1710, and proved before "Honrble Coll Robert
Gibbes Esqr. Governr &co" September 26, 1710, gave the
minister, for the time being, of the French Church in
Charles Town, £5. currency per annum; gave the poor of
Charles Town £20 currency, gave friend, Peter Fillion,
cooper, of Charles Town, £20 currency, gave wife, Mary,
one-third of his real estate for life, at her death to go to
her three daughters, Mary Wragg, Judith DuBose and Ann
DuBose, also one-third of his personal estate, gave Judith
DuBose £842 currency; gave Ann Dubose a like sum,
gave remainder of estate to Mary Wragg, Judith DuBose
and Ann DuBose, but in case of the death of either without issue her share was to go to the survivors, gave Elias
Bissett, £5; gave Ann Hester Poinsett, £5., gave Thomas
Satur, son of Jacob Satur, £10, gave Mary Guerin, daughter of Mathurin Guerin, £10, gave Jacob Satur a mourning ring of forty shillings value; gave Peter Manigault a
mourning ring of twenty-five shillings value; appointed

wife, executrix Witnesses John Simmons, John Jordin, Jacob Satur and Mary Satur. (Pages 163-165)

Will of Richard Prize, of South Carolina, Indian trader, made May 19, 1707, and proved before Governor Gibbes, September 22, 1710, gave an Indian woman by whom he had two children, Elizabeth and Sarah Prize, her freedom and two Indian slaves (a woman, Fortuna, and a girl, Jeany); gave his said two daughters the remainder of his real and personal estate, gave friend, Matthew Porter, a gold ring of the price of twenty shillings, gave James Peartree and Elizabeth, his wife, a gold ring each of the value of twenty shillings and appointed them his executors, requesting them to take charge of his said two daughters Witnesses: David Ferguson, David Rize and Patrick P Ballentine (Pages 165-166)

December 8 1710, Francis LeBrasseur and George Logan executed a bond to Governor Gibbes for LeBrasseur's faithful discharge of the trust of "Guardian and Tutor of the P'son & Portion of Christopher Arthur" during his minority   (Page 167)

In the Name of God Amen I Abraham Isack of Cyty of New Yorke Being bound to Sea and therefore being present in good health, but not knowing when it may please the Almighty God to take me out of ye world my Will is yt after my just debts are paid I bequeath all my Estate whatsoever be it in houses Lands Good Chatles or what else unto my Dear and Loveing Sister Sarah Isack & to her heires for ever shee paying out of ye same ye Sum of ten Pounds New Yourke mony to my Brother Henry Isack if Liveing, after my Deceas and I do Constitute and appoynt my dear Sister Sarah my whole and Sole Executrix of this my Will, revokeing all Wills by me heretofore made and this alone to Stand in Force   In Testimony whereof I have hereunto Sett my hand and Seale in New Yorke this Twenty Sixth day of May Anno Dom One Thousand Seven hundred & Nine

Signd Seald published and
Declared by ye said Abra· Isack
in ye presence of us

Edmd Creiswell
Jno Basford

Abraham Isack   (Seale)

Recorded Febry 20th 1710 per J H D Secy   (Page 168)

February 22, 1710, Richard Capers and Richard Reynolds executed a bond to Governor Gibbes for Capers's faithful performance of his trust as " Guardian and Tutor of y' person and portion of Thomas Capers" during his minority   (Page 169)

Will of "Edward Tynte, Esqr Constituted Governor of Carolina in America being about to take a speedy voyage thither", made July 19, 1709, gave Frances Kilner, of Browlow Street, in the parish of St. Giles in the Fields, in the county of Middlesex, spinster, all of his estate, after the payment of his debts and funeral expenses, and appointed her, executrix   Witnesses the Earl of Craven, Palatine of Carolina, Denbigh Reimon, William Morgan and Abel Ketelbey   (Page 170)

July 13, 1711, John Cooper, vintner, as a creditor of John Todd, gent, entered a caveat in the Secretary's office against a nuncupative will, or pretended nuncupative will, which "One John Charlton would insinuate & Endeavor to have pass'd the Accoustom'd Seal in his favour for that the s' nuncupative Will or pretended nuncupative Will is void of those necessary Qualifications and Circumstances the Law in Such Cases requires"   (Page 171)

August 3, 1711, Henry Bruneau and Michael Durazeaux executed a bond to Governor Gibbes for Bruneau's faithful performance of his trust as administrator of the estate of Paul Bruneau, deceased   Witness Thomas Hepworth, Deputy Secretary. (Pages 171-172)

August 3, 1711, Peter Cattell and George Evans executed a bond to Governor Gibbes for Cattell's faithful administration of the estate of Margaret Cattell, relict and administratrix of the estate of John Cattell, of the province, deceased   Witness William Stone (Pages 172-173)

December 17, 1711, William Cattell and Peter Cattell executed a bond to Governor Gibbes for William Cattell's faithful administration of the estate of John Cattell, gent , deceased   Witness· William Stone   (Pages 174-175)

August 7, 1711, Mary Grimball, Thomas Grimball and James Burtt executed a bond to Governor Gibbes for Mary Grimball's faithful performance of her trust as "Guardian and Tutor" of Christofer Linkley, a minor   Witness· Thomas Hepworth, Deputy Secretary   (Pages 175-176)

John Faucheraud Grimké.

August 1778 to May 1780.

(Continued from the January Number.)

A RETURN OF THE OFFICERS IN THE CONTINENTAL SERVICE
IN THE STATE OF SOUTH CAROLINA.

*Names, Regiments, Dates of Commissions, Dates of Resig-
nation or Promotion and Remarks:*

Note—*ry* signifies Regiment; *r,* Resigned; *p,* Promoted.

Major General Robert Howe.
Brig⁺: General Wᵐ. Moultrie.

COLONELS.

Isaac Huger, 5 *rg,* 25 March: 1776.
Wᵐ. Thompson, 3 *rg,* 16 Sepʳ: 1776.
Owen Roberts, Artⁿ, 16 Sep: 1776.   Killed 20 June 1779,
     Stono Ferry.
C. C. Pinckney, 1 *rg,* 16 Sep. 1776.

LT. COLONELS.

Alexʳ. MᶜIntosh, 5 *rg,* 25 March 1776.
——— Marion¹, 2 *rg,* 6 Sepʳ: 1776.
James Mayson, 3 *rg,* 16 Sepʳ: 1776.
Barnard Elliott, Artⁿ, 16 Sepʳ: 1776.   Died 25 Oct. 1778.
Wᵐ. Henderson, 6 *rg,* 16 Sepʳ: 1776.
——— Scott², 1 *rg,* 2ᵈ May [?] 1776.

MAJORS.

Benjamin Huger, 5 *rg,* 25 Mar: 1776.   Killed before
     Charles Town.

¹Francis Marion, *see Roll of Society of Cincinnati.*
²Willia

Peter Horry, 2 *rg,* 6 Sep 1776
Samuel Wise. 3 *rg,* 16 Sep' 1776
Barard Beckman, Art , 16 Sep' 1776, *p* 25 Oct' 1778
W'" Brown. 6 *rg,* 16 Sep' 1776
Thos Pinckney, 1 *rg,* 2 May 1778

CAPTAINS

Isaac Harleston. 2 *rg,* 4 Nov' 1775
Edmund Hyrne. 1 *rg,* 4 Nov' 1775.
Roger Saunders, 1 *rg,* 4 Nov' 1775, *r* Oct 6 1778
Charles Motte, 2 *rg,* 4 Nov' 1775
James Ladson, 1 *rg,* 15 Nov' 1775
John Vanderhorst, 1 *rg,* 11 Dec' 1775
John Donaldson, 3 *rg,* 6 Feb' 1776
Samuel Taylor, 6 *rg,* 25 March 1776
Felix Warley, 3 *rg,* 24 May 1776
James Conyers. 5 *rg,* 10 June 1776
Glen Drayton, 1 *rg,* 9 Aug' 1776
W'" Charnock, 2 *rg,* 29 Aug' 1776
Richard Brown. 3*rg,* 14 Sep' 1776
David Hopkins. 3 *rg,* 15 Sep' 1776
Thomas Lesesne, 2" *rg,* 16 Sep' 1776
John C Smith, 3 *rg,* 16 Sep' 1776
John F Grimké, Art , 16 Sep' 1776, *p* 25 Oct' 1778
Thomas Moultrie, 2 *rg,* 22 Oct' 1776
Ephraim Mitchell, Art:, 1 Nov' 1776
Robert Lyell. 3 *rg,* 7 Nov' 1776
Richard Doggett 6 *rg,* 14 Dec' 1776
John de Treville, Art 10 Jan' 1777
W'" Davis, 5 *rg,* 14 Mar" 1777
George Turner, 1 *rg,* 22 April 1777
Daniel Mazyck, 2 *rg,* 6 May 1777
R B Roberts*, Art , 4 June 1777
Jos" Warley, 3 *rg,* 10 June 1777
Jeremiah Theus, 1 *rg,* 18 Aug': 1777
Uriah Goodwin, 3 *rg,* 1 Sep' 1777
Ale' Petrie, 5 *rg,* 9 Sep' 1777, *r* Oct 6 1778
James Mitchell, Art , 11 Sep'

Thomas Dunbar, *2 rg*, 21 Nov' 1777
George Warley, *6 rg*, 26 Dec' 1777
Harman Davis, Art , 6 Jan' 1778
Thomas Shubrick, *5 rg*, 15 Jan' 1778
W'" Caldwell, *3 rg*, 22 Jan' 1778. Prisoner of War
Thomas Hall, *2 rg*, 16 Feb 1778
Joseph Elliott, *1 rg*, 7 Mar 1778 Brevett
Oliver Fowles, *3 rg*, 19 Mar 1778 Prisoner of War
—— Hext', *1 rg*, 1 May 1778 Brevett
W'" Blamyer, *5 rg*, 15 May 1778, *r* 5 Nov' 1778 No
  Commission
Alex Bonie, *6 rg*, 28 June 1778 No Commission
John Armstrong, *6 rg*, 10 Aug' 1778 Dead Oct 3ᵈ
  1778 No Commission
Joshua Leacy, *6 rg*, 3 Sep' 1778 Dead Sep 20 1778
  No Commission
Dan' Lewis Martin, *5 rg*, 30 May 1778 No Commis-
  sion
Derrill Hart, *3 rg*, *r* 3 Oct 1778 No Commission

FIRST LIEUTENANTS

W'": R Thompson, *3 rg*, 6 June 1776, *r* 3 Oct 1778
—— Lining', *1 rg*, 31 Aug' 1776, *p* 20 July 1778
Richard Baker, *2 rg*, 16 Sep' 1776, *p* 25 April 1778
Isaac Crouther, *3 rg*, 1 Oc' 1776, *r* 3 Oct' 1778
Adrian Provaux, *2 rg*, 22 Oct' 1776, *p* 27 April 1778
Thomas Gadsden', *1 rg*, 31 Dec' 1776, *p* 6 Oct' 1778
Field Farrar, *3 rg*, 1 Jan' 1777
George Liddell, *3 rg*, 2 Jan'. 1777.
John Hennington, *3 rg*, 4 Jan' 1777
Lewis de Saussure, *3 rg*, 22 Jan' 1777
Richard Mason, *2 rg*, 27 Jan' 1777
Joel Hardway, *3 rg*, 19 March 1777
Richard Jones, *3 rg*, 25 March 1777
Luke Mayson, *3 rg*, 20 April 1777
—— Williamson', *1 rg*, 22 April 1777

'Wm Hext, *see Roll of Soci'y of Cincinnati*
'Charles Lining, Ibid
'Son of Gen Christopher Gadsden
'John Williamson *Roll of Cincinnati*

—— Wetherly, 1 *rg*, 8 May: 1777.

John Hart, 2 *rg*, 21 May: 1777.

—— Smith[7], 1 *rg*, 26 May: 1777.

—— Jackson[8], 1 *rg*, 18 Aug[t]: 1777.

Peter Gray, 2 *rg*, 28 Aug[t]: 1777.

—— Lavacher[9], 1 *rg*, 22 Oct[r]: 1777.

Albert Roux, 2 *rg*, 5 Dec[r]: 1777.

Alex[r]: Keith, 5 *rg*, 10 Dec[r]: 1777, *p* 7 Sep: 1778.

Thomas Gordon, 5 *rg*, 22 Dec[r]: 1777, *p* 6 Oct[r]: 1778.

Henry Hampton, 6 *rg*, 23 Jan: 1778, *p* Sep[r]: 20, 1778. No Commission.

John Buchanan, 6 *rg*, 23 Jan: 1778, *p* Oct[r]: 3, 1778. No Commission.

John Martin, 2 *rg*, 16 Feb[y]: 1778.

Jesse Beaker, 6 *rg*, 20 Feb[y]: 1778. No Commission.

W[m]. Capers, 2 *rg*, 24 Feb[y]: 1778.

Benj[o]: Postell, 1 *rg*, 7 March: 1778. No Commission.

Wilson Glover, 1 *rg*, 7 March: 1778. No Commission.

Stephen Guerry, 5 *rg*, 16 March 1778, *p* 6 Nov: 1778.

James Kenny, 5 *rg*, 4 April: 1778.

Will[m]: Fishburn, 1 *rg*, 1 May: 1778. No Commission.

John Hogan, 5 *rg*, 15 May: 1778.

Thomas Weaver, Art:, 27 May: 1778, *p* 25 Oct: 1778. No Commission.

Basil Jackson, Art:, 28 May: 1778. No Commission.

John S. Budd[10], Art: 29 May: 1778.

W[m]. Tate, Art:, 30 May: 1778.

Richard Pollard, 6 *rg*, 28 June: 1778.

Paul Warley, 2 *rg*, 25 April: 1778.

Benj[o]: Brown, 6 *rg*, 3 Sep[r]: 1778.

Andrew Redmond, 6 *rg*, 3 Sep[r]: 1778.

SECOND LIEUTENANTS.

Samuel Guerry, 2 *rg*, 8 May: 1777, *p* 27 April, 1778.

John Davis, 3 *rg*, 10 Aug[t]: 1777.

John Goodwyn, 3 *rg*, 1 Sep[r]: 1777.

---

[7]John Caroway Smith, Ibid.
[8]William Jackson, see this *Magazine*, vol. 9, p. 207.
[9]St. Marie Lavacher, *DeSaussure's List of Cont. Officers.*
[10]John Shivers Budd, surgeon 4th Regt. Art'y, *DeSaussure's List.*

Benj: Hodges, 3 rg, 10 Sep[t]. 1777.

John Jones, 3 rg, 20 Sep[t]: 1777.

Peter Foissine, 2 rg, 6 Dec: 1777. p 1st. July. 1778.

Charles Skirving, 1 rg, 20 Dec[r]: 1777. p 20 July. 1778.

Alex[r]: Fraser, 1 rg, 20 Jan[y]: 1778. p 6 Oct: 1778.

W[m]. Taggart, 3 rg, 3 Feb[y]: 1778.

—— Bradwell[1], 1 rg, 13 March: 1778.

—— Parham, 1 rg, 14 March: 1778.

James Robinson, 3 rg, 24 March: 1778.

Robert Gaston, 3 rg, 25 March: 1778.

Aaron Smith, 3 rg, 26 March: 1778.

Benj[a]: Newson, 3 rg, 27 March: 1778.

Joel Doggett, 6 rg, 8 May: 1778.

Jos[h]: Kolb, 2 rg, 14 July: 1778. p 15 July: 1778.

Henry Ramsay, 3 rg, ... No Commission.

—— Milling[2], 6 rg, ... p Sep[t]. 20. 1778.

—— Adair[3], 6 rg, ..., p Oct: 3. 1778.

—— Langford[4], 6 rg, 30 Oct: 1778.

John Wickom, 2 rg, 6. Nov[r]: 1778.

Henry Moore, Art:, p 25. Oct[r]: 1778.

Alex[r]: Fotheringham, 5 rg, p 20. June 1778.

Samuel Warren. 5 rg, p 10 July 1778.

OMITTED.

W[m]. Mitchell, Art:, 27 May: 1778. p 25 Oct[r]: 1778.

John Weekly, Art:, 28 May: 1778. No Commission.

Barnard Elliott, Art:, 29 May: 1778. No Commission.

John Gorgett, Art:, 30 May: 1778. No Commission.

James Wilson, Art:, 31 May: 1778. No Commission.

W[m]. Donnom, Art:, 1 July: 1778. No Commission.

1st. Lieut Platen[5], Art:, 31 Oct: 1778. No Commission.

OCTOBER. Head Quarters Charles Town

1: Parole, Clergy.

[1] Nathaniel Bradwell, *Devonssure's List of Cont. Officers.*
[2] Hugh Milling, Ibid.
[3] W[m]. Adair, Ibid.
[4] Daniel Langford, Ibid.

2:    Parole, Ladson.

The General Court Martial ordered to try Charles Turberfield, J. B. Taylor, both of the Second Regiment & John Pinker of the 5ᵗʰ Battalion of Desertion have reported as follows, that Charles Troblefield alias Turberfield is guilty & that they therefore Sentence him to receive 90 lashes on the bare back with a cat of nine tails & that he be picketted for a quarter of an hour that John Barnett Taylor is also guilty of Desertion & that they therefore Sentence him to receive 100 lashes on the bare back with switches, the General approves of & ratifies these sentences which the Commanding officer of the Brigade to which they belong will have executed at such time & place as He shall think proper, of John Pinker of the 5ᵗʰ Regiment they reported that no Evidence appearing against him they remanded him to the Guard: He is therefore to be delivered to the Commanding officer of the Regiment to which He belongs to be tryed if he thinks proper by Regimental Court Martial.

The Court Martial is Disolved

3:    Parole, Bretigny.

4:    Parole, Sullivan.

The Returns for this Month are expected at Head Quarters, for Commanding Officer of Brigades.

The Commanding officer of the Corps of Artillery will have a report made to the General of the fixed Ammunition & other Artillery Stores that were returned after the late Expedition.

5:    Parole, Montgomery.

6:    Parol, Ellis.

Colᵒ: Francis Huger having resigned the Commission of Depᵘ: Quᵃ: Mʳ: Genᵉ: to the State of South Carolina is no longer to be respected or obeyed as a Continental officer.

Colᵒ: Stephen Drayton is appointed to act as Depᵘ: Qʳ: Mʳ: Genᵉ: to the Continental Troops in the State of South Carolina until the Pleasure of Congress can be had, with the rank of Colᵒⁿᵉˡ

Cap!. Roger Saunders of the first Continental Battalion in this State, having resigned his Commission, is no longer to be respected or Obeyed as a Continental officer.

Cap!. Alexander Petrie of the nith Continental Battalion in this State having resigned his Commission is no longer to be respected or obeyed as a Continental Officer

7: Parole, Arnold.

8: Parole, Dry.

Lieu!. James Crowther of the third Continental Battalion in this State, having resigned his Commission on the 3ᵈ. Oct!. is no longer to be respected or Obeyed as a Continental officer

9: Parole, Pitt.

10: Parole, Washington.

The Engineers are immediately to Survey Fort Johnson & Fort Moultrie, & report their Situation to the General.

Commanding officers of Brigades are to Report to the General the Quantity of Cartridges with which their Brigades are furnished; The Ammunition Chests & other Military Requisites they have & those wanting, & as the present aspect of affairs requires that we should be in the best state of defence possible They & all other officers are to Exert themselves to the utmost to effect a purpose in which the Honor of the Army & Good of the Common Cause are So essentially concerned.

The Comdt Officer of the Corps of Artillery will as immediately as possible report to the General the State of the Military Stores in his department & also those Articles with which it is necessary he should be furnished.

The Dep: Qu: Mr Gen: is to Report the Number & State of the Ammunition Waggons that more may be ordered if necessary. He is to have everything in his Department put in the best order with all possible Expedition.

11: Parole, Lillington.

12:   Parole, Hancock.

Brigade Majors are ordered to attend Head Quarters at orderly Hour, every day, until further orders.

13:   Parole, America

The General observes that many of the Soldiers appear without Bayonets. Commanding officers of Brigades will therefore take care that a standing order issued some time since relative to the loss or injury of Arms & accoutrements otherwise than by inevitable accident in actual Service is Strictly & immediately carried into Execution (Nov': 4: 1777.)*

14:   Parole, Carolina

15:   Parole, Maryland.

Brigadier General Moultrie & Col': Commandant Huger will report as immediately as possible the Military & other Stores wanting for the defence of their respective Commands.

The Dep: Commissary General to report the Provisions of every kind he has on hand & at what places stored.

16:   Parole, Virginia.

17:   Parole, Abingdon.

One Subaltern, One Sergeant & eight R & F: from Fort Moultrie,One Sergeant, & twelve R & F. from Fort Johnson to hold themselves in immediate readiness to go on Command they are to act as a Covering Party to some Public Workers upon Dewee's Island. They are to be furnished with Tents, 24 Rounds & a weeks Provision. They will receive & Obey such Orders as his Excellency the President shall issue & are to be relieved weekly in the same proportion.

18:   Parole, Gadsden.

Adjutant John Downs of the Second Continental Bat-

*Order of that date.

talion in this State having resigned his Commission of the 6th. October is no longer to be respected or Obeyed as a Continental officer.

19: Parole, North Carolina

Abstracts of back rations ordered to be stopped from officers upon the late Southern Expedition, are to be made up & certified by Commanding officer of Regiments & Corps, who were upon that Command, down to the date, when Susistence Money was allowed by Congress; these back Rations are to be paid by the Deputy Commissary General; & Subsequent to that time, these officers are to be allowed Subsistance Money, agreable to the resolution of Congress.

20: Parole, Senf.

21: Parole, Eveleigh.

The Engineers are as immediately as possible to Report to the General the Situation of the batteries in & about the Town.

An Order of the 10th & another of the 15th. Instant respecting Brigades has not as yet been complied with.

22: Parole, Rutledge.

23: Parole, Livingston.

24: Parole, Morris.

25: Parole, Harnett.

26: M: O:

All Soldiers in Town except those on Duty are to appear upon their regimental Parades at twelve o'Clock to day precisely, when officers of Companies are to attend the Rolls are to be called over & the men who are missing are to be reported to the General & will certainly be punished. They are not to be dismissed until they receive orders. Brigade Majors & Adjutants are immediately to make men acquainted with this order.

Brigadier General Moultrie & Col° Commandant Huger will give notice to the officers at Fort Moultrie & Fort Johnson that they are invited to & as many as can be spared from those Posts may attend the Funeral of Lieut' Colonel Elliott tomorrow Morning at o'Clock [sic] in Charles Town

General Moultrie will order the Grenadier Company of the 2ᵈ Regiment to attend upon this Melancholy occasion & to bring with them those standards which were presented to the Regiment by Mʳˢ Elliott.

Parole, D'Estaign

L' Col"· Elliott of the Corps of Artillery deceased will be buried tomorrow with the Honors of War due to his rank

The Detail of the officers & Men for this Duty will be given out by the Dep Adj Gen the whole to be ready by eight o'clock in the Morning

The officers of the Army will be present upon this Melancholy occasion

The Field officers of the Corps of Artillery & other Field-officers of Similar Rank with the deceased will attend as Pall-Bearers; if not enough of equal rank the deficiency to be made up out of the Field officers next in Rank

The General condoles with the Army upon the loss of so truly valuable, so much to be lamented an officer, whose Spirit & abilities would have done Honor to any Service

Col° Roberts, L': Col" Marion, L' Col° Henderson, Major Huger, Major Beckman & Major Brown are appointed Pall-Bearers

The 1ˢᵗ & 6ᵗʰ Regiments with the Grenadier Companies of the 2ᵈ & 5ᵗʰ Regiments are ordered to hold themselves in readiness for this duty

Major Pinckney will command the Party

The Guards not to be relieved until the Funeral Procession is over

27   Parole. La Fayette

Order

of Procession observed at the Funeral of Barnard Elliott
Esq Lieut' Col" of the Continental Corps of Artillery in
South Carolina

Brigade Major

———————————————————————

Grenadier Company of the 5th Regiment, in 3 divisions;
each, 9 men abreast   An officer to each division   the
youngest officer at the head of the party, the Captain in the
rear

——————— · · ·   ———   · - · - · ·

Grendier Company of the 2d Regiment (formerly commanded by L' Col° Elliott)   in 4 divisions; each 10 men
abreast   An Officer to each division   the youngest officer
leading the Company, the Cap' in the rear

———————————————————————

The Standards of the 2d Regiment
(presented by M" Barnard Elliott* after the Engagement
at Fort Moultrie)
the Ensigns carrying them over their shoulders, the Pavilion
hanging unfurled behind their backs, the ferril of the Spear
pointing to the front, the head of the Spears bound with
Crape

—   —

Band of Music
Muffled. Drums and Fifes playing dead March

———————————————————————

The Sixth & First Regiments in similar divisions &
officered in the same manner as the Grenadiers making 10
divisions

———————————————————————

The officer appointed to command the Party

———————————————————————

The Adjutant General

———————————————————————

— —   -   —————   ——— ——

*She was Susannah Smith, dau of Benj Smith, Esq, and mar-
ried Barnard Elliott Jan 1776, after his death she married Patrick
Carnes   For an account of her, and the flags which she presented
to the 2d S C Regiment see vol IV of this Magazine, page 250

Band of Music

Hautboys, Clarinets, French-Horns & Kettle-Drums playing a dead March composed by M'. Beck for this mournful Occasion.

The Corpse

Supported by the Field officers of artillery, & by their equal & next in rank (after the Infantry) to the deceased.

The Mourners
Two by Two

The Masons
Two by Two

The President & the General.
Col': C: C: Pinckney & The Vice President.
The Speakers of both houses.
The Members of the Privy Council:
The Members of the Legislative Council.
The Members of the Assembly.
Captains & Subalterns of the Army.
The Remainder of the Invited.

The Troops were drawn up before L'. Col': Elliotts House, who, as soon as the Corpse was brought out & laid in the carriage, Rested their Firelocks. They then proceeded to Reverse their arms & wheeling by division to the left marched off the ground. When they approached the Church the Division filed off from their flanks in Indian File & formed a rank on each side off the Street: The whole Procession Halted. The Two ranks were then ordered to face inwards & to Rest on their arms reversed. the Procession went on thro the ranks & proceeded into Church: The Troops Shouldered their Firelocks, wheeled up from the Right & Left & formed again their Divisions. They then proceeded to the Funeral Ground*, where being drawn up Two deep, They, after the Service was over, fired three volleys.

*St. Philips Church'd

The Troops were marched back to their Barracks, the Eldest officer in rank at their Head.

All the officers trailed their Firelocks, carrying the butts foremost. The officers on Horse-back dropped the points of their Swords.

28: Parole, Green.

A detachment from the first & Sixth Regiments consisting of one Subaltern, One Sergeant, & 12 rank & File is to Relieve the guards at Dorchester on Fryday next.

The officer Commanding the Party will receive his orders from the Dep: Adj: Gen.

The Death of L: Col: Elliott of the Corps of artillery occasions the following Promotions

Major Beckman to be Lieut: Col: vice L: Col: Elliott deceased.

Cap: John F: Grimké to be Major, vice Major Beckman promoted.

Cap: L: Wm: Mitchell to be Captain, vice Captain Grimke Promoted

First L: Thomas Weaver to be Captain Lieu: vice Cap: L: Wm: Mitchell Promoted.

Adjutant Henry Moore to be first Lieu: vice first Lieu: Thomas Weaver Promoted

Cap: Lieut. Barnard Elliott is appointed Adjutant to the Regiment of Artillery

The appointment of these officers takes place from the 25: Instant: & They are to be respected & obeyed accordingly.

29: Parole, Moultrie.

Sir, you will proceed with the Detachment under your Command to Relieve the officer & guard Stationed at Dorchester, for the Security of the Magazine & Stores.

You will be careful to post your Centinels at such places as will best tend to Promote the Service you are detached on.

You will be particularly attentive to the Health of Your Men & that their Arms & Accoutrements are always kept in the best order possible & fit for action

You will without further Orders from Headquarters receive a Detachment from Orangeburgh to relieve you & you will return to Town as immediately as possible after the relief has taken place.

For further orders & such as have a local tendency you will apply to the officer you relieve who has directions to deliver his orders, which I transmitted him some time ago, to the officer relieving him & you will in turn deliver them to the officer who relieves you.

I am Sir etc J: F: Grimke Dep: Adj: Gen:

To the officer Marching with a Detachment from the 1st. & 6th. Regt. to relieve the Guard at Dorchester.

Sir. The officer who will deliver you this has marched to Relieve you & your Guard, you will therefore deliver the Care of the Magazine etc into his Charge & leave with him the Orders which Some weeks ago transmitted you. You will march immediately to Orangeburgh the Quarters of your Regiment & produce these orders to the Commanding officer as a Certificate that you have been properly relieved by a Detachment from Town.

I am Sir etc: J: F: G: Dep: Adj: Gen.

To the officer Commanding the Guard at Dorchester.

Sir.

Application having been made by the officer of your Regiment who Commands the Guard at Dorchester to be relieved & giving information at the same time that the bad health of his men had induced him to take that Step, the General ordered his Party to be immediately relieved from Town & that He should repair to his Regiment quartered at Orangeburgh with all the Expedition the Situation of his Men would allow & has commanded me to inform you that the present State of the Troops in Town does not permit that the Detachment which relieved Lt: Mayson should be continued at Dorchester. You will therefore immediately upon the receipt of these orders detach a Party equal in Number and officered in the same manner as the Detachment under Lt: Mayson & without delay relieve the officer Commanding at Dorchester for which Duty this will be the proper & sufficient order. Your officer will receive other local instructions from the officer He relieves to whom I have already given particular Instructions for that Purpose.

I am Sir etc: J: F: G:

Dep: Adj: Gen:

To Col: Wm Thompson or Com: officer at Orangeburgh.

30: Parole, George Town

If the Main Guard Should be composed of only of the Men of one Brigade & Soldiers of any other Brigade should be committed to the guard, the Commanding officer of that Brigade of which the guard is Composed is to order his Brigade Major immediately to inform the Commanding officer of the Brigade to which the Prisoner belongs of his confinement.

31: Parole, Prussia.

Philip Frederick Platin, Gent: is appointed a first Lieut: in the Continental Corps of Artillery in this State: He is therefore to be respected & obeyed accordingly.

REGISTER OF
ST. ANDREWS PARISH, BERKELEY COUNTY, SOUTH CAROLINA

1719-1774

Copied and Edited by MABEL L WEBBER.

(Continued from the January Number)

CHRISTNINGS

John the Son of John & Mary, Free negroes, formerly belonging to M' John Godfrey bap⁴ May 31 1730

John the Son of Tho' & Mary Mell bap⁴. June 5ᵗʰ. 1730

Mary the Daughter of Benjⁿ. & Margaret Godfrey pr bap⁴ June 5ᵗʰ 1730

James the Son of Cap' James Goodby of Goosecreek bap⁴ June 21 1730—

Catherine the Daughter of Paul Mazyck of Goosecreek bap⁴ June 21, 1730

Christopher the Son of Arthur & Martha Hall bap⁴. July 5 1730

Francis the Son of Francis & Lydia Yonge p' bap⁴ July 21, 1730

Tho'. the Son of Samuel & Elizabeth Stocks bap⁴. July 26. 1730

Tho' the Son of William & Martha Ladson bap⁴ July 26 1730

Charles the Son of Wᵐ & Deborah Webb p' Bap⁴ Aug'. 10 1730

Jonathan the Son of Joseph & Constance Fitch p'· Bap⁴ Aug' 15 1730

John the Son of M' Ralph Izard of Goose Creek bap⁴. Aug' 17 1730

Mary the Daughter of John & Mary Delony bap⁴ Aug'. 24 1730

Williamson the Son of Joseph & Constance Fitch bap⁴ p'· Sep. 3ʳᵈ 1730

Elizabeth the Daughter of James & Sarah Streater bap^d.
   p^r Sepr 13. 1730

Charles the Son of Charles & Rachel Jones bap^d Novr 15
   1730

John the Son of John & Sarah Cattell bap^d Decr 27 1730

John the Son of James & Hester Taylor bap^d. January 17
   1730/31

Martha the Daughter of William & Mary Chapman bap^d }
   Febry 14th 1730/1   }

Anne the Daught^r. of Joseph & Eliz Dell   }

Rachel the Daug^r. of Francis & Mary Ladson bap^d March
   7 1730/1

James the Son of Thos & Hester Hayward bap^d March
   30 1731

Nathaniel the Son of Thos & Hester Hayward bap^d
   March 30 1731

Joseph the Son of Peter & Elizabeth Perry bap^t p^r y^e
   Revd Mr Varnod Ap 16 1731

William y^e. Son of William & Martha Fuller Junr bap^d
   Augt 5 1731

Sarah the Daughter of Joseph & Eliz · Heap bap^d pr Aug^t
   22^d. 1731.

Mary the Daug^r of John & Martha Rivers bap^d Sepr 7th
   1731

Sarah the Daught^r of Richd Smallwood bap^d Sepr 7
   1731

Elizabeth y^e. Daught^r of Edwd & Rosemund Perry bap^d
   Sepr 26 1731

Robt ye Son of Robt & Gibbon Wright bap^d Octr 5th
   1731

Mary the Daug^r of Willm & Eliz Lamboth bap^d Octr 9
   1731.

Anne the Daugh^r of Willm & Mary Miles bap^d p^r
   Oct^r: 12th 1731

Daniel the Son of Joseph & Sarah Blake of Dorchest^r
   bap^d Oct 24. 1731

Thos ye Son of Thos & Eliz Drayton bap^d Octo^r 27th
   1731

Hepziba the Daugh^r of Henry & Eliz Wood Senr bap^d
   Octr 31 1731

Joseph the Son of Henry & Eliz Wood Senr bap^d Octr. 31 1731.

George the Son of Robt & Sarah Wood bap^d Octr 31. 1731

Robt the Son of Robt & Sarah Wood bap^d Octr 31 1731

Ruth ye Daugh^t of W^m & Ruth Holman bap^d Novr. 20th. 1731

Mary the Daugh^r of John & Mary Haydon bap^d January 2^d 1731/2

Mallory the Son of Robt & ——— Rivers bap^d January 10th 1731/2

Joseph Son of Jacob & Eliz Ladson bap^d. February 13 1731/2.

Willm the Son of Stephen & Martha Bull bap^d February 21 1731/2

Hannah ye Daughter of Saml & Eliz Rivers bap^d March 5 1731/2

David Miller an Adult bap^d March 10th 1731/2

Samuel the Son of Samuel Stocks & Eliz his wife bap^d March 12th 1731/2

Mary Holman an Adult bap^d March the 20th 1731/2

Bathsheba ye Daughter of Isaac Battoon & Sarah his wife bap^d March 24 1731/2

James the Son of James Manning & Sarah his wife bap^d. March 24 1731/2

John the Son of Benjn Godfrey & Margaret his wife bap^d March 31 1732.

William the Son of John Delony & Mary his wife bap^d March 31 1732

Charles the Son of Francis Stokes & Margaret his wife bap^d April 2^d. 1732

Samuel. an Adult Negro man belonging to Mr Thos Drayton bap^d Apr^l 9 1732

Susannah the Daugh^r of Henry Wood Senr & Eliz his wife bap^d April 23. 1732

Thos the Son of Henry Wood Senr & Eliz· his wife bap^d April 23 1732

Elizabeth the Daught^r. of Henry Wood Junr & Anne his wife bap^d Apr 23 1732

Jane Baynes the Daught^r of Wm Guy & Rebecca his wife bap^d pr June 10 1732

Frances, a little Negro Girl belonging to D^r Ed^d. Ord bap^d. June 18 1732

Hester ye Daug^r of Edmund Bellinger & Eliz his wife bap^d. June 30. 1732

John the Son of John Champneys & Mary his wife bap^d July 10 1732

Magnus the Son of Magnus Brooks & Mehitabel his wife bap^d July 16 1732

Hester the Daug^r of James Taylor & Hester his wife bap^d July 23 1732

Gabriel the Son of William Brandford & Anne his Wife bap^d. Aug 3 1732

Sarah ye Daugh^r of Francis Ladson & Sarah his Wife bap^d Augt 9th 1732

Elizabeth ye Daug^r of Charles Brett & Rebecca his Wife bap^d Augt 11 1732

Robt the Son of John Gibbs, & Mary his wife of St Paul's | bap^d Sepr 17 1732

Susannah ye Daug^r of Arthur Hall & Martha his wife bap^d. Sepr. 26 1732.

Charles the Son of Francis Yonge & Lydia his wife bap^d p Octo^r 6 1732

Stephen the Son of Stephen Russell & Jane his wife bap^d October 25th 1732

Sarah the Daughter of Charles Crubin & Elizabeth his wife bap^d Octo^r 11 1732

Hester the Daug^r of Charles Jones & Rachel his wife bap^d Novr 5 1732.

Martha the Daugh^r of Thos Mell & Mary his wife bap^d Novr 14 1732.

William the Son of Josiah Canty & Eliz his wife bap^d Novr 14 1732

Lucina the Daugh^r of Thos Barlow & Susannah his wife bap^d January 7 1732/3

Elizabeth Warren a Young girl belonging to Wm Street bap^d March 2^d 1732 3

Sarah ye Daught^r of Wm Chapman & Mary his wife bap^d March 4 1732 3

Martha y' Daught' of Elizabeth Dell bap' March 4 1732/3

Joseph Stent a poor Boy belonging to y' Parish bap'. March 4 1732/3

Arthur the Son of John Cattell & Sarah his wife bap' March 7. 1732/3

Elizabeth the Daught' of Tho' Butler & Elizabeth his wife bap' March 19 1732/3.

Martha the Daug' of Tho' Whaley & ——— his wife bap' March 23 1732/3

Tho' the Son of Benj" Godfrey als Garnier & Martha his wife bap' March 23'. 1732/3

William the Son of Peter Fushee & Margaret his wife bap' March 23' 1732/3

Samuel the Son of Thomas Heyward & Hester his wife bap' April 1". 1733

Moses the Son of John Cockfield an Adult bap' April 3'. 1733

Susannah the Daughter of Edmund Bellinger an Adult bap' May 6. 1733

William the Son of Tho'. Drayton & Eliz'h his wife bap' May 6 1733

Sarah the Daught' of W'" Ladson & Mary his wife bap' May 13 1733

Anne the Daughter of Peter Perry & Elizabeth his wife bap' June 3' 1733

Anne the Daughter of W'" Stocks and Rachel his wife bap' June 3' 1733

John Son of John Delony & Mary his wife bap'. June 10, 1733

FUNERALS.

Anne the Daughter of Henry Wood Jun' bur' Dec' 6. 1732

William Webb Sen' & Sarah his Wife bur'd February 3' 1732/3

William Gibbs bur'd March the 14 1732/3

Eliz the Daughter of Tho' Butler & Eliz his wife bur'd March 20, 1732/3

An Indian Woman, named Eliz. belonging to Mr Godfrey's Family—bur'd March 26 1733—

Eliz Butler, wife of Thos Butler, Son of Rich^d—Bur'd March 27. 1733

Martha Hall, Wife of Arthur Hall burd June 5th 1733

Joseph the Son of Thomas Mell & Mary his wife bur'd Augt 26th 1733

Edwd Smith, Bookkeep^r to Mr Cattell, burd Sepr 14 1733.

Wm Bull, Fishmonger, bur'd at Mr Burnaby Bulls Sepr 14 1733

James Manacke burd Sepr 24 1733

Thos. the Son of Samuel Stocks bur'd Octob^r 4 1733

John the Son of John Delony burd October ye 13 1733

Thos Rose Senr Burd Decr 3 [?] 1733

Jonathan James Schoolmaster at Mr Wm Cattell Buried Jan^{ry}. 19 1733/4

Richard Son of Benjn Godfrey Bur^d Jan^{ry} 31—1733 4

Willm Orge Alex^d Parris Parrot [sic] Buried Feb^r 18th 1733/4

Mulrey Gill Servant to Wm Cattell Esqr Burried March 1st 1733/4

William Jefries Son of Charles & Eliz Hill Burd April 5—1734

Anne Daught^r of William Cattell Junr. April 6: 1734

Eliz^{bth} Daughter of John & Eliz Mell Bur^d. June 17th 1734

John Haydon Son of Thos Haydon Bur^d July 12 1734

Charles Hill Esq Buried p^r ye Revd Mr Thompson July 27 1734

Catherine Wilson widow Sister to Coll. William Bull Burried p^r the Revd Mr Varnad—Sep^{br} 1 1734

Eliz^{bth} Daught^r of Charles Crubin & Eliz his Wife Bur^d p^r ye Revd Wm Guy Sepr 3 1734

Jonathan Son of Joseph Fitch and Constant his Wife Bur^d Sepr 9 1734

Benja Godfrey Buried Octo^{br} 1. 1734

Petter Ripos Buried p^r the Revd Wm Guy he belong^d to Capt Henry de Jersey Junr Octo^{br} 17 1734

Margaret Daughter of John Haydon & Mary his Wife
  Buried pr Wm Guy Octr 19 1734
Margaret Daughter of Samuel Stock^sr & Eliz· his Wife.
  Bur^d p^r Wm Guy Octo^br 23 1734
William Smith Buried Overseer to Mrs Yonge Octo^br
  24 1734
Manly Williamson Buried Nov^br: 3^d 1734
Rachel the Daughter of Capt ffrances Ladson & Mary his
  Wife Bur^d Dec^br 1 1734
John Mason Burd Dec^br: ye 13 1734
Charles Crubin Buried Jan^r 31 1734/5
David Johnson Bur^d March 25th 1735
John Wood Bur^d Oversear to Mr Cartwright May ye 10
  1735
Sarah Daugh^r of Edwd Sympson Bur^d May 13 1735

MARRIAGES

Manley Williamson, & Hannah Hogg Widd Mard, April
  12th 1733
Isaac Stewart, & Elizabeth Dingle Widdow of St Barthol-
  omews—Mard Ap^l: 12 1733
Henry Hyrne & Susannah Bellinger Sp^r mard May 8
  1733
Joseph Payne & Eliz Bacalesk Sp^r mard May 17 1733
Thos Tew & Mary You Sp^r mard July 12 1733
Lewis La Fountain, & Mary Galloway Widd mard Aug^t
  26 1733
Francis Varnod, Clerk, & Mary Dodson Sp^r mar'd Sep^r.
  4 1733
Thomas Sissons, & Mary Storey widdow mard Octr 3.
  1733
Robert Rivers Junr & Anne Parrott Sp^r mard Octr 23
  1733
Robert Young & Hepsey Wood Sp^r Mar^d Novr 23 1733
Charles Leslie & Nancie Elmes widdow mard Jan^r 14th
  1733/4
Archib^ld Neale & Mary Wilkins Widd mard Jan^r 19th
  1733/4

Joseph Norman & Margaret Webster Spr mard Jan' 24ᵗʰ 1733/4

Samuel Burgess & Mary Givens Spʳ Mar'd Jan' 26 1733/4

Stephen Carter & Sarah Barton Spʳ Marᵈ April 16 1734

Nathaniel Payne & Elizᵇʰ Worral Spʳ Marᵈ April 18 1734

*Thomas Tatnell & Eliz Barnwell Spʳ.

*Samuel Underwood, & Margaʳ Mellichampe Spʳ both marrᵈ pʳ the Revᵈ. Mʳ Thompson April 23, 1734

Willᵐ Holman & Rachel Clare Spʳ Marᵈ. June 2 1734

James Boswood & Martha Wood Daughtʳ of Benja: Wood Marᵈ. June 11ᵗʰ 1734

George Smonin [sic] & Martha Hull Widd Marᵈ June 12 1734

Samuel West & Mary Dandridge Spʳ marᵈ. June 27ᵗʰ 1734

Jonathan Fitch & Frances Nelson Spʳ Mard July 22 1734

John Boswood & Nancy Wood Spʳ marᵈ. Jan' 21 1734

John Miles & Eliz Ladson Spʳ mard. Febʳʸ· 10 1734

Samuel Rome & Christian Mason widow marᵈ pʳ the Revᵈ Wᵐ Guy April 4: 1735

Robert Bowman & Eliz Crubin Widow mard June 7ᵗʰ. 1735

Stephen Hamilton & Eliz Verdal Spʳ Mard June 16, 1734

*Henry Williamson & Margʳ Rose Spʳ mard June 17 1735

Samuel Jones & Mary Vincent Spʳ mard June 27ᵗʰ 1735

Nathaniel Beacon & Anne Holman Spʳ married July 17ᵗʰ 1735

Christopher Linkly & Mary Holman Spʳ mard July 31 1735

Thomas Miles Junior & Ann Ladson Spr Marᵈ August 4ᵗʰ 1735 St Pauls parish

*William Bowman & Anne Young Widdow Married by Revᵈ. Mʳ Guy 12ᵗʰ Sepʳ 1735

---

*Written in on opposite page and not with the regular entries

Stephen Beadon & Ruth Rivers Sp^r Mar^d Sepr 16. 1735

John Mullrein & Clodia Cattell Sp^r Mar^d Octo^br 23 1735

Isaac Chardon & Mary Woodward Sp^r. Mard Nov^br 6 1731.

William Wood & Sindinah Boswood Sp^r Mar^d Octo^br 7th 1735

Acton Rowland & Anne Boswood Sp^r. M^d Feb^ry 3^d 1735/6

John Daniel & Sarah Raven Sp^r Marr^d January 22^d 1735-/6

Paul Jenys & Elizabeth Raven Widd mar^d January 25 1735/6

Beltshazzar Lambwright & Mary Anne Smith Sp^r Married 14th October 1736

*Patrick Norris & Mary M^c gilvray Spinster Married by Rev^d M^r. Guy Octr 1736

*William Elliott Junr & Francis Guering Sp^r married ⅌ Revd Mr Garden 20 Jany 1725† [sic]

---

*Written on opposite page and not with the regular entries
†William Elliott and Francis Gearing married Jan 20, 1725/6
(*Reg of St Philips Parish*—Salley)

(*To be continued*)

HISTORICAL NOTES

INSCRIPTIONS FROM ST ANDREWS CHURCH-YARD—Copies of all the Inscriptions on the Tombstones at the old Church in St Andrew's Parish, taken April 5th, 1912, by N A Chamberlain *

Marble Tablet over door on West side of Church has this Inscription

J F.   T R

Supervisors

1706

Here | Lies the remains of | Daniel Kirkpatrick   who departed this life | on the 2nd of June 1829 | aged 58 years 9 months | and 17 Days
   [Stone standing N W of Church]

To the Memory | of Evan W Calvitte | Died June 6th 1838 | aged 47 years | and of his consort | Mary Ann Cal- vitte | Died Nov 29, 1840 | Aged 27 years, and 9 Months | Also | Frederick W Calvitte | Died Oct 1 1832 | aged 2 Years and 5 Months | Rebecca Ann Calvitte | Died June 1839 | Aged 9 Months
   [Stone fallen. N. W of Church]

Sacred | to | The Memory | of William Heriot | Son of | Robert & Maria F. Heriot | He departed this life | 4th January 1841 Aged 24 Years 8 Months | and 16 Days
   [Stone standing N W of Church]

Sacred To the Memory of | Little Jimmie | Son of | Dr J M & E R Meggett | who departed this life on the 9th of Jan'y. 1863 | Aged 1 year 9 months and 16 days
   [Stone fallen   In Clement enclosure N of Church]

Pinckney | Son of Dr J M & E R Meggett | Died Oct 15, 1873 | Aged 3 Years 9 Mos 21 Days |
   [Stone standing in Clement enclosure N of Church]

*Poetry not copied

Sacred to the Memory | of | Roger Moore Smith | who departed this life | 6th July 1808 | Aged 57 Years and Eleven Months

[Slab covering tomb displaced N W of Church]

To the Memory of Mary Elliott | Wife of Benjn Elliott Esq | Who died the 3rd. Novr. 1706 Æt 31

[Stone standing in N W angle close to Church wall]

In Memory of | Joseph Williams | who died the 1st September | Ann 1768 | Aged 65 Years | Also | Elizabeth his wife | who died after a long and painful illness | on the 18th June 1796 | Aged 70 Years

[Stone fallen & broken W of Church]

Elizabeth Holman | Moreland | Departed this life | on 3rd November 1829 | aged 18 Months

[Stone standing, close to E wall of Church]

Sacred | To the Memory | of | Susan Helena Moreland | who departed this life | August 9th 1838 | aged 9 Months | and 3 days

[Broken, close to E wall of Church]

Isabella Pinckney Moreland Died on the 22nd February 1844 | Aged 4 Years and 5 Months | ———— Julia Evelina Moreland | Died on the 21st May 1854 Aged 11 Years, 2 Months | and 5 Days

[Standing close to E wall of Church]

In Memory | of | our young friend | Harriett Bee | Born August 9th 1844 | Died January 6th 1833 | Aged 9 Years 4 Months 28 Days

[Standing close to E wall of Church]

In Memory | of | Joseph Bee | Born May 22nd 1800 Died August 20th 1850 | Aged 50 Years 2 Months and 29 Days

[Close to E. wall of Church]

This Stone Marks The Spot Where are interred The remains of | Simon Magwood | a native of Armagh | County of Monaghan Ireland | He died after a life of | Eminent usefulness | on the 4th day of August 1836 in the 73rd Year of his Age | Also | The remains of | Mary Elizabeth Magwood | consort of Simon Magwood | who departed this life | on the 1st day of February 1833 | in the 63rd Year of her age

[Slab over tomb displaced In enclosure E of Church]

Glorvina | Consort of | Henry C Bissell | Died 20th February 1839 | aged 22 Years

[Standing in Magwood enclosure E of Church]

Beneath | This Stone in Hope of A Glorious Resurrection | Rests the Mortal remains of James Magwood a native of the County of | Armagh. Ireland. | Who departed this life | October 30th Ann Domi 1824 Aged 27 Years

[In Magwood enclosure E of Church]

In Memorian Maham Haig | Born Nov 10 1837 | Died | Sept 24 1884 | Charleston S C

[Granite monument in enclosure N E of Church]

Sacred | To the Memory of | Benj Fuller Jr | Born in Coosawhatchee S C | April 8th 1804 | Died in Charleston S C Feby 10 1873 | Also, his wife | Caroline Savage Fuller | Born in Charleston S C | Sept 27 1819 | Died in St Pauls Parish | March 27 1881 | [On the reverse] Christopher Innes | Son of | Benj and Caroline Fuller | Born 1846 | Died 1893 | Interred at | South Amboy N J

[Standing N E of Church]

Sacred to the Memory of | Mrs Ann Blake Fuller | Consort of Benj. Fuller Jr. | who died 7th Oct' 1851 | Æt. 25 Years 1 Month

[Slab covered tomb N E of Church]

Sacred to the Memory | of | Catherine O'Hear | Consort of Dr John O'Hear | who died on 27th December 1835 | Aged 23 Years 6 Months and 20 days

[Slab covering tomb broken N E. of Church]

Sacred | To the Memory | of | Benjamin Fuller | who died on the 4th Oct' 1832 | Aged 56 years 7 mts and 21 days | and | Of his two infant Children | Jane Porteous | Born on 25th July 1807 | Died on 26th June 1811 | and | John Alexander. | Born on 28 August 1815 | Died on 21 August 1817.

[Slab covering tomb displaced. N E of Church]

In Memory | of | Mrs. Sarah Green Fuller | Daughter of the late | Robert Porteous | of Beaufort | and relict of the late | Benjamin Fuller Sr. | of this Parish | Born 20th April 1778 | Died 17th April 1850 | in the 72nd year of her age

[Slab covering tomb displaced N E of Church]

Sacred | To the Memory | of | Edward W. Clement | who was born 16th Sept' 1800 | Obit. 30th Sept'. 1836 | Also of | His three Children | Emma Eliza | was born 3rd Jan'y 1833 | Obit 7 Oct' 1836 | Edward Wilkinson | was born 14th Feb'y 1835 | Obit 3rd Feb'y 1838

[Fallen & broken N E of Church]

In Memory | of | Andrew Moreland | Born in County Down, Ireland | Oct 22nd 1789 | Died Feb'y 16th 1863.

[Standing E of Church]

In Memorian | Donald Sams. M D | Born April 7th 1820 | Died April 13th 1898

[Standing East of Church]

Sacred to the Memory | of | William Roach | who departed this life | on the 10th of September 1838 | Aged thirty-eight years 11 months | and 14 days

[Slab covered tomb E of Church]

Sacred to the Memory | of , Our Beloved Mother | Mary C. Roach | wife of | William Roach who died May 28th 1868 | Aged 58 Years 6 Months and 27 days
[Stone fallen E of Church]

Beneath This Stone | lies the remains of | Emma Carroll | who died Jan'y 23rd 1839 | aged 4 years 26 days | and of her | Infant Sister | who died Nov 10th 1835 | Daughters of | B R and Eliza Carroll
[Stone fallen. E of Church]

Here Lieth * * * | of Thomas Nairn born y* 15th of January 1697 and dyed y* | 30th of Novem. 1718
[Cement cover to tomb broken & displaced E of Church]

Here Lyes the Body | of Mrs Elizabeth Nairn | who dyed the 9th day of | March 1720 1 aged 63 years | She was Eldest daughter of | the Learned and Religious Divine | Robert Edward A M | of Dundee, and Minister of Murrose. She was married first | to Henry Quintine, by whom She | had one son Henry, | who died in the Service of his Country | in the year 1716 And | two daughters Mary and | Posthuma | Her second husband was | Thomas Nairn —Judge of | the Vice Admiralty of this | Province who was | barbarously murdered ' by the Indians while he was | treating with them in the | year 1715 and | by him she had | one son Thomas
[Slab covering tomb broken E of Church.]

Here Lies the Remains | of | Charlotta Drayton | Daughter of the Honourable William Bull Esq | Lieutenant Governor of South Carolina | and Mary—His wife She was married to John Drayton Esquire | By whom she had two Sons | William & Charles | on the 30th day of December, A D 1743 in the 23rd year of her age | she died | Sacred to the Memory ' of her conjugal virtues and merit this Marble is erected by her | afflicted Husband
[Large tomb E of Church]

Susan Hunter Robinson | Died on the 27th March 1854 aged 22 Years.
[Standing E of Church]

Randal Robinson | Died the 2nd March 1854 | Aged 69 Years
[Standing E of Church]

LIST OF PUBLICATIONS

OF THE

SOUTH CAROLINA HISTORICAL SOCIETY.

COLLECTIONS.

Vol I., 1857, $3.00; Vol. II., 1858, $3.00; Vol III 1859, out of print. Vol IV., 1887, unbound, $3.00, bound $4.00; Vol. V., 1897, paper, $3.00.

PAMPHLETS.

Journal of a Voyage to Charlestown in So. Carolina by Pelatiah Webster in 1765. Edited by Prof. T. P. Harrison, 1898.   75c.

The History of the Santee Canal. By Prof. F. A Porcher. With an Appendix by A. S. Salley, Jr , 1903
75c.

THE SOUTH CAROLINA HISTORICAL AND GENEALOGICAL MAGAZINE.

Volume I, 1900, Edited by A. S. Salley, Jr. Complete Volume. $10.00

Single copies of Nos 2-4, $1.25 each.

Volume II to IX, 1901-1908, Edited by A. S. Salley, Jr.
Unbound $5 00 each

Volume X to XII, 1909-1911, Edited by Mabel L Webber   Unbound $5 00 each.

Single copies of No. 4, Vol. XI, $2.50 each   Members get a discount of 25 per cent. on the above prices

Address: South Carolina Historical Society,
Charleston. S C

THE

SOUTH CAROLINA

HISTORICAL AND GENEALOGICAL

MAGAZINE

PUBLISHED QUARTERLY BY THE

SOUTH CAROLINA HISTORICAL SOCIETY

CHARLESTON, S. C.

VOLUME X111., NO. 3.   JULY 1912.

Entered at the Post-office at Charleston, S. C., as
Second-Class Matter.

PRINTED FOR THE SOCIETY BY
WALKER, EVANS & COGSWELL CO.
CHARLESTON, S. C.
1912

PUBLICATION COMMITTEE.

JOSEPH W. BARNWELL,   HENRY A. M. SMITH,
                  A. S. SALLEY, JR.

EDITOR OF THE MAGAZINE
MABEL L. WEBBER

CONTENTS.

N. B —These Magazines, with the exception of No. 1 of Vol. I and No. 4 of Vol. XI, are $1.25 each to any one other than a member of the South Carolina Historical Society. Members of the Society receive them free. The Membership fee is $4 00 per annum (the fiscal year being from May 19th to May 19th), and members can buy back numbers or duplicates at $1.00 each In addition to receiving the Magazines, members are allowed a discount of 25 per cent. on all other publications of the Society, and have the free use of the Society's library.

Any member who has not received the last number will please notify the Secretary and Treasurer,

Miss Mabel L. Webber,
South Carolina Historical Society,
Charleston, S C

CONTENTS.

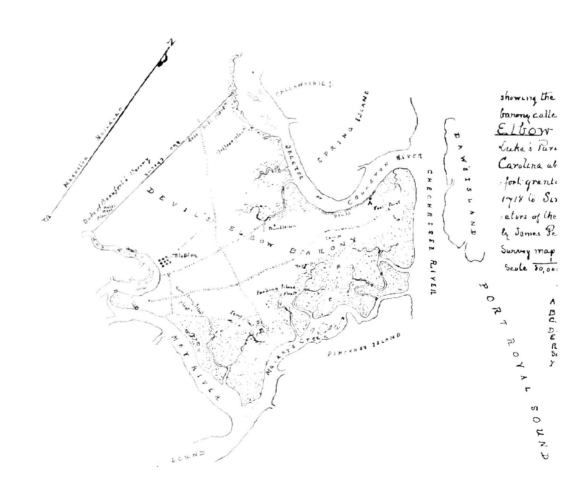

The South Carolina Historical and Genealogical Magazine.

VOL XIII   JULY, 1912.   No 3

THE BARONIES OF SOUTH CAROLINA

By Henry A M Smith

IX

THE OKETEE OR DEVILS ELBOW BARONY

By the original Fundamental Constitutions, as proposed by the Lords Proprietors for the Province of Carolina, each of the eight Proprietors was to have a signiory of 12.000 acres in each and every county[1] At the first settlement of the colony the attempt was made by means of "temporary laws" and "instructions" to the Governor and Council to shape the laws and government of the country so as to accord, as near as practicable, to the provisions of these Fundamental Constitutions until the latter could be put in full operation[2] It soon developed that from the physical difficulties, and from the temper of the settlers, the Fundamental Constitutions were wholly unsuited for and could never be put in force over the country In proportion with the recognition of this fact the departure from the observance, or recognition, of the Constitutions became more marked. and after the rejection by the popular assembly of the Province in 1702,[3] of the final revision of the Fundamental

[1] Carroll's Hist Coll" vol 2 p 363
[2] ...ers' Sketch of S C. pp 341. 347. 348. 351. 359. 366
[3] Stats of S C ... ...

Constitutions, they were practically wholly abandoned The Proprietors, treating the whole country as their own, deemed they could have baronies set out to them as they saw fit. without reference to any limitations contained in the Fundamental Constitutions, but with regard of course to grants already made by them

As early as 1711 plans had been made of 119,000 acres to be laid out in baronies to the Proprietors,[1] but nothing farther seems to have been done at that time

After the Yemassee war had freed the country of those troublesome neighbors these plans were again taken up and on 14th Novr, 1718. the Proprietors ordered that four baronies of 12,000 acres each should be laid out in Granville County by cross lines drawn from the river May northward to the river falling into Port Royal river   These four baronies with others ordered at the same time (aggregating in all 119,000 acres) were to be drawn for among the Proprietors by lot. and this was done at their next meeting on 21 Novr, 1718,[6] and on 5 Decr, 1718, the grants were ordered to be executed[7]

Sir John Colleton the grandson of Sir John Colleton, one of the original proprietors, and the then owner of his proprietorship, evidently drew the barony which is the subject of this Article. for on that day (5th Decr, 1718) a grant for it to him was executed with attached the usual map of the land granted[8] It lay between the river May and a river, the Indian name of which as variously given in the old grants and deeds was "Oketee," "Okeetee" or "Okatie," the latter river forming the northern boundary for the entire length of the barony

The name "Devils Elbow" creek or river was given to this stream apparently from the elbow shape of its course from the point where it joined Port Royal sound or Broad river to a point around Spring Island and back into the country   The barony while owned by the Colletons, and

[1] Trans Hist Soc of S C, vol 1, p 191
[6] Ibid p 192
[7] Ibid
[8] Ibid
[5] Off Hist Com'n Memo Bk 4, p 118

until its final partition, was commonly called the "Devils Elbow" barony or "Colleton Neck," and the Oketee river where it bounded the barony was called "Colleton" river

The situation was an ideal one in many respects It could be reached from the sea by the deepest and most accessible natural channel south of Norfolk in Virginia, and its shores afforded deep water up to the very wharves, with a land locked harbour in which any fleet could ride in safety

Such were its natural advantages in this respect that the extreme northeastern point of the barony on deep water called "Foot point" was at quite an early period in the last century regarded as the coming site of a great commercial city

The lands from the agricultural point of view were very fine Up to the war of the Revolution indigo seems to have been largely planted by the Colletons In after years the culture of sea island cotton flourished on them, and the barony had become the seat of a wealthy and cultivated community of planters, when the social, political, and financial destruction consequent upon the War of 1861-1865 turned a region sparkling with agricultural opulence into an abandoned waste, inhabited by a thriftless and ignorant negro population

The family seat of this branch of the Colletons in South Carolina was at Fairlawn Barony[9] in Berkeley County and the Devils Elbow Barony in Granville County was much later brought under cultivation

On 28 Sept' 1726, Sir John Colleton transferred the Devils Elbow Barony to his second son Peter[10] Little appears on the record concerning this Peter He came to and lived in South Carolina, for prior to 1733 he purchased a plantation of 400 acres called Epsom lying on Biggon creek at Biggon bridge and between Fairlawn and Wadboo baronies[11] He was certainly in Carolina in 1739 when he is a witness to a deed[12] He died prior to 1748, for in that year his brother executed a codicil disposing of the Devils Elbow

[9]S C Hist & Geneal Mag vol 1, p 330
[10]"Off Hist Com" Memo Bk 3, p 195
[11]Ibid. p 453
[12]M C O Charleston, Bk T, p 290

barony as his own   His will was dated in 1740 and was probated in England in 1754   (S C Hist & Geneal: Mag , vol. XI, p 131) In 1751 his father, in a letter to Mess". Nathaniel and Thomas Broughton, speaks of him as "my late son Peter" who "bought a little plantation by "Fairlawn I think called Epsom and gave £300 sterling for "it which he left to his brother Robert'"[13]

At Peter's death, probably under the limitations of the deed of gift from his father, the Devils Elbow barony went to his brother, the Honorable John Colleton of Fairlawn barony, who by a codicil dated in June, 1748, devised the "Barony at Port Royal'"[14] to his son John

The Honorable John Colleton died in 1750   Shortly before his death he had made provision for the development of the barony as his widow and Executrix in an agreement with Morgan Sabb dated 8ᵗʰ Sept , 1750, recites that

> "for the cultivation & improvement of a certain barony
> "belonging to the said John Colleton situate and being
> "at a place called the Devils Elbow in Port Royal river
> "in Granville County" the said John Colleton had

agreed with Morgan Sabb that John Colleton would put in 61 slaves and that Morgan Sabb would put in 53 slaves and that the same would be used under the direction of Morgan Sabb for 7 years from 1ˢᵗ. January, 1751, "to clear and

> "cultivate and make plantations and work & labour up-
> "on the said Barony by improving and breeding flocks
> "planting rice corn and other grain sawing timber
> "making pitch tar turpentine Indigo & other commer-
> "cial commodities thereon'"[15]

Under the Will of the Honorable John Colleton his lands, including this barony, upon the death of his eldest son Peter, who died about 1756, (S. C Hist & Geneal: Mag·, vol IV, p 236) passed to his son John   The latter was a minor at his father's death, and his mother dying a few months after his father, the child seems to have been sent to England to his grandfather, upon whose death he succeeded to the title.

---

[13] Prob Ct Charleston, Bk 1751-54, p 185
[14] Ibid, Bk 1747-1752 p 310
[15] Prob Ct Charleston Bk 1749-51 p 365

During the life of this last Sir John the Devils Elbow
barony seems to have been well developed and improved
M" Graves, his daughter, states that the property had been
devoted largely to the cultivation of indigo In 1762, Moses
Lindo, "Inspector and Surveyor General of South Carolina
Indico" states that he has granted certificates for the first
sort "equal in quality to the best French" to several growers
of indigo, including Sir John Colleton, whose indigo had
sold at 30 s (currency?) per lb "

M" Graves also states that the value of the live stock on
the Devils Elbow barony taken and destroyed during the
revolutionary war amounted to over £8,000 As it lay
near the theatre of hostilities from 1779 to 1782 it is probable that it was largely swept clear of its labour in the shape
of slaves, and of its provisions and buildings

Sir John Colleton died in 1777 and under his will the
property went to his only daughter Louisa Carolina Colleton   Before his death however the disintegration of the
barony had begun as he seems to have disposed of about
6,199 acres of it," viz to William Fripp   1668 acres

Thomas Farr	700 "
Benj". Walls	680 "
James Stanyarne	1200 "
Edmund Bellinger	1667 "
George Hipp	284 "

Of Louisa Carolina Colleton who married Admiral Richard Graves of the British Navy an account has been given
in an article on the Colleton family in South Carolina published in this Magazine in vol 1, p 339, for October, 1900

During the lifetime of M" Graves she retained the
barony practically as devised to her, but on her death it was
divided up and sold Prior to her death she seems to have
disposed of a part of the barony lying on Colleton river to
Benjamin Guerard, which part seems afterward to have
become the property of M" William Wigg Barnwell by
whom it was called "Trimbleston "

After her death, under proceedings in the Court of Chan-

"Elzas, Jews of S C, p 57
"M C O Charleston, Bks T 6, p 47, O 3 p 2, O 5, p 247

cery for foreclosure of mortgage the rest of the barony was disposed of," viz

On .... the Rose Hill tract, 800 acres to James Kirk

On 25 Sept, 1828, the Hunting Island tract, 946 acres to James Kirk.

On 11 Novr, 1828, the Camp tract, 1,370 acres to M^{rs}. Pinckney & Mrs Izard

On 3 Feby, 1829, the Foot Point tract, 1,055 acres to John Stoney

On 3 Feby, 1829, the Ferry tract, 942 acres to John Stoney

On 3 Feby, 1829, the Fording Island tract, 750 acres to W J Grayson.

On 3 Feby, 1829, the Toppin tract, 790 acres to Misses Pinckney

Making a total of 6,653 acres

The barony had evidently, for the purposes probably of more efficient supervision and cultivation, been subdivided into tracts during the Colleton ownership and when sold off the plantations, into which it was subdivided for sale, carried the names by which they had been before designated The village or summer settlement of "Bluffton" is on a part of the barony (apparently on that part conveyed to Benjamin Walls) on a bluff fronting the river May Colleton Neck is distinguished botanically by the fact that many forms of a more southern flora are found as far north as that locality It was also the scene of much of the botanical work of Stephen Elliott, who frequently refers to it in his "Sketch of the Botany of South Carolina and Georgia" In later years it was the field for the botanical observations of that most excellent of field botanists as well as skilful physician, the late Dr James H Mellichamp who for many years lived at Bluffton

As the family home and mansion of the Colletons was at Fairlawn barony it is improbable that there was on the

Devils Elbow barony a larger dwelling than was required for the resident overseer; certainly none on the extensive scale denoted by the ruins at Fairlawn It's more favorable situation and finer lands constituted it from the financial standpoint a much more valuable property than the Fairlawn barony

The map published with this article represents the map as taken from the lines of a map made in 1786 by James Peart for Miss Louisa Carolina Colleton, but located and laid down on the map of the locality published by the U. S Coast Survey

The final sales of the barony show that it exceeded largely in its actual contents the 12,000 acres it was originally laid out for, but this excess was a usual feature of large surveys made at that early period

STOCK MARKS
RECORDED IN SOUTH CAROLINA, 1695-1721

Contributed by A S Salley, Jr.

In the office of the Historical Commission in Columbia there is a small manuscript volume bearing the following inscription on the fly leaf preceding the index

"A Booke for Recording of Cattle Markes & others Given by the Hono^ble: Thomas Smith Esqr Landgrave & Govern^r In September 1694"

Notwithstanding the good intentions of Governor Smith, very few marks were recorded and the purpose for which the book was given was almost nullified, the greater part of the book was soon given over to other uses The few records that were made, however, are now quite valuable historically and genealogically

---

Record of Cattle Markes & others

1694/5 March 8th	This day came Mr John Hamilton of Edestoh Island in Colleton County. & Recorded his marke of Cattle Hoggs & c^t· being as followeth, In each Eare two halfe Moones The Topps of both Eares Cropt & Soe Slitt down to bottom of each Eare this Brand
H	Marke as ⁊P Margent
March 8th 1694/5	This day came Mr John Hamilton of Edestoh Island in Colleton County and Recorded; His daughter Mary Hamilton her Marke of Cattle & Hoggs (& c^t) (being as followeth)
M H	The right Eare a halfe Moon cutt out in each side, The Top of said eare Cutt of and soe Slitt downe in ye midle to the bottom of the Eare The Left Eare only Cropt. Her Brand Marke, on ye Left buttock as ⁊P Margent

---

¹Previously to this time a few marks had been recorded at random in other volumes

1694/5
March—8th

P II

This day Came Mr John: Hamilton of Edestoh Island in Colleton County And Recorded his Sonn Paul Hamilton his Marke of Cattle & Hoggs & c' (as followeth) In Each Eare a Swallow Taill cutt out in the Topp thereof and under the Swallow forke a round Hole cutt out in Each Eare his brand marke as 7^H margent being on the Left buttock

1694/5
March—8th

This day came Mr John Hamilton of Edestoh Island in Colleton County and Recorded his daughter Anna Hamilton her Marke of Cattle & Hoggs & c'. (as followeth) The Topp of both Eares cutt of, and two Slitts in each Eare from ye Topp to the bottom her brand marke on ye Left buttock as 7^H Margent —

1694/5
March 8th
J B

This day Came John Berrisford Esqr and Recorded his Cooppers Brand marke for barrells as 7^H Margent

1695
May 30th

This day came Samuell Stent of James Island in Berkeley County and Recorded his Marke for Cattle & Hoggs (as followeth) The Right Eare an upper Keel on the outside of the said Eare, and ye Left Eare an under Keell on the outside of the said Eare. and his Horne Marke S S. branded

1695
July—19

This day Came Major Charles Colleton, and Recorded his Marke for Cattle, Horses & Hoggs as followeth. Both Eares two under Keells. His Brand marke X on the Neer Buttocks

1695
August—6

This day Came James Bard and Recorded his Marke for Cattle & Hoggs as followeth, The Right Eare a Crope & Two Slitts downe almost to ye roott of said eare. The Left being a Swallow forke and an under keele. his brand marke being J B

1695
August—6

This day came Richard Shaw of Berkley County & Recorded his Marke for Cattle & Hoggs (as followeth) The Right Eare a hole in y middle of y eare and said Eare Cropt, And an upper keell cutt of said eare, The Left Eare a Crope and a Slitt, his Brand Marke is R S

1695 /
October 29
M N

This Day Came Moses Norman of Berkley County recorded his marke for Cattle & Barrells as Ᵽ Margent

1695
Novemb' 27

This Day Came John Raven of Colleton County & recorded his Marke for Cattle & hoggs as followeth Two Slitts in y Right Eare & one in y Left his Brand Marke being J R

1695/6
January y' 11

This Day Came Thomas Rake of Edistow Island & recorded his marke for Cattle & hoggs, as followeth one slitt in y Right Eare & & upper Keele in y Left & in y Left a Side Slitt

1695/6
January y' 17

This Day Came John Alston of Chachan in Colleton County & recorded the marke of John Harris, Jun' for Cattle & Hoggs as followeth Two und' Keeles in Boath Eare
This Day Came John Brea of Edistow Island & recorded his marke for Cattle & Hoggs as followeth y topps of Both Eares Cutt of & three Slitts Downe to y botom of them both

ffebry—5
1695/6

This Day came Richard Benett of ffrips Island & recorded his marke for Cattle & Hoggs as followeth halfe of y Eares Cutt of & Two peaces cut out

March 2ᵈ
1695/6
W B

This Day Came M' Wᵐ═Bolow & recorded his marke W B with a Slitt in y Right Eare & a Hole in y Left

March 21" 1695/6 T P	This Day came M' Thomas Pinkny & Entered y' marke of his cattle & Hoggs it being 2 und'=Keeles one; in Each Eare which was formerly y' Marke of Thomas Rose which is now assigned unto y' s' Pinckny (and also branded on the Right Buttock as ᛏᒆ Marg')
Aprill 3 1696	This Day came M'=Nathaniel Law & Entered his mark which is Three halfe Moones cutt out of Each Eare & his Brand marke being as ᛏᒆ Merg'=
Aprill 6 1696	This Day came Cap'=W'"=Smith & recorded his marke for Cattle and Hoggs Viz' is a Hole in the Midle of Each Eare with a forke cutt out of the Tipp of Each Eare and his Marke for Horses is a figure of Seaven
1696 Aprill 16 J S	This Day came John Sanders of Wando River and recorded his marke for Cattle & Hoggs Viz'=Two upper Keeles and his Brand marke being as ᛏᒆ Merg'=
1696 May 11	This Day came Robert Britewell of Cumbohee and recorded y' marke for Cattle & Hoggs which is one fforke Cutt out of Each Eare & a Slitt, ffor Sarah Bures Jun'
1696 May 23	This Day came M' Nicholas DeLongemar Jun and recorded his mark which is a ᛏᒆ Merg'=who Lives above Tee in the Eastern branch of Couper river neare pumpkin hill
1696 June 22	This Day came M' John Branford of the North Side of Ashley river and recorded his marke for Cattle & Hoggs Viz'=one Slitt in Left Eare & a figure of seaven in y' right & his brand marke beeing as ᛏᒆ marg'=
1696 June y' 22	This Day came Peter Manico of Santee & recorded his marke for Cattle & Hoogs which is y' Eare Cutt of boath sides as ᛏᒆ

P M
1696

marg'=& his Brand marke as 𝔓 merg'=P M
which cutt is in y° Left Eare

June y° 27

This Day came John Burke of Bowatt and recorded his marke for Cattle and Hoggs which is a Cropp Slitt and und° Keele in y° left Eare and a Swalow forke in y° Right and

J B
1696
July y° 16

his Brand marke as 𝔓 merg'=
This Day came Joseph Ellott of Stono river & recorded his marke for Cattle & Hoggs which is both Eares Crop'=and a Slitt in the Right Eare and his Brand marke as 𝔓 marg'=

July y° 27ᵗʰ
1696
M T

This Day Came Mʳ Mathew Talartha of Berkley County & recorded his Brand marke which is 𝔓 merg'=& a swallo forke in the Right Eare & a noch in the Left Eare Cropt

August 3ᵈ
1696

This Day Came Richard Blake of Coupe River Head & recorded his marke for Cattle and Hoggs which is y° Left Eare Cropt & y° Right Eare an und° Keele & his Brand

R B
1696
octobʳ 29

marke as 𝔓 merg'=
This Day Came Joseph Marbuff Jn² LaBrosse of Couper river & recorded his marke for Cattle and Hoggs which is boath Eares Slitt

LB M
29
L J

& his Brand marke as 𝔓 marg'=
and this Day Came Lewis Juin of Couper River & recorded his marke ffor Cattle & Hoggs which is the Left Eare Cropt & Three Slitts in the right

1696
Novembʳ 16

This Day came Shem Buttler & recorded the marke of Wᵐ. Smith for Cattle & Hoggs which is the Left Eare Cropt & Three Slitts & the Right Eare Cropt & Two Slitts and his Brand marke as 𝔓 margent

---

²This should have been de   La Bruce, or La Brosse, de Marbeuf or Marbeuf de La Brosse or La Bruce, were the usual forms in which the present La Bruce family name was written in that day

Novemb' 16   This Day Came Shem Buttler & recorded his
marke for Cattle & hoggs which is the Left
Eare Cropt & Three Slitts & the Right Eare
with a Single Slitt in the midle & his Brand
marke as $\maltese^{\text{D}}$ mergent

1696
January 7th.   This Day Came Jn° Mackfashion & recorded
his Marke for Cattle & Hogs which is a Crop
& a Whole in the Right Eare and a Crop &
a Slitt in the Left

(To be continued)

DIARY OF TIMOTHY FORD

1785-1786

With notes by Joseph W Barnwell

Timothy Ford, Esq was born December 4th, 1762, and was the son of Jacob Ford and Theodosia Johnes of Morris Town, New Jersey In 1880 when a mere youth he was twice wounded at Springfield, N J, while acting as a volunteer under Capt Coalfax His patriotic feelings as a soldier of the Revolution remained with him to his dying day[1]

He received his education at Princeton, where he graduated with honors He was admitted to the Bar in New York, having studied his profession in the office of Robert Morris

His sister, Elizabeth Ford, having married Henry William De Saussure, afterwards Chancellor De Saussure, one of the most learned and distinguished Judges of South Carolina, Mr Ford came to Charleston with him in 1785, and was admitted to the Bar of this State in 1786 He was very soon in active practice, his name appearing on the briefs in many important causes before the Appellate Courts For many years, however, he confined his practice mostly to the Equity Court

He found not a few graduates of Princeton, or "Nassau

---

[1]Will Book G, page 470
I Timothy Ford of the City of Charleston being about to go to the Northern States for the residue of the present season for the benefit of my health, confid management of my estate to my Executrix— the house on Tradd Street belongs to my wife, wife estate for life then to my two daughters Louisa Catherine and Mary Theodosia, subject only to a legacy of $1,000 to my grand child Mary Louise when 21 or day of marriage, wife & daus to care for the orphan Library to be sold, but the sale not forced Wife & daus to select such books as they may wish

"My father's Revolutionary sword is in my possession after his death my beloved mother girded it on my thigh at the age of sixteen and I wore it in the field of Battle It is a Sacred family Relic of the Revolution and Should descend in the name of Ford, I bequeath this sword to my nephew Frederick Ford, the Son of my brother Jacob "   Wife Mary Magdalene Ford to be sole executrix 25 July 1827 Proved January 27—1831

Hall," among the lawyers and men of position in Carolina Chancellor Richard Hutson, Thomas Stanyarne Gibbes, John McCrady, Patrick Noble and others had received their education there To his work as a lawyer in the higher ranks of the profession, he added important work as a citizen of the city and State, while his zeal for every literary, benevolent and religious object was prominent throughout his life He was a member of the City Council, a member of the South Carolina Legislature, Trustee of the College of Charleston, President of the Charleston Library Society, of the Literary and Philosophical Society, and of the Bible Society He died December 7th, 1830 He was twice married, his first wife being Sarah Amelia DeSaussure, sister of the Chancellor, and his second, Mary Magdalen Prioleau, daughter of Samuel Prioleau He had issue by both marriages, but his descendants are now extinct Through the kindness of Mr Frank Ravenel Frost, the administrator of Dr Edmund Ravenel, the last descendant of Mr Ford, and with the consent of the family, for both the brothers of Timothy Ford, Jacob Ford and Gabriel Ford, have descendants in South Carolina, we are permitted to publish this diary found among the family papers

DIARY

Saturday October 1ˢᵗ 1785.

This morning at 9 o'clock my Sister with her husband' Miss DeSaussure' & my Self take leave of my mother to go to Charleston, which was a melancholy scene My dear Mother parted with her only daughter as tho' for the last time It was a scene of tears indeed, and such was its effect on me that it moved my tears which however I may be effected Seldom flow As a consolation however in the midst of this distress we had the chearful company of our charming friends the $++725++={}^\prime+\frac{n}{m}$ as far as brunswick to which place we arrived in the evening without any event that need be particularized and were received at Mʳ.

'Married Lately in New-Jersey. Mr William Desaussure, son of the Hon Daniel Desaussure Esq, of this city to Miss Ford, of Morristown in that State *State Gazette of South Carolina*, Thursday, Sept 1st, 1785 The family record gives May as the month of marria--

'Marri

Dunhams wth their usual kindness & hospitality. Here I found Mrs Forman on her way to visit my mother which tends to alleviate our common gloom knowing it it will also assuage her grief

Sunday 2^d.

Early in the morning we prepare to prosecute our journey intending this day to reach Burlington and nine o'Clock with tears the girls take the last kiss & after the benedictions of our friends we were off—& in order to avoid Doct Scott whose zeal for religion or love for money invariably inter-rupts the traveller under the Sanction of law we take a road which runs thro' Middlesex County out of the sphere of his jurisdiction We proceed unmolested to Princeton where I meet with many of my college & other acquaintances with whom I spend an hour & renew the round of unpleasant feelings incident to parting with friends—We dine in tren-ton & have the happiness of the comp^y. of A D Woodruff my worthy friend After dinner we Start for Burlington & my friend Woodruff takes me in his Chair as far as the ferry that we may be together as long as possible We fill up the few remaining moments in talking upon our mu-tual intentions for future Life & at the ferry bid adieu!

In the morning we arrive at B [?] & cross over to Bur-lington where our amiable friends regale us not less by their cordiality of reception than a good dish of tea We have the mortification to find Fanny confined to her chamber by indisposition, Miss R. not very well but not prevented from exercising her favorite virtues of friendship & hospitality.

Monday 3^d   This day we spend at Mr Randolphs sociably & of course agreeably Fanny is able to come down and & mix with us The weather boistrous & disagreeable we hope for a change by to-morrow as we expect to go down to Phila in a boat

Tuesday 4th

Contrary to our expectations & hopes the inclemency of the weather is rather augmented but for our consolation so exceedingly boistrous that no boat will go down the river we are of course gratified with one day more at this agreeable place By this time I have made an acquaintance with M^r

Randolph having never before had an opportunity He and I sit up 'till 12 oclock reading Pope

Wednesday 5th

At 3 o'clock we are roused by an ambassador from the boat with information that we are to sail in an hour, the winds very high Anne wth her usual goodness has breakfast prepared for us in the mean time & we accordingly take leave of them & go on board having partly obtained the promise of M^r. Randolph to bring the Ladies by land to Philad^a should their feelings & the day favor it in order that my sister & Miss De Saussure may spend the remainder of the time on land as much as possible We arrive at Philad^a at 9 oClock after a boisterous passage & are received by our friends with every mark of kindness & hospitality M^r M^{rs} & Miss De Saussure take bed and board at Mr Wm Clarksons—I dispose of my self between his house & M^r. Snowdens According to our sanguine hopes our Burlington friends arrived at 2 o'Clock viz M^r R Miss R Miss F & Mrs Hayter My acquaintance with the last lady had hitherto been slight and the pleasure I dirived from it led me to regret that circumstance not a little She is by nature blessed with a good face, a fine eye & a comely person —a fertile mind not a little improved, and a hospitable disposition She seems calculated however to display the dignified rather than the softened parts of her nature, and to excite admiration rather than love Invited by a number of friends in Philad^a wee seem to regret the circumstances of leaving them so soon—but Capt Allibone tells us we shall sail on Saturday

Thursday 6th

M^r DeSaussure & myself imploy the fore part of this day in providing sea stores—I dine at Mr Clarksons where love presided at each end of the table & that cheerfulness which flows from a mutual friendship divested of all the unwholesome restraints of formality run its pleasant round This amiable couple form a striking instance of conjugal felicity, being evidently at first designed for each other Fine feelings, smooth & conforming dispositions, and a mutual desire that the sight of the one should see the pleasure of the

other form a part of the fuel that keeps alive & in its original lustre the fire of love   Though the short time that they
have been united has not given opportunity for the full
trial of the constancy of their tempers, there is the most
plausable presumption of their surviving in their present
purity, if not of being improved by the cares of life or the
vicissitudes of fortune   In the afternoon we all visit M^r
Peales exhibition room (except M^rs. Huyter) where we are
entertained by a novel display of transparent paintings done
in a masterly manner.   Day & night, light and shade in a
very masterly manner   A part of market Street is at first
represented in the midst of night the lamps lighted the day
comes on in its natural gradation from its first blush at
dawn to the full irradiation of the rising sun   Many other
scenes are as exquisitely performed & the whole interspersed
with interludes—but I cannot pay any compliments to the
musick

Our Burlington friends spent the afternoon & evening
at Mr Clarksons—to add *agreeably* w^d be superfluous —

Friday 7th.

Our time is chiefly passed at M^r. Clarksons and I find
myself in improving an acquaintance wth Miss Cornelia
Clarkson the sister of our friend, who partaking largely of
that friendly disposition which is so eminently characteristic
[of] her brother & sister spends her time with us   She is
16 years old; and through the goodness of her heart not less
than the modeling counsels of her parents seems exempted
from many foibles of her sex which makes their first if not
their plainest appearance at her age   I should do her injustice in confining myself to a negative description—for
she is not more meritorious for being untainted with the
common foibles of her age than for possessing the virtues
of much more advanced years   Her heart seems to be as
nature first made it, tender humane & susceptable—her
manners & understanding not unimproved in proportion to
her years—though her capacity promises & taste assures us
they will both be improved to advantage in time   Her easy
& artless manners point out a correctness of disposition
void of that vanity peevishness and severity too frequent

among her sex & too perceptible at her age   And to crown
the whole there appears in all her deportment a degree of
well timed morality which sheds a luster upon all her other
properties at the same time that it proves them to be genuine
In such company as this it would be my own fault if my
time did not pass agreeably—In truth it did so in so much
that I was not displeased with the disappointment when
Capt. Allibone informed us he should not sail to-morrow,
as his workmen on board had not finished their business—

Saturday 8th

This day passed like the rest in the circle of our friends
where sociability presides in all its pleasing forms   To re-
count the variety of amusement, conversation and pastimes
would be endless—the time seemed to steal imperceptibly
away   In the midst of all my happiness I am shocked with
the catastrophe of a young man who unfortunately fell by
his own hands   His name was Shipping of the respectable
family of that name in this City   His prospects of patri-
mony not rendering necessary his application to business, he
took the two frequent resort of young men of fortune and
became early attached to pleasure   He unfortunately made
such acquaintances as led him to excesses which smothering
the seeds of reason & morality soon let loose the reigns of
his passions & he became abandoned to vice & debauchery.
No doubt he had better counsels from his friends, but not
proped with that force & soliciture which they w^d. have
been had they forseen where his courses would land him
Passing thus through the several vicissitudes of vice his
mind and intellectual faculties became victiated in extreme
so that his time was divided and measured by actions the
most brutal   In this degree of vice a person never stands
long at the same point   Either some happy and unforseen
event reaches his conscience with conviction & alarms him
into a reformation, or he is pushed to the last enormity
which soon or later concludes the dreadful scene   This was
the case with this unfortunate young man. Not content to
carry on revelling & carousing in all its bestial forms he
fancied himself in love with one of them and married her
unknown to his friends   But why did they not anticipate

this event or some other as shocking to them? Surely the use of means cannot more directly point us to the end, than his actions demonstrated the dreadful issue to which he would be brought   But his vices previous to this being fashionable ones could be palliated and even be applauded for his spirit & address!   Solicitous now to dissolve a connexion which disgraced it, his family & friends plyed him on all sides with reproaches; and represented to him what he could not understand the dishonor he had done himself and the wounds he had given to delicacy & all the finer feelings—he still retained a regard for his friends, and they proposed a voyage to the East indies to forget the harlot, and when he returned to form a better connextion he refused & declared he could not live without her   They urged —and finally brought him to a dilemma from w" he resolved to extricate himself by Death   Either to break the union or be abandoned by his family—he took a dose of Laudenum   Of this they got notice and prevailed on him to take an Emetic which brought it away   But finding himself in a folorn state he could not endure his life and after writing a letter to that effect addressed to his friends he took a portion or arsenick & closed a life stained with every vice by a most tragical and exemplary death

Sunday 9th

The forepart of this day I pass at Mr Clarkson's not feeling disposed for church—In the afternoon wait on Miss Cornelia to Mr Sproats Church in Arch Street—the rest of the company not using dicision enough in their choice go to no church at all   In the Evening the Miss Randolphs drink tea at Mr Clarksons & we pass the time as usual very agreeably

Monday 10th

Still our Captain defers sailing; we attend the ladies on board the ship who admire very much her accomodations and almost wish themselves of our party

Tuesday 11th.

The forepart of the day is devoted to getting our baggage & Stores on board the ship the Capt having signified that we shall sail tomorrow.

Wednesday 12ᵗʰ

However agreeable it is to Stay among such an agreeable circle of friends still we find the inconveniences of a state of suspense for our sailing is disposed until tomorrow and indeed some of the Charms of the visit are this day dissipated by the departure of our Burlington friends; and Mʳ. DeSaussure & myself in addition to the regret of their leaving us had also that of our not being on the spot to take leave of them   This mortifying circumstances was occasioned by our taking a mornings walk & staying beyond our time   I confess however I found some consolation in its affording me occasion of writing to them

Thursday 13ᵗʰ

Accustomed to be deceived from time to time I this morning expected it as usual; & that very expectation was itself a cause of it; for in fact we are this morning arrested with a short notice to be on board & we accordingly leave our friends in the utmost hurry   At 10 oClock the ship hawls ot [sic] and in about 2 hours we were under way— a rainy disagreeable day prevented us from viewing the opposite shores as we passed down the deleware

We have a clever company of passangers but no ladies except my Sister & Miss Sally   Very few scenes could take place during the passage—my time was chiefly divided by seasickness & sleep which induces me to conclude I shall never go to sea for pleasure   In eight days we arrived at Charleston bar, but the wind setting from the land we could not get in, a few of the passengers went on shore in the pilot Boat   The succeeding day the same boat cruising off the bar the pilot on board of us hailed her & ordered her alongside for the purpose of taking to shore those passengers who should chose to go   Mʳ DeSaussure, Betsy & Sally got on board with two other passengers; but the sea running high it broke her fast & She went off leaving three of us on board—we consoled ourselves under the disappointment with a good dinner and a glass of wine; and the custom house boat coming the next day on board of us, we embrassed that opportunity of coming on shore; and arrived in Charleston on Saturday the 22ᵈ. October; and after hav-

ing my head adjusted by a barber went up to M' DeSaussure's where I was very kindly & friendly received & was
introduced to a large circle of company a process at the
same time agreeable and disagreeable—the former from
the circumstance of making acquaintance the latter from
the embarrasment usual on such an occasion The vertigo
occasioned by the motion of the ship made me feel rather
awkward & unsociable tho I endeavoured to counteract it
Sleep however dissipated in a principal degree the remains
of my maritime feelings and in the morning I felt myself
on the land; and disposed to look around me & view a city
so remote from my native place & of which I have heard so
much

Charleston is situated much like New York at the con-
fluence of two Rivers (viz Cooper and Ashley named after
one Ashley Cooper an original Proprietor in this country)
It's Southeastern prospect is the Atlantic ocean which is not
more than 10 miles, separated from the bay by a bar of
sand over which no ships but small burthen can pass; and
larger vessels steer through the inlet which of itself is
dangerous except when the tide is up The harbour is
replete with shoals which render it both intricate and
dangerous for strangers, tho the inhabitants rather value
it on this account as an Enemy's navy in time of war cannot find so easy an access & they alledge that the due attendance of pilots may always obviate difficulties in time of
peace For my part I rather question the validity of this
reasoning In the first place a country that intends to defend itself effectually against foreign invasion will find
all dependiences short of a navy very ineffectual; and where
they are led to depend on the natural inaccessibility of a
harbour they will be the more remiss in providing themselves In the second place a fleet of enemies ships during
the present state of human nature would find no difficulty in
alluring by their gold even from the bosom of their own
country a sufficient number of wretches whose knowledge
of the harbour would obviate all difficulties And lastly in
case of storms & tempests an unskillful vessel on the coast
might nearly as well run on shore elsewhere, as to try to

make this harbour where the chance is almost as bad, and
where tho' in sight of land they cannot reach it The streets
of Charleston are straight & generally regular but like New
York again very narrow most of them A portion of the
streets on each side, generally about 4 feet is paved with
brick w" makes it pleasant walking; the intermediate space
is in it's natural state mostly sandy & therefore disagreeable
crossing the streets But this is attoned for by the inoffen-
sive quietness with which carriages pass along; for being
accustomed to having my ears strained by the rattling of
carriages in New York I was struck most agreeably by seeing them pass here without leaving behind them noise or
disturbance—tho sometimes they leave dust The city
covers a great deal of ground in proportion to the number
of houses, even more so than Philadelph" This admits of
the freer circulation of air Their yards & in many
instances their gardins also are large & convenient This
however is more to be found in the interior than in the
front parts of the town the places more particularly of business A small majority of the buildings are of brick tho
many are of wood

None of the dwelling houses rise higher than three
stories, and by no means a majority so high; tho a pretty
good proportion of the buildings, those especially of brick,
may be termed *tolerably good* In some instances the pro-
jectors seem to have studied intricacy, & have of course been
led from uniformity, indeed their external appearance would
almost persuade a person that they sprung undeliberated upon from the hand of chance herself and the inside appears as
void of taste as the outside of design Such buildings are
however to be more or less found in every city The police
is pretty good, it consists of an intendant & corporation I
admire their precaution in case of fire—for they are not
only provided with engines, & the people taught to throw
themselves into lines immediately upon their assembling for
the purpose of conducting water; but every warden (of
whom there are 13) is obliged to keep 5 hogsheads, strongly
made & painted full of water which on the first alarm are
immediately to be rolled out to the place to supply the

engines until the lines can be formed   By this means 65 hhds of water may reach the place of fire as soon as the engines themselves & thereby they are prevented from the delay & loss of time in the confusion, of the peoples getting into order   This instant supply may sometimes check or extinguish a fire in its early stages which might otherwise make a great headway.

The most obvious division of the inhabitants of Charleston is into *Black* & *White,* the former being to the latter as 5 to one.[5] This sight occasions a reflection rather painful; that, in a land of Liberty & Christianity, that boasts & builds upon the irrefrayable [sic, irrefutable?] rights of human nature; so many of the species should be torn from the enjoyment of them, & devoted to perpetual slavery for no other cause but that God has formed them black   It begets a strange confusion of ideas & contradiction of principles—the general rule is Liberty, but the Exceptions form a majority of 5 to 1

It would readily be supposed that the people require a great deal of attendance: or that there must be a vast superfluity of Servants. Both are true though not in equal degree   From the highest to the lowest class they must have more or less attendance—I have seen tradesmen go through the city followed by a negro carrying their tools—Barbers who are supported in idleness & ease by their negroes who do the business, & in fact many of the mechaniks bear nothing more of their trade than the name

In the higher classes every body must have a vast deal of waiting upon from the oldest to the youngest   One or more servants (in many places) plant themselves in the corners of the room where they stand & upon the slightest occasion they are called   Every child must be attended, & whenever the whim takes it the servant is dispatched on its service At dinner it w⁴. seem as if the appetite were to be whetted

---

'This was probably intended to apply to Charleston County, or District, where by the U S census of 1790, the number of the blacks was not indeed "five to one" but 51,583 and that of the whites 15,402   We have no figures for the city in 1785, but in 1790 the blacks by the U S census, in the Parish of St Philip and St Michael which included Charleston City and what was then called Charleston Neck, were 8,270, and the whites 8,089

& the victuals receive it's relish in proportion to the number of attendance They surround the table like a cohort of black guards & here it appears there is a superfluity, for no sooner is a call made than there is a considerable delay either from all rushing at once, or all waiting for one another to do the business From the multiplicity of servants & attendance arises more than from the climate that dronish ease & torpid inactivity which are so justly attributed to the people of the Southern States, accustomed to have every thing done for them they cannot or will not do anything for themselves With many life is whil'd away in idleness, or consumed in dissipation The great majority possessing independance will not even take the trouble of directing their own business There are many who call themselves planters who know little about the process & art of planting—some ignorant of its most ordinary courses All is committed to overseers & drivers In fact they owe their wealth neither to art, genius, invention, or industry— but it seems to be showered upon them in the copious productions of a fertile soil & a prolific climate As might naturally be supposed arts & manufactures have but little cultivation & of course no great existance here Planting itself the very life of this country is done with little art and in the most round-about manner The number of slaves supply the almost total want of instruments of husbandry; & the dint of muscular force the want of invention & improvem' They import from the northern states what might as well be produced in their own country if they would only use the necessary industry and application—nay I have seen fruits & vegetables brought from thence & sold here at a very high rate to which their own soil is better adapted and wants nothing but the opportunity of producing in higher perfection & greater abundance With regard to some kinds of improvement they would seem to be in an early period of Society, and with regard to manners and customs to have reached their climactric I have an idea that State can scarcely ever be enabled to stand by itself unconnected with, or unsupported by others A great portion of its inhabitants now are & likely for time to come will be com-

posed of African slaves   Of consequence the proportion of
subjects to the quantity of Land or extent of territory cannot be so great as in other countries differently circumstanced; & therefore not able to make a proper defence.
To arm & embody their slaves would be impolitic & dangerous, for that would be no less dangerous in another case
wherein it w^d be an obvious policy in the enemy to tempt
to insurrections & rebellions   In the one case finding them
selves embodied & armed they would be emboldened; in the
other unrestrained by their absent masters & allured by
promises & prospects they would be encouraged to shake off
that unwarrantable joke under which they languish, & assert
that Liberty which nature, reason [illegible] & prejudice
all concur to represent to them their most sacred & involu-
able birth right.

Friday 4th Ap^l This day set out in a chair with M^r De
Saussure for Beaufort about 70 miles where the circuit
court is to be held   We rode through very heavy sandy
roads with fatigue & difficulty until we reached Ashley
ferry,* and after crossing it had very good roads causways
only excepted which are frequent in this country & generally bad   As our rout was for some distance on the side
of the river we were often entertained with the prospect of
country seats of which there is a number and some of them
fraught with taste and magnificence   In the evening we
reached the plantation of Mr Waring where I had the
pleasure of finding M^r. Benjn. Waring with whom I made
an acquaintance in philad^a and found him to be as I then
supposed him a very clever fellow   We stay all night at
this mansion & are most hospitably intertained   In the
morning we set off at 8 o'Clock upon our journey I having
previously promised Mr Waring a visit at his friendly
request   We ride Eleven miles to Pompon ferry   The
roads in general good except as before the intervention of
causways—but the traveller in this country has it but little
in his power to indulge his eye in prospects; the roads being
ever bordered by very thick hedges so that we can have
nothing but a glympse now & then thro the interstices   and

*Now Drayton Station on the Atlantic Coast Line Railroad

the country being always level are cut off from the advantages of iminences   The greatest part of the country lies in an uncultivated state—low lands are appropriated to rice & the good upland to indigo   The planters all fix at a distance from the road with avenues cut thro' the woods leading up to their houses   The negro houses are laid out like a camp & sometimes resemble one   After riding 11 miles we reached Ashepoo ferry—this country is happy in a number of navigable rivers which facilitate the transportation of the crops to market   We proceed 11 miles farther & cross Cumba ferry— the Country much the same as that thro which we have already passed, a small part cleared a still smaller cultivated; & the greatest part pine-barren   We arrive late in the evening at the widow DeSaussure's where we are regaled with a dish of tea and spend the night. This is a very pleasant place but very solitary, no neighbors in less than 4 or 5 miles w". induced me to recommend to Miss DeSaussure to get married in self defense   In the morning we accompany the Ladies about 6 miles to church where Billy meets with many of his friends & relations & after service was begun previous to which we made an apology to the parson we rode off designing ourselves next for the Island of port Royal, & the town of Beaufort where the court was to be held   I remarked to Billy that I thought the spirit had not lately visited this parish; the Shattered & forlorn condition of the Church gave but too much room to question their zeal; & the few that attended it (about 50 whites) to doubt the ardor of their devotion   We rode about 12 miles to port royal ferry where we found all the gent" of the Bar that rode this circuit ready to cross (viz Mess" Holmes,' Colhoon, Maj". Frazier & Maj" Pinckney brother to the Gen'. who is considered the greatest Lawyer in this State)   We all cross'd together dined at the tavern & just at dusk rode into the little village of Beaufort   It consists of about 30 houses— stands on an arm of the sea very pleasantly & is stiled a very healthy place   The inhabitants are almost all connected by

'John B Holmes, John Ewing Calhoun afterwards Senator from South Carolina, Alexander Fraser and Thomas, afterwards General Thomas Pinckney

some family relation; which makes them sociable & friendly
A stranger taken notice of by one gains an early access to
all—I experienced the most agreeable marks of hospitality
The next day (Monday) I had an invitation to dine with
Gen'. Bull⁵ I was politely treated & made an acquaintance
with Edanus Burk Esq' the justice in Eyre Chance seated
me near him at the table & a good deal of conversation ensued between us & I found him a striking instance of the difference men sometimes make in their appearance in company
& on paper About 18 months ago I had read a pamphlet of
his on the Society of the Cincinnati'; fraught with solid
learning & good sense, & dressed in a very good stile I had
formed an idea of his being a very great dignified &
Learned judge I found him an arrant Irish man whose
conversation though well enough aimed never contained a
sentence of good english but on the contrary abounded with
blunders vulgarisms & Hibernianisms The same was vis-
ble on the Bench—his ideas seem'd amazingly confused &
he neither look'd spoke nor acted like a judge In short he
carries with him less dignity than I have seen for a man of
his learning & station—I am told however that he is a
Lawyer Gen' Bull is a militia officer & he seems in character to conform to Gen' Furman of New Jersey—with all
his activity & whigism rather of an aristocratical turn At
this table I met also a Miss Garden¹⁰—she is an heiress
*   *   *   *   *   *   *   *   *   *   *
However she was sociable Here I feasted on oranges of
the finest kind the growth of this Island

The next day I had an invitation to dine with M' Barn-
well¹¹ Here I met many of the company I dine with yesterday; and among the rest the Irish Judge The table was
well spread & the company genteely treated Court having

---

⁵General Stephen Bull of Sheldon Brigadier General of State
troops in the Revolutionary War
⁹*Considerations upon the Society or Order of Cincinnati* Charleston S C 1783 This pamphlet was re-arranged and re-written
in French by Mirabeau in his own style and published as his in
1785 It was translated by Sir Samuel Romelly
¹⁰Dau of Col Benj Garden, she was 2ᵈ wife of Dr Robert
Pringle a son of Robert Pringle, a Provincial Judge
¹¹Probably General John Barnwell then living in the Town

risen after only two days session & the trial of one civil cause, we prepare to set out for Charleston in the morning In the morning notwithstanding rain we set out accompany'd by Mr Holmes (a very liberal, clever young fellow) & without any event worthy of particular enumeration arrived on thursday evening & found the family well — I will only observe upon the whole of this jaunt—1 that it is unpleasant travelling because the houses all stand a great distance from the road & the country all obscured by the thickets on each side of it There is no variety to amuse the traveller 2 The ferry's are but illy attended & the roads too much neglected 3 Houses of entertainment are very rare, their accommodations very bad, & their charges most enormously high 4 But the people are generally hospitable & polite, the District of Beaufort most remarkably peaceable & industrious Six months had not afforded business enough to detain a court 3 days It is so much the boast[12] of Carolina that it would be thought rudeness to say a word ag^t it

---

[12] It is interesting to note what the condition of this small "Village" of Beaufort was in 1857, 72 years after Mr Ford's visit A letter to the Charleston Mercury written by the late Capt Geo P Elliott on Sept 24th, 1857, and signed "Veritas" gives the following statistics The white population of about 1,200 did not contain a single adult who could not read and write From among its young men there had been a graduate with the first honors at Harvard, Yale, Princeton, the South Carolina College and the College of Charleston It had sent two Senators to the U S Senate and five members to the U S House of Representatives from natives of the Town Two Presidents of Colleges, a Bishop, and thirteen "other Clergy" were then alive, who were natives of the town Judge Thomas Heyward, a signer of the Declaration of Independence, Stephen Elliott the Botanist, and first Editor of the Southern Review, John A Stuart of the Charleston Mercury, and many other distinguished men were born there In a single year were distributed from its Post Office 33,120 news papers, and 3,406 magazines and periodicals Almost entirely of English, Scotch and Irish descent there were more than 30 among its 150 voters who were six feet in height, and their average weight was even greater in proportion The beauty of its women was as remarkable as the stature and talents of its men It would seem that the community continued to be the "boast" of the State, till destroyed in the Confederate War, as much as it was in 1785

(To be continued)

ORDER BOOK

of

John Faucheraud Grimké.

August 1778 to May 1780.

(Continued from April Number)

Head Quarters Charles Town
NOVEMBER 1778

1:   Parole Meade
It is observed that many Corporals bring up Reliefs &
relieve Sentinels in a negligent unsoldierly manner Officers
of Guards are strictly to order their Corporals to correct
this error as those Corporals who in future are found negligent will certainly be punished.

2:   Parole, Neglect

3:   Parole, Mercer.
Adjutant Robert Simpson of the fifth Continental Regiment in this State, having resigned his Commission is no
longer to be Obeyed or Respected as a Continental Officer.
The Honble. the House of Assembly of this State have
resolved that all officers of the 1, 2^d, 3, 5, & 6th Reg Continental to the rank of Captain should rise regimentally &
that all officers of & above the rank of Captain should rise
in the line.

4:   Parole, Nelson.

5:   Parole, Pinckney.
Capt. Hawthorn of the Sixth Continental Battalion in
this State having resigned his Commission on the 9th. Augt.
last & Capt. Coil^d of the Same Reg^t: on the 3^d September
last, first Lieut Armstrong was Promoted to be Captain in
the room of the first & first Lieut Leacey to be Captain in
the room of the Second: & Second Lieut Brown was Promoted to be a first L^t. vice L^t. Armstrong Promoted &

There in Lieut Coil. D. Smith etc. *High Court* of *Officers*
go in the State etc.

ORDER BOOK

of

John Faucheraud Grimké.

August 1778 to May 1780.

(Continued from April Number)

Head Quarters Charles Town
NOVEMBER 1778

1:    Parole Meade

It is observed that many Corporals bring up Reliefs &
relieve Sentinels in a negligent unsoldierly manner Officers
of Guards are strictly to order their Corporals to correct
this error as those Corporals who in future are found negligent will certainly be punished.

2:    Parole, Neglect

3:    Parole, Mercer.

Adjutant Robert Simpson of the fifth Continental Regiment in this State, having resigned his Commission is no
longer to be Obeyed or Respected as a Continental Officer.

The Hon[ble]. the House of Assembly of this State have
resolved that all officers of the 1. 2[d]. 3. 5. & 6th Reg Continental to the rank of Captain should rise regimentally &
that all officers of & above the rank of Captain should rise
in the line.

4:    Parole, Nelson.

5:    Parole, Pinckney.

Cap[t]. Hawthorn of the Sixth Continental Battalion in
this State having resigned his Commission on the 9th. Augt.
last & Cap[t]. Coil[t] of the Same Reg[t]: on the 3[d] September
last. first Lieut Armstrong was Promoted to be Captain in
the room of the first & first Lieut Leacey to be Captain in
the room of the Second: & Second Lieut Brown was Promoted to be a first L[t]. vice L[t]. Armstrong Promoted &

[1]Captain James Coil, DeSaussure's *List of Continental Officers*
gives the names as ....

Where Stationed.	Officers Presents.												Effectives Se...						
	Commissioned.					Staff.						Present fit for Duty.			Each Brigade			
	Colonels	Lt Colonels	Majors	Captains	Lieutenants	2d Lieut.	Chaplains	Adjutants	Q. Masters	Paymasters	Surgeons	Surg. Mate	Sergeant	Drummers	Rank & File	Sergeant	Drummers	Rank & File	Sergeants	Rank & File
Charles Town.	1	1	1	9	8	6		1	1	1	1	1	11	14	112				3	20	1
Fort Moultrie.	1	1	1	8	9	4	1	1	1	1	1	2	18	13	156				3	13	
Charles Town		1	1	6	6	1		1	1	1	1		18	10	124					1	
1 Brigade	1	3	3	23	23	11	1	3	3	3	3	3	47	37	392	47	37	392	6	34	1
Orangeburgh	1	1	1	11	9	10	1	1	1	1	1	1	18	12	194				6	138	1
Fort Johnson	1	1	1	6	7			1		1		1	16	12	202						
2 Brigade	2	2	2	17	16	10	1	2	1	2	1	2	34	24	396	34	24	396	6	138	1
Infantry.	3	5	5	40	39	21	2	5	4	5	4	5	81	61	788	81	61	788	12	172	2

Stationed at Georgetown.	Officers Present.								Artillery											
	Commissioned.					Staff.			Present fit for Duty		Effective Sergeants, Corporals, Dra...				On Command			On Furlough but fit for leave	Sick.	
	Colonel.	Lt Colonel.	Major	Captains	Capt Lieut	1st Lieut.	Adjutant	Surgeon.	Paymaster	Sergeants	Corporals	Drummers	Gunners	Matrosses	Sergeants	Corporals	Gunners	Matrosses	Invalids	Invalids	Matrosses
Artillery Volunteers	1	1	1	6	6	4	1	1	1	6	6	7	13	39	3	4	4	20	1	9	3

Head Quarters Charles Town; Septr 4: 1778.

Officers. | Effectives, Sergeants, Drummers, ...

	Commissioned.					Staff.					Present fit for Duty.			On Command.			absent sent Recruit			Sick.			Total Effecti...
Where Stationed.	Colonels	Lt Colonels	Majors	Captains	Lieutenants	2d Lieut.	Chaplains	Adjutant.	Qr Master	Pay Master	Surgeon	Mate	Sergeants	Drummers	Rank & File	Sergeants	Drummers	Rank & File	Sergeants	Rank & File	Sergeants	Rank & File	Sergeants	Drummers
Charles-Town.	1	1	1	9	10	4		1	1	1	1		14	17	120			9		8	1	34	15	17	56
... Maultrie.	1	1	1	8	9	3	1	1	1	1	1	2	17	12	180	1	2	5	1	2	1	26	20	14	24
Charles Town.		1	1	6	7	1	1	1	1	1			18	14	79	6		22		22	1	29	18	14	75
1st Brigade.	1	3	3	23	26	8	1	3	3	3	3		49	43	376	7	2	36	1	32	3	86	53	45	53
Orangeburgh.																								
Coll. Johnson.	1	1	1	4	6			1		1			14	15	197					13	2	43	17	17	25
2d Brigade.																								
Infantry.																								

Artillery.

	Officers						Effectives. Sergeants. Corporals, Drummers						
...at Beau...	Commissioned.				Staff.		Present fit for Duty.			On Command		absent sent Recruit	Sick
Georgetown.													
Artillery.	1	1	1	6	6	1	1	1	1	4	7	6	129	4	5	2	4	30	1	6	2	1	2

Head Quarters Charles Town
October 1778.

State of the Division of the Army of the United States of America under the Command of the...

Officers.

Where Stationed.	Commissioned.						Staff.					Present Fit for D.			On Command.			Absent by Leave & recruiting			Prisoners.			&c.
	Colonels	Lt. Colonels	Majors	Captains	1st Lieut.	2d Lieut.	Chaplain	Adjutant	Qr. Master	Paymaster	Surgeon & Mate	Sergeants	Drummers	Rank & File	Sergeants	Drummers	Rank & File	Sergeants	Drummers	Rank & File	Sergeants	Drummers	Rank & File	Sergeants
1 Charles Town.	1	1	1	8	10	4	1	1	1	1	1	14	15	187			1			9			3	4
2 Fort Moultrie.		1	1	8	9	3	1	1	1	1	1	16	15	184	2	2	8			9	in goal 1		3	4
6 Charles Town.		1	1	6	6	2		1	1	1		11	14	102	5		21			15			2	
Total 1st Brigade.	1	3	3	22	25	9	2	3	3	3	2	41	44	473	7	2	30			24		1	8	4
3 Orangeburgh.	1	1	1	10	10	8	1	1	1	1	2	16	10	153	9	4	144	1	1	38			7	1
5 Fort Johnson.	1	1	1	5	2					1	1	17	15	165				2		7			4	1
Total 2d Brigade.	2	2	2	15	12	8	1	1	1	2	2	33	25	318	9	4	144	3	1	45			7	4	2
Total Infantry	3	5	5	37	37	17	2	3	4	5	5	2	74	69	711	16	6	174	3	1	69			8	12	6

Artillery.

Attached to Beaufort & George Town.	Officers.									Effectives, Sergeants, Corporals, Gunners,			On Detachment.			Sick.			Prisoners.			Tot. Officers.		
	Commissioned.					Staff.																		
	Colonel	Lt. Colonel	Major	Captain	Capt. Lieut.	1st Lieut.	Adjutant	Qr. Master	Paymaster	Sergeants	Corporals	Gunners	Drummers	Matrosses	Matrosses	Matrosses	Corporals	Gunners	Sergeants	Corporals	Gunners			
Total Artillery	1	1	1	6	6	6	1	1	1	11	13	15	8	60	6	13	2	1	11	15	16	8		

Head-Quarters, Charles Town. November. 1778.

Second Lieu'. Redmond to be a first Lieu'. vice L'. Leacey Promoted

Cap'. Leacey having died on the 20ᵗʰ September & Cap'. Armstrong on the 3ᵈ. October last, first Lieu': Hampton was Promoted to be Captain in the room of the First, & first Lieu'. Buchanan to be Captain in the room of the second; & Second Lieu'. Milling was Promoted to be first Lieu'. vice Hampton Promoted, & Second L'. Adair to be first Lieut'. vice Buchanan Promoted.

First L'. Pollard takes rank as such on the 28 June 1778; Second L'. Doggett takes rank as such on the 8ᵗʰ. May, & Second L'. Langford on the 30ᵗʰ: October, 1778. These officers are to be respected & Obeyed accordingly.

Cap'. Wᵐ. Blamyer of the fifth Continental Regiment in this State having resigned his Commission, is no longer to be respected or Obeyed as a Continental officer.

6:    Parole, Mifflin

7:    Parole, DeBouillie.

8:    Parole, Taarling.

9:    Parole, Williamson.

10:    Parole, Oliphant.

The General Chooses to Republish an order issued July 16, 1777, which He then meant & now intends to be observed as a Standing Order. Regimental Surgeons are, for the future when they find it necessary to Remove the Sick of their Several Regiments to the General Hospital, to obtain orders for that Purpose from their Colonel or Commanding officer for the time being & to transmit to the Director of the General Hospital a signed return of the Sick in which shall be specified the names of the Men, the Companies they belong to, the nature of the Disorder, the time they have been ill and & the manner in which they have

---

²Deaths: Capt. John Armstrong and Capt. James Lacey, both of the 6th. regiment. *South Carolina and American General Gazette*, October 8, 1778. DeSaussure's *List* and the news-paper both give Capt. Lacey's name as James, while the Order Book gives him as Joshua

been treated   The Director General will furnish the Surgeons of each Corps with a proper form of the Return Whenever it becomes necessary to send sick men from Regiments to the General Hospital the Quarter Master of the Regiment or their Sergeants are to Report to the Purveyors of the Hospital what Provisions the Men sent are provided with, that Unnecessary Provisions may not be served to them before those they have on hand are expended

Regimental Surgeons are to keep an exact account of the Expenditure of the Medicine received from the general Hospital, which they are to lay before the Director General of the Hospital whenever He requires it

An immediate Report is to be made by Surgeons of Regiments to Head Quarters of the Present State of their Several Chests

---

11:   Parole, Philadelphia
No officer Commanding a Division of the army in this Department or any Regiment or Corps at any Post or Garrison distinct from Head Quarters shall accept Resignation of any officer under his Command or shall give leave of absence to officers beyond the bounds of this Department upon any occasion whatsoever without the Consent of the Commander in Chief in the Department for the time being be first had   The Deputy Adjutant General is immediately to transmit this Order to Commanding officers of Divisions Regiments or Corps distant from Head-Quarters

D' Colonel
I have enclosed you an order as directed to transmit it to the Commanding officers of Divisions Regiments or Corps distinct from Head Quarters Enjoining the Commanding officers of Divisions in the army in this Department or of any Regiment Corps at any Post or Garrison distinct from Head-Quarters not to acceept the Resignation of any officer, nor to give leave of absence to officers beyond the bounds of this Department without leave first obtained from the Commanding officer in the Department

I have also subjoined an order signifying to you my appointment to the Post of Adjutant General for the Two States of South Carolina & Georgia.

I am Sir, etc:

John F: Grimké.

To Col": Com': Elbert
    Georgia

12:    Parole, Demeré.

First Lieut'. W"". Thompson of the 3ᵈ. Regiment & First L'. Derril Hart of the same Regiment having resigned their Commissions on the 3ᵈ: Oct: last in the Continental Service, are no longer to be respected or Obeyed as officers.

The General Postpones for a Day or Two publishing in Orders the Promotions in the Army for very particular Reasons.

13:    Parole, S': Domingue.

14:    Parole, Lincoln.

All the Men unprovided with Powder Horns are as soon as possible to be furnished with them; Commanding officers of Brigade will give orders accordingly: They are also to apply to the Deputy Quartermaster General for the ammunition chests necessary to the Men under their Command, who is directed to furnish them with all possible Expedition

A Report of the Number of Ammunition Carts & waggons belonging to the Army immediately to be made to the General by the Deputy Q'. M'. General.

The General calls upon the officers of the Army of every degree to Exert themselves to the utmost to have the men under their Command & every thing in their several Departments in the best order possible for immediate action.

15:    Parole, Thompson

16:    Parole—Promotion

The Hon"'. House of Assembly having resolved that the Continental Regiments should remain on the usual

Establishment, Except the Corps of Artillery until the Pleasure of the Honble. Continental Congress be known thereupon the following Promotions therefore take Place

1st Lt Joseph Elliott is promoted to be Captain in the 1st. Regiment vice Capt Ioor lost in the Randolph on the 7 March, 1778

2^d Lt Benjamin Postell to be first Lieu^t vice Lieut Elliott Promoted

2^d Lt Wilson Glover to be first Lieut^t vice Lt Gray lost in the Randolph on the 7th March 1778 *

1st Lt William Hext to be Captain vice Capt Pinckney Promoted to be Major on 1st. May 1778

2^d Lt Wm Fishburn to be 1st Lieut vice Lieut^t Hext Promoted

1st Lieut^t Charles Lining to be Capt vice Capt Cattell resigned on the 20 July 1778

2^d Lieut^t Charles Skirving to be first Lieut^t vice Lieut^t Lining Promoted

1st Lieut^t Thomas Gadsden to be Captain vice Capt. Saunders Resigned on the 6th October 1778

2^d Lieut^t Alexander Fraser to the first Lieut^t vice Lieut^t Gadsden Promoted

1st Lieu^t. Bohun Baker of the Second Regiment to be Captain vice Capt Blake Resigned 25 April, 1778

2^d Lieut^t Paul Warley to be first Lieut^t vice Lt Baker Promoted

1st Lieut Adrian Provoaux to be Captain vice Capt Jacob Shubrick deceased 27 April 1778

2^d Lt Samuel Guerrey to be first Lieut^t vice Lieut^t Provoux Promoted

2^d Lt Peter Foissine to be First Lieut^t. vice Lt Peronneau resigned, 15 July 1778

John Wickom Gent is appointed an Ensign in the Second Continental Battalion in this State & his Commission is to bear date, 6 Nov: 1778.

Those Officers are therefore to be respected & obeyed accordingly, & take rank from the Day the Several vacancies happened

---

*George Gray, of 1st Regiment

17:   Parole, Girard.

18:   Parole, Louis.

19:   Parole, D'Orvilliers.

20:   Parole, Brest.

Captain George Turner of the first Continental Battalion is appointed Aid de Camp to the General, with the Rank of Major, in the room of Col.: Stephen Drayton Promoted.

Ensign Josiah Kolb of the Second Continental Battalion is promoted to be first Lieutenant vice Lieut.: Galvan resigned 15 July 1778 until the pleasure of Congress is known thereupon: These officers are to be respected & Obeyed accordingly.

Names [of officers on leave] and
where to be found.

Cap.: Lesesne. 2d. Regt. [at] Dan.: Lessenes St. Thomas Parish, 20 miles from Town: departed 10 Oct 1778; leave of absence, 3 or 4 weeks.

L.: Col.: McIntosh, 5th Regt. [at] Cheraws; departed 20 Oct. 1778: leave of 2 months.

L.: Glover, at Ponpon; departed 28 Oct: 1778; leave, 2 or 3 weeks.

Cap.: Baker 2d. Regt. at Ashepoo; departed 31 Oct.: 1778, leave of 2 or 3 weeks. Returned 17 Nov.. 1778.

L.: Col.: Henderson, 6th Regt., departed 2d. Nov. 1778.

Major Shubrick, 5th Regt., at his House in Town; departed 17 Nov.. 1778, leave of 3 weeks.

Cap.: Gadsden, 1st Regt., at George Town: departed 17 Nov.: 1778; leave unlimited.

Cap.: Proveaux, 2d. Regt., at Ashepoo; departed 17 Nov.: 1778; leave unlimited.

(To be continued.)

REGISTER OF
ST ANDREW'S PARISH, BERKELEY COUNTY,
SOUTH CAROLINA

1719-1744

Copied and Edited by MABEL L WEBBER

(Continued from April Number)

CHRISTNINGS

Anne the Daughter of Edward Sympson & Sarah his wife
bap⁴ July 15 1733

Benoni-Peter yᵉ Son of Peter Hoskins & Rebecca his wife
bap⁴. Aug 26 1733

Mary the Daughter of John Man, & Anne his wife bap⁴
Octʳ 15. 1733

Susanah the Daughter of Joseph & Martha Croskeys Bap⁴
Octoʳ. 23 1733

Anne the Daughter of Joseph & Martha Croskeys his Wife
Bap⁴ Octoʳ 23 1733

Martha Daughter of Edwᵈ Pickrin & Mary his Wife Bap⁴
Octoʳ 23 1733

John Son of William Chapman & Mary his wife Bap⁴
Octʳ 23 1733

William Son of Thoˢ & Eliz ᵇᵗʰ Whaley Bap⁴ Janry 1733
/4

Anne the Daughter of Robert & Sabina Ladson Bap⁴ Janʳʸ
yᵉ 20 1733/4

Richard the Son of Benja Godfrey & Margaret his Wife
Janʳʸ 23ᵈ 1733/4

Anne Daughter of James Manning & Sarah his Wife Bap⁴
Febʳʸ 10 1733/4 . . . . . .Born Decᵇʳ the 14ᵗʰ 1733. . . . . .

Anne the Daughter of William Cattell & Anne his Wife
Feb 11 1733/4

Sarah Daughter of Willᵐ & Mary Miles Receᵛᵈ into the
Congregation Baptᶻᵈ before private Bptm April 12ᵗʰ
1734

Margaret Daught of John & Mary Haydon Bap^{td} April
10th 1734

Tho⁸ the Son of Joseph & Mary Barton Bap^d April 16
1734

Elizbth Daught^r of Joseph & Mary Barton Bap^{td} 16 1734

Susanah Daught^r of Joseph & Mary Barton Bap^d 16:
1734

Joseph Son of Joseph & Mary Barton Bap^d 16 1734

Ann Daughter of John & Martha Rivers Bp^d May ——
1734

Isabella Daugh^r. of John & Easter Silvant Bap^d June 4 [?]
1733 [sic]

Eliz bth Daughter of David & Catherine Russ Bap^d June
y⁸ —— 1734

Sarah Daughter of James Taylor & Hester his wife Bap^d
James Island July 21—1734

Martha Daughter of James Carr & Hester his wife July
21 1734 James Island

Eliza^{bth} the wife of Thomas Butler Bap^d. July 23^d: 1734

Tho⁸ the Son of Tho⁸ & Eliz ^{bth} Butler Bp^d. July 23 1734

Mary the Daughter of Tho⁸ & Eliz^{bth} Butler Bap^d July
23 1734

Anne the Daughter of Tho⁸ & Eliz^{bth} Butler Bap^d July
23 1734

William the Son of Tho⁸ & Eliz^{bth} Butler Bap^d July 23
1734

Eliz^{bth} the Daughter of Tho⁸ & Eliz^{bth} Butler Bap^d July
23. 1734

Anne the Daughter of Josiah Canty & Eliz^{bth} his wife
Bap^d July 31 1734

Sarah the Daughter of Benja Godfrey als garnier & Martha his wife Bap^d. August 20. 1734

Mary Daught^r of John Champneys & Mary, his wife
August. 26 1734

Constant Daughter of Joseph Fitch & Constant his Wife
Bp^d Sep^{tr} 9 1734

Joseph Son of Joseph Fitch & Constant his wife Bap^d
Septr 9 1734

William Son of Edmund Bellinger & Eliz[beth]. his wife Bap[d]
Sept[br] 11 1734

Martha Daught[r]. of Sylas Wells and Mary his Wife Bp[d]
pr[t] bap[tm]. Sep[t]. 21 1734

Benjamin Son of Cap[t] William Fuller & Martha his wife
Bap[d] [September?] 22 1734

Margaret Daughter of Samuel Shock Sen[r]. & Eliz: his
wife Bap[d] p[r]. W[m] Guy Oc[tr]. —— 1734

Benjamin Son of Tho[s] Mell & Mary his Wife Bap[d] Nov[br].
21, 1734

Henry Son of Henry Wood Jun[r] & Anne his wife Bap[d].
Nov[r] 21, 1734

William Ellis an adult Bap[d] Dec[r] 15. 1734

Mary Daugh[tr] of Thomas Drayton & Eliz. his wife Bap[d].
Feb[y]. 4th 1734/5

Mary Daugh[tr] of ffrances Ladson & Sarah his Wife Bap[d]
March 12 1734/5

Anne Daught[r] of Charles Jones & Rachel his wife Bap[d].
March 19th 1734/5

Anne Daughter of Charles & Eliz:[beth] Crubin Bap[d] March
19 1734/5

Will[m] son of William Field & Margaret his Wife Bap[d]
March 19[tb] 1734/5.

Arthur Son of John Deloney & Mary his wife Bap[d] March
26 1735

William Stock Son of Will[m]: Stock & Rachel his Wife
Bap[d]· May 11: 1735

Mary y[e] Daughter of Petter Perry & Eliz: his wife May
y[e]: 25th. 1735

Mary Daught[r] of W[m] Cattell Jun[r] & Anne his Wife Bap[d]
July 19th 1735

Martha Daugh[r]. of Isaac Battoon & Sarah his Wife Bap[td].
prvt July 19th 1735

*Thomas the Son of Joseph Heap & Eliz· his Wife Bap[d].
May y[e] 13th 1735

*Mary Daught[r] of Margrey Ervin June y[e] 18th 1735

*Margaret Daught[r] of Burnaby Bull & Lucy his Wife Bap[d].
July y[e] 31 1735

Eliz:^bth Daughter of Willm Chapman & Mary his wife Bp^d.
   Aug 24th 1735
Eliz·^btn Daughter of Jacob Ladson & Eliz: his Wife Bap^d
   Sep^r —— 1735
Sabina & Mary Daughters of Samuel Stock & Eliz ^btn his
   Wife Bap^d p^r Octo·^r 14th 1735
Sophia-Sarah Daught^r: of William Guy & Rebeca his wife
   Bap^d Octb^or 28th· 1735
Cathrine Daught^r of John Man & Anne his Wife Bap^d.
   Nov^r: 4th. 1735·

Mary-Anne ⎫
Joseph   ⎪   Children of Joseph Elliott and Edeth his
Sarah   ⎬   wife Bap^d. Octo^br the 24th: 1735 p^r y^e.
Eliz.^bth ⎪   Rev^d. Wm Guy
Thos   ⎭

Samuel Ladson an Adult Bap^d. Dec^br 31 1735
Willm: Son of Pett Hoskins & Rebeckah his wife Bap^d
   Feb^ry 31 [sic] 1735/6
Mary Daughter of John Boswood & Nancy his wife Bap^d
   Feb^ry 3^d. 1735/6.
Thomas Son James Kerr & Hester his wife Bp^d. March
   14th 1735/6
Thomas the Son of Thos Barlow & Susannah his wife Bp^d.
   April 9th: 1736
Joseph the Son of Wm Miles & Mary his Wife Bp^d May
   2^d. 1736
Anne the Daught^r of Jonathan Fitch & Francis his wife
   Bap^d May 14 1736

FUNERALS

Christian the wife of Samuel Rome Bur^d pr Wm Guy May
   ye 16 1735
Ann Crubin Daught^r of Charles Crubin Bur^d· p^r Wm Guy
   June 12th 1735
Joseph Fitch Bur^d July ye 26 1735
Wm Son of Mary Middleton Bur^d. Sepr y^e· 4th. 1735
Alice the Wife of Thos: Hudson Bur^d ye 18th: 1735
Eliz^bth Daught^r of Jacob Ladson & Eliz ^bth his wife Bur^d
   Oct^r· ye 15th 1735

Rebecca Capers Daughter of Richard Capers of St Pauls parish Bur^d p^r Wm Guy Octob^r: 25 1735

Benjamin, Son of Thos Mell & Mary his wife Bur^d Novr ye 2^d. 1735

John Kitchen Bur^d Overser to Mrs Monger Nov^{br} ye 29 1735

Zacheus ffuller Bur^d De^{br} ye 5th 1735

Eliz:^{bth} daughter of Joseph Elliott & Ede his wife Bur^d Octb^r. 25: 1735

Joseph Son of Joseph & Constant Fitch Bur^d Jan^{ry}· 16th 1735/6

William Miller buried Lived with Mr James Manning Feb^{ry} 25 1735/6

Philis Barnet Sp^r Burd Feb 27th: 1735/6

Eliz^{beth} Butler wife of Thomas Butler (son of Rich^d) Bur^d Daught^r of Wm Gibbs Feb^r 29th 1735/6

Edwd Hill Burd March 19th 1735/6.

Mary Johnson Burd March 20 1736

Joseph the Son of Jacob Ladson Burd June 5 1736

Isabella Jones Burd June 30th 1736

John Wood apprentice of John Haydon Buried July 13th 1736

William Street Buried Augt. 2nd 1736

Anne ye Daughter of Wm Brandford & Anne his Wife Buried Augt. 12th 1736—

Isaac Battoon Buried Augt 17^{tb}. 1736

Priscilla Hodgson Buried Augt 19th 1736

Eliz^a Samways Buried Augt 27th 1736

Revd Francis Varnod Buried 25th Septr 1736

Thomas Mann Senr Buried 29th. Septr 1736

Eliza Canty [Sindinia erased and Eliza written over] buried 2nd Octob^r 1736

Constant Fitch Junr buried 3^d Novr 1736

Thomas Marquess buried 17th. Novr. 1736

Samuel Young Buried 17th. Novr 1736

CHRISTININGS

Benjamin the Son of James Boswood & Martha his wife
Bap⁴ p⁵. the Rev⁴ M⁵ Wm Guy May y⁵ 16th 1736.

Elizabeth the Daugh⁵ of Rob⁵ Ladson & Sabina his wife
Bp⁴ May 16 1736

John the Son of William Ladson & Mary his wife bap⁴
May 16 1736.

Anne, the Daughter of W^m. Branford & Anne his wife
Babp⁵ June 2⁴ 1736

Elizabeth the Daught⁵. of Tho⁵ Stocks & Rachel his wife
bap⁴ June 4 1736

Mary-Anne ⎫
Samuel   ⎪
Benjn   ⎪
Susannah ⎬   Children of Sam⁵. Ladson & Eliz⁵ his wife
Henry   ⎪   bap⁴ June 10, 1736
Sarah   ⎪
Elizabeth ⎭

Eliz. the wife of Samuel Ladson bap⁴. (p⁵. Dipping) June
22⁴ 1736

Elizabeth the Daught⁵ of Samuel Boswood & Martha his
wife bap⁴. July 11th 1736

William Son of Wm Cattell Jun⁵ & Anne his wife bap⁴
July 19th 1736

Peter son of George Simmons & Martha his Wife Baptized
25th July 1736

James Son of Thom⁵ Mell & Mary his Wife Baptized Aug⁵
27th 1736

Esther Daughter of James Taylor & Esther his Wife Baptized Aug⁵ 29th 1736.

Thomas son of Tho⁵ Sisson & Mary his wife Baptized
Aug⁵ 29th 1736

Richard Son of Sam⁵ Jones & Mary his wife Baptized
Septem⁵ 1st 1736

George the Son of Josiah Canty & Eliz^a his Wife Baptized
2nd October 1736

William the Son of John Champneys & Mary his wife
Baptized 20th Oct⁵ 1736

Rich⁰ & Susannah Son & Daughter of Mʳˢ. Seabrook Baptized 23ᵈ Octʳ 1736.

Susannah the Daughter of John Gibbs & Mary his wife Baptized 24ᵗʰ Octʳ 1736

Sarah yᵉ Daughter of Isaac Chardon & Mary his Wife Baptized 24ᵗʰ. Octʳ 1736

Stephen yᵉ. Son of Thomas Drayton & Elizᵃ his Wife Baptized Novʳ. 6ᵗʰ. 1736.

Sarah yᵉ Daughter of John Cattall & Sarah his Wife Baptized 25ᵗʰ. Janʸ. 1736 [1737].

MARRIAGES

John Billiald & Mary Robinson Spinster Married 25ᵗʰ Novemʳ 1736

John Watson & Abigail Butler Spinster Married 30ᵗʰ November 1736

John Barksdale & Anne Hepworth Spinster married 12ᵗʰ. December 1736

Samˡ Sandiford & Mary Jones Spʳ Married 20ᵗʰ Decemʳ 1736

Samˡ Morray & Anne Fitzgerald Spʳ married 2ⁿᵈ Janʸ 1736 *

Zaccheus Ladson & Sarah Battoon Spinster married 12ᵗʰ Janʸ 1736*

John Drayton & Sarah Cattell Spinster Married 17ᵗʰ Febʸ 1736 *

John Shepherd & Elizᵃ Wickham Spinster Married 13ᵗʰ March 1736 *

Benjᵃ Seabrook† & Mary Bonneau Spʳ married 7ᵗʰ Aprill 1737

Thomas Lamboll & Margaret Edgar Spʳ Married 14ᵗʰ. Aprill. 1737

John Brown Junʳ & Judith Hull Spʳ married 5ᵗʰ May 1737

John Unckles & Anne Drayton Spʳ Married 2ⁿᵈ June 1737

James Ogelbee & Mary-Anne Beaver Married 11ᵗʰ July 1737

---

*Old style, 1737 new style
†Thomas erased

Joseph Edw⁴. Flower & Elizabeth Woodward Spins*
    Married 22ⁿᵈ Dec* 1737
John Cattell Jun* & Margaret Livingston Sp*. married 3ᵈ
    Jan* 1737*
James Smith & Rachel Hardihorn widow Married 25ᵗʰ
    Feb** 1737*
Nathan*¹ Sterling & Margaret Gibbons widow Married 5ᵗʰ
    March 1737

FUNERALS

John Mell buried 4ᵗʰ. Decem* 1736
Anne Mann buried 28ᵗʰ Decem* 1736
Isaac Chardon buried 14ᵗʰ Jan* 1736
Richard son of Edmund & Elizabeth Bellinger Buried 20ᵗʰ
    Jan*. 1736*
Thomas Heyward Buried 11ᵗʰ. March 1736*
Sarah y* Daughter of Benj* Godfrey & Martha his Wife
    Buried 23ᵈ. Aprill 1737
Mary y* Daughter of John Rivers and Martha his wife
    Buried 24ᵗʰ Aprill 1737
Hannah the Wife of John Skene Esq* Buried 10ᵗʰ. May
    1737
Anne y* daughter of George Young & Anne [Elizabeth
    erased] his wife Buried the ninth day of June 1737
Charles y* Son of Maurice Lewis & Jane his wife buried
    10ᵗʰ June 1737
Richard Son of Benj* Godfrey & Martha his Wife Buried
    20ᵗʰ June 1737
———————— Wife of an Overseer at M*. Cattell's buried 1*ᵗ
    July 1737
Richard son of Edmund Bellinger and Elizabeth his wife
    buried 3ᵈ July 1737
William Son of William Cattell Jun* and Anne his Wife
    buried 15ᵗʰ July 1737
Jacob Moll Overseer to M** Eliz* Hill buried 27ᵗʰ. July
    1737
Phebe Peters buried 11ᵗʰ. August 1737
Anne y* daughter of Charles Jones & Rachel his wife
    buried 5ᵗʰ. Sep* 1737

*Old style

Mary ye Daughter of John Champneys & Mary his wife buried 25th Septr 1737

Mary ye Daughter of Francis Ladson and Sarah his Wife buried 18th October 1737

William Son of Jno Rivers & Martha his wife Buried 2nd. Novem^r 1737.

(To be continued)

ALL-SAINTS WACCAMAW

Mural Tablets and Tombstone Inscriptions

Copied and Contributed by the Rector,
Rev J E H Galbraith

This Parish was taken off from Prince George's Winyaw, by Act of Assembly passed May 23, 1767 It was to consist of "all the lands which lie between the Sea and Waccamaw River, as far as the boundary line of North Carolina" William Allston, Joseph Allston, Charles Lewis, William Pawley, Josiah Allston, William Allston, Jun, and John Clarke, were appointed Commissioners for building a Church, Chapel of Ease, and Parsonage-House, at such places as they should approve, within the Parish[1]

The existing registers begin in 1819, during the rectorship of Rev Henry Gibbes, who was rector 1819-29. Dalcho states that neither Journals nor Register were extant when he wrote, which was about 1820, but some of the earlier records existed then, for they were lost when the house of Dr. Flagg, a warden, was swept away by the storm of 1893; a badly defaced copy of the minutes of the vestry was rescued from the sea

The corner stone of the present church has been mutilated in the past by some one in search of treasure

There is very little information to be obtained in regard to this Parish before 1800 —*Editor*

[Inscription on Corner Stone of All Saints]

The first edifice built of wood before the | Revolution was taken down about 179— | The second also of wood was built aboy A D 1—— | By Capt John Allston; was repaired in 1813 | and was taken down in 1843 | This third edifice will be erected chiefly | with the funds bequeathed to this Church by | Mrs Mary Huger daughter of the above | Capt John Allston. | Building Committee Edmund T Heriot | Francis M Weston Joshua J Ward T Pinckney A E S' —— | Architect and Builder Lewis Rebb |

---

[1] Dalcho, p 321

Stone of the third Edifice erected on this site under the
appellation of | Parish Church of All Saints | The Rev^d
Alex^r. Glennie A M | Rector of this Parish Dec 27, 1849 |
Glory be to God | Father, Son—

Mural Tablet

In Memory | of Mildred | Born 4th July 1777—died 1st
Aug 1822 | and of | Mary | Born 13th Nov· 1779 died
19th Ap 1856 Daughters of Charles Weston | of Kursley
[?] Warwickshire England | and wives of Francis M
Weston Esqr | of Laurel Hill in this Parish | Farewell!
farewell! born from the womb of one | By th' other nur-
tured in the fear of God | I here again unite your sister
dust | and lay ye both beneath the quiet sod, | Myself to
rest beside you, ere't be long | Repose awhile, till renovat-
ing life | a heavenly spring shall summon ye from hence, |
Warm the chilled vigor of the buried sense | and join
again son, sister, husband, wife | A loving household mid
the gathering throng.

Mural Tablet

In Memory | of | Francis Marion Weston | of Laurel
Hill in this Parish | Born June 1783, Deceased Nov 21,
1854 | [Eulogy omitted] Erected by his widow & son

Mural Tablet

This humble Memorial is the public Tribute of | a
widow'd Mother's affection to an exemplary & only child |
William Haddrell Hart | son of | Robert Smith & Sarah
Mary Hart | who died at Waccamaw on the evening of
the 6th August 1817 | aged 8 years and 14 days [Eulogy
omitted]

Mural Tablet

Sacred to the Memory of Benjamin Huger Esqr | Eldest
son of Benjamin Huger deceased | Sometime | Major of
the 5th S C Regt | on the Continental Establishment |
He died on the 7th day of July in the year | of our Lord

1823 | and of his age the 55ᵗʰ | To the well understood piety
of a Christian and to a spirit of | Patriotism & a zeal for
the public good | worthy of one whose much respected
father had laid down his life in the service of his | country,
to the experience of a Statesman & to the acquirements of
a scholar, were found in this greatly beloved & lamented |
individual the most courteous manners, the most extensive
Charity | and benevolence, a hospitality which knew no
distinction of ranks | a deep sense of the sacredness of
friendship | and the spotless integrity of an honest man |
His friends & neighbors holding his memory dear to | Their
hearts and cherishing a grateful sense of his services as
their | representative in Congress and in the Legislature of
the State | hoping too that a tribute however humble in
testimony of their love | and respect for so much merit
graced with so many amiable qualities might tend in some
degree to alleviate the sorrow of | his afflicted widow for
the loss of one so deservedly dear to her | might have a
salutary effect on the feelings of the rising generation
hence erected this.

MDCCCXXIV

Mural Tablet

In Memory | of | Major Charles | Brown | who died in
April 1819 | a pious and zealous Christian | who contrib-
uted much | To the advancement of | Religion | In this
parish | and | To the Establishment | of this Church

Mural Tablet

Sacred | to the Memory of The | Rev. Hugh Fraser |
native of Scotland, | Formerly Rector of this Parish | un-
der whose pastoral charge | this Church was re-established
| He died in November 1838 | aged 75 years

This tablet has been erected | By the vestry in gratitude |
for his past services

Mural Tablet

Sacred | To the Memory of | General Joseph Waties Allston | who departed this life | August 13ᵗʰ. 1834 | at the Red Sulphur Springs | Virginia | in the 37ᵗʰ year of his age | In endearing qualities | few equaled none excelled this eminently useful | and sincerely pious Christian | This tribute of affection is | erected by his afflicted | widow.

Mural Tablet

Sacred | To the Memory of | Mary | widow of the Hon Benjamin Huger, | and daughter of Capt John Allston | She died in Charleston | 30th June 1836 | aged 76 | This tablet has been erected | By the vestry of All Saints | In gratitude to her | for her munificence to this Church

Mural Tablet

Sacred to the memory of | Robert Withers | a native of this Parish who died at the | Bowling Green, Kentucky 22ᵈ September 1825 | aged 43 years 10 months and 21 days | This tablet is erected by one who had the | privilege of his friendship for upwards of | twenty years and who saw in him the | virtues | of the Christian Character exemplified He was honest in all his actions. | He was never known to deviate from the truth | He was a kind and affectionate husband | and father, and a ready friend to the poor and | the stranger, and to his servants a kind | and indulgent master | "Behold an Israelite indeed in whom is no guile."

Sarcophagus

To the Memory | of | Susan Elizabeth Smith | daughter of | William and Jane Ladson | and widow of | John Rutledge Smith | who departed this life | on the 1st of March 1857 | In the eightieth year of her age. | Born to affluence and enjoying in early life | much temporal good it pleased God | in training her for the heavenly inheritance | to bring her through many tribulations | and with her as with many | tribulation worked patience | and patience experi-

ence and experience hope, | even that hope which maketh
not ashamed | Because the love of God was shed abroad |
in her heart by the Holy Ghost, | which was given her |

"Pure are they which come out | of great tribulation and
have washed | their robes and made them white | in the
blood of the Lamb " | "Therefore are they before the
throne of God " Rev VII, 14, 15

[Below on side]   Here also rest the remains of Charles
Freer Smith | Son of | Mrs Susan E Smith | who died
September 1839 | In the 32ᵈ year of his age

[On the other side]
Within this enclosure also are interred | the following
children of Dʳ Benj Huger Smith | Catherine Farr Smith |
who died July 12ᵗʰ 1839 aged 2 years | John Rutledge
Smith | who died Decʳ 14ᵗʰ 1843, aged 2 months | John
Rutledge Smith | who died April 21st 1845, aged 3 days

[Obelisk]

To the revered memory | of | John Ashe Alston | whose
remains lie in the same grave here | with the remains of
his beloved wife | Sarah M'Pherson | under this monu-
ment erected by his grandson | Joseph Alston

Thomas Alston | Son of John Ashe Alston | died July
16 1835 | at the Red Sulphur Springs Va | in his 29ᵗʰ year |
and his body was removed to the cemetery here of his
father |

Josephine | the wife of Thomas Alston | and daughter
of Wm Algernon Alston | died June 17ᵗʰ 1831 at Green-
ville | in her 21st year | and her ashes now lie under | this
marble
[Obelisk]

Sarah H Tucker | born Allan | on the 25 of April 1833 |
Departed on the 16 of September 1857

Sacred | to the memory of | Mrs Mary K. Allston widow of the late | Gen¹ Joseph W. Alston | who departed this life | Oct 7ᵗʰ 1841 | [Eulogy omitted]

[An unmarked grave in same lot]

Charles Albert Stuart Post | Son of | William and Mary Stuart | Post | aged 15 months and 15 days | "of such is the kingdom of heaven "

Arthur Lee Stuart | Son of | William and Mary Stuart | Post | aged 13 months and 10 days | "And he took them up in his arms and blessed them "

[Slab]

In Memory | of | Robert Nesbit | Planter | Born in Scotland (Berwick upon Tweed) the 17ᵗʰ Nov' 1799 | He resided in this parish since 1808 | and died 17ᵗʰ. Oct'. 1848 | Justly beloved by his family | for his domestic virtues | He was respected and valued | by the Community | for his unpretending sincere | and useful qualities | Never in vain was he calleld upon | by his friend or his country. | In the performance of public duty | he was habitually industrious | energetic and patient | honest true Independent

[6 other graves in the same iron fenced enclosure]

Sacred | to the | memory of | Joseph Taylor | who departed this life | 13ᵗʰ Oct'. 1833 | aged 15 years & 6 Months | 3 days | "not lost but gone before" |

[A large gum tree has grown up through this grave]

Charles Delamer | Infant son of | D D and H P Rosa | Died May 27ᵗʰ 1858 |

This inadequate memorial | of a sister's love | marks the spot where is buried | Mary Rutledge Smith | daughter of John Rutledge Smith | and his wife Susan Elizabeth | she died on the 17ᵗʰ of June 1846 | in the 43ᵈ. year of her age. | One so long and so much separated | from the world, and who had for some years | more experience of the trials and sorrows | of life than of its fruition requires no | memorial beyond the recollection of the | worth and virtues which endeared her | to the few who knew and loved her | Nor need there be other record than this that | confessing her weakness and meekly | submitting her sins to her Savior | relying on his merit alone she lived | in humble imitation of his example | and died we trust in the hope of a "joyful resurrection" | "through faith in" "His name "

In memory | of | Fannie | daughter of | J P & A H. Tooker | Died May 9ᵗʰ 1878 |

David D Rosa | Born Oct 14ᵗʰ 1814 | died Feb 17ᵗʰ 1885 | .   .

Weston | Beloved son of C W & L S | Rosa | April 22 1895 | Oct 27, 1901

Annie | daughter of | D D & H T Rosa | Born Jany 9, 1864 | died June 21, 1890 | .   .

To the memory | Laura Spring | daughter of | Charles & Eliza Crouch | who departed this life | on the 6ᵗʰ Augᵗ 1848 | aged 5 years, 11 months, and 3 days

[Slab.]

Charles Alston Jr | born | April 18ᵗʰ 1826 | died | October 2ⁿᵈ 1869 |

Sacred to the Memory | of | John Richardson, | died Sept 11ᵗʰ 1873, | aged 57 years

In Memoriam

| Philip R Lachicotte June 2 1824, | May 15 1896 | | Mary J Lachicotte Feb 18, 1830, | April 26, 1895 | |

Sacred to the Memory | of | Louisa C Morel | consort of | Dʳ James S Morel | of Savannah, Ga | who departed this life | at Magnolia Beach | Aug 25ᵗʰ 1859 | aged 39 years |

Mary H Lachicotte | wife of | W W. Muckenfuss | Oct 27 1865 | Sept 16, 1888

William F Lachicotte | May 27 1871 | Dec 19, 1891 | . .

Baby | Baby
1886 | 1898

Children of F W & L S Lachicotte

Lillie | daughter of | L C & E S Lachicotte | Died Sept 21st 1885 | aged 1 month and 18 days |

In memory | of | James Lamble (Engineer) a native of | Odern Canton De. A. Arnarin | Department Du Heul— | Rhine France | He died in Charleston | the 23ᵈ Novʳ 1852 | aged 33 years 8 months 11 days | He was a man of unexceptionable character | and was beloved by all who | knew him | In a strange land he made friends | and this Tablet is erected | by one who knew his worth | and valued him

I H S

Sacred | To the memory of | Francis Valentine | Infant son of | James and Cecilia Lamble | Born the 25ᵗʰ of April | Died the 3ʳᵈ of May 1849 |.

Georgie Alberta | Daughter of | J. J & M L. Ward | April 17 1905 | Dec. 16. 1905 | .   .   .   .

Infant daughters | of | J L & E. R LaBruce | Born Feb 5. 1904

Robt Bruce | Son of | J L & C. A. LaBruce | Jan 3 1900 | March 25 1900 |

Georgie Alberta | wife of | J L. LaBruce | Feb 26 1862 | Aug 24 1901 | .

Joseph Llewellyn | Son of | W. S & M A Oliver | Died March 7ᵗʰ 1888 | aged 18 years & 7 months |

Charles Alexander | Son of | W S & M. A Oliver | died May 29ᵗʰ 1885, | aged 18 years and 6 months |

Jane | wife of | Alfred Gordon Lloyd | daughter of | St J M & Emma S Lachicotte | Born April 18 1885 | died at Detroit Mich Apr 8 | 1907 and Alfred G Jr died at birth Apr 1 1907

Sacred | to | Memory | Mary McDowell | consort of Davison McDowell | who departed this transitory life | on the 4ᵗʰ of Oct 1822 aged 30 years | 1 month & 3 days |
[Eulogy omitted]

Sacred | to the memory of Dʳ. B. Clay Fishburne | Born Feb 16ᵗʰ 1835 | died November 8ᵗʰ 1870 Blessed are the pure in heart | for they shall see God |

Sacred | to the Memory | of | Mrs Mary Allston Fraser | Relict of | Peter William Fraser | Born | September 15ᵗʰ 1808 | Died Oct 1st 1849 | aged 41 years and 16 days |

Sacred | to the Memory | of | William Buford Fraser | Son of Mʳ William Fraser | and of Mary Allston his wife | Born 11ᵗʰ of January 1834 | Died 26ᵗʰ of May 1836, | aged 2 years and 15 days |

Sacred | To the memory | of | Peter William Fraser | Born Feb 2ⁿᵈ 1806 | Died | May 1st 1819 | aged | 16 years 12 months and | 29 days |

Sacred | to the Memory | of | Mrs Agnes | consort of Benjamin P Fraser Esq | who died | Sept 29 1823 | age 26 yrs 9 mo 18 | d |
Also to her | Infant daughter, Elizabeth—

Sacred | to the Memory | of | Hugh Fraser | Son of Benjamin and Agnes Fraser | who died at Richmond Va | Nov 21st 1852 | aged 32 years

Sacred | to the Memory | of | Benjamin Porter Fraser |
Son of | The Revd Hugh Fraser | and of | Ellizabeth his
wife | who departed this life | on the 19ᵗʰ December 1832 |
aged thirty two years 3 months and 19 days

Simply to Thy cross I cling | Paul W Fraser

In | Memory of | Thomas M'Crea | Son of | Davison &
Catharine | M'Dowell | who departed this life | July 21st
1842 | aged 4 years and 10 months | It is well with the
child | It is well.

In | Memory of | Davison Son of Davison and Catharine
D | M'Dowell | who departed this life | Aug 19ᵗʰ 1843 |
aged 4 years and 6 months |

In | Memory of | Davison M'Dowell | who departed this
life | Jan 29ᵗʰ A D 1842 | aged 58 years and 10 months |
He was born in Newry Ireland | where he resided until
nearly grown | Then removed to this country | and settled
in Georgetown district S C | where he spent the remainder
of his life |. He was an affectionate husband | a loving
father, a faithful friend | a kind master and a true Chris-
tian | In him the church and community | lost a valuable
member |

A husband weeping | hath placed this marble in sacred |
remembrance of his beloved wife | Mrs Francis
Jane Fraser | who died in Charleston | on the 12ᵗʰ of March
1836 | aged 56 years | [Eulogy omitted]

In | Memory of | Hester M'Crea | and Benjamin Alls-
ton | Infant children of | Davidson and Catharine | D. Mᶜ
Dowell |.   .

In Memory | of | Joshua John Ward | Eldest son | of |
Joshua and Elizabeth Ward | who was born at Brook
Green | The 24th Novʳ. 1800 | and who died there | The
27ᵗʰ Febʸ 1853

[Long eulogy omitted]   This Monument is erected | by his afflicted widow and sons.

Joanna Douglass | daughter of | G. P Bond Hasell | wife of | Col J J Ward | Born in Edinburgh | June 4, 1805 | Died Dec 14, 1878

Beneath | is the Remains | of | Major Joshua Ward | Long a respectable inhabitant of this parish |

Anne Allston | June 20, 1877 | Dec 9, 1878 | Jane Mc-Crady | June 20 1877, Dec 2 1878 | Children of | B H. & J McC Ward

J J Ward | Son of S M & K L Ward | died July 10, 1886 | aged 6 mos | Safe in the arms of Jesus | . Salina Mortimer | who died June 20th 1895 | aged 6 days

"I go to my Father." |
Joshua John | eldest son of | J. & E Ward | died Aug 11th 1857 | aged 3 years | and 7 months |—

God is love | Elizabeth Ryan | Eldest daughter of J & E Ward | died Aug 11th 1856 | aged 1 year | and 8 months—

Sacred to the memory | of | Joshua Ward | eldest son of | J J and J D Ward | Born at Brook Green Waccamaw | Dec 11th 1827 | Departed this life Dec 7th 1867

In memory of departed worth | The remains of Mayham Cook Ward | rest beneath this stone | He died on the 9th of June | 1838 | in the 22nd year of his age | at his residence Magnolia, | of bilious inflammatory fever |

Fanny | daughter of F W & L. S Lachicotte | Dec 13, 1878 | aged 34 days | Gone before

Philip | Son of F W & L S Lachicotte | July 21st 1881 | aged 5 days | Safe in the fold | .

Arthur | Infant son of L C & E S Lachicotte | Died
Dec 10th 1886 | aged one month | and four days | .

"The Lord is mindful of his own " | Fanny Buford |
daughter of the late | Rev Hugh Fraser | of Scotland | and
widow of | John Ashe Alston | of Waccamaw, Georgetown
Co S C | Feb 17, 1820—Feb 20 1897—[Eulogy omitted]

[This monument has coat of arms, a shield with triangle
of ten stars and the mottoe Immotus.]
Theodosius Alston M D | Born June 13, 1841 | Died
Oct 25 1879

[A small flat tombstone]
Algernon | Infant son | of | John Ashe and Fanny Alston
| Born 23rd March 1825 | Died 15 June 1848 | —
[Scripture verse indecipherable.]

[A tombstone with coat of arms]
John Ashe Alston | son of | William Algernon Alston |
Died October 8 1858 | In the 42nd. year of his age

John Ashe Alston | M D | Born August 21, 1842, | died
May 2, 1882

Helen | daughter of | Dr John Ashe & Emma R | Als-
ton | aged 11 months

[Monument with Sun dial Face]
In memory | of | Plowden C J. Weston | Fell asleep Jan-
uary 25th 1864 | aged 44 years |
"The Lord gave and the Lord | hath taken away, blessed
be | the name of the Lord "
[Right side]
Mary Weston | April 19th 1856 | aged 76 years |
My flesh shall rest | in hope
[Reverse]
Mildred Weston | August 1st 1822 | aged 43 years |
"Our days upon earth | are a shadow "

[Monument]

George B Weston M D | March 19, 1840 Oct 24 1881
A graduate with honors of the | University of Edinburg
[Reverse]
Bentley Weston | April 19, 1842 | Feb 4, 1883—
"Until the day break"

Beneath | lie the remains of Elizabeth C Rutledge | daughter of | Benjamin H and Alice A Rutledge | From her birth this infant | was distinguished by a robust | constitution and exuberant | animal spirits | amid all these flattering indications of a long life | she died suddenly of a violent | inflammatory sore throat and | fever on the 12ᵗʰ December 1827 | AET, 12 months and 18 days | Memento mori

Benjamin Huger

Thomas | Pinckney Huger | Third son | of | Francis K. Huger

[The Pawley Monument is enclosed by an iron railing and has the name Pawley on the front & back of the base, Carr & Graham on the sides inscription in front]

Thomas George Pawley | son of Percival Pawley & Anne Shory | born Dec: 16, 1669 | Married Mary Allston Dec 31 1719 | who died Sept· 24, 1742 | Leaving 5 sons and 3 daughters | Elizabeth the youngest married | David Graham |

This land was given by Thos Geo Pawley | for a church and cemetery with the | privilege of retaining this burial place for his descendants

[Left side]
Elizabeth Pawley | youngest daughter of | Thos· Geo· Pawley & Mary Allston, | born June 26, 1741, and died 1815 | married David Graham who died in 1807 | and is interred here alongside | of his wife leaving one child | Mary Allston Graham

"Blessed are the dead who die | in the Lord"

[Right side.]

Thos Geo Pawley & Mary Allston | had 5 sons and 3 daughters; | two daughters lie buried here; | also his second and third wives, | three of his sons and their | families also rest here | . He left a large estate to his | surviving children | . This monument is erected by his | last great grand daughter, | Sarah Esther Carr, who died Aug 6, 1892 | in the 77th year of her age | and is also interred here

The | infant daughter of | Rev: Alexande'. and | Harriet B Glennie | Dec 26 1837

Rev Alexander Glennie | Born | in Surrey England | July 8th 1804 | Died in Virginia | All Saints day 1880 | Rector | of All Saints' Parish | from 1832 to 1866

In Memoriam | Harriet B Glennie | wife of | Rev Alex'. Glennie | born August 29th 1801 | Died September 9th 1866 | "I know in whom I have believed | and am persuaded that He is able | to keep that which I have committed | unto Him against that day "

This monument | is erected to the memory of | the two infant children of | Ralph E. & Martha Ann Durr | who both died Sept 11 1840 |

Charlotte Ann Durr	Madaline Glennie Durr
born Aug 16	1839	Born Feb 1	1837

Sacred | to the Memory of | Edward Thomas Heriot | born June 27th | 1834 | died Sept 1st 1840 | .

HISTORICAL NOTES

CALHOUN'S STUDENT FEES—The following item is taken from a cash book of the Law firm of DeSaussure and Ford:

1804 Dec' 24th. Mr John C Calhoun Entered our office as a Student, fee 100 Guineas
[No] 26

RECORDS OF GEORGETOWN COUNTY—The following notes taken from some blank books in the Clerk of Courts office, and in the Probate Court at Georgetown, S C, explain why there are no records for Georgetown County before 1862

"Ordinary's Office

July 1863

This Book appears to have been used in the subsequent pages by the late Henry Frederick Detyens, who departed this life on Sabbath morning 26 July, as a Book of Records of the office of Mesne Conveyance, and as a temporary place of the Books appertaining to that office   In April 1832 [sic it is evidently 1862] all the public records in this town, by order of the Executive Council, were removed to the interior of the State

I am persuaded in my own judgment, that the good sense of our Legislature will regard the entries herein made as valid, as though they had been made in the regular book of the office, which in the present perilous condition of the country have been removed, as it is hoped beyond the reach of the invading and beleaguering and mercyless foe

E. Waterman Ordinary
Aug 25th. 1863

Book of temporary records

A.

Henry Frederick Detyens, a native of the City of Amsterdam, Holland, was born in the year 1812, and died in Georgetown S C Sabbath morning July 24th 1863   At the time of his death he was Clerk of the Court of Common Pleas & Gen'l Sessions, Register of Mesne Conveyance, Locator, and Clerk & Treasurer of the Town Council of Georgetown, and Clerk of the Board of Commissioners of the Roads

He filled all these offices with credit to himself and with usefulness to the State and district

Paul Tamplet was elected Clerk of the Court October 7ᵗʰ. 1863, and qualified by taking the office on the back of his Commission December 1, 1863

E Waterman, Ordinary
Georgetown, December
7ᵗʰ 1863 "

The first 32 pages of the blank book in which the above is written are taken up with the Constitution and Minutes of the Georgetown Lyceum, from March 16, 1859, to May 18, 1860

The first record in the book is a power of Attorney, dated September 2, 1862, the last record in book B, the second of the two temporary blank books is a title to real estate, dated 28 April 1866, and recorded May 1st. 1866.

In the Probate Court, is a small book of records of the Court of Ordinary which was used for miscellaneous records, for the first pages are filled with lists of Alien Enemies of the Confederate States, with the defendants, kind of process, date and name of person lodging the accusation, when and to whom returned and how served, other pages are taken up with minutes of the Court of Ordinary

On the back Cover is the following.

"(Copy)

Executive Council Chamber Columbia S C April 17ᵗʰ 1862

Resolved, That the Clerk of the Court of Common Pleas and General Sessions   Sheriff   Register of Mesne Conveyance and Commission of Equity for Georgetown be instructed by the Chief Justice and P lies to move the books

and respective office and other valuable papers in their possession to the town of Cheraw, or such other safe place as may be approved by Messrs F S Parker, R F W Allston and R. I Middleton or a majority of them

Official Copy
Signed B F Arthur
Secty Ex Council

State of South Carolina }
  Georgetown Dist   }

I do hereby certify that the above is a true and correct copy of the original in possession and addressed to F S Parker Esq

Henry F. Detyens
C. C. P. & G S

April 22ᵈ 1862
[In another hand]

The above order is intended to include the books & records of the Ordinary's office.

Francis S Parker

22ᵈ April 1862 "

General Sherman's army occupied Cheraw in March, 1865, so it is not necessary to say why the records were never returned to Georgetown

CORRECTIONS—The name of Maj Barnard Beckman, so spelled on pages 42, 90, and elsewhere in the two previous issues of this volume, should be Barnard Beekman

The date of the death of Mary Elliott (page 114) is 1760, not 1706

LIST OF PUBLICATIONS

OF THE

SOUTH CAROLINA HISTORICAL SOCIETY.

COLLECTIONS.

Vol. I., 1857, $3.00; Vol. II., 1858, $3.00; Vol. III. 1859, out of print. Vol IV., 1887, unbound, $3.00, bound $4.00; Vol. V., 1897, paper, $3.00.

PAMPHLETS.

Journal of a Voyage to Charlestown in So. Carolina by Pelatiah Webster in 1765. Edited by Prof. T. P. Harrison, 1898. 75c.

The History of the Santee Canal. By Prof. F. A. Porcher. With an Appendix by A. S. Salley, Jr., 1903. 75c.

THE SOUTH CAROLINA HISTORICAL AND GENEALOGICAL MAGAZINE.

Volume I, 1900, Edited by A. S. Salley, Jr. Complete Volume. $10.00

Single copies of Nos. 2-4, $1.25 each.

Volume II to IX, 1901-1908, Edited by A. S. Salley, Jr. Unbound $5.00 each.

Volume X to XII, 1909-1911, Edited by Mabel L. Webber. Unbound $5.00 each.

Single copies of No. 4, Vol. XI, $2.50 each. Members get a discount of 25 per cent. on the above prices.

Address: South Carolina Historical Society, Charleston. S C.

THE

SOUTH CAROLINA

HISTORICAL AND GENEALOGICAL

MAGAZINE

PUBLISHED QUARTERLY BY THE

SOUTH CAROLINA HISTORICAL SOCIETY

CHARLESTON. S. C.

VOLUME XIII., NO. 4.   OCTOBER 1912.

PRINTED FOR THE SOCIETY BY
WALKER. EVANS & COGSWELL CO
Charleston, S C.
1912

CONTENTS.

The South Carolina Historical and Genealogical Magazine.

| VOL. XIII | OCTOBER, 1912 | No 4 |

DIARY OF TIMOTHY FORD

1785-1786

With notes by Joseph W Barnwell [1]

(Continued from the July Number)

Nov'. 28th. At the request of Doc[t] Waring & the invitation of his agreeable family I accompany him to his father's to spend a day or two principally with his Brothers Benj & Peter [2] In the progress of this jaunt I improve my acquaintance with the Doct and found him in fact what I had before judged him to be an amiable man endowed with good sense and merit His heart seems calculated for friendship, his mind for improvement & his manners for sociability We arrived at M[r] Warings in

---

[1] In the issue of this Magazine of July, 1912 (page 132), Mr Ford mentions General Furman of New Jersey This was probably Moore Furman (1728-1808) a distinguished lawyer of Trenton, N J and Philadelphia, Pa, first mayor of Trenton, Judge of the Common Pleas of N J, owner of mills and manufacturing establishments at Pittstown, N J, a village founded by him He was Department Quartermaster General in the Revolutionary War

The respectable family of "Shipping" mentioned (page 137) by the diarist was probably meant for "Shippen," of which family the wife of Benedict Arnold was a member

[2] John Beamer Waring and his three sons by his first wife, Katherine Smith None of these sons married The plantation mentioned was probably "Pine Hill" the same at which the author was entertained on his trip to Beaufort (page 144) John Beamer Waring was a son of Richard Waring, and a grandson of Benjamin Waring, who came to the Colony in 1683

the evening. The next morning the gent" proposed to
spend the day in hunting and fowling—We do so & commit
considerable slaughter   The next day we spend in the same
manner very agreeably—I admire the harmony of these three
brothers & their hospitality   Here I have an opportunity
of learning something of the nature & process of cultivat-
ing rice; a piece of information which I readily embraced
I was told that planters adopted divers modes, differing
from one another sometimes, thro difference of situation,
soil & judgment   Indeed the same mode will not always
do—it must in some degree be regulated by caprice of
season   The first peculiarity that strikes a northern person is the lands being tilled by the Dint of manuel labour
without the assistance of machines—'tis neither plowed
nor harrowed, but hoed; the hoe being the only instrument
used not only in rice, but indigo, corn &c —

Rice is generally planted in April—the ground is yet
wet & marshy when they begin to dig their trenches, which
are at the distance from 8 to 12 inches apart   If a crop
has come off the last year they make the new rows between the old ones, & a smart negro will plant his half
acre per day   The average of seed to the acre is one
bushel, this however is various according to the degree of
fertility.   It is from 3 days to a week in making its appearance & being invariably attended with weeds & grass
must soon after to wit 2 or 3 weeks be hoed & weeded   Little use can however be made of the hoe at this period except
to loosen the soil between the rows   the weeds must be
pulled up by hand   This is a critical time & requires the
vigilance & judgment of the planter, for heavy rains, or
severe droughts prove equally fatal, & put him to the necessity of re-planting   In the one case the banks around his
field must be opened, & every possible drain made use of
to draw off the incumbent water; in the other case the
sluices must be opened from the reservoirs & the water
brought upon the field taking care that it remain not too
long—ordinarily from 6 to 18 hours   Shortly after this
the stalk forms a joint like oats at about 4 inches from
the ground & once this is fairly formed & the stalk is pro-

ceeding to its second joint the planter thinks himself pretty safe & the crop mostly out of danger. At this period it requires a second dressing & now the hoe may be used whereby they cut up the grass & weeds & turn them over between the rows After this the crops are generally again overflowed & the water suffered to remain on some days; but this and indeed the flowing it at all depend much on the season & situation of the ground Every planter has his reservoirs or ponds of water which are so attended by drains & ditches that he can at any time set his plantation afloat, or vice versa; & he must know more from his own judgment & observation than anything else, when, how often, & how long his fields must be under water When the stock forms its second joint when it begins to branch out and set it needs the third hoeing which done it is left to fill and ripen The stock grows, branches, kernels & much resembles oats; & when it is fit to cut looks yellow like any other field of grain In September about the middle the negroes enter the field each with a small sickle in his hand & cutting up the rice lay it upon the Stubble where it remains for one day to dry & cure or until it is dryed & cured, it is then bound up in sheafs & put in small cocks, & then at leisure transported into the Barnyard & put up in large stacks ready for threshing This is the time for fine butter in the country, the cows are turned upon the rice field where they fatten & give the richest milk in great plenty—the butter is called by way of eminence rice-butter There is no particular set season for threshing; it is however the interest of the planter to thresh soon because he has his crops the sooner to market and if they do not command a good price & he is not so necessitated for money but that he can wait it is stored in Charleston and waits for a rise of the market

The crop being now ready for threshing it is laid on an earthen floor in the barnyard and threshed just as our farmers do the wheat And as in other respects it resembles oats, so in this the kernel, husk and all is beaten from the stalk, the husk closely adhering to the kernel To separate them is another distinct process; and is done by friction between two blocks which are thus prepared They are cut from live oak, about 2 feet through, the under one 2½ feet high the uper one 12 to 16 inches   These are cut from their centers to their edges into threads or nuts much like a millstone and in every respect work like them (tho by hand) the grain being fed in at the center & thrown out at the circumference together with its disengaged chaff. The next procees is to separate the grain from the chaff; this is effectually and expeditiously done by a winnowing mill in every respect resembling ours at the northward   The grain has now a yellowish hue, & looks rough & unpleasant   This is caused by a coat or incrustation it still has on it, & the next process is to take this off & give the grain that whiteness & polish which it is always observed to have, when at market   For this purpose wooden mortars are provided to hold about half a bushel; & fitted with large pestles with which the rice is beaten; & by a great deal of attrition this crust is disengaged from the grain & becomes a dark brown flour, which is separated by sieves for that purpose   The quantity bears a proportion to that of the clear rice as 1 5—at this season every thing on the plantation gets fat—the fowls round the barn, & even the wild fowls find a rich supply of food   The rice flour mixed with the chaff or cut straw forms the most luxurious feeding for hogs & horses—they are invariably fatned   The negroes are inspired with alacrity in beating & preparing the rice by the certainty of their coming in for shares with the rest of the *stock* on the plantation   For here it must be noted that what is called the clean rice is not the *merchantable* rice, for it is easy to conceive that the beating must break many of the grains in pieces; and this divides it into, *rice, midlings, & small rice*   These are all separated by sieves; the first is put up in barrels for market; the second reserved for family use; & the third for the consumption of the plantation

The proportions of these three kinds are as follows— [The rest of the page blank]

At the invitation of M' Holmes & of M' Edwards I prepare to spend the Christmas holidays at his seat at Washington about 33 miles from Charleston and on Saturday 24ᵗʰ Dec' we set off M'ˢ Holmes & Miss Beckworth in the Carriage & M' Holmes & Myself in the Chair & the two M' Edwardses on Horseback We had the threatning prospect of a rainy day which added to the badness of the roads must necessarily occasion a disagreeable ride The issue was no better than our apprehensions—the roads could not well be worse & it rained with very little intermission from 11 to 2½ o'clock from which tho the Ladies in the carriage were sheltered, & we in the chair by means of a large umbrella was very disagreeable & the gent" on horseback got considerably wetted. At 12 o'clock we reached Mr Garrets' Seat a former governor of this state where we stopped with an intention if the rain continued to tarry all night Here I had the pleasure of an introduction to Gov' Garret & we were regaled by some generous liquors & the rain subsiding we concluded to prosecute our journey on which we entered after a repast at 2½ oClock The clouds broke away and after many plunges thro slough and mud holes we arrived in the evening at M'ˢ Edwards's plantation to whom I had an introduction & whose easy manners affability & politeness enable me to make a speedy acquaintance In the morning I had an opportunity of casting my eye around this place which differs from many parts of the country in that it is somewhat interspersed with hill & valley & does not exhibit that dead uniformity which though it may in some measure please the eye at first glance does not so much delight & exercise the imagination one of the boundaries is the Cooper river, another a large creek & each of their banks afford an agreeable walk

The garden is spacious, & animated by the taste & in-

'John Edwards, who married the widow of Isaac Holmes Her maiden name was Rebecca Bee and she was the mother of John B Holmes, so often mentioned by the author Washington plantation belonged to her, was afterwards owned by her son, Henry M Holmes, and remained in the family until a few years before the Confederate War

'Benjamin Guerard Governor, 1783-1785

genuity of M[rs] Edwards, exhibits its various walks, flowers, vegetables, trees & springs in the most pleasing view

The plantation produces everything in the greatest perfection mediately under her direction but immediately under that of an overseer & driver But in regard of the food it is difficult to say whether its production or cookery & dressing is in the greatest perfection. This day we are all engaged to dine at Major Hamiltons[5] about 2 miles from here; and at 2½ oClock our company all set out for that place

Here I have the pleasure of an introduction to himself & Lady, Governor Moultrie & his Lady & M[rs] Hyrne[6] We all pass the compliments of the season—dinner is served up & I have the honor of a seat by the side of the Goverer The afternoon & part of the evening are passed agreeably. I ride home with Miss Beckworth with whom I have a great deal of conversation She is a Lady from England her father & Brother are in the british army. She posseses a brilliancy of understanding far above even the improved part of her sex—has read a great deal, has seen much of the world at least the principal parts of Europe been conversant with the best of company in each, and really displays in an easy sociable manner all that knowledge & good sense which a mind like hers would necessarily collect from so many advantages She has philosophy enough to think nothing that passes unworthy her attention—She scrutinises into the minutia of things, & makes the meanest parts of agriculture, botany, domestic Oconomy &c the objects of her inquiry There is no subject either of religion, philosophy, history belles lettres or arts & sciences with which she does not appear to have been in some degree conversant. She posseses equal independence of mind & complaisance in conversation Removed at an infinate distance from the pets, flirts affectations & prudery which are practised by the weaker part of

[5]"The Villa" the place of Major James Hamilton father of Gen Hamilton of 'Nullification" days, who married the widow of John Harleston, Jr, and daughter of Thos Lynch

[6]Probably Mrs Sarah Hyrne, widow of William Alexander Hyrne, who was the owner of "Umbria" plantation, near Wash-

her sex, she seems to unite depth of understanding & so-
lidity of thought with the delicacy of her sex. In short I
have before seen very sensible women but in my estimation
the palm belongs to Miss Beckworth I like all others
have found myself highly pleased with her acquaintance
& Society

On Monday M^{rs}. Edwards invites the company we were
with yesterday to dine with her The governor Maj^r
Hamilton & Mrs Hyrne attend—the Ladies of the two former being indisposed The afternoon & evening are spent
agreeably—necessarily so since presided over by Mrs Edwards who is an exception from the formality of this
country & dispenses of her sociability & attention in so
easy & agreeable a manner as to leave the most pleasing
impressions on the company & even cause them to be
more sociable with each other We employ much of our
time in sporting with our guns, which also give me an
opportunity of seeing the different plantations in the vicinity of Washington They are chiefly rice plantations &
of course there prevails a sameness thro the whole—but
still there is a variety in regard of buildings, avenues walks
& gardens There is a common taste for improvements of
this kind among the planters here about On Wednesday
Mr Edwards being informed that Col^o Moultrie brother
of the governor & Att^y Genl of the State has arrived at
his seat about 2 miles hence with some company from
town proposes that we all take tea there in the afternoon by
which means I have an introduction to him his Lady, Miss
Smith & Mr Moultrie his nephew from England Miss
Smith knows well that she is thought handsome; she pos-
sesses accomplishments, some sense. & a great deal of vanity She has a great flow of spirits, talks a great deal
without conversing, & intersperses profanities which I
think would come much better from the mouth of a sailor
than from one whose external appearance would lead us
to look for delicacy and moral excellence How much
may we err in allowing the face to be an index to the mind!
Since under the most pleasing features often lurks a gross-
ness of feelings, corruption of Sentiment & severity of
disposition

M^{rs}. Edwards invites the company to dine with her on friday Thursday we spend in romping about the plantation Barns &c & in viewing the negroes at work at the rice—On Friday the company dine with us & in the evening we attempt to dance but find the music so bad that we are obliged to desist I am more confirmed in my opinion of the rattling disposition of Miss Smyth, of the innumerable merits of Miss Beckworth & the hospitality, generosity, affability & goodness of Mrs Edwards M^r & Mrs Holmes are no less entitled to my highest esteem & gratitude On Saturday we all received an invitation to dine on Sunday at Col^l Moultries, where we meet an accession of company from Charleston Dinner is served up at 4½ oClock & the desert by candle light—On Monday we form a maroon party to visit some saw mills about 8 miles hence which in this country are considered an object of curiosity like all other pieces of machinery—water works are seldom to be heard of the levelness of the country not admitting of them

But here I must note that this parish (of St John's) is an exception being very frequently interspersed with hills & valleys & the champaign country lies chiefly on the river This has occasioned the superior order of planters to choose their plantations here, seeing they can at the same time cultivate rice & enjoy the pleasures & improvements that may be attained from the variety of hill & vale, eminences pleasant situations prospects & water courses The soil on the uplands (for that distinction will hold here) seems much like ours at the northward only not stony & in some places spontaneously produces clover, tho in small perfection seeing it is not cultivated Nor indeed need they cultivate it seeing their corn blades stripped off when green & cured with their native substance in them form a very Luxuriant feed for horses The hay they cut is but little better than dry leaves—however their pastures are good the greater part of the year, & the rice straw is both agreeable & serviceable to horses & cattle.

Within sight of Washington is the seat & plantation of his excellency Henry Laurens,^{7} agreeable prospect of which

Mepkin Plantation

induces us to visit it today (tuesday) Contrary to our
expectations he had gone to Town we were not however
disappointed of viewing the place which displays the beau-
ties & advantages of nature no less than the ingenious
improvements of its owner He is a rare instance of
method, whereby his plantation raises itself above those
of this country in which everything is done immethodically
by the round about means of force & Labour One may
here & there be found who rising above the prejudices &
shaking off the supine carelessnes of the country ventures
into the use of machinery & the contrivances of art; and
what makes it still more surprising that they are not im-
itated more is that they are generally very successful and
find their account in such undertakings Mr Mr Holmes
& myself get into a boat & return to Mr Edwards's by
water about 3½ miles

The Cooper river at this place winds itself very beau-
tifully into a serpentine course, is navigable a considerable
distance above Strawberry, and its banks afford a number
of fine situations & prospects, which are generally improved in this country seeing they are so rare. This day
is closed by preparations to set off tomorrow early for
Charleston Mr Edwards to accompany us We all set
out at 8 oClock & I take leave of a place with a degree
of gratitude which for 10 days past has afforded me much
pleasure The day is very pleasant, but nothing occurs
worthy of relation except one incident which may seem in
a degree to illustrate some of the maxims of this country
As we were dining under the trees by a bridge a gent on
horseback hove in sight who appeared by his dress his air
& the goodness of his horse to be of some note & distinction As we were all surveying & querying who he should
be one of the company finished the enquiry by saying "he
cannot be a gentleman for he is riding without servants"
At this instant I transported my self to the northward &
tacitly remarked how many would lose their titles, were
such to be the test of gentility there But so it is that in
this Country a person can no more act or move without
an attending servant than a planet without its sattellites
If they only cross their plantation they must have a sub-

servient follower, and if they ride out their horse might as well want a leg as they the necessary equipage which is their recourse in their frequent helpless situations And which as they advance serve as ensigns of their rank and dignity The person however regained his lost honours by two servants heaving in sight who had been concealed by the woods, and it was agreed on all sides that he is a gentleman. Our ride to town would have been very agreeable but for bad roads of which S Car has very ample share—some almost impassable

We got in in the evening & there I finished my Christmas jaunt—A Season when the country is most lively partly by means of the vast imigration from the city & partly of the relaxations from rural concerns, the hurry of business being chiefly over It is almost vulgar to spend the Christmas holidays in the city, and of course the gay part of its inhabitants pour into the country where like birds uncaged they scarcely allow rest to their feet, but range thro the plantations & the barn yards & beat up the game; the ladies mount the rice stacks, with emulous dexterity, & perch'd upon their summits in triumph vaunt at the gent" below, who at length investigate them, & having gained the summit a contest succeeds which either brings them down in succession, or the mass of rice unable longer to sustain the load rushes down hurrying in its common fall its intrepid riders

The citizens as would naturally be expected relax in some degree that rigid formality for which they are remarked—but still they retain more than enough It is hard that hospitality should thus want its most essential part (sociability) and that a person cannot be made an object of politeness without being also made an object of formality The ladies carry formality & scrupulosity to a considerable extreme, a stranger makes his female acquaintance by slow gradations interspersed with niceties & punctilios w". often disconcert the forward & intimidate the bashful. The maxims of the country have taught them & custom has forced them to almost consider a sociability on their part with gentlemen as an unbecoming forwardness— & they are by this means circumscribed within such nar-

row bounds as exclude the frankness & care which are
necessary to put people on the most agreeable footing and
constitutes the principal charms of Society

The gentlemen are more sociable and I must confess as
agreeable as any I have ever seen after a person has made
an acquaintance with them. But they are generally very
dissipated, little inclined to study & less to business

A young man of 22 has often by his excesses wracked
his constitution to such a degree as to commence his de-
cline & be obliged to prop himself up by medicines And
this is not to be wondered at since spiritous liquors are
often used instead of wines—and brandy, gin & cordials
the circulating companions of their social meetings This
practice is the parent of many evils, destructive to health
& happiness First it causes a habitual Love of strong
liquors & excess in the use of them And I must note that
I have heard & seen more of this here than in any place
I have ever been acquainted with

Another consequence of this habitual excess in strong
liquors is an indifference to business or study Far be it
from me to charge all who fall under this description with
being drunkards—this would comprehend too many—but
still the disposition the young fellows have for shew and
pastime, & not a few for carousing, makes them disregard
improvement, & a young fellow of fashion looks down
from the height of his ignorance upon the man of study
with a mixture of pity & contempt for his consuming that
time in the study *"he does not know what"* which he de-
votes to the offices of gallantry and to all the nobler pur-
suits of a beaux *d'esprit* Business is too irksome & he
fails not to shift it off upon his overseer, or negroes &
betake himself to sports or ease as the humor of the
moment shall direct him—

Another consequence of this intemperance is the disorder which it frequently occasions in private families
Of the truth of this I am also convinced by the experimen-
tal testimony of this country; where I must again remark
that I hear of more family troubles & especially of the
conjugal kind than in any other place I every day hear of

unhappy marriages both in time past and present. This
however I fancy may be partly attributed to the share
which sinister views are apt to take, among people who
plume themselves on rank & fortune, in the making of
matches   But it seems not unnatural to suppose that their
confirmed habits of idleness & dissippation being but illy
suited with the duties of the married state, & tending to prodigality, & neglect of domestic Oeconomy (to say nothing
worse) must rouse the appprehensions, the regret &
sometimes the reproaches of those who are nearly connected   In confirmation of this it is acknowledged that
many men large as their incomes may be are living above
them, and a plurality of instances are not wanting wherein men of the first fortunes are much reduced by an imprudent prodigality   That there is but little of the spirit
of Education here is evident (if it needs to be made more
so) in that there has been ample provision made for the
endowment of a College by persons who saw with regret
the unletter'd situation the State was in on their death
beds; and yet nobody has the spirit to draw them forth
into utility⁵   This appears the more extraoidinary after
reflecting that many send their young sons to England for
education from whence they generally return but little
more improved & much more dissipated than they went—&
after this much expense has been lavished upon them   This
however may be in some measure the consequence of the
connexions the people have with England which I take to
be much greater here than at the northward   Many of the
inhabitants came originally from great Britain, many of
them are british merchants who indeed form by no means
a small part, and many have very strong connexions there,
all w⁴ together with the want of improvements in their
own country sufficient to make them independent, conspires
to keep alive their prejudices in favor of whatever is english
And notwithstanding this there exists in this country an in-
veterate enmity against g⁴ Britain which appears at first view
to savor of the paradox   The causes of this additional hatred

⁵Act of March 19th, 1785, chartering colleges at Winnsboro,
Charleston and Ninet -Six

arose at the conclusion of the war° A number of british merchants found means to remain in the country & foreseeing the great demand there w^d be for slaves & being the only persons possessed of cappital they early imported vast cargoes from Africa The planters impelled by their necessities to procure slaves eagerly grasped at the first opportunities that offered; & unable to pay down the cash supplied themselves on credit, at whatever rate the british Merchants were pleased to fix, & they failed not to take advantage of their necessities and advanced upon them from 50 to 75 p^r Cent In a short time they became the creditors of a great part of the State; and the infatuated debtors began to view their situation with a degree of regret & concern, to the prospect of which they had been put too easily or voluntarily blinded by their necessities at the time of contract The time of payment began to draw nigh & they then began to perceive (as they might or perhaps did foresee) how far they must fall short of their engagements

The merchants influenced by no particular feelings of generosity to their late enemies, or pressed by their credit to make remittances, or as likely as either, expecting to get into their possession the plantations of their debtors for much less than their value, insisted rigidly upon the punctual fulfillment of their contracts The crisis was important & melancholy for the planters & many of them were torn to pieces by legal process. An universal alarm took place—it became a common cause on both sides The courts of justice being the resort of one became the terror & hatred of the other The sheriff & his officers were threatened in the execution of their duty, and at length the people in the district of Camden grew outrageous— planted out centinels to intercept the sheriffs, & put the laws at defiance; and one Col° Mayham being served by the sheriff with a writ obliged him to eat it on the spot^10

News of these transactions being brought the Govern^r

°See the account given by Ramsey of the legislation as to debtor and creditor just after the Revolutionary War (Ramsey Hist of S C, Vol 2, page 425)

^10Col Hezekiah Mayham of Marion's Brigade

he immediately assembled the legislature, laid before them the proceedings in the language of a frightened man, & requested them to deliberate on the subject & strike out some mode either of restoring to the laws their wonted efficacy or of abating their rigor

They took into consideration the distresses of the people the necessities which first impelled them to forego the dictates of judgment & discretion, & the character of the persons who had thus taken advantage of them   On the one hand it was urged that no precedent is more dangerous to society or more destructive of public credit, than that of the legislatures interfering in private contracts fairly made, that it unsettles all confidence between man & man, renders property uncertain, breaks down the pillars of commerce, & makes the people licentious & ungovernable That the acts already passed with regard to old debts, arose from a very singular & uncommon necessity, which alone could have justified them; as contracting parties before the war could not foresee the great depredations that were about to be committed on their property, & that the fate of war had so disenabled them to pay their debts Circumstances were now different   They had contracted their late debts with their eyes open & could make no such plea   If they were able to pay they ought to be compelled to it— if not, they knew it before hand, & therefore deserved to be distressed for their fraudulent contracts   In a word that the legislature could not afford them countenance or relief without flagrantly invading the rights of individuals who having already been treated like citizens (tho' they became so by sufferance) ought now to enjoy the privileges of such

On the other hand it was alledged—that the people after several years suspension from business, after the loss of a great part of their property & a consumption of their fortunes in exile viewed their forlorn situation as the prelude of their speedy ruin unless they immediately availed themselves of their plantations, which having been stripped of their stock could yield no relief unless they could fall on some mode of procuring negroes

That when the british merchants threw out the bait they took it as their only resource; & that it was no wonder their necessities got the better of their judgment   They represented them as harpies preying upon those distresses & misfortunes to which themselves had been necessary; and using the word *tory* as a weapon (much as the zealots in the times of fanaticism used the word heretic) suggested that they had premeditated the design of getting into their hands extensive property thereby to infuse british influence into the government of this country and lastly that they might well afford to delay the recovery of their debts seeing they sold at such exorbitant prices & that the debts were now at interest   These & the like arguments applying to the prejudices, the passions & the interests of the legisl.ʳ inclined them to interpose in behalf of the debtors; and being furnished with a plausible pretext for so doing from the recent meetings in the State, they easily brought themselves to pass " an act for the regulation of sheriff's sales," commonly called the pine barren act" because it authorises the dʳ in case of prosecution to tender any kind of lands in payment (to be valued by persons chosen for that purpose) at 2/3 their value, & if they exceed the debt the Cʳ to give his bond & security for the remainder payable in six months   Thus the legislature at one stroke put an end to all civil prosecutions by this most impolitic & iniquitous law   Such is the nature of a republican government! And it is hard to decide which is most blamable the premeditated fraud of the debtor, or the weak & unsuspecting confidence of the creditor   The person who had committed this daring abuse upon the sheriff was prosecuted & tryed in Charleston—the Court sentenced him to 4 months imprisonment, a heavy fine & him-self & two securities to be bound to the peace for 6 years   The govʳ suspended the sentence until the meeting of the Legislature who (upon his submissions) entirely reversed the decree

These are the causes of the great jealousies between the parties—for everything will now depend upon whose interest will be the greatest in the legislature; & it is alleged

"Act of Oct 12, 1785   It was limited by its terms to the end of the next session of the Legislature, and was never re-enacted

that the british merchants by indirect means have made a
considerable progress already   The politics of the State
are very confused, opinions & interests various & adverse,
& legislative councils possessing all the instability & un-
certainty of republican caprice   Altho the foregoing accounts for the animosities which subsist between the B
Merchants & the people of this country, yet this unwarrantable interposition of the Legislature was produced by
some other concurring causes   The same imprudence in
accumulating debts had been exercised by every class of
people amongst each other from 1782 to 1785.   To this
they might have been the more easily deluded by the ease
with w[b] they had ever been accustomed to make & obtain
money in this country & never having known the difficulties
of necessity   Debtors were equally tardy & refractory to
all their creditors as well as to the british Merchants who
were put at the head as persons with whom the least delicacy was to be observed   This was equally cruel & per-
fidious   So true it is that war corrupts the human mind,
& tends to erase the salutary ideas of honesty & good faith.
And when a legislature has once broken through the bounds
of equity, the precedent becomes dangerous & no man can
tell at what point it will stop   The constitution seems to
be in general pretty well framed on the republican plan,
except one clause which displays their english prejudices
wherein the sole right of levying taxes is vested in the
house of representatives to the exclusion of the Senate
who are equally the representatives of the people   And
the house of represent[*] are as tenacious of this unmeaning
perogative as the convention was preposterous in the initiation.   There is another clause exceptional for it's illib-
erality which excludes the clergy from a seat in either of
the houses   Although it is not probable that the people
w[d] be disposed to elect them, or that clergymen of good
sense would accept the appointment, still it is illiberal to
exclude them by an express clause & inconsistent with
liberty to refuse them a seat should they be made choice of

by the people for that purpose   I am told that it got a place
in the constitution chiefly to exclude one parson Tennant[12]
(a presbyterian) & who opposed with great eloquence &
finally with success the attempts that were made to establish hierarchy & fix the episcopalians as the only Legal &
Supreme Church in this country

He carried his point, but his opponents in return fixed
on him & his cloth a political silence forever   From hence
it is manifest that the church of england is the pre-eminent
and fashionable mode of worship here—especially in the
city & lower parts of the country   The interior being much
peopled from the northward & from Scotland partakes
most of presbyterianism.   There subsists but a poor understanding among the clergy from a variety of causes but
chiefly from the two leading sects—the episcopalians not
having forgotten their overbearing & assuming dispositions
on the one part, nor the presbyterions their obstinacy &
biggotry on the other   Although the constitution after
the above exceptions seems tolerably well framed the laws
are in a very confused & uncertain state—the best lawyer
does not really know what is law at present   There is but
one complete copy of the Laws of the State in existance—
the british Statutes are retrenched by a defining act of the
Legislature made since the war which specifies what particular statutes shall be in force   This has been rather in-
judicially done, for it is clear that to make so great an
innovation required a full & complete view of the judicial

---

[12]The clause excluding clergymen is found in the constitution
of March 19th, 1778, Section XXI and was continued substantially
in the constitutions of 1790 and 1865, but was omitted from those
of 1868 and 1895   It reads as follows

"And whereas the ministers of the gospel are by their profession dedicated to the service of God and the cure of souls, and
ought not to be diverted from the great duties of their function—
therefore no minister of the gospel or public teacher of any religious persuasion, while he continues in the exercise of his
pastoral function and for two years after, shall be elligible either
as Governor, Lieutenant-Governor, a member of the Senate, House
of Representatives, or Privy Council in this State "

The words "and for two years after" and the reference to the
'Privy Council" were striken out of the constitutions of 1790
and 1865   This clause however skilfully drawn did not reconcile
the clergy to their exclusion   Rev William Tennent certainly
delivered a strong argument, which has been published, in favor
of the disestablishment of the Episcopal Church

code in one prospect, a deep & accurate investigation, and a great deal of time to deliberate   The legislature have however been made sensible of the imperfections & errors of the present establishment, and in order to remedy them have it is to be feared laid the foundation of greater evils They have appointed three commissioners, Judges Pendleton Burk and Grimke with full powers to draw up digest & organize a complete code of Laws *a capite ad calcem* which they are to present to the Legislature in three years, having furnished them with the surviving copy, & all the documents which can be obtained for this purpose " This is clearly making these men lawgivers   For although it may be said that the laws are to have the revision & approbation of the Legislature before they are valid, still the difficulties are not removed   For if they are to be contemplated in detail the extreme ardency [sic] of the task & the inadequateness of the greater part of the legislature to examine & pass a proper judgment upon so immense a fabric will beget impatience & haste incompatible with business so momentous & important   Unless the magnitude of the object working upon the spirit of liberty should beget a jealousy which it is easy to conceive would issue in the most violent factions & oppositions when the code if passed would be a mere compound between parties & of consequence be cut & mangled into the most distorted shape imaginable   Or if this code is to be swallowed at a gulp which is the present idea of the commissioners themselves as well as of many others the government is for the time being (& what cannot be expected afterwards) changed into a complete aristocracy

Lastly I conceive that it must be both deficient & faulty. Laws are suggested by occasions & are co-ordinate with political circumstances running parallel with the progressive exigencies of the State   It is easy to apprehend & institute them when the causes strike our senses, but it is not in human nature to contemplate unite & adjust the present past & future in one complete & corresponding system—unless where it might relate to the confined juris-

---

"Such a "code" was, however, not adopted until 1870 under the provisions of the constitution of 1868

dictions of Solon or Lycurgus   Besides the diversity of
the materials, letting alone the objects, seem to me to
threaten difficulties & confusion—the common & statute
law of England, the bulky statutes of this country, & the
recent revolutions of government   To them may be added
the looseness & irrigularity of legal Practice; owing I believe partly to the method of administering justice in the
several parts of the state and partly to the carelessness of
practitioners.   Perhaps the latter proceeds from the former   The State is divided into two districts the Northern
& Southern, each of which is subdivided into circuits;
where circuit courts are held twice a year including sessions common pleas goal delivery & presided over by one
of the associate judges of whom there are four   For these
Courts all the business is prepared & causes brought to
issue in Charleston; & then the lawyers & judges set off
together taking the requisite papers with them & are generally absent about 5 weeks   The consequence of this
mode is that all the attorneys centre in Charleston, are acquainted with one another & practice upon so liberal a
footing as only to adopt so much of the english practice
as suits their case & convenience & compound for the rest—
so that no errors or omissions of that kind are taken advantage of; & the judges do not make it their business to
scrutinize into these niceties   The practice is of consequence
as slovenly & unsettled as the laws themselves.   But the
late introduction of county courts in two or three of the
districts, by distributing the attorneys through the country
will probably retrieve the practice in some measure from
this state of confusion; at least as far as the deviations
from the english mode of administering justice will admit
of   This deviation is however considerable   Hitherto
there has been but one court of common Law from which
there lay no appeal except in the form of a new trial in
Charleston if such could be obtained.   This still remains;
but there lies an appeal from the county court to the circuit
court of its respective district when all causes so removed
must be concluded

Next to this there is a court of chancery presided over
by *four* judges who sit four times a year in Chas". wherein

no cause can be protracted longer than one year except by special indulgence upon good cause shown   This seems an improvement upon the english plan, where delays are so great and so expensive as almost to defeat the equitable ends of its institution   However there are so many resorts for justice independently of it before the cause arrives to it that it will not be retarded if pursued in a proper manner   There is another mode of administering justice called a summary process, & is commenced by petition to the associate judge to summon the defend' to shew cause why he should not immediately pay the sum demanded (which must not exceed £20 sterling) upon which one of the judges endorses his approbation   The party must have at least 10 days notice, & appear at the court into which it is returnable prepared to answer or pay the money   A hear' is had & excution thereon   Inferior to this is the jurisdiction of justices of the peace which takes cognisance of any demand under £10 & proceeds in the ordinary way   From his decision recourse may be had to the Superior Court in the usual form of appeal   The Salaries of the judges are adequate to the office being a year those of the courts of Law £500 and of Equity £500 St' besides the usual fees of office

These salaries render the judges very independent, & as a necessary consequence the bench is reputable both for learning & dignity   Attempts have however been made to curtail these salaries by that spirit of parsimony not to say envy which too frequently attends democratic governments   It was however rejected by the last legislature tho' the number of advocates who appeared for the measure may give their honors no small ground to apprehend a stroke of the kind at some future day   Their legislature seems to be composed of a diversity of characters; many directed by party as well as private interests   The debtor interest is however prevelent, and operates in all the forms of injustice oppression; the laws are enacted not by principle of *right*, but by maxims of interest, & while men are madly accumulating enormous debts, their legislators are making provisions for their nonpayment

The almost universal advantage which is taken of these iniqutous laws at once illustrate & confirms the maxim that a corrupt government necessarily bespeaks a corrupt people This State having sustained a considerable share of the war has in a no less proportion partaken of its concomitant corruptions—men are ever astonished at each other when they see instances of fraud finesse & deceit where they have been accustomed to find the utmost punctuality honor & rectitude; but while they blush for the Crimes of their neighbors are themselves in one shape or another guilty of the same Perhaps the contrast of principles between the present and past times is more striking in this, than in the Northern States It had been the custom of the merchants to sell their goods negroes &c to the planters at one years credit, and so universally did it obtain that the planters scarcely pretended to deal on any other terms It was convenient for both—for the planter because when he got his crop to market in the fall he could command money—for the merchant because that was the time of making remittance, so that the planter had nothing to do but to draw on his factor for his arrears in rice or indigo, & the merchant rec^d and shipped it off But this habit of giving & obtaining long & extensive credit implied or begot a great deal of honor & punctuality in dealing—'twas the merchants to cultivate it because he rec^d a proportional profit on his goods—it was the planters interest to support it because he got goods at his pleasure & paid at his leisure. Besides, once in arrears always so—for that he might obtain the supplies of the current year he must necessarily anticipate it's crop having already disposed of the last except that portion of it which he had sequestered for the support of his own etiquette His credit of consequence became a very delicate & important part of his interest; & in a degree little inferior to that of the merchant himself Perhaps the principle of commerce has seldom if ever entered more into the genius of the planting interest In fact credit had wrought itself up into a principal of honor which uniting with that of interest had given to So Carolina an extraordinary character for mutual confidence in their domestic intercourse & punctuality in their foreign

trade   Credit being thus the great medium of business it
is easy to conceive the situation most men must have been
in at the commencement of the war   viz   that the denomi-
nations of debtor & creditor must have included all the
men in the State—all were included in a less or greater
degree; and most men as much as their fortunes would
closely bear   Another division of the inhabitants seems
as obviously to be into merchant & planter which was the
general proportion between debtor & creditor; and thus
circumstanced, the one charged with debts across the water
the other indebted to the merchants, they dropped business
& went to war   As war in one view is a temporary return
to a state of nature, as it calls forth into action all the
latent principles of cruelty & barbarity which had been
buried under a polished & civilized education; as it employs
in its operations actions of cruelty & ferocity; and thro
the arbitary power of military establishments fills the mind
with similar ideas, & suspends for the time being the exercise of justice & the cardinal and social virtues & super-
sedes the jurisdiction of the municipal laws—it has with
propriety been said to corrupt mankind.   On this principle
has a state of nature been called a state of war, and history
represents nations that are purely warlike as little better
than savages

What then might not be expected from a civil war? when
a brother was often called to imbrue his hands in a
brothers blood—where civil contracts were broken up &
property set afloat upon the sea of a fluctuating paper,
which tendered the strongest temptations to fraud & dis-
honesty under sanction of law   All the baneful effects
which could be supposed to flow from this fountain of evil
are visible here   The planter who had been accustomed
to live at his ease found himself much distressed at the
conclusion of the war; involved in debt, his plantation torn
to pieces; his stock of negroes gone, & his creditors push-
ing for payment, the legislature immediately interfered &

opened a new source of hope as well to the imprudent &
fraudulent as to the unfortunate   They learnt new lessons
of fraud from legislative interference; improved the idea
without loss of time as has been already mentioned by
obtaining large supplies of negroes & goods at exorbitant
prices upon long credit and as now appears without the
design of paying until they have made their fortunes
Having thus deviated from the salutary principles of integrity & learnt to practice over the lessons of deceit one
species became the parent of another & chicanery as much
their study as the support of their credit had been before
the war   Thus their apostacy is magnified thro the medium of their former integrity and the man sometimes
blushes to find himself so much fallen from what he boasted
to be his original character

What ever disease this country may labour under its
staples will still ensure it a considerable rank in a commercial point of view—the planting interest & the various
modes of lucritive business must still invite to imigration
But while the facility with which money may be made
invites to population; it has also a very considerable influence upon manners & customs   The inhabitants possess
not that keenness & sagacity which are visible in countries
more difficult to subsist in, and which tends to make them
famous for ingenuity & improvements   Pleasure becomes
in a great measure their study, Science but little patronized
or pursued, & activity to habits of study looked upon as the
retreats of the tasteless or melancholy resorts of the needy
While science is thus in a state of degradation the arts can
scarcely be expected to flourish   Manufactures are neither
patronized encouraged or pursued, and they seem to be
perfectly content to supply themselves from foreign markets   The military art goes fast to decay; dwindling apace
into empty pajeantry and artless parade   They seem willing to forget the dangers & hardships of war amidst the
alluring baits of pleasure; and vountarily to sink from the

active spirit of the soldier into the effeminate spirit of luxury and dissipation   It seems strange that while they lavish so much money upon the objects of luxury they are still but illy & imperfectly supplied   A person walking thro the market would have an idea of many of the commodities being but the mere cullings from the tables of those who supply them   Flesh coarse & seldom very fat or delicate; fish in no state of perfection, always dead & sometimes stale; and all sold at very exorbitant prices

(The end)

ORDER BOOK

of

John Faucheraud Grimké

August 1778 to May 1780

(Continued from the July Number)

November, 1778
Head Quarters, Charles Town

21   Parole, Steuben

The Honble Cont· Congress having appointed Lt Col Turnant[1] Inspector of the Confederal Troops in the States of S° Carolina & Georgia. He is to be respected & obeyed accordingly   Congress also orders that until a Plan of Regulations for the Inspectors Department now under Consideration shall be finally arranged & transmitted that He shall train, Exercise & Discipline the Army in this Department in the manner Introduced and Practised in the grand Army by the Inspector General   The General therefore requests that officers of every Degree will Chearfully aid & assist the Inspector in a Matter so Consistant with the good of the Service, for which purpose Battalions & Corps will Parade when He shall require it   And Adjutants of the Battalions in Town are by turns to leave a Copy of the General Orders of the Day at the Inspectors Quarters

22   Parole, Sunbury

(Col^n. Thomsons Reg^t ordered to march into Georgia)
The Sixth Regiment is to be put into immedite readiness for Marching   Brig^r General Moultrie will give orders

---

[1] Jean de Ternant, a French officer who started to America with LaFayette, de Valfort and others in 1777   He took service in the American army in March 1778   He was a man of wit and talent according to the memoirs of de Chastellux, drew well and spoke English as well as he did French   He was made prisoner at Charleston, and did no further fighting in America, but saw service later in Holland as Colonel of the Legion of Maillebois   Congress appointed him Lieutenant-Colonel, Sept 25, 1778, with orders to repair forthwith to South Carolina as Inspector of the South Carolina and Georgia troops, with pay and subsistence dating from March 26th   Balch *The French in America* and *Journals of h C*

to have them Supplied with waggons, ammunition, Tents. Canteens etc & will Report to the General when they are ready

The Com' officer of Artillery will give orders that Twenty Five Matrosses hold themselves in immediate Readiness, to March from Beaufort with two Field Pieces Ammunition, etc at the shortest notice after orders

The Irruption of the East Floridians happened at this Juncture of time L' Col" Prevost with a body of 600 men penetrated within 5 miles of Ogéchee River Col Fuser possessed himself of the Town of Sunbury which he quitted with precipitation the Day after This Expedition broke up the Settlements on the other side of Ogeechee the Enemy burnt almost every House in the County of Liberty, & drove off a large number of Cattle, Sheep, Hogs &c²

---

23 Parole, Turnant

Col° Pinckneys Battalion will Parade at Ten o'clock on Wednesday Morning for Inspection, when the Inspector will attend

The Command at Pritchards² is to be relieved tomorrow morning from the Sixth Regiment

First L' Daniel Louis Martin is promoted to be Captain in the First Regement, vice Capt Edward Walsh resigned 30 May 1778

First L' Alexander Keith to be Captain vice Cap' George Cogdell resigned 7 September 1778

---

²The above paragraph is evidently a later insertion, and is written in a blank space at the bottom of the page It was during this invasion that Col Fuser of the 60th (British) regiment demanded of Col John M'Intosh the surrender of Fort Morris, and received the well known and plucky reply "Come and take it" Col M'Intosh with a force of 127 Continental troops, some militia and citizens from Sunbury less than 200 men in all, held Fort Morris the town of Sunbury being otherwise unprotected. Jones' *History of Georgia* V 2, pp 309-310, gives an account of this invasion, and prints in full Col M'Intosh's letter to Fuser It is dated "Fort Morris, Nov 25 1778," and signed "John M'Intosh, Colonel of Continental Troops."

M'Crady, *Hist of S C* 1775-'80, p 324, states that Col Lachlan M'Intosh commanded at Fort Morris and sent the famous answer, and Gregg, *Hist, of Old Cherawas* (p 294, new ed) makes Col Alexander M'Intosh the author Alexander M'Intosh was apparently on leave of absence, (see page 153) and the letter in Jones' history seems to settle the point

Col Pritchard Liprvad

First L' Thomas Gordon to be Captain vice Captain Alexander Petrie resigned 6 October 1778

First L' Stephen Guerry to be Captain vice Captain W'' · Blamyer Resigned 6 November 1778

Second L' James Kenny to be first L' vice First L' David Dubose resigned 27 April 1778

Second L' John Hogan to be first Lieut' vice first Lieut' John Jones resigned 15 May 1778

These officers are to Rank agreable to the above dates when the vacancies happened & are to be Obeyed & respected accordingly

Alexander Fotheringham Junr [?] & Samuel Warren Gentleman are appointed first Lieutenants in the fifth Continental Regiment. the First to take rank from the 20 June, the Second from the 10 July 1778 They are therefore to be respected & obeyed as Continental officers

---

Camp at Great Ogéchee Hill

29 Parole, Elbert

A General Parade is to be immediately marked out by the Dep Adj Gen' where the Troops of every Corps are to Parade at 4 o'Clock this afternoon No man to absent himself

The Commanding officers of Reg'' & Corps are to Report to Morrow Morning at 9 o Clock to the General the number of Horses appertaining to their several Corps either of Public or Private Property, Exactness is Requisite & will be Expected upon this occasion for very particular Reasons

The Com' officer of artillery will Report exactly & immediately the quantity of fixed & other ammunition under his care

No Guns are to be fixed either in or about Camp upon any occasion except upon Duty those transgressing this order will be punished

John F Grimke Esq having been appointed Dep Adj Gen' for the States of South Carolina & Georgia with the the rank of Colonel, & George Turner Esq aid de Camp to the General with the rank of Major They are to be respected & Obeyed accordingly

Christian Senf Esq. having been appointed Cap' Engineer in the Continental Service, He is to be received & obeyed accordingly

Col° John Stirk of the 3ᵈ Continental Battalion in the State of Georgia having resigned his Commission on the 9ᵗʰ October Ultmo He is no longer to be respected or Obeyed as an officer in the Service of the United States

After Orders

The review of the Troops which was ordered this morning is postponed on account of the bad weather until further orders

Camp at Ogechee River
November 1778

30   Morning Orders

The Troops are to March as immediately as possible; Commanding officers of Battalions are to prepare for moving off accordingly

The Commandant of Artillery is also to be in readiness to March

The waggons are to be ready to Receive the Baggage, which is to packed up

Orders will be given when the Tents are to be Struck

Parole, Walton

Order of March

Advanced Guard to consist of

1 Sub · 1Sarg': & 19 Rank & File

One brass Field Piece

The Troops in Platoons

Artillery

Baggage

One Small Iron Field Piece

Rear Guard to Consist of

1 Sub 1 Sarg' & 12 Rank & File

Camp at Slades Plantation
December 1778

1   Parole, Ternant

Returns will be made by all Persons who draw Forage to the Commanding officer for the time being without which they are not to be entitled to Forage——

These Orders so far as they relate to the Men are to
be read to them Company by Company

After Orders.

Doct' William Shud is appointed Surgeon to the 4ᵗʰ
Continental Battalion of this State, and he is to be respected
& obeyed accordingly

Headquarters: Sunbury 6ᵗʰ Dec'
1778

6   Parole, Sunbury

The Commanding Officer of Fort Morris is immediately
to Report to the General the State of his Garrison, the
Number of Ordinances & quantity of Stores of every kind
in the Fort or any other place under his command.

The Firing of Morning, Evening & 8 O'Clock guns is to
be discontinued; nor are guns of any sort to be fired except
on Duty

The assistant Dep Commissary Gen' of purchases at
this Post is to Report the quantity of Provisions of every
sort He has on hand, & also such as He has contracted for

The Assistant Dep Commissary of J Jones [sic] to report what is now in his Hands & also what He has received for a month past & the manner of its Expenditure

An orderly Serg' to attend the General daily

Head Quarters, Sunbury's
December 1778

7   Parole, Morris

A Detachment of one Sub one Serg': one Corporal &
Ten Privates are to be warned for Duty tomorrow Morning at Sun rise They are to be furnished with 20 Rounds
of Ammunition & Six Days Provisions The officer Commanding the Party will receive his Orders from the Dep
Adjutant Gen at Head Quarters

The Col° Com' of the Continental Georgia Brigade is
immediately to recal all absent officers to join their respective Corps

A Detachment of 1 Capt 2 Sub 3 Serg': & 20 rank &
file are to March from Camp to Head Quarters to-morrow
Morning

Orders to the officer Com[g]. a Detachment marching to the bluff on Colonels Island.

Sir:

You are to proceed to the bluff at Timons's upon the back part of Colonels Island with the Detachment under your Command, where you will be Extremely Vigilant & Observant least the Enemy should approach undiscovered. Upon the first appearance of any Hostile Force you are to Dispatch a Messenger to the General with an Acct: thereof & should they be formidable you are to Retreat with your Detachment bringing off with you all such Persons as can give any information to the Enemy; but should they less than, or only equal to your force you will Defend your Post as long as possible & should occasion require retreat as much order as possible.   I am etc:

John F. Grimké D: A: G.

8:    Parole,

9:    Parole,

10:    Parole, Roberts.

One Capt: 2 Sub[s], 3 Serg[t]: 3 Corporals & 30 Privates to be taken by Detachment from the Troops at Midway Meeting House are to immediately to proceed to M[r]. Spencers Hill where they are to act according to the Orders they will receive: They are to take 3 Days Provisions & 20 rounds of Ammunition.

One Sub: 1 Serg[t]: 1 Corporal & 10 Privates from the Troops in Fort Morris are immediately to proceed to Newport Ferry where they are to act according to the Orders that will be given them.

Sir:

You are to order the Detachment from the Troops under your Command mentioned in General Orders to proceed & take post at M[rs]. Spencers Hill where the roads fork: They are to act as advanced Guards to prevent your Camp from Surprise. The officers are to be directed to post Centinels in a manner the best calculated to answer this purpose & to be particularly enjoined to be Vigilant & Active. From this Post a Detachment of 1 Sub: 1 Serg[t]:

1 Corp & 10 Privates are to be ordered to take post at North Newport Bridge   They are to encamp on this side of the bridge & to act as an advance Party to the guard to which they belong   They are to keep a Sentinel upon the bridge both Night & Day & at Night to pull up post of the bridge that they may not be attacked by surprise   Should the Detachment at the Bridge be attacked by a body too considerable for their force they are to retreat to their Main Guard & should the Main Guard be attacked by a force too powerful they will retreat slowly to the Army to which they belong, giving information of their retreat to the Com^r officer by Express and sending notice to the Detachment at the Bridge to make their retreat good by a different rout

As the Safety of your Camp & the Honor of the Troops may depend upon the Alertness of their Advanced Parties I rely upon the Execution of the officers to answer these ends so essential to Service   I am Sir etc

    (Signed)   Robt Howe Maj Genl

To the Com^r office at
    Medway Meeting House

Sir

You are to proceed with your Command to Newport Ferry about 5 miles distant from Sunbury   You are to take post on this side of the ferry, where you are to exert the Utmost Vigilence to prevent the Enemies surprising your guard or approaching the Town without being perceived   You are very right to keep the flat & other Boats on this side of the River & place over them a proper Sentinel   Should you be attacked by a Party superior to you. you will retreat to the Fort first sending an Express to inform the Garrison of your retreat & of any other circumstances beneficial to Service   Relying upon your Vigilence & good Conduct

    I am Sir Etc J F Grimké D A G

To the officer Com^r A
Detachment marching to
take post at Newport Ferry

Camp at Slades Plantation 1st: Decr 1778

Sir

You will proceed with the Troops under your Command to Medway Meeting House or any other place the situation of which is safe & defensible & calculated to cover the Plantations whilst they collect the Property, the Enemy has left them   You will fortify the Camp so as to be able to make a proper defence in case of accident & take every measure in your power to aid & assist the Inhabitants of this State in general & this distressed County in particular   You will keep out Scouting & Patroling not only to prevent Surprise & retard the Progress of the Enemy should they advance to annoy this State, but also to prevent wicked & designing men from Maruding the Inhabitants & encreasing their distresses by an embezzlement of the remaining Property   Good order & strict discipline is to be kept up among the Troops & Severe Punishment be inflicted upon those who shall insult the Persons or injure the Property of their fellow Citizens

Constant Intelligence of your Proceedings is to be sent to me or the Commander in Chief of the Department for the time being & of every important Event information is to be sent by Express   Should any officer superior to you in command arrive, you are to Deliver him these Orders, which are by him to be observed

I am Sir &c (Signed) Robt Howe Maj Gen
To Lt Col^o Rae

(To be continued)

REGISTER OF
ST ANDREWS PARISH, BERKELEY COUNTY, SOUTH CAROLINA

1719-1774

Copied and Edited by MABEL L WEBBER.

(Continued from the July Number)

CHRISTENINGS

John the Son of Robert Rivers & Anne his wife Baptized
9th Jan' 1736*

Richard the Son of Benj' Godfrey and Martha his wife
Baptized 27th Feb'' 1736*

John y' Son of John Shepherd & Eliz' his wife Baptized
13th March 1736 *

Sarah y' Daughter of John Mulryne & Claudia his wife
Baptized 17th April 1737

Sarah y' Daughter of Thomas Butler Sen' & Elizabeth
his wife Baptized 8th [?] May, 1737

Richard Son of Edmund Bellinger and Elizabeth his Wife
baptized 25th June 1737

Charles Son of James Rattary & Mary his Wife baptized
29th. July 1737.

Eleanor Daughter of Elding King & Eleanor his Wife
baptized 31st July 1737

Mary y' Daughter of James Manning & Sarah his Wife
baptized 11th. Sep' 1737

Susannah y' Daughter of Francis Ladson & Sarah his Wife
baptized 18th October 1737

William Son of Jn° Rivers & Martha his Wife baptized
30th. Oct'. 1737.

Frances y' Daughter of John Champneys & Mary his Wife
baptized 13th Decem' 1737

Stephen Fox Son of John Drayton Jun' & Sarah his Wife
baptized 31st Dec' 1737

*Old style, 1737 new style

Thomas Son of William Chapman & Mary his Wife baptized 1ˢᵗ Janʸ 1737†

William Son of Charles Jones & Rachel his Wife baptized 16ᵗʰ Janʸ 1737 †

Anne yᵉ Daughter of Willᵐ Brandford & Anne his Wife baptized 24ᵗʰ Janʸ 1737†

Samuel yᵉ Son of Jeremiah Fickling & ―― his wife baptized 29ᵗʰ Janʸ 1737†

FUNERALS

Frances yᵉ Daughter of John Champneys & Mary his Wife Buried 14ᵗʰ Decemʳ 1737

Priscilla yᵉ wife of Edward Doyell Buried 17ᵗʰ December 1737

Dʳ. Thoˢ Hodgson buried 14ᵗʰ Janʸ. 1737†

Jane Moll Daughter of Jacob Moll Overseer at Mʳˢ Hills buried 10ᵗʰ July 1738

Robert Son of Robᵗ Ladson Junʳ and Sabina his Wife buried yᵉ 9ᵗʰ Augᵗ 1738

William Son of John Champneys and Mary his wife buried 11ᵗʰ Augᵗ 1738

Martha Jennings Buried, a poor woman, Augᵗ.

Martha yᵉ Wife of Geo. Simony Buried 19ᵗʰ. August 1738

Charles Hill Guerard Son of John Guerard & Elizᵃ his Wife buried 25ᵗʰ. August 1738

Mary the wife of John Champneys buried 17ᵗʰ Sepʳ 1738

Sarah & Thomas Son & daughter of Joseph Heape buried 18ᵗʰ Sepʳ 1738

Sarah Daughter of Zaccʰˢ Ladson & Sarah his Wife buried 23ʳ 7ber 1738.

Joseph Heape buried 25ᵗʰ 7ber 1738

Christopher Son of Benjᵃ. Godfrey burᵈ. 13ᵗʰ 8ᵇʳ 1738

Anne Falkinham buried 15ᵗʰ. Octʳ 1738

Esther Campbell Buried 26ᵗʰ Octʳ. 1738

Elizabeth Stock Buried 29ᵗʰ. Decʳ. 1738

Mary yᵉ Daughter of Wᵐ. Cattell Junʳ. and Anne his Wife buried 22ⁿᵈ. Janʸ. 1738‡

---

†Old style 1738 new style
‡Old style 1739 new style

Susanna ye Daughter of Saml Ladson and Eliz^a his Wife
Buried 27th Jany 1738‡
John Rivers Buried 18th. March 1738‡
J Grall of James's Is^{ld} Burd February 1st. 1738/9

CHRISTENINGS

Caesar an adult negro Man belonging to Mr Edmund Bel-
linger Baptized 12th. February 1737†
Thomas Son of Thos Drayton & Eliz^a. his Wife baptized
26th Feby 1737 †
Joseph Son of Jno Billiald & Mary his Wife baptized 10th
March 1737 †
Margaret ye Daughter of James Boswood & Martha his
wife, Baptized 10th. March 1737†
George Son of John Boswood & Nancy his Wife baptized
21st March 1737†
Jonathan Son of Henry Wood Junr & Catherine his Wife
baptized 21st March 1737†
Nancy a Molatto belonging to Henry Wood Junr Bap-
tized 21st March 1737†
David Son of Fra^s Hext & Sarah his Wife of John's Island
baptized 22nd March 1737†
Martha Daughter of Thos Tilley & Willoughby his Wife
baptized 8th April 1738
Sindiniah Daughter of Wm Boswood & Susanna his wife
bapt^d 28th April 1738
Naomi Carlisle baptized being an Adult Woman 13th June
1738
Samuel Son of Saml Jones & Mary his Wife baptized 24th
June 1738.
Robert Son of Robt Ladson Junr and Sabina his wife
Baptized 8th Augt 1738.
Edward Son of William Miles & Mary his Wife baptized
15th August 1738
Anne Sarah Daughter of Jacob Ladson and Elizabeth his
Wife baptized Septr 1st 1738

‡1739 new style
†Old style 1738 new style

MARRIAGES

Nathaniel Barnwell & Mary Gibbes Spin^r Married 7th April 1738

Thomas Butler & Constant Fitch Widdow married 16th. Aprill 1738

John Kelsal & Mary Bellinger Spin^r of St Pauls parish married 24th May 1738

Hugh Ferguson & Sarah Burley Married 1st June 1738.

Joseph Hasfort & Naomi Carlisle Married 13th June 1738

William Clifford & Mary Parker Sp^r married 22nd June 1738

Thomas Elliott Junr & Mary Butler Spinst^r married 20th July 1738

Sampson & Reb [?] 2 free Negroes & George & Eliz free Negroes Married 3^d Septem^r 1738

Elisha Butler & Eliz^a Miles Widow Married 24th Septr 1738

William Butler & Elizabeth Elliott Sp^r. married 1st Decr 1738

John Rivers & Eliz^a. Godfrey Sp^r married 26th Decr 1738

James Fitchett & Jane Armstrong Sp^r married 18 Jan^r 1738$\frac{1}{4}$

Alexander Mc Gregor & Margaret Mc Elvin Sp^r married 13th Feb^{rr}, 1738$\frac{1}{4}$

William Heape & Sarah Drayton Spinster Married 11th March 1738

Joseph Spencer & Keziah Rivers Married 15th March 1738$\frac{1}{4}$

Samuel Stock & Hannah Haydon Married 4th Aprill 1739

Joseph Izard & Eliz Gibbes Sp^r Mar^d Sepr 28. 1738¶

CHRISTENINGS

Eliz^{eth}· Anne the Daugh^{tr} of Maurice Lewis Esq & Jane his Wife Bap^t Sepr 13 1738

William Son of George Simony Baptized 4th Septem^r 1738

‡Old style. 1739 new style
¶Inserted on the opposite blank page

Sampson & Pompey 2 free negroes & their Wives baptized 23ᵈ July 1738

Sarah yᵉ Daughter of Zachᵗ Ladson and Sarah his Wife baptized 9ᵗʰ Sepʳ. 1738

Robert the Son of Robert Rivers & Anne his wife Bapᵈ Sepʳ yᵉ 25ᵗʰ 1738*

Susannah the Daughter of Samuel Boswood & —— his wife Bapᵈ. Sepʳ yᵉ 28, 1738*

Mary Daughter of Samˡ Ladson & Elizabeth his Wife baptized 1ˢᵗ Octʳ 1738

John-Samuel Son of Thoˢ Barlow & Susannah his wife Bapᵈ Octʳ yᵉ 5ᵗʰ 1738*

Christopher Son of Benja Godfrey alias Garnear & Martha his Wife Bapᵈ Octʳ yᵉ 5ᵗʰ 1738*

Mary Daughter of Jehu Stanyarn Octoᵇʳ yᵉ 8 1738*

Mary Daughtʳ of Joseph Laws & Sarah his Wife Bapᵈ Octobʳ yᵉ 8ᵗʰ 1738 *

John Son of John Rivers & Martha his wife bapᵗ Novʳ yᵉ 19 1738

Thomas Son of Wᵐ Hare and —— his Wife of Goose Creek bapᵈ 26 Decʳ. 1738

William Son of John Drayton Junʳ & Sarah his Wife bapᵈ 1ˢᵗ Janʳ 1738‡

Sarah yᵉ Daughter of Wᵐ Cattell Junʳ and Anne his Wife baptized 22ⁿᵈ Janʳ 1738‡

William Son of William & Mary Flood Baptized 13ᵗʰ Febᵘ 1738‡

Elizabeth Daughter of Edwᵈ Simpson & Sarah his Wife baptized 10ᵗʰ March 1738†

Jonathan Son of Jonathan Wood & Rebeca his Wife Bapᵈ March yᵉ 16 1738/9.**

Joseph Son of Stephen Carter and Sarah his wife baptized 8ᵗʰ Aprill 1739

Sarah Daughter of James & Sarah Manning Baptized 22ⁿᵈ Aprill 1739

Sophia yᵉ Daughter of Dʳ Mᶜ Gilvrey bapᵈ. Aprill 29 1739

*Inserted on opposite page, not with regular entries.
‡1739 new style
**Inserted

Sarah Daught'. of William Fuller & Martha his wife Bap^d May ye 13th 1739

Katherine the Daugt^r John Green & Phebe his Wife bap^d May 17th 1739**

Catherine the Daught^r of John Mulryne & Claudia his Wife bap^d May 17, 1739**

Edwd the Son of Saml Burgess [? page worn] & Mary his wife bap^d May 20, 1739**

Margaret Daught^r of Thomas & Mary Mell Bap^d May ye 27 1739: Born Aprill ye 1 1739

Robt.—Hall the Son of John Cattell & Sarah his wife bap^d July 13 1739

Susannah the Daught^r of Wm Murray & Eliz his Wife bp^d. Oc^t. 2, 1739

Martha Daugh^r of Benj Godfrey & Martha his wife bp^d 6 1739

Nathaniel, the Son of Nathaniel Barnwell & Mary his wife bap^d Octr 7th 1739

FUNERALS

Mary the wife of the Honb^{le} Wm Bull Esqr Buried 21st. March 1738.⁊

Edith Elliott widow of Joseph Son of Thos Elliott Buried 24th March 1738‡

Mary-Anne, Daughter to Samuel Ladson & Eliz^{beth} his wife Buried 24th April 1739

Magdalen ye wife of John Stanyarne of John's Island, Burd April 21st 1739

Joseph Son of John Billiald & Mary his wife Bur^d June ye 3—1739

Charles Gervais Armorer of the Hawk man of War Burd June ye 11 1739

Joseph Son of Stephen Carter & Sarah his wife Buried July ye 11th 1739

Sarah Daught^r of Willm Cattell Junr & Anne his wife Buried August ye 4th. 1739

**Inserted on opposite page
173...

John-Samuel Son of Thomas Barlow & Susannah his wife Buried August ye 23 1739

Allice Gibs widow of William Gibs Buried Sep^t ye 1st 1739

Capt John Bowles Master of a vessel at Wm Cattells Buried Sep^t ye 6th 1739.

Mr William Bowles Brother to Capt Bowles buried Sepr ye 6th 1739

Stephen-Fox Son of John Drayton Junr and Sarah his Wife Buried Sep^{tbr} ye 9th 1739

Maurice Lewis Esqr Buried Sep^t ye 23^d 1739

Mary the Wife of John Billhald Buried Sep^{tr}. ye 25th 1739

Benja Board Servt to Mr William Cattell Junr Burd Sep^t ye 29th 1739

Sabina Daught^r of Samuel Stock Buried Octob^r ye 3^d 1739

Susannah the Daughter of Wm Murray Bur^d Oct 5 1739

John McDaniel Buried at Mrs Sereaus Octo^{br} ye 13th 1739

John Burn Bur^d 8^{br} 14th 1739

Dorothy the Wife of John Hewson Buried Octob^r ye 15th 1739

Mary Daught^r of Samuel Stock Buried Octo^{br} ye 16th 1739

Thomas Son of Thomas Drayton Esqr & Elizabeth his wife Buried Octob^r ye 19th 1739

Robert Anderson Buried at Mr Stanyarns Octo^{br} ye 29th 1739

William Capers Son of Richard Capers Buried Nov^{br} ye 26 1739

MARRIAGES P^r W^m GUY

Edward Hussey & Mary Barton Widow married 8th Aprill 1739

George Cook & Eliz^{btb} Hull sp^r Married June ye 2^d 1739

George Simony & Anne Hutchins Sp^r Married June ye 19 1739

Joseph Simcock & Hannah Moll marr^d June 4th 1739

D^r. John Lining & Sarah Hill Sp^r Married June 28 1739

Wm Harvey Junr & Mary Seabrook mar^d Augt 23^d 1739

Doc[tr] William Simson & Martha Rivers Widow Married
    Feb[ry] y[e] 12th 1739

Frances Holmes & Elizabeth Brandtord Sp[r] Married
    March y[e] 20th 1739

Bethel Dews & Margaret Croskeys Sp[r] Married May y[e]
    8th 1740

Thomas Holman & Mary Wells Sp[r] Married May y[e] 15th
    1740

John Stanyarn & Sarah Harvey Widow Married August
    y[e] 18th 1740

John Morrick [?] Eliz[bth] Lock Sp[r] Mar[d] August y[e] 23
    1740

William Walter & Mary Cattell Sp[r] Married Sep[r] y[e] 2[d]
    1740

Thomas Radcliff & Elizabeth Warren Sp[r] Married Sep[r]
    y[e] 13th 1740

John Cockfield & Anne Barton Sp[r] Married Oct[br] y[e] 6
    1740

Will[m] Rivers son to Cap[t] Robert Rivers & Susanah-ffrances
    Maverick Sp[r] Nov[br] y[e] 6th 1740   James Island

Will[m] Cockfield & Sarah Carter Wd[w] Married De[hr] y[e]
    24th 1740

John Champneys & Sarah Saunders Sp[r] Married Jan[ry] y[e]
    7th 1740°

John Burford & Susanah Wood sp[r] Married Feb[y] y[e] 1
    1740/1

William Chapman of James's Island & Mary Guy Sp[r] mar-
    ried p[r] Rev[d] M[r] Orr May y[e] 10th 1741

George Lee & Elizabeth Godfrey Sp[r] Married p[r] the Rev[d]
    M[r] Guy June y[e] 10th 1741

John French & Sarah Johnson Sp[r] Married p[r] the Rev[d]
    M[r] Guy July y[e] 1st 1741

Tho[s] Pritchard & Sarah Hutchins Sp[r] Married July y[e]
    30th. 1741

Will[m] Bee & Eliz[abeth] Witter Sp[r] Marr[d] August y[e] 20th
    1741

°1741 new style

CHRISTENINGS

John-Vincent Son of John Man & Anne his wife Bap^d Oct^r
  ye 23. 1739

Mary Daughter of Robert Ladson & Sabina his Wife Bap^d
  Feb^ry ye 17th 1739 ||

Mary Wells an Adult Baptized &
  John, Sylas, Thomas
  Martha, Margaret & Mathew } Children
  of Sylas Wells & Mary his wife Bapt^ed Feb^ry ye 22^d
  1739 ||

Robert an Adult negro Man belonging to Thomas Drayton
  Esqr Bap^d March ye 14th. 1739 ||

Thomas Son of Samuel Stock Rec^d into the Congregation
  June ye 1 1740 Bp^d privat Bapt^em before

May-acke Daughter of Zaccheus Ladson & Sarah his Wife
  Bap^ted June ye 8th 1740

Dorcas, Nehemiah,   } Children of Eliza^bth.
  Sarah, Catherine } Rivers widow to
                    } Sam^el Rivers Deces^d
                    } [Date not given]

Dewe Son of William Chapman Sn^r & Mary his wife
  Bapt^ed —— 1740

Samuel Son of Edwd Pickrin & Mary his wife Bapt^ed
  August ye 10th 1740

Frances Son of Ibid

Elizabeth Daught^r of Thomas Drayton Esqr & Elizabeth
  his wife Bap^d Sepr ye 9th 1740

Richard Son of Griffith Bullard & Hepsey his Wife Bap^d
  Decr ye 12th 1740

Sarah-ffrancis Daughter to Henry Campbell & Sarah his
  wife Bapt^ed Feby ye 3 1740/1

Richard Son of Richard Martin & —— his wife Bapt^ed
  Priva^t B^m Feby ye 12th 1740/1

Elanor Daugh^r. of James Taylor & Hesther his wife Bapt^ed
  Feby ye 22 1740/1

Hannah Daugh^r to John & Eliz^bth Rivers March ye 15th
  1741

||1740 new style

Martha-Phebe Daughter of Elizabeth Ladson widow to Sam^{el} Ladson Deces^d Bap^d March ye 29 1741

Frances Daught^r to Benjamin Stone & Elizabeth his wife Bapt^ed April ye 19th 1741   James Island.

Nancey the Daught^r of John Boswood and Nancey his Bapt^{ed}. May ye 5th. 1741

Willm the Son of John Kelsal & Mary his wife, & Mary Daughter to Ditto Bap^d August ye 6th 1741

FUNERALS

Mrs Jane Munger Widow Buried p^r the Revd Mr Guy Decem^{br} ye 2^d 1739

Jane the Daugh^{tr} of William Cattell Esqr Buried Decem^{br} ye 14th 1739

Jonathan the Son of Henery Wood Junr & Catherine his wife Buried Decemb^r ye 17th 1739

William Ladson Buried Decemb^r ye 22^d 1739

William Heape Buried Jany ye 5th 1739||

John Son of John Rivers & Eliza his wife Buried Janr^{r}y ye 25th 1739 ||

Elizabeth the wife of John Purkis Buried Janry ye 31 1739

Mr Benjamin Perry Bur^d Feb^{ry} ye 1st. 1739

Mrs Crawford widow Bur^d: Feb^{ry} ye 6th 1739

Sindimah the wife of William Wood Buried Feb^{ry} ye 8th 1739

Martha the Daught^r of Martha Ladson widow Buried Feb^{ry} ye 10th 1739

Margret Daught^r to Mrs Crawford Buried Feb^{ry} ye 12th 1739

Mr Samuel Ladson Buried Feb^{ry} ye 19th 1739

Thomas Honehan Buried at Mrs Anne Cattells Feb^{ry} ye 20th 1739

Landgra^{ve} Edmund Bellinger Buried March ye 5th 1739

Benja^m· Son of Benja^m Godfrey als Garnier Buried March ye 18th 1739

Elizabeth The Daughter of Joseph Barton Dec^d and Mary Barton his wife Bur^d March ye 24th 1739

||1740 new style

Thomas Son of Thomas Booth & Hannah his wife Buried March y* 25th 1740

Hannah the wife of Samuel Stock Buried Aprill y* 6th 1740.

Sylas Wells Buried April y* 16th 1740

Mrs Grace Stantin widow Buried April y* 19th 1740

Mr Benjam Godfrey Alice [sic] garner Burd April y* 30th 1740

John Son of John Champneys & Mary his Wife Buried May y* 3 1740

John Hewson Buried May y* 11th 1740

Joseph Richards Buried July y* 9th 1740

Susanah Daughter of Frances Ladson & Sarah his Wife Buried August y* 11th 1740

Mr Samuel Stock Buried August y* 21" 1740

Capt James Sutherland at Johnsons Fort y* 26 Aug 1740

William Son of John Drayton Junr & Sarah his wife Buried Sepr y* 9th 1740

To be continued)

STOCK MARKS

RECORDED IN SOUTH CAROLINA, 1695-1721

Contributed by A. S. Salley, Jr

(Continued from the July Number)

1697
January 15   This Day came M* Peter Roberts of Santee
and recorded his marke for Cattle an Hoggs
which is as followeth a Cropp of the Left
eare and a Slitt from the Top to the Bottom
and halfe of the upper part Cutt away of the
P R   Right Eare and his Brand marke as ℔
Merg*·

15   This Day came John Peter Pelett and recorded his marke for Cattle and hoggs which
is as followeth The Right Eare Cropt & an
J P P   upper Keele in the Left and his Brand marke
as ℔ merg*

May 1697 12   This Day came Edward Howard & recorded
his Marke for Cattle & Hoggs Viz*=the
Right Eare Crop* & Two Notches in the
E H   upper Side of the Left Eare

     This Day came David Evans & reEntered
12   his Marke for Cattle & Hoggs Viz*=The
Left Eare Cropt & Two peeces Cutt out of
E   the upper Side of the Rite Eare

     This Day Came Christopher Beech & Re-
C B 12   corded his Marke for Cattle & Hoggs Viz*=
The Left Eare Cropt & an upper Keele & an
und* Keele & the Right a Swallowes forke

12   This Day Came Peter Conley & Recorded
P C   his Marke for Cattle & Hoggs Viz* The
Left Eare Cropt & the Right Eare a Square
Cutt out

12   This Day Came John Guppell & Recorded
G   his Marke for Cattle & Hoggs Viz* The
Left Eare Cropt & a Slitt in the Same

July th 15
1697
I C

This Day Came Jobe Chamberlin & Recorded his mark for Cattle & hoogs &c; (ass followeth) a Croop of the right Eare & a slitt in the Same Eare & a halfe penny out of the back side of the other Eare his brand mark ass Pr margent being on the left buttock—he liveing up Ashly Reaver in Barkly County

July the 15
1697

H S

This Day Came Henry Spray of ashly Reaver in Barkly County & Recorded his marke for Cattell & hoggs &c (ass followeth) the right Eare Cutt Close home the left Eare wth a Swallow fork & a slitt of one side his Brand mark being on the left buttock ass P margent—

August the 12th
1697

P M

This Day Came Mr Peter Mecho of Sante Planter & recorded his mark of Cattell & hoggs &c, ass followeth, boath yeares Crapt & the right yeare three Slitt, his brand mark being ass P mergent

August th 12th
1697

D H

This Day Came Daniell Huger of Sante Planter & record his mark of Cattell & hoggs &c: followeth, the left yeare Cropt the other wth an under & upper Keele, his brand mark ass P margent

August the 16
1697

This Day Came Robert Wood of barkly County & recorded his mark of Cattell & hoggs &c; ass followeth, the left yeare wth one under Keele & a slitt & the right yeare a slitt

August the 16
1697

This Day Came Henry Wood of Barkly County Cordwinder & recorded his mark of Cattell & hoggs &c; ass followeth, a Slitt in each yeare an under keele in the right yeare

August the 19
1697

This Day Came Salamon Brimmer¹ of Barkly County & recorded his mark of Cattell & hoggs ass followeth the right yeare wth an under keele & ye left a Deep Slitt

¹Solomon Bremar

August yᵉ 19   This Day Came Lewis Dutark of Barkly
1697   County & recorded his mark of Cattell &
                 hoggs as followeth the right yeare wᵗʰ a large
                 Slitt & one halfe of the halfe Cutt of & the
                 left wᵗʰ a Deep Slitt

August yᵉ 20   This Day Came Nicolas Bochet of Barkly
1697   County & recorded his mark of Cattell &
                 hoggs ass followeth boath yeares with a Slitt
                 from the top halfe wayes to the root & one
                 part of the Slitt Cutt of—

August the 30   This Day Came Joseph Cooper of Colliton
1697   County & reCorded his mark of hoggs &
                 Cattell as follow (viz) the right yeare three
                 Slitts wᵗʰ a Crop in each yeare his brand
                 mark ass ☿ margent—²

August the 30   This Day Came Henry Samwayes of
1697   Barkly County & recorded his mark of hogs
S   & Cattell as followeth (viz) the left eare wᵗʰ
                 a Swollow fork the right yeare a Croop &
                 two Slitts his brand mark as ☿ margent
                 being on the right buttock the horses being
                 on the right sholder

August the 30   This Day Came Henry Samwayes of Barkly
1697   County & recorded his horne mark as ☿ᵉ
H S   margent—

September 10ᵗʰ   This Day Came George Burnett of Barkly
1697   County & recorded his mark of hoggs & Cattle
G B   (viz) the left Eare wᵗʰ Swollow foark the
                 right Eare a Cropp & two Slitts, his brand
                 mark as ☿ margent—

September 10ᵗʰ   This Day Came John Jones of Barkly
1697   County & recorded his mark of Cattle &
                 hoggs (viz) the left Eare wᵗʰ a Swollow fork
                 the right Eare wᵗʰ a Cropp & one Slitt, his
                 brank mark as ☿ mergent—³

---

²A T over an inverted U.
³A circle around an I

Septem 17
1697

This Day Came Henry Baly of Colliton County & recorded his mark of Cattle & hoggs (viz) one under keele in each eare & the right eare Cropt,

September 18th
1697

This Day Came Anthony Bourau & recorded his mark of Cattle & Swine (viz) the right eare an upper keele & the left an under keele, likewis a parcell of Cattle bought by yᵉ sᵈ Bourau of the Widdow Horry marked as followeth boath Eares wᵗʰ an upper Keele & the brand as 7ᵖ margent—

≺ B

ffebrewary
the 16th. 169⅞

A M

This Day Came Abraham Mechos & recorded his mark of Cattle and Swine & horses (viz) boath Eares Cropt & the left Slitt in three parts & his brand mark & per margent—

Aprill- 15th
1698 |
X

This Day Came William Branford of yᵉ South Side of Ashly River near Accabee & Recorded his Marke of Cattle & Swine viz' the right Ear wᵗʰ a Cropp & a Hole & one upper Keel in yᵉ Left Ear and Burn't Marke as pʳ Margent

May - - - 16
1698

This day Came Mʳ Isaac Mazeque and Recorded his Brand Mark for Cattle &c wᶜʰ is a Flower-de-Luis upon yᵉ Right Buttock, Mark as pʳ. Margent.⁴

Novembᵈ- 21
B W

This day Came Benjamin Willman of Edistoe Island Cooper. & Recorded his Brand-Marke—for Barrells, wᶜʰ is B W as pʳ Margent

Novembʳ 21

This Day Came Jeremiah Varreen & Recorded his Marke for Cattle, Hoggs &c being a Spade in both Ears ⁵

March 14

This Day Came Mʳ Stephen Fox & Recorded his Ear Marke for Cattle & hogs, viz' one Crop in yᵉ. Left Ear and a Halfpenny under yᵉ Right Ear and two under Latches under both Ears & Burn'd Mark'd wᵗʰ an O

---

⁴A fleur-de-lis
⁵A spade in the margin

Aprill 27   This Day came Mr Edmund Jarvis & Recorded his Ear-marke for Hogs & Cattle,
viz' a Slitt in ye Left-Ear & a Crop in the
Right |

May 12   This Day Came John ffripp & Recorded his
Marke for Cattle & Hoggs wch is a Cropp &
a Hole in ye right Ear and a Cropp and a
Slitt in ye Left, being formerly ye Marke
of William Macfashion upon Edistoe-Island,
& by him Assign'd to ye s^d ffripp for all
Cattle & Hoggs on ye s^d Island of that
Marke   Tes^t Henry Wigington

(To be continued)

HISTORICAL NOTES

VALUE OF THE OFFICE OF PUBLIC TREASURER IN 1776—The case of Henry Peronneau may be found printed in the *Second Report, Ontario Archives*, 1904, Part II, p 1201

He had been appointed Public Treasurer of South Carolina in 1770 to succeed Mr Jacob Motte, whose daughter he had married, and in 1771 Benjamin Dart was made with him a joint-holder of the office

On 26 March, 1776, he was dispossessed of the office by the adoption of the Constitution on that date, and he paid over to the "Rebel Governor Rutledge" the balance of the public moneys then in his hands   Refusing to take the "Oath of Allegiance and Abjuration," he was imprisoned and in April, 1777, he was banished from the State and went to Holland, and thence to England

From the British Treasury he received an allowance of £200 per annum, dating from 1 January, 1778; but when Charles Town was taken by Sir Henry Clinton in 1781, he was ordered to return   Arriving there on 3 June, 1781, he remained until the evacuation in December, 1782, and during this period held a little office of the value of 10 Shillings a day

He stated the loss of the office at £800 per annum and that this arose from 2½ per cent on all sums paid in and out of the Treasury

His brother, Robert Peronneau, testified as to the emoluments of the office, and estimated the commissions of 2½ per cent on moneys received and paid out at £500 per annum, while the fees of 5 shillings each for entering and 20 shillings each for clearing ships amounted to about £400. These emoluments were independent of interest, which amounted to at least £1000 more

The witness recollected no commission on taxes

Mr Robert William Powell testified that the reputed income of the Treasurer's office was £2000 per annum, of which Mr Peronneau had the half

The Board allowed Mr Peronneau £400 per annum for the half profits of the office of Treasurer, but apparently off-set this partially by the allowance from the Treasury of £200 per annum   From the statements of this case the items only have been abstracted which go to show the value of this office at that period, but the case is full of interest in other respects

The valuations seem all to have been made in Sterling
(*Contributed by D E Huger Smith*)

RICE SHIPMENTS IN 1743—The following letter in the possession of this Society, is from a firm of merchants in Charles Town to their London agent, and is of interest because it gives the value of rice and the freight charges, for that year

[*Addressed*]   To
              Mr James Pearce
                    In
                        London
    ⅌Capt Chads
          Q D C
                        Charles Town 8th July 1743
Mr James Pearce
              The Foregoing is third Copy of what we had the favour of writing you the 16th ultimo, since which we have not had any of your further favours, this God Willing Comes Handed to you by the Ship Grayhound Thomas Perkins master, and Covers invoice and Bill of Lading, for one Hundred and fifty barrells of Rice shiped on the same for our account and risque   Amounting to £1423 16 10 which be pleased to Dispose of to the best advantage and pass the proceeds to our Acco^t this parceel of Rice is very good, it has all been screened and we hope it will Keep its Collour and that the Quallitye will recommend it (if not other advantage) to a Quick Sale and that you will have but Little Trouble with it —Inclosed we remitt you M^r. David Montaguit [sic] first bill of Exchange for £20 Sterling on Messrs. Peter & H Simmonds of London payable to your order £15 10. thereof is for your and Company account and Exactly Ballances their account Current here annex'd, the remainder £4 10 . be pleased to pass to our Credit   We have Endeavoured to Dispose of the beans both by private and Publick Sale but Cant as yet

Effect it, no body would offer any thing for it   Rice is still at 30| and Freight for London at £4 ℔ ton, the Rice Crop on the Ground is very promising having Lately had fine Season, of Rain, and if we have the Like Continuence to the Earing Time we shall have a Large Crop, we shall advice you how it will prove, and as we have nothing further at present to offer, we take Leave to assure you of our best respects and are ————————

[*On the same sheet, in different hand*]

Charles Town 13 July 1743

Sir

In foregoing Copy of what we wrote you the 8ᵗʰ Curr' ℔ Capt Perkins who pass'd our Barr the 10ᵗʰ to wᶜʰ please to Lett us referr you, This Serving only to hand you another of his Bills of Lading for the 150 Barrels Rice as mentioned in Copy and Mʳ David Montaguit Second Bill of Exchange for £20 Sterᵍ in your favor on Messʳˢ Peter & H Simmonds, and is for account as is Express'd on the other side wᶜʰ being the present Needful we remain

Sir Your most Humble Serᵗˢ

Hill & Guerard

INDEX

INDEX

LIST OF PUBLICATIONS

OF THE

SOUTH CAROLINA HISTORICAL SOCIETY.

COLLECTIONS.

Vol. I., 1857, $3.00; Vol. II., 1858, $3.00; Vol. III 1859, out of print. Vol IV , 1887, unbound, $3.00, bound, $4.00; Vol. V., 1897, paper, $3.00.

PAMPHLETS.

Journal of a Voyage to Charlestown in So. Carolina by Pelatiah Webster in 1765. Edited by Prof. T. P. Harrison, 1898
75c.

The History of the Santee Canal By Prof. F. A. Porcher. With an Appendix by A. S. Salley, Jr., 1903.
75c.

THE SOUTH CAROLINA HISTORICAL AND GENEALOGICAL MAGAZINE.

Volume I, 1900, Edited by A. S. Salley, Jr. Complete Volume.
$10.00

Single copies of Nos. 2-4,
$1.25 each.

Volume II to IX, 1901-1908, Edited by A. S. Salley, Jr.
Unbound $5 00 each.

Volume X to XII, 1909-1911, Edited by Mabel L. Webber.
Unbound $5 00 each.

Single copies of No. 4, Vol. XI, $2.50 each. Members get a discount of 25 per cent. on the above prices.

Address: South Carolina Historical Society,
Charleston. S C

THE
SOUTH CAROLINA
HISTORICAL AND GENEALOGICAL
MAGAZINE

PUBLISHED QUARTERLY BY THE

SOUTH CAROLINA HISTORICAL SOCIETY

EDITED BY
MABEL LOUISE WEBBER

VOLUME XIV.

PRINTED FOR THE SOCIETY BY
WALKER, EVANS & COGSWELL CO.
CHARLESTON, S. C.

OFFICERS

OF THE

SOUTH CAROLINA HISTORICAL SOCIETY,

MAY 19, 1911—MAY 19, 1912

President,

HON JOSEPH W. BARNWELL

1st Vice-President,

HON HENRY A M SMITH,

2nd Vice-President,

HON THEODORE D JERVEY

3d Vice-President

HON. F. H WESTON

4th Vice-President,

HON JOHN B CLEVELAND

Secretary and Treasurer and Librarian,

MISS MABEL LOUISE WEBBER

Curators

LANGDON CHEVES, ESQ,   D E HUGER SMITH, ESQ,

CHARLES W KOLLOCK, M D,

PROF. YATES SNOWDEN,   CAPT. THOMAS PINCKNEY.

PROF. C. J. COLCOCK,   M ALSTON READ, ESQ,

A. S. SALLEY, JR., ESQ.,   HENRY S HOLMES, ESQ

Board of Managers,

ALL OF THE FOREGOING OFFICERS

Publication Committee,

HENRY A M SMITH,   JOSEPH W BARNWELL,

A. S SALLEY, JR

THE

SOUTH CAROLINA

HISTORICAL AND GENEALOGICAL

MAGAZINE

PUBLISHED QUARTERLY BY THE

SOUTH CAROLINA HISTORICAL SOCIETY

CHARLESTON, S. C.

VOLUME XIV., NO. 1,   JANUARY 1913.

PRINTED FOR THE SOCIETY BY
WALKER, EVANS & COGSWELL CO
CHARLESTON, S. C.
1913

PUBLICATION COMMITTEE.

Joseph W. Barnwell,   Henry A M Smith,
                A S. Salley, Jr

EDITOR OF THE MAGAZINE.
Mabel L Webber

CONTENTS

N B—These Magazines, with the exception of No 1
of Vol I, are $1 25 to any one other than a member of the
South Carolina Historical Society   Members of the Society receive them free   The Membership fee is $4 00 per
annum (the fiscal year being from January to January),
and members can buy back numbers or duplicates at $1 00
each   In addition to receiving the Magazines, members are
allowed a discount of 25 per cent on all other publications
of the Society, and have the free use of the Society's library
    Any member who has not received the last number
will please notify the Secretary and Treasurer,
                        Miss Mabel L Webber,
            South Carolina Historical Society,
                        Charleston, S C

The South Carolina Historical and Genealogical Magazine.

VOL. XIV   JANUARY, 1913   No 1

AN ACCOUNT OF
THE TATTNALL AND FENWICK FAMILIES
IN SOUTH CAROLINA

By D E Huger Smith

Strolling through the hospital at Greenwich in England, I once found myself in what was called the "Painted Hall," a gallery filled with portraits of Naval Commanders and pictures of sea-fights

Although the only visitor, I was not alone. An ancient mariner in his seaman's dress stood at attention and volunteered no information, but answered courteously my few questions When passing out of the Hall, I stopped to thank him, and I noticed that his breast was covered with service-medals and clasps He carried there as many of bronze as Field-Marshal Roberts might show of gold.

This easy way of rewarding a veteran has always amused me, and I asked what war or battle each one represented The old man's "bosom swelled with pride" as he answered

One, he said, had been gained at the fight with the Peiho Forts.

"The Peiho?," said I.

"Yes! don't you know that it was there that the American Commodore said, 'Blood is thicker than water!,' when he towed our boats into action?" Thereupon the old sailor

went on with a full narrative of the event, and I learned
how Commodore Tattnall had been ordered to take no part
in the attack, how the British Admiral changed his flag
four times, from ship to ship, as each was disabled, how
he lay badly wounded on the deck of his third flag-ship;
how his reserve force in boats could not stem the tide to
reach him; how an officer from these boats visited the
American Commodore, who cried out, "Well! blood is
thicker than water!," and towed the boats up the river

All of this I have since read more at large, but the account by Lieutenant Johnston [see Jones' Life of Tattnall]
has never displaced from my memory the unpolished narrative of the old British Tar, and his pleasure in telling of
the timely use of the old proverb that "blood is thicker than
water"

THE TATTNALL FAMILY

Commodore Tattnall's family connections in South Carolina were of the best   We find under date of the "13th day
of the 11th month of 1687" that James Beamer devised to
his step-son Joseph Tattnall certain property to be delivered
to him at the age of twenty-one, and we are left in doubt
whether Mrs Beamer's first husband ever came to this
country

Joseph Tattnall married Martha Patey, the daughter
of Edward Patey by his wife Elizabeth Gibbes   This
Elizabeth Gibbes was the daughter of Thomas Gibbes, an
elder brother of Robert Gibbes, Governor of Carolina,
1709-1712 [See McCrady's Proprietary Government]

Edward Patey was the son of Theophilus Patey, and one
of his sisters, Sarah, had married Robert Fenwick   Another, Elizabeth, was the wife of Major John Boone, of
whom there are many descendants

Martha Patey was certainly unmarried on 4th February,
1706, for on that date a grant of land on James Island was
made to her under her maiden name   This land was conveyed on 10th October, 1709, to William Rivers by her
husband, Joseph Tattnall, and herself, and we can thus fix
at   the

We cannot fix the date of his death, but in 1727 we find his widow, Martha, bearing the name of a third husband, Hext, while acting as administratrix of the estate of her second husband, Michael Beresford

All of this is confirmed by the will of M⁣ʳˢ Sarah Fenwick (widow of Robert Fenwick) dated 26ᵗʰ January, 1726/7 She makes bequests to Thomas Tattnall, son of her niece, Martha Hext, and to Michael Beresford, of whom the survivor was to inherit from the other This Michael Beresford was the half-brother of Thomas Tattnall, who speaks in his will, dated 20ᵗʰ March, 1743, of a bequest to his son by that son's uncle, Michael Beresford

No opinion can be given as to the correct spelling of the name. It is written Tatnell or Tatnall in the earlier wills and deeds In the will of Thomas *Tatnell*, recorded in Charles Town in 1746, it is spelled as given. After the removal of his son Josiah to Georgia, it is generally spelled *Tattnall*

This son Josiah, seems to have grown up in what is now called Beaufort County, among his mother's relations She was Elizabeth Barnwell, a daughter of Col John Barnwell, who settled in South Carolina about 1701, and left a name metaphorically written across the history of that colony until his death in 1724 [See South Carolina Hist & Gen Magazine, Vol II. p 47]

St. Andrew's Parish Register gives the marriage of Thomas Tatnell and Elizabeth Barnwell on 25ᵗʰ April, 1734

The compiler of St Helena's Register has given us 8ᵗʰ Feb, 1740, as the date of birth of Josiah, son of Thomas and Elizabeth Tattnell of Stono The same birth is given in St Philip's Register as on 1ˢᵗ Feb, 1739/40, and this is probably the correct date, as his baptism on 27ᵗʰ Feb, 1739/40, is there recorded. In this he is called "Josias" In St Helena's Register his marriage to Mary Mullryne is given, as well as the birth of a son John Mullryne Tattnell

This Mary Mullryne was born 19ᵗʰ October, 1741 [St Helena's Register] and was the daughter of Col John Mullryne and of Claudia, his wife John Mullryne had some time before 1735 come to Carolina from Montserrat. one ⟨illegible⟩ 35.

he married in St Andrew's Parish Claudia Cattell, the daughter of John and Catherine Cattell.

Josiah Tattnall is said to have followed his father-in-law, Col Mullryne, to Savannah, soon after 1762, and his second son, Josiah, is said to have been born at Bonaventure, the beautiful seat of his grandfather   The career of this son, Josiah, forms a good part of the early State history of Georgia, and need not be narrated here   His marriage to Harriet Fenwick is to be found in the South Carolina Gazette of 9th February, 1786—"a few days ago married, etc "

Of this marriage was born, on 9th November, 1795, Commodore Josiah Tattnall, whose "Life and Services" have been well written by Charles Colcock Jones, Jr

THE FENWICK FAMILY

Harriet Fenwick, wife of Josiah Tatnall, Jr, was the daughter of the Hon Edward Fenwick, who in 1747 was made a member of His Majesty's Council in South Carolina   He married 1st Martha Izard, daughter of Hon Ralph Izard, by whom he had a daughter, Elizabeth   This daughter became the wife of John Barnwell, a grandson of John Barnwell heretofore mentioned, on 30th January, 1766, and died within the year, leaving no issue   [See South Carolina Hist and Gen Magazine, Vol II, pp 54-211]

Edward Fenwick married 2nd on 27th February, 1753, [see South Carolina Hist and Gen Mag , Vol X, p 231], Mary Drayton, the daughter of Thomas Drayton, by whom he had a numerous family.

By the kindness of Mr Charles E Jackson, a descendant, I am able to extract from a genealogical table the following list of their children

1 Edward Fenwick b 12 Dec , 1753
2 John Fenwick, b 12 Aug , 1755
3 Sarah, b 3 Dec , 1756
4 Mary, b 7 Jan , 1757
5 Thomas, b 19 Dec , 1758
6 Martha b 15 Jan , 1760   .

8   Charlotte Elizabeth, b 4 Nov , 1762
9   Selina, b 18 April, 1764.
10 Robert William, b. 16 May, 1765
11 Charlotte, b 21 July, 1766.
12 Matilda, b 12 Dec 1767
13 Harriette [sic], b 5 Mar , 1769
14 George, b 5 Jan , 1771
15 John Roger, b 13 Jan , 1773

The same table gives the date of Edward Fenwick's birth as 22 Jan., 1726, and of his death as 8th July, 1775 [Note, the Gazette gives this as 7 July, 1775] Also Mary Drayton's birth is given as 21 Dec , 1735, and her marriage date as 19 Feb , 1753 [Note, St Andrew's Register gives her birth as on 21 Dec , 1734, and her baptism on 4th Feb., 1734/5, while Col Hayne gives her marriage as on 27th Feb , 1753]

In the Gazette of 21st July, 1775, there is a rather full notice of the death of Hon Edward Fenwick His remains were brought from New York to Charles Town for interment [See South Carolina Hist & Gen Mag , Vol XIII. p. 64.]

His will, dated 15th April, 1775, with a codicil 2nd June, 1775, was proved on 5th August 1775 It mentions the following children

Sons Edward, Thomas, Robert William, George, John Roger
Daughters Sarah, Mary, Martha, Selina, Charlotte, Matilda, Harriet

His widow, M[rs] Mary Fenwick, married on 18 Feb , 1776, John William Gerard de Brahm, an engineer officer of distinction in the service of the Crown and of the Colonies of South Carolina and Georgia [See South Carolina Hist. and Gen. Mag , Vol XI , p 160.]

Mary de Brahm's will, recorded in Charleston, is dated 20 May, 1805, and was proved on 27th March, 1806 She describes herself as of Charleston, the widow of John William Gerard de Brahm, and mentions in her will her daugh her daughter, Martha Gadsden, her grand-daughter, Mary Edwardina Fenwick, her nephew, Jacob Drayton; the grandson of her late husband, de Brahm, Frederick Wm Mulcaster; four nieces of said husband, viz Marie Wallburgh de Brahm, Francesca de Brahm, Baroness de Wenz, and Ann Louisa de Brahm, who are said to have lost their whole property by the ravages of war; her daughter, Selina Fenwick, her grand-daughter, Claudia Tattnall; her son, John Roger Fenwick; she leaves Matilda Giles one shilling in lieu of any claims against her estate; to Thomas Sparks of Exeter, G B., and to Thomas Thompson of Nether Compton in Dorsetshire, a piece of plate each, to the Charleston Orphan House a bequest

Her daughter, Selina Fenwick is made sole executrix, and in case of her death, then her son, John Roger Fenwick

JOHN WILLIAM GERARD DE BRAHM

Mary Drayton's second husband, de Brahm, is said to have been a Captain in the service of the Emperor before coming to America   In 1751 he aided in establishing a colony of Germans at Bethany in Georgia   In 1755 he was employed by South Carolina to reconstruct the fortifications of Charles Town, and thenceforward was constantly engaged in important military engineering and surveying work   In 1756 he assisted in building Fort Loudon on the western slope of the Appalachian mountains   In 1757 he fortified Savannah, and erected a fort at Ebenezer, and in the same year he combined his surveys with those of Lt Gov Bull, to which we owe the first comprehensive map of South Carolina and Georgia   In 1761 he constructed Fort George on Cockspur Island in the Savannah River In 1764 he was appointed His Majesty's Surveyor General for the Southern District of North America, and in 1765 was engaged in further survey of the Atlantic and Gulf coasts   When Sir Henry Clinton and Sir Peter Parker made their attack upon Charles Town in 1776, we are told that Capt de Brahm had erected on the eastern end of Sullivan's Island the breastwork and battery behind

which Col Thomson (of the South Carolina Continentals)
foiled the British General's attempt to cross Breach Inlet—
an important part of what is known as the battle of Fort
Moultrie   [See McCrady, 1775-80, p 145, and Weston's
"Documents connected with So Ca", p 204]

De Brahm must have removed to Philadelphia towards
the end of his life, for, on 29th July, 1791, in a conveyance
by himself and Mary his wife, he is described as "of Philadelphia, late of Charleston."

THE CHILDREN OF EDWARD FENWICK

Before entering on an account of the children of Edward
Fenwick, I give here an abstract of a deed recorded in the
Mesne Conveyance Office (Book A 8, p 225) and dated
1 August, 1785, conveyance by the Master in Equity to
Arthur Middleton   *   *   *   Whereas William Gerard
de Brahm of Charleston, Esq, and Mary his wife, late
widow of Edward Fenwick esq dec'd, and Mary, Martha,
Selina, Charlotte, Matilda, and Harriet Fenwick, infants
under 21, by Mary de Brahm, their mother and next friend,
did on or about 10 May, 1777, exhibit their Bill of Com-
plaint against Robert Gibbes and John Gibbes, the only
qualified executors of the last will of Edward Fenwick;
and also against Edward Fenwick and Thomas Fenwick
(then an infant under 21) by Robert Gibbes his guardian,
devisees under the will of their father, said Edward Fenwick   *   *   *   *   and whereas Macartan Campbell of
Charleston, Esq and Sarah his wife one of the daughters
of said Edward Fenwick, and Thomas Gadsden and Martha his wife, another of his daughters, and Walter Izard
Esq, late husband of Mary, now deceased, another of his
daughters, and William Leigh Pierce and Charlotte his
wife, another of his daughters   *   *   *   did about 22
December, 1784, file their supplemental Bills   *   *   *   *
did adjudge that the remainder of Thomas Fenwick's estate be sold   *   *   *   *

[Note—The wording of the deed has not been closely
followed]

Sarah, the eldest daughter of Hon Edward Fenwick, married in February, 1777, Macartan Campbell. [So Ca. Hist and Gen Mag, Vol XI., p 162]

He bought from his brother-in-law, Edward Fenwick, on 16 July, 1777, the Hon Edward Fenwick's residence on the lower part of Meeting Street. The lot still measures, as described in the conveyance, 132 feet on the street and runs through to Church Street, and on it stands the large house built by the late Mr George W Williams   Mr Campbell's will, dated 13 Nov, 1793, and proved in Richmond Co, Georgia, on 21st December, 1793, describes him as of Augusta and speaks of Charles Cotesworth Pinckney and Charles Drayton as the trustees of his wife Sarah

M^{rs}. Sarah Campbell married 2nd D^r. George Jones of a distinguished family in Savannah   She left issue by both marriages

Mr Macartan Campbell conveyed on 1 September, 1788, the Fenwick residence on Meeting Street to Col Charles Pinckney   .

Mary Fenwick, the second daughter of Edward Fenwick, married in November, 1779, Walter Izard, son of Ralph Izard and a brother of Lady William Campbell, whose husband was the last royal governor of South Carolina

Mrs Izard pre-deceased her husband and left no issue [See So Ca Hist and Gen Mag., Vol II, p 234]

Martha Fenwick, the third daughter of Edward Fenwick, married about 15 October, 1778, Thomas Gadsden, Captain in 1st Regiment South Carolina Continentals   [See So Ca Hist and Gen Mag, Vol XI, p 167]

Captain Gadsden was a son of Gen Christopher Gadsden, a most distinguished personage of the Revolution He pre-deceased his father, dying in 1791, when his will was proved   The will of Gen Gadsden, proved in 1805, mentions Martha Gadsden, the widow of his late son, Thomas, and directs that four shares of certain property be given to his son Thomas' children

Selina Fenwick, the fourth surviving daughter of Hon Edward Fenwick, was still unmarried at the date of her mother's will (1805)

Charlotte Fenwick, the fifth surviving daughter of Hon Edward Fenwick, married 1st William Leigh Pierce

From Heitman's Continental Officers we learn that he was from Virginia and was commissioned a Captain in 1st Regiment Continental Artillery on 30 November, 1776, and that he served on the staff of Gen Greene until the end of the war

After the Battle of Eutaw Springs Congress voted him a sword "in testimony of his particular activity and good conduct" during that action   In Gibbes' Documentary History may be found a letter from him signed William Pierce, Jr , Aide-de-Camp

He must have settled in Georgia soon after the Revolution, for in 1787 he sat as a delegate from that State to the Convention that framed the Constitution of the United States

Charlotte Fenwick's second husband was Ebenezer Jackson   Heitman gives Massachusetts as his State   He was commissioned 2nd Lieutenant of 3rd Continental Artillery on 27th June, 1781   He served to 3rd November 1783   Mrs Jackson's daughter, Harriet Jackson, became in 1821 the wife of Commodore Tattnall, her first cousin

Of Matilda Fenwick little is known   She is mentioned in her mother's will (1805) as Matilda Giles   Robert Giles in his will, proved in 1803 mentions his wife Matilda, with apparently no children by her

Harriet Fenwick, the seventh surviving daughter of Hon Edward Fenwick, married Josiah Tattnall, Jr , in 1786, the marriage appearing in the Gazette of 9th February   Her husband, Governor Tattnall died in 1804

We come now to the surviving sons of Edward Fenwick   Two of the five, viz   Robert William and George, probably died before 1785, for the petition of Robert Gibbe   he

Court of Chancery, requests that one-third of certain property be allotted to testator's son, John Roger, another to the representatives of Robert William, and the remaining third to the representatives of George This petition complains of the injury to the three minor sons by the misconduct of Edward and his brother Thomas "when the British Army came into this State in the year of our Lord 1779" [See So Ca Hist and Gen Mag, Vol VIII, p 222]

In Moultrie's Memoirs, Vol I, pp 122-123, we are told that in 1776, 3d Feby, it was ordered by the Provincial Congress that the wife and daughter of Capt John Stuart, the Superintendent of Indian Affairs, be restrained from absenting themselves from his home in Charles Town, but that on 2d February Mr Fenwick obtained "leave to take his wife into the country" Somewhat later Mrs Stuart escaped, and Mr Fenwick was sent to gaol on suspicion of aiding her This was clearly Edward Fenwick, although the index of McCrady's volume, 1775-1780, calls the lady Mrs *Thomas* Fenwick, which could hardly be correct, as Thomas was only seventeen years old at the time

But McCrady is probably right in stating that it was Thomas who guided the British in their attack on Captains Matthews and Barnwell on John's Island in 1779; and it seems certain that it was Thomas, who, as Col Fenwick of the British Militia, was captured by Col Harden at Pocotaligo Harden, under date of 18th April, 1781, gives a detailed account of this and other matters connected with his capture of Fort Balfour [See Gibbes' Documentary History, 1781-1782, pp 53, 54, 55]

In the lists pertaining to the Confiscation Act of 1782 Edward Fenwick is found among those who congratulated Lord Cornwallis upon his success at Camden in 1780, while Thomas Fenwick was banished and his estates declared confiscated because he held a military commission under the Crown By an Act of Assembly, on 24 March, 1785, Edward Fenwick's property was restored to him, but he was required to leave the State within a year Nothing is now

The career of John Roger Fenwick, described as of South Carolina is thus given by Heitman

2nd Lieutenant Marine Corps 10 Nov , 1799 ,
1st Lieutenant, 1 December, 1801 ;
Captain, 13th August, 1809 ;
Resigned, 1 April, 1811 ;
Commissioned Lieutenant Colonel Light Artillery 2 Dec , 1811 ;
Brevet Colonel and Adjutant General, 18 March, 1813 to 15 June, 1815 ,
Colonel 4th Artillery 1 June, 1821 ,
Brevet Brig General 18 March, 1823 , died 19th March, 1842

HON JOHN FENWICK

The father of Hon Edward Fenwick was Hon John Fenwick

In an appendix to Jones' "Life and Services of Commodore Tattnall" there is printed a letter dated London, 27 July, 1726, from Edward Fenwick, a merchant of London, and a brother of Col John Fenwick This letter is addressed to Roger Fenwick Esq , of County Cork, Ireland, and is intended to give an account of the name and family

To the lineal descent there given have been added the marriages from the family record in America

William Fenwick of Stanton, born at Stanton in Northumberland, 22 September, 1581
Edward Fenwick of Stanton, born at Stanton, 29 October, 1606, died 14 August, 1689, married Sarah Neville
Robert Fenwick, a younger son of Edward, married Ann Culcheth
Hon John Fenwick of South Carolina youngest son of Robert, died probably in 1747, as his will was proved in London, 23 July, 1747; married Elizabeth Gibbes, daughter of Gov Robert Gibbes of South Carolina
Hon Edward Fenwick, died July, 1775, married 1st Martha Izard, 2nd Mary Drayton.

The families of Neville and Culcheth are well known in the north of England, where branches of the first named have been ever found among the great noble families. When the High Constable heard the famous suit between Le Scrope and Grosvenor, as to their respective rights to the arms "Azure, a bend or," a certain Gilbert de Culcheth was one among the many gentlemen called to bear witness in the case. Chaucer, too, was a witness, and it is perhaps due to this fact that the frescoes in the drawing-rooms at Eaton Hall show his Canterbury Pilgrims, while a great mantel-piece in the hall bears a bas-relief of the scene of the trial.

At what date John Fenwick came to South Carolina is not known, but it was about the beginning of the eighteenth century. During the French invasion of 1706 he commanded a company of militia and, with Capt Cantey, destroyed at Wando Neck a party of the invaders, and captured at Hobcaw, some days later, another party [See McCrady's Proprietary Government, pp 398-399-400.] That it was John Fenwick and not his contemporary Robert Fenwick would seem to be settled by an Act of 19 July, 1707, which names, among the Commissioners for regulating the Indian trade, Mr. [sic] Robert Fenwick and Major [sic] John Fenwick.

The relationship between the two is not known.

John Fenwick was a planter and merchant with a business on a large scale, but like other men of that day he found time to serve the public in many capacities.

When the Commons House of South Carolina, on 7 August 1712, decided to send a second expedition to assist the North Carolinians in the Tuscarora War, we find him on a committee to advise with Col John Barnwell as to the best means of so doing, and also to suggest a commander. In the course of the discussion between the Commons and the Council, Governor Craven finally suggested Fenwick himself, or else James Moore, and the latter was chosen [In So Ca Hist and Gen Mag, Vol X, may be found an excellent account of this expedition, by Hon Joseph W Barnwell]

In 1721 Col Fenwick was appointed an Associate Justice. [McCrady's Royal Government, p 802]

In 1730 he was appointed a member of His Majesty's Council in South Carolina, and in the Gazette of 26th June, 1740, there is a notice of his promotion to the rank of Major-General and of the appointment of Col. Charles Pinckney to the command of his regiment

In the So Ca. Hist. and Gen Mag, Vol VII, p 27, there is an abstract of John Fenwick's will, dated 27th Feb, 1745/6 and proved in London, 2 July, 1747. He mentions his son-in-law, Isaac Whittington Esq, his kinsman, Robert Fenwick, of Lincoln's Inn—his late brother, Edward Fenwick Esq—his daughter, Deloraine—his daughter, Sarah—his son, Edward Fenwick   A codicil on same day mentions his brother-in-law, Col. John Gibbes, and Andrew Rutledge Esq., both of South Carolina—his nephew, Culcheth Golightly of South Carolina—his nephew, John Gibbes, son of his late brother-in-law, William Gibbes—and his grandson, John Scott   The administration of the will was granted 23 July, 1747, to the Right Hon Elizabeth, Countess dowager of Deloraine, the daughter of the deceased   Administration was also granted 2 Nov, 1749, to Edward Fenwick Esq

The nephew mentioned, Culcheth Golightly, died in South Carolina in 1749, leaving two daughters and co-heiresses, who married respectively, Maj Benjamin Huger, killed in front of Charles Town in 1779, and William Henry Drayton, who died a member of Congress in Philadelphia in 1779

The Countess of Deloraine was Elizabeth Fenwick, who had married at Charles Town, on 11th August, 1734, the Hon Henry Scott, Captain of His Majesty's Ship Seaford [See St Philip's Reg']

When James, Duke of Monmouth and Buccleugh, was beheaded on 15 July, 1685, in pursuance of an Act of attainder without further trial, his title of Duke of Monmouth became consequently extinct   He had married the heiress of the Scotts of Buccleugh, and, as his wife held in

her own right the peerage of Buccleugh, her title was not
affected by his attainder   Lord Henry Scott, the second
son of the unhappy Monmouth, was created Earl of Deloraine by Queen Anne, in 1708   His eldest son, the second
Earl, died without issue, and was succeeded by his brother,
Captain the Hon. Henry Scott, whose son Henry became
the 4th Earl, and at his death in 1807 the title became
extinct.   [See Collins' Peerage, III, p. 388.]

Hon John Fenwick's wife, Elizabeth Gibbes, was born
4 Feb, 1691   Her mother's name is not now known   It is
interesting to remember that she was the first cousin of
M"° Patey, the mother of M"° Joseph Tattnall, from whom
is descended the Tattnall family   [For a genealogy of the
descendants of Gov Gibbes see So Ca Hist and Gen
Mag, Vol XII, p 78]

THE EARLY DRAYTONS

Mary Drayton, the wife of Hon Edward Fenwick, was
born 21 December, 1734 [St Andrew's Reg'] and was the
daughter of Thomas Drayton by his wife Elizabeth Bull
The immigrant of this Drayton family came to South
Carolina from Barbadoes
  a   There is recorded in Columbia the recital of a land
warrant to Thomas Drayton, dated 18 May, 1678, and of
the grant dated 2 November, 1678, of 200 acres on New-
town Creek
  b   Hotten, in "The Original Lists, etc," under date of
25th April, 1679, mentions the sailing in the ship Mary
from Barbadoes to Carolina of Thomas Drayton, Jr, and
in the same ship came Stephen Fox
  c   On 12 May, 1699, Thomas Drayton and Elizabeth his
wife conveyed to Stephen Fox 300 acres on Stono, and one
of the witnesses to this deed was Thomas Drayton, Jr.
  d   In the Probate Court in Charleston is recorded the
granting of the administration with will annexed of the
estate of Thomas Drayton to Thomas Drayton, with Steph-
en Fox joining in the administration bond
  e   On 16 August, 1703 Thomas Drayton and his wife,
Ann conveyed 154 acres on Pon-pon

i An Elizabeth Drayton is recorded in St Philip's Reg'
as having been buried on 12th May, 1722

For the facts marked a, c and e we are indebted to M'
Drayton Hastie, who found them recorded in Columbia

Unluckily the wills of Thomas Drayton (1700) and of
Stephen Fox have not been found, and without further information we can only make inconclusive surmises on the
following points:

1st Was Thomas Drayton to whom a grant was made
in 1678 identical with the Thomas Drayton, Jr, who came
to Carolina in the ship Mary in 1679?

2nd. Was Thomas Drayton, Jr., who came to Carolina in
1679 identical with the Thomas Drayton, Jr, who witnessed a deed in 1699?

3rd. Was the Thomas Drayton, who died about 1700 that
Thomas to whom there was a grant in 1678, and whose
wife was probably Elizabeth, and/or was he the Thomas,
Jr, who arrived in the Mary?

4th Was Thomas, the administrator in 1700, the
Thomas, Jr., who came in the Mary, and/or the Thomas
who married Ann and died in 1717?

5th. Was Ann's maiden name Fox or Booth, or was her
husband's mother born Fox?

6th The first four queries may be reduced to one—were
there *two* or *three* Thomas Draytons in Carolina down to
and including him, who married Ann and died in 1717?

In considering this question No 6, it must be remem-
bered that all of Thomas and Ann's children *seem* to have
been born after 1700; and that, if we assume the husband
of Ann to be identical with Thomas, Jr, who arrived here
in 1679 as a grown man, he must have been quite advanced
in life when he married Ann

As a strictly temporary hypothesis it may be conjectured
that the Thomas of the grant in 1678, the Thomas, Jr, of
the Mary in 1679, the Thomas of the conveyance in 1699,
and the Thomas of the administration in 1700 were all one
and the same man: and that the Thomas, Jr, who witnessed
in 1699, the Thomas who was the administrator in 1700,
and the Thomas, husband of Ann, dying about 1717, were
identical

This conjecture reduces the number to two, and leaves it an open question whether they were father and son, and which (if either) married a daughter (or sister) of Stephen Fox Nothing appears to sustain the suggestion that Ann Drayton, the wife of Thomas (1717), was a daughter of Fox, beyond the fact that Thomas Drayton had a son and a grandson who bore the name, Stephen Fox Drayton In the absence of proof, it is of course possible that his mother may have been a Fox.

The assertion that Ann Drayton, the wife of Thomas (1717), was born Booth is made in a family chart shown by a descendant of her grand-daughter, Mary Drayton, who married Hon Edward Fenwick This is supported in a measure by the fact that M" Ann Drayton in her will (proved 1742), mentions her grand-daughter, Ann Booth Fuller (Query Was the one named after the other?) Further, M" Ann Drayton makes Thomas Elliott, Sr , an executor and trustee for her daughter M" Fuller Now this Thomas Elliott, Sr , (born 1699 and died 1760) was the son of Thomas Elliott, who with Thomas Booth, were called his brothers by William Cooke in his will, proved 23 Jan' , 1689 These facts *may* indicate that M" Drayton was born Booth, with possibly also an Elliott origin [For Thomas Elliott's family see So Ca Hist and Gen Mag , Vol XI, p 57]

The first wife of Thomas Drayton (son of Thomas and Ann) was Elizabeth Bull, who was a daughter of William Bull, (Lieut -Governor from 1738 to his death in 1755), by his wife Mary Quintyne

William Bull, born 1683, died 21 March, 1755, was the son of the no less eminent Stephen Bull, one of the first settlers of South Carolina His wife, Mary Quintyne, was the daughter of Richard Quintyne (died 1695) and his wife, Elizabeth Edward, who married later Thomas Nairne, who was murdered at the outbreak of the Yemassee War in 1715 M" Nairne died 9 March, 1721, and lies buried at St Andrew's Church

William Bull's daughter Elizabeth was born 9 March, 1712/13 and married Thomas Drayton 26 Dec , 1730 Her sister, Charlotte Bull, married as his 2nd wife on 14 Nov., 1741, (Hon) John Drayton, a brother of her sister's husband. [See Bull Genealogy by Langdon Cheves, So Ca Hist and Gen Mag , Vol 1, p 76, also St. Andrew's Reg^r]

Thomas Drayton's 2nd wife was Lady Mary Clarke, born Mackenzie, widow of Captn Clarke and daughter of George, Earl of Cromartie, whom he married in 1757   Her father had been convicted of high treason after the rebellion of 1745, but the death sentence was remitted by the King Lady Mary married later John Ainslie, and her last husband was Henry Middleton (sometime President of the Continental Congress) whom she married in January, 1776, and by whom she had no issue   She died at sea in 1788, returning from England to Charleston.

REGISTER OF

ST ANDREW'S PARISH, BERKELEY COUNTY, SOUTH CAROLINA

1719-1774

Copied and Edited by MABEL L. WEBBER

(Continued from the October Number)

FUNERALS

James Parmenter School-master at Major Fullers   Buried
Sep[r] y[e] 15th 1740

Petter Goodman a Little boy under the care of M[r] Robinson Buried Octo[br]. y[e] 13th 1740

Elizabeth the Daughter of Thomas Drayton Esq & Elizabeth his wife Buried Nov[r]. y[e] 9th 1740

M[rs]. Sindiniah Boswood Buried Dec[r] y[e] 9th 1740

M[r] Robert Stansmore Buried Dec[r] y[e] 12, 1740   Died at
M[rs] Sereau's

Hester the Wife of James Carr Bur[d] Octo[br] y[e] 28 1740*

William Clay Buried Dec[r] y[e] 15th 1740

Sarah the wife of John Drayton Jun[r]   Buried De[br]. y[e] 24th
1740

Richard the Son of Richard Martin & his wife Buried Feb[ry]
y[e] 14th 1740†

Sindiniah Daughter of William Wood   Bur[d]   March y[e]
13 1740 †

Will[m] Viser Buried at M[rs] Hills April y[e] 1 1741

Benjamin Son of William Cattell Jun[r] & Anne his wife
Buried April y[e] 18th 1741

Maj[r] William Fuller Buried April y[e] 26, 1741

M[r]. John Purkis Buried May y[e] 23[d] 1741

Mary Daught[r] of James Manning & Sarah his wife Buried
July y[e] 7th 1741

Hanah the Daugh[tr] of John Rivers & Elizab[th] his wife
Buried July y[e] 8th 1741

---

*Inserted on blank side of page
†Ob... ...

Mr John Casper Young Buried July ye 30th 1741 bur^d from Mr Gorings

John Son of John Guerard & Eliz^{bth} his wife Buried August ye 24th 1741

Mary Williams Buried from M^r. Robinsons August ye 31-1741

Thomas Visser Bur^d at Mrs Hills he was the Son to Willm Visser Octo^{br} ye 9th 1741

William Son of William Walter & Mary his wife Bur^d Octo^{br} ye 10th 1741

Roger Saunders Buried Octo^{br} ye 13th 1741

Martha Daught^r of Mr John Guerard & Eliz his wife Bur^d Octo^{br} ye 22, 1741

Sabina the Wife of Robert Ladson Buried Nov^{br} ye 7th 1741

Charles ye Son of Thos Drayton & Elizabeth his Wife Buried Nov^{br} ye 10th 1741

Rebecca the wife of the Revd William Guy Buried Dec^{br} ye 1st 1741 p^r the Revd Mr Orr of St Pauls

CHRISTENINGS

Thomas Son of John Miles & Elizabeth his wife Bap^{tsd} June ye 21 1741 of St Pauls Parish

Margaret Daughter of Ditto Bap^{tsd}. June ye 21st 1741

John Son of John McIntosh & —— his wife Bap^d August ye 20th. 1741

Anne the Daught^r to John Cattell & Sarah his wife Bap^d August ye 21 1741

Charles the Son of Thos Drayton & Eliz^{bth} his wife August ye 31 1741

Willm Son of William Walter & Mary his wife Bap^{tsd} Sepr ye 4th 1741

Keziah the Daughter of William Rivers & Susanah-ffrances his wife Bap^d Nov^{br} ye 1 1741 James Island

Thomas Son of John & Mary free negroes formerly belonging to Mr John Godfrey Bap^d Novr ye 1 1741

Sabina Daughter of Robert Ladson & Sabina his wife Bap^d Nov^{br} ye 7th 1741 & born ye 5 Day

Charles Son of William Chapman & Mary his wife Bap^{td} Decr ye 11th 1741

Martha daughter of James Manning & Sarah his wife Bap^d
    Feb^ry ye 7th 1741/2

Sarah ye Daugh^r of John Champneys & Sarah his wife
    Bap^td Priv^t Bp^tm Febry ye 3 1741/2

Ralph the Son of Henry Izard & Marg^t his wife Bap^d
    Feb^ry ye 9th 1741/2

Ann the Daugh^t of Samuel Burgess & Mary his wife Bap^d
    Feb^ry ye 25th 1741/2 James's Island

Mary Daugh^t of Willm Chapman Junr & Mary his Wife
    Bap^tzd pr the Revd Mr Orr March ye 6 1741/2

Robert the Son of Jacob Ladson & Eliza^bth his wife Bapt^d
    May ye 11th 1742

Ralph Son of Henry Wood & Anne his wife Bap^td May y^e
    12th 1742

John Son of John Burford & Susanah his wife Bap^d May
    ye 12th 1742

Elizabeth Daugh^r of George Lee & Elizab^th his wife Bap^tzd
    May ye 23 1742

Elizabeth Daugh^tr of John & Eliz^bth Rivers Bap June y^e
    20th 1742

Robert the Son of Robert Rivers & Ann his Wife Bap^t
    August ye 8th 1742

Elizab^th the Daughter of Willm Boswood & Margaret his
    wife Bap^td August ye 17th 1742

Whitmarsh Son of Martha Fuller widow to Willm Fuller
    Deces^d Bap^td August ye 17th 1742

William Son of George Coock & Eliza^bth his wife Bapt^td
    August ye 27th 1742

Samuel Son of Sam^ll Maverick & Catherine his wife Bap^t
    [worn away] Sept^r ? 1742 James Island

Judith, an Adult negro woman & Seven of her Children
    Slaves belonging to Capt Richard Fuller Namely,
    { Mary   &c Bapt^td April ye 16 1742
    { Charles
    { Catherine
    { Abraham   adults
    { Phebe
      Judith
      Isaac

Likewise Saml [worn away] of Capt R^hd Fullers Bap^td
    April y [worn away]^th   ?

MARRIAGES pr the Revd Wm Guy

Thomas Hudson & Elizabeth Mell Sp^r Married p^r the Revd Mr Melechamp Octo^r ye 1741

William Godfrey & Ann Saxbey Sp^r Married p^r ye Rev^d W^m. Guy Octo^br ye 22 1741

John Drayton Junr & Charlotta Bull Sp^r Married Nov^m ye 14th 1741

Thomas Witter & Judith Banbury widow Married Nov^{mr} ye 26 1741

James Roulang & Catherine Boyden Married Decr ye 15th 1741

Joseph Robinson & Jone Merideth Sp^r Mar^d Feb^{ry} ye 4th 1741/2

John Bonetheau & Mary Banbury Sp^r Marr^d Feb^{ry} ye 25th 1741/2

David Stiles & Ann Reid Sp^r Marr^d May ye 6 1742

Isaac Ladson & Rachel-Ladson Perry Sp^r Marr^d May ye 20th 1742

Richard Wright & Mary Butler Sp^r Mar^d p^r The Revd Mr Guy May ye 25th 1742

Benja^n Perry & Susana Rawlings Spr Mar^d June ye 27th 1742

Willm Chapman & Margarett Parsons Sp^r Mar^d July ye 12th 1742

Allen Wells & Mary Joyce widow Marr^d July ye 22 1742

John Beswicke & Mary Hill Sp^r Married Nov^{br} ye 17th 1742

William Freeman & Jane Lewis widow Marr^d. Deb^r y^e 22^e 1742

John Page & Sarah Battoon widow married Feb^{ry} y^e 9th 1742*

Robert Ladson & Martha Ladson Sp^r Married Feb^{ry} y^e 10th 1742

Frances Ladson Sn^r & Margaret Musgrove widow Married June y^e 28th 1743

Thomas Wright & Elizabeth Bellinger Sp^r Married July y^e 17th 1743

_____

*17.1

John Goodin & Elizabeth Street widow, Mar^d August y^e 29th 1743

John Clark & Eliz^bth Bowman widow Marr^d Sep^tr y^e 10th 1743

Patrick Mol-holand & Anne More widow Marr^d Septr. y^e 14th 1743

William Ross & Anne-Booth Fuller Sp^r married Deb^r y^e 10th 1743

Richard Godfrey & Rebecca Guy Sp^r married p^r the Rev Mr Orr Jan^ry ye 31 1743†

John Smith & Mary Delony widow married Jan^ry ye 28th 1743†

FUNERALS P^r THE REV^d W^m GUY

Susannah the wife of Willm Gough School-Master on James Island Buried De^br ye 1 1741

Susanah the Daughter of Mary Delony Widow buried Jan^ry ye 17th 1741

Sarah the Wife of John Cattell S^nr Buried Jan^ry ye 20th 1741

Anne Drayton w'do^w Burd July ye 31 - 1742

Cap^n Robert Rivers Sn^r Buried Sepr ye 5th 1742 James Island

A Swis Servant boy belonging to Doct^r Bull Buried Sep^tr ye 13th 1742

Mary Wells Widow Buried Sepr ye 18th 1742

—— Son to Edwd Hussey & —— his wife Buried Sep^tr ye 19 1742

John Son of Cornelius Vangelder [?] & Eliz^bth his wife Burd 1742

Robt Bowman Bur^d Decr ye 21, 1742

Thomas Inns Buried Decr ye 27th 1742

Richard Clay Buried March ye 24th 1742/3

Mary Daugh^r of Doct^r John Lining & Sarah his wife Buried April ye 24th 1743

Ann the wife of William Cattell Junr Buried Augus^t ye 23^d 1743

Martha Daugh^r of James Manning & Sarah his wife Buried Sepr ye 6th 1743

†1744 new style

John Son of John Burford & Susanah his wife Buried
Sep^tr ye 15th 1743.

Thomas Lockyear Buried Octo^br 5th 1743

William Bowman Buried Octo^br 8

Thomas the Son of Thomas Holman & Mary his wife
Buried Octob^r ye 9th 1743

Thomas Fitch Buried Octob^r ye 19th 1743

Mary the wife of William Chapman Sn^r Buried Nov^br y^e
5th 1743

Martha the wife of Robert Ladson Burd Nov^br ye 10th 1743

Paul   a Swiss boy Servt to Dr Bull Buried De^br y^e
24th 1743.

Charlotta the wife John Drayton Junr Buried Janry ye 1st
1743†

Thomas Booth Buried Jan^ry y^e. 13th 1743/4

Sarah Daughter of James Manning & Sarah his wife Buried
Janr'y ye 21st 1743/4

George Cook Buried Jan^ry ye 22 1743†

Elizabeth Clay widow Buried March ye 23 1743†

Sarah Daught^r of Doct^r John Lining and Sarah his wife
Buried May ye 8th 1744

Elizabeth the wife of John Guerard Buried June ye 7th
1744

Benja^mn the Son of William Godfrey & Anne his wife
Buried Sepr ye 3 1744

CHRISTENINGS P^r THE REV^d M^r GUY

Malachi Son of William Branford & Ann his wife Bap^td
Sep^tr ye 8th 1742

Thomas the Son of Thomas Holman & Mary his wife
Bap^tzd Sep^tr ye 18th 1742.

Thomas the Son of John Man & Anne his wife Bap^td
Septr ye 19th 1742

Jane the Daught^r of William Cattell Junr & Anne his wife
Bap^td Octo^br. 4th 1742

Henry the Son of Thomas Tapley & Martha his wife Bap^td
Octo^br ye 25th 1742

---

†1744 new style

Zacharias Son of Zacheus Ladson & Sarah his wife Bapt^{zd}
    April ye 1st 1743

Sam^{el} & Charles [Samuel erased] Sons of Samuel Jones &
    Mary his wife Recev^d. in the Congregation May ye 1743

Abraham Son of Thos Radcliff & Eliz^{bth}. his wife Baptz^d
    May ye 29th 1743

Benjamin Son of William Godfrey & Anne his wife Bapt^{td}
    July ye 10th 1743

William Henry Son of John Drayton & Charlotta his wife
    Bapt^{zd} August ye 1st, 1743

Henrieta-Charlotta Daugh^r of Thomas Drayton & Eliza-
    beth his wife Bapt^{zd} August ye 1st 1743

Elizabeth Daugh^r of Isaac Ladson & Rachel his wife
    Bapt^{zl} August 16th 1743 Prv^t Bap^{tsm}

Sarah Daugh^r of Edwd Simpson & Sarah his wife Bap^{td}
    August ye 22 1743.

Mary-Ann Daugh^r of Mary a Negro Slave belonging to
    Capt Richard Fuller Bap^{td} August ye 22· 1743

William the Son of James Boswood & Martha his wife
    Bap^{td} August ye 26 1743

Thomas Son of Nicholas Wescoat & Mary his wife Bap^{ttd}.
    Sepr ye 5th 1743 James Island

Jemima Daugh^r of James Manning & Sarah his wife
    Bapt^{td} Sep^{tr} ye 6th 1743 Priv^t Baptism

Peeter the Son of Cornealus Vangelder & Eliza^{bth} his wife
    Bapt^{td} Sepr ye 25th 1743

Rebecca the Daught^r of William Chapman Junr & Mary
    his wife Bapt^{td} Jan^{ry} 1st. 1743/4

Charles the Son of John Drayton Junr & Charlotta his
    wife Bap^{trd} Jan^{ry} ye 15th 1743/4

Elizabeth the Daught^r of John Clerk & Eliz^{bth} his wife
    Bap^{td} Jan^{ry} ye 27th 1743*

Elizabeth the wife of William Butler Bap^{ttd} p^r Diping Feb^{ry}
    ye 29th 1743* (of St Pauls Parish)

BIRTHS

William-Henry Son of John Drayton and Charlotta his
    wife born   1742

Charles the Son of John Drayton Junr & Charlotta his

Rebecca the Daugh'' of William Chapman Jun' and Mary
  his wife born Nov'' y' 30'''. 1743

Elizabeth the Daugh' of John Clerk & Elizabeth his wife
  born Jan'' y' 3' 1743*

Anne the Daughter of Thomas Mell & Mary his wife Born
  May y' 23 1743

John Son of John Champneys & Sarah his wife Born Deb'.
  28''' 1743.

Jane & Mary Twins Daught'' of Thomas & Elizabeth
  juks born July y' 9''' 1743

Benjamin Son of Benjamin Perry & Susannah his wife
  born Jan'' y' 17''' 1743

Thomas Son of Robert Rivers and Anne his wife Born
  Feb'' y' 19''' 1743

Judith Dagh'' of Stephen Russel and Jane his wife Born
  Feb'' y' 1'' 1739 [sic]

William Son of William Rivers born June y' 3'. 1744

Jane y' Daugh' of John Deveaux & Sarah his wife Born
  March y' 6 1742

Susanah Daught' of John Rivers & Elizab''' his wife Born
  Octo''' y' 17''' 1744

Luci the Daught' of Will''' Walter & Mary his wife born
  May y' 14''' 1744

{ Maacah Daugh' of Zacheus Ladson & Sarah his wife
    Born Octo''' · y' 20''. 1739
  Zacahrias Son of D° Born April y' 4 1742
  Elizabeth Daugh'' of Zacheus Ladson & Sarah his wife
    Born Jan'' y' 22' 1743

Richard Son of John Burford & Susanah his wife born
  March y' 26 1744

Mary Daught' of Charles Cattell & Kathrine his wife born
  Dec''' y' 26''' 1744

Robert the Son of Frances Rose & Mary-Anne his wife
  born Jan'' y' 1'' 1744

Mary Daug'' of Richard Wright of S' Pauls parish Deceas' & Mary his wife born March y' 12''' 1744

William Son of Christoph' Guy & Mary his wife born
  March y' 23' 1744

William Son of William King and Susanah his wife born
  M . . . . :

Sarah Daugh^r of William Chapman Junr and Mary his
   wife Born [date omitted]
Anne Daugh^d of John Man & Anne his wife born August
   ye 11th 1745
Constance Daugh^r of William Reynolds & Elizabeth his
   wife (of St Helen's Parish) and James Son of Ibid born
   9th of March 1744

CHRISTENINGS P^r THE REV^d M^r GUY

Anne the Daughter of Thomas Mell & Mary his wife
   Bapt^{zd} March y^e . 3^d 1743*
Jemimah the Daught^r of James Maning Rec^d into the
   Congregation Bap^{tzd} before March ye 23 1743/4
Joseph a negro Man belonging to Mrs Perry Bapt^{zd} March
   ye 23 1743
Benjamin Son of Benjamin Perry Bap^{tzd} March ye 25th
   1744
Thos Son of Captⁿ Robert Rivers & Anne his wife Bapt^{zd} .
   April ye 29th 1744
Judith Daugh^{tr} of Stephen & Jane Russel his wife Bap^{td}
   April ye 29th 1744
John Son of John Champneys & Sarah his wife Bapt^{zd}
   April ye 15th 1744 prv^t Bapt^m
Mary Daugh^{tr} of Robt Allan & Rebecca his wife Bapt^{zd}
   April ye 22 1744 prv^t Bapt^{zm}
Jane the Daughter of John Deveauxe & Sarah his wife
   Bap^{tzd} May ye 11th 1744
Luci Daught^r of Willm Walter & Mary his wife Bapt^{zd} July
   ye 2^d 1744
William Son of William Rivers. Son of Robt Bapt^{zd} July
   22 1744
Elizabeth Daught^r of Zacheus Ladson & Sarah his wife
   Octo^{br} ye 5th 1744
Susanah Daught^r of John Rivers & Elizahth his wife Bapt^{zd}
   Nov^{br} ye 25th 1744
Emanuel Tobias an Adult Bap^{tzd} (the son of Mary Tobias
   widow) Dec^{br} ye 10th 1744
John Son of Willm Miles Junr & Elizabeth his wife Bap^{tzd}
   Jan^{ry} ye 4th 1744

*1744 new style

Petter Son of John Deveaux & Sarah his wife Bap^{td} Feb^{ry} ye 11th 1744.

Richard Son of John Burford & Susannah his wife Bap^{td} March ye 31 1745

Mary Daughter of Charles Cattell & Katherine his wife Bap^{ted} May ye 3^d 1745 prv^t. Bap^{tm}

Robert the Son of Frances Rose & Mary-Anne his wife Bapt^{ed} May ye 17th 1745:

William Son of Christopher Guy & Mary his Wife Baptized May ye 19th 1745

William Son of William King & Susanah his wife Bapt^{ed} June ye 19th 1745

Sarah Daught^r of William Chapman Junr & Mary his wife Bap^d· August y^e—1745 priv^t Bap^{tm}

Deborah Daught^r of Aurthr [sic] Tucker & his wife Bapt^{ed} August 11 1745 Prv^t Bap^t

Mary Daugh^{tr} of Mary Wright (widow of Richard Wright Deces^d) Bapt^{ed} —— 1745

MARRIAGES P^r THE REV^d W^m GUY

Frances Rose & Mary-Anne Elliott Sp^r married p^r the Revd Mr Guy Feb^{ry} ye 23 1743.*

Daniel Haward† & Mary Miles Sp^r married March ye 8th 1743*

Charles Cattell & Catherine Cattell Sp^r married March ye 25th 1744

John Godfrey & Mary Chapman Sp^r Married May ye 14 1744

Charles Pinckney & Elizabeth Lucas Sp^r. Married May ye 27 1744 p^r Revd Mr Guy

Christopher Guy & Mary Godfrey Sp^r June 21

John Friley & Margaret Dent widow Marr^d June ye 23^d 1744

Frances Thompson & Martha Simpson widow married July ye 21st 1744

Josheua Lankestir & Sibella Grey wd^o mar^d August ye 16 1744

---

*1744 new style
†D.

William Ford & Keziah Cartret w^{dd} married Septr ye 11th 1744

William Dues & Lois Wilkins Sp^r married Oct^{br} ye 10th 1744

John Witter & Hannah Collins widow mar^d Dec^{br} ye 20th 1744

Frances Ladson Junr & Elizabeth Manning Sp^r Married Decb^r ye 22^d 1744

Thos Elliott Sn^r of St Paul parish & Eliza^{bth} Bellinger widow married Jan^{ry} 30 1744†

Joseph Page of St Bartholomews Parish & Elizabth Battoon Sp^r Marr^d March ye 21st 1744 †

John Miles & Anne Butler Sp^r Married May ye 21st 1745

Andrew Cattell & Sarah Toomer Sp^r married July ye 14th 1745

John Gordon & Bridget Batsford Married August ye 10th 1745

George Bodington & Sarah Crubin Sp^r married Octo^{br} ye 13th 1745

James Chesheiar & Mary Davis married Octo^{br} ye 14 1745

Richard Bedon & Martha Fuller widow Married Octo^{br} ye 17th 1745

George Ducat Junr & Anna Ullett Sp^r. married Octob^r. ye 24th 1745

George Welsh & Ann Bowman Widd^o Nov ye 2^d 1745

Thomas Rivers & Sarah Atkinson Sp^r Married Novr ye 27th 1745

Thomas Jones & Hanah Fidling widow Married Jan^{ry} ye 30th 1745‡

Colsheth Golightly & Mary Elliott widow Married March ye 30th 1746

Thomas Heyward & Ann Stobo widow marr^d March ye 30th 1746

FUNERALS

George Finlayson Buried at Mr Saxbeys p^r the Revd Mr Guy Sepr ye 10th 1744

†1745 new style
‡1746 new style

Robert Ladson Buried Sp' y° 16ᵗʰ 1744

Mary Daught' of (Elizabeth Ladson, widow of Samˡˡ. Ladson Decesᵈ) Burᵈ· Nov' y° 21 1744

Mary Wife of John Beswick Burᵈ. Decbˡ. y° 8ᵗʰ 1744

Elizabeth Heap widow Buried Janʳʸ y' 2ᵈ 1744 †

Jane Clerk Buried Janʳʸ y° 24ᵗʰ 1744†

Charles the Son of John Beswicke & Mary his wife Buried March y° 7 1744 †

Joseph Batsford Buried April y° 14ᵗʰ 1745

Mary the Daugh' of John Drayton Sn' & —— his wife Buried May y° 27ᵗʰ 1745

William Son of William King and Susanah his wife Buried June y° 26ᵗʰ 1745.

Rebecca Ryne the wife of Dʳ Ryne buried p' y° Revᵈ. Mʳ Thompson Rector of Sᵗ Georges Parish Burᵈ. July y' 18ᵗʰ 1745

Anne Daughter of John Man & Anne his wife Buried August y° 19ᵗʰ 1745

Sarah Daught' of John Champneys & Sarah his wife Buried August y° 23ᵈ 1745

Elizabeth Cheeseman widow Buried August y° 26ᵗʰ 1745.

Charles-Hill Son of Doct' John Lining & Sarah his wife Buried Sepʳ 13ᵗʰ 1745

A Servant of Mʳ John Drayton Buried Sep' y° 30ᵗʰ 1745

Elizabeth Daught' of John Rivers & Elizabeth his wife Buried Octoᵇʳ y° 16ᵗʰ 1745

Jane the wife of Thomas Goreing Buried Octoᵇʳ y° 17ᵗʰ 1745

Daniel Son of James Clemens & Elizabeth his wife Buried Octoᵇʳ y° 19ᵗʰ 1745 from Mʳ Cheshieres (Interrᵈ without a minister Mʳ Guy absent)

Susanah Daugh' of John Rivers & Elizabeth his wife Buried Octoᵇʳ y° 20ᵗʰ 1745

Thomas Son of Rober' Rivers & Anne his wife Buried Octoᵇʳ 19ᵗʰ 1745

Whitaker Son of William—George Freeman & Jane his wife Buried Octobʳ y° 24ᵗʰ 1745

†1745 new style
†1745 new style

Obediah Wood Son of Jnᵒ Wood Decesᵈ Buried at Mʳ
    Mannings Novʳ yᵉ 8ᵗʰ 1745 (interᵈ without a minister)

Elizabᵗʰ Daughᵗ of Frances Ladson Junʳ & Elizᵇᵗʰ his wife
    Buried Novʳ yᵉ 19ᵗʰ 1745

James Drummond Buried from Mʳˢ Sreaus Novʳ yᵉ 10ᵗʰ
    1745.

BIRTHS

John Son of John Godfrey & Mary his wife born — 1744

Elizabeth Daughᵗ of Thomas Radcliff & Elizabeth his
    wife Born March 10 - 1744

John Son of William Miles Junʳ & Elizabeth his wife Born
    Novᵇʳ yᵉ 14ᵗʰ 1744 Sᵗ Bartholomews parish

Grace Daughᵗ of James Taylor & Hesther his wife Born
    174 [sic]

Francis Son of Robert Rivers & Ann his wife Born Sepᵗʳ
    yᵉ 13ᵗʰ 1745

Petter Son of John Deveaux & Sarah his wife Born Feb
    yᵉ 11 1745

Elizabeth the Daughᵗ of Frances Ladson Junʳ and Elizaᵇᵗʰ
    his wife Born Sepᵗʳ yᵉ 11ᵗʰ 1745

Richard Son of Richard Godfrey & Rebecca his wife Born
    [date not given]

Edmᵈ. Son of Landgrave Edmᵈ Bellinger 2ᵈ, was born at
    Mʳ Shem Butler's, a Baptist the 9ᵗʰ April 1719 [sic]

Mary Daughᵗʳ of Thomas Holman & Mary his Wife Born
    Octoᵇʳ yᵉ 15ᵗʰ 1744.

Esther Daughᵗ of Thomas Elmes and Rebecca his wife
    born Sepʳ. yᵉ 6 1744

{ William-Parsons Son of William Chapman & Margaret
    his wife Born August yᵉ 29, 1743.
{ Anne Daughter of Do Born Novᵇʳ yᵉ 5 1745

Samuel Son of Cornelus Vangelder and Elizaᵇᵗʰ his wife
    Born Sepᵗʳ yᵉ 28ᵗʰ 1745

John Son of Thomas Hudson & Elizabeth his wife Born
    Janᵗʳ yᵉ 10ᵗʰ 1745

David Son of Samuel Jones & Mary his wife Born Janᵗʳ
    yᵉ 14 - 1745

Benjamin Son of Isaac Ladson & Rachel his wife Born
    1746

Mary Daught^r of Thomas & Elizabeth Williams born June 1745

Thomas Son of Thomas & Elizabeth juks born Nov^{br} ye 17th 1745

Anne Daugh^{tr} of John Miles & Anne his wife born April ye 16th 1746

Rebecca Daugh^{tr} of Thomas Weaverly & Mary his wife Born April ye 22^d 1745

Thomas Son of Francis Rose & Mary-Ann his wife Born April ye 14th 1746

William Son of John Champneys & Sarah his wife Born Nov^{br} ye 7 1745

John Son of John Champneys & Sarah his wife born Dec^{br} ye 28th 1743

CHRISTNINGS P^r THE REV^d WILL^m GUY

Ann Daught^r of John Man & Anne his wife Bapt^{zd} August ye 16th 1745

John Son of John Godfrey & Mary his wife Bapt^{zd} Augus^t ye 26th 1745

Elizabeth Daugh^{tr} of Thomas Radcliffe & Elizabeth his wife Bapt^{zd} Septr ye 19th 1745

John Son of Thomas Drayton & Elizabeth his wife Bap^{tr} Sepr ye 3^d 1745

Samuel Son of Jacob Boman & Barber his wife Bapt^{zd} Sep^{tr} ye 24th 1745 (Lives at Mr Roses)

Constance & James Daugh^{tr} & Son of William Reynolds & Elizabeth his wife of St Helen's Parish Bapt^{zd} Octo^{br} ye 7th 1745

Grace the Daugh^{tr} of James Taylor & Hesther his wife Bapt^{zd} Octob^r ye 19th 1745

Frances Son of Robert Rivers & Ann his wife Bapt^{zd} Octo^{br} ye 19th 1745

Benjamin Son of Samuell Maverick & his wife Bapt^{zd} Octo^{br} ye 19th 1745

Richard Son of Richard Godfrey & Rebeca his wife Bapt^{zd} Nov^{br} ye 15th 1745

Elizabeth Daught^r of Frances Ladson Junr & Eliz^{bth} his wife Bapt^{zd} Nov^{br} 1st [?] 1745

Edmond, Son of Landgrave Edm^d Bellinger 2^d & Elizabeth his wife, Daughter of Mr Shem Butler, an Adult,
Bapt^d Novr 11th 1745

Mary the Daught^r of Thomas Holman & Mary his Wife
Bapt^zd. August ye 20th 1745

Esther Daught^r of Thomas Elmes and Rebecca his wife
Bapt^zd Dec^br ye 22^d 1745

John Son of Thomas Hudson & Elizabeth his wife Bapt^ta
Jan^ry: ye 11th 1745*

David Son of Samuel Jones & Mary his wife Bapt^ta Priv^t
Bap^tsm Jan^ry ye 14th 1745 *

Benjamin Son of Isaac Ladson & Rachel his wife Bapt^ta
Feb^ry ye 1st 1745*

George the son of Erik Schafus & ——— his wife Ser^nt to
Dr Bull Bapt^ta Jan^ry ye 29th 1745*

Eleanour Daug^r of Willm Hare of Charles Town & ———
his wife Bap^td March ye 17th 1745*

Thomas the Son of Thomas & ——— juks Bapt^ta April y^e
6th 1746

Anne Daugh^tr of John Miles & Anne his wife Bap^tza April
ye 23^d 1746

Mary Daugh^r of Thos Williams & Eliz his wife Bapt^ta
April ye 4th 1746

Rebecca Daugh^r of Thomas Weaverly and Mary his wife
bapt^td May ye 13th 1746

Thomas Son of Frances Rose & Mary-Ann his wife Bapt^td
June ye 1st 1746 Priv^t Bapt^sm

William Son of John Champneys & Sarah his wife Bap^tzd
June ye 7th 1746 Priv^t. Bap^tsm

Samuel Son of Samuel Burges & Mary his wife, Bapt^td
June ye 29th 1746

MARRIAGES

William Brandford & Mary Bryan Sp^r married April y^e
18th 1746 p^r ye Revd Mr Guy.

Henry Wood & Elizabeth Ellmes widow Married May y^e
13th 1746

Joseph Williams & Ann Deloney Sp^r Married June ye 13th
1746

*1746 new style

Benjamin Parrott & Ann Rivers Sp' Married August y'
7ᵗʰ 1746

Will" Cattell Jun' & Ann Frasier Sp' Married at Goose
creek p' y' Rev' M' Guy July y' 31" 1746

M' Samuel Ladson & Sarah Norton Sp' Married July y'
7ᵗʰ 1746

James Cosing & Mary Godwin Sp' Married Octo'' y' 23ᵈ
1746

Jacob Markey & Jane McKelvey Sp' married Dec'' y' 3
1746 of St James Goose Creek

Petter Edwards & Mary Smith Sp' Married Nov'' 19
1746

William Smith & Griszel Agneau Married Jan'' y' 13"
1746 †

Thomas Goring & Mary Cheshire widow Married March
y' 1", 1746 †

Nathaniel Alexander & Rebecca Elmes widow marr'' March
y' 3ᵈ 1746 †

Petter Girerdeau & Elizabeth Heap Sp' Marr'' March y'
19ᵗʰ 1746.†

Benjamin Heep & Mary Wood Sp' married in Charles
Town April y' 7ᵗʰ 1747

Thomas Elliott Jun' & Mary Bellinger Sp' Married p' y'
Rev' William Guy May y' 19ᵗʰ 1747

William Rivers & Mary Dill married August y' 2ᵈ 1747

The Rev' William Guy & Elizab'' Cooper Sp' of S' James
Goose Creek Married p' the Rev' M' Commis'' Garden
in Charles Town August   1747‡

Daniel How & Eliz'''. Guines wᵈᵒ mard· Dec'' y' 18"
1747

Elisha Butler & Mary Wright wd° Mar'' Jan'' y' 17"
1747

Nathaniel Brown & Sarah Elliott Sp' marr'' Feb'' y' 4ᵗʰ
1747

Thomas Hayward & Anne Miles Sp' married Feb'' y' 14ᵗʰ
1747**

---

†1747 new style
‡Married August 6th, 1747   *St Philips Register*
**1748 new style

(To be continued)

SOUTH CAROLINA LOYALISTS

Contributed by Mabel L. Webber

The claims advanced by the Loyalists on account of services in connection with, and arising from, the Revolutionary War, were investigated by Special Commissioners appointed by the British Parliment in 1783, two of whom, viz. Col Thomas Dundas and Mr Jeremy Pemberton, were sent to Canada, to meet the claimants there in person and obtain evidence on the spot The evidence thus secured is contained in a number of manuscript volumes, which were retained by Col Thomas Dundas, at his home, Carron Hall, Stirlingshire, a transcript of them having been placed in the Public Record Office in London

About 1864, Sir Henry Lefroy, who had married a grand-daughter of Col Dundas, saw the original manuscript, and being then much interested in the Smithsonian Institution, which at that time was doing much to collect manuscript material relating to American History, he advised that these papers be sent to that institution This was done, and the papers remained there until an Act of Congress was passed transferring the manuscripts in the Smithsonian to the Library of Congress, and the above manuscripts are now in the Manuscript Department there

The Province of Ontario had them copied exactly, and have printed them in the *Second Report of the Bureau of Archives for the Province of Ontario, Alexander Fraser, Provincial Archivist,* 1904, (in two parts) without alteration

The manuscript reproduced differs from the transcript preserved in the Public Record Office in London in that it contains marginal notes and references made by the Commissioners during the proceedings, many of which are characteristic and sum up the position more pungently than appears in the official record

This *Second Report of the Bureau of Archives* of Province of Ontario, is out of print, but our Society was fortunate enough to obtain a copy some time ago, and it is from this that the above information is taken

The evidence on the various claims throw much light upon the Royalist side of the struggle, and it forms a valuable source of material for the personal history of those who remained loyal to the Crown

In the New York Public Library there are some 58 Folio manuscript volumes of transcripts of memorials and claims of loyalists, copied from the records in the Public Record Office in London, these are arranged according to the states from which the memorialists came Volume twenty-six contains the memorials of the South Carolina loyalists taken in Nova Scotia, and the list of names, as copied for this Society, agree, with a few exceptions, with those from South Carolina found in the printed Ontario Archives

The memorials taken in London, of the South Carolina loyalists, are to be found in volumes 52 to 57 of the manuscript transcripts in the New York Public Library, and we now print below, the names of the memoralists, with reference to the manuscript volumes in which the claims are to be found

The claimant appeared in person or by proxy and gave an account of his service, of trials endured, or losses suffered, for the Loyalist cause, and a schedule of property lost, these all being testified to by reliable witnesses

SOUTH CAROLINA

Vol 26

Transcriber's LIST of CLAIMANTS

[This is the list of the S C Memorials taken in Nova Scotia, as stated above, and most of these claims are to be found printed in the Ontario Archives]

Alexander Robert	204	Bond John	279
Anderson George	479	Bower Adam[1]	58
		Bowers Charles[1]	38
Blakely Chambers	156	Brison John[2]	259
Bleackney David	469	Brison William[2]	254
Bond George	298	Brown James	459

[1] Probably Bauer
[2] Or Bryson

Bullein Nathaniel   275

Carey James [Col]   75
Carter James   233
Chisholm John   496
Commander Thomas   182
Crum Nicholas³   126
Cumine Alexander⁴   501
Cunningham William   42

Dawkins George   5
Dores John   66
Drew Joseph   452
Dunsmore David   216

Fannen, Lt Col John   352
Fratick Adam⁵   192
Fritz Abraham   35
Fritz Peter   31

Garrett Joshua   117
Graham Arthur see Han-
  nah Lumb widow of
Green Henry   324

Hamilton John   474
Henderson Jean (wo)   92
Henry (now Dores) Eliz   71
Hudson Joel   335

Jones James   320

Lively Reuben   248
Long George   49
Lumb Hannah, wife of
  Joseph Lumb wo of
  Arthur Graham   171

Lumb Joseph   151
Lyndon Annabella wo &
  Henry, son of Henry
  dec'd   491

McAlister Samuel   285
McEowen Patrick⁶   464
Mail Peter, see Mary Shed-
  die wo Marks Conrad   25
Marks Lawrence   133
Meek William   314
Migler Daniel   20
Moffat James   420
Murphy John   238
Myers Andrew⁷   161

Nielley Christopher
  [Maj]   386
Nickels James   198
Nunkaser Adam   187

Pearis, Col Richard   362
Pearson Thomas [Col]   290

Rittenhouse William   139
Robinson Joseph Lt Col   402
Rupert Cath & Barbara⁸   434
Rupert Christopher⁸   426

Sanderson John   176
Shalnet George   166
Sheddit Mary, widow of
  Peter Mail   145
Siteman Henry⁹   329
Sloane Robert   346
Snell George   209

³Or Crane
⁴Or Comyne
⁵Probably Fralick or Frelick
⁶Or McCune
⁷Or Meier
⁸Or Ruprecht
⁹Or Citeman

Song Christian	103		Wallace Wm	242
Spence Robert	441		Weaver George	110
Strum Henry	99		Whitley, St Moses	411
			Williams Edward	305
Thornton John	486		Withrow John	227
Thornton Thomas	221		Wright James	14
Walker Thomas	446		Young Thomas	264

SOUTH CAROLINA

Vol 52 to 57

Transcriber's LIST of CLAIMANTS

[The following list is of the S C Memorials taken in London, and so far as we can ascertain, are to be found only in the manuscript vols in the New York Public Library]

	Vol	Page		Vol	Page
Alexander James	54	5	utor of William		
Arters William	53	221	Wragg wch see		
Askew Leonard	56	142	Brailsford John for		
Atkins Charles	55	457	self Mother and		
			Sisters	53	510
Balfour Mary Ann	54	340	Bremar John	57	450
Ball Elias Senr	55	87	Brisbane James	53	356
Ballingall Robert	54	360	Broadhead Thomas	52	453
Ballmer, Major James	56	86	Brown Christopher	57	240
Barber James	52	134	Bull Wm Lieut		
Beard Robert	53	240	Govr	57	160
Begbie James	56	284	Bulman Rev John	54	85
Begbie William, see			Burke Redmund	52	5
Danl Manson and			Burn John by son Jas		
Benson Capt			& brother &Exr Dr		
George	55	326	Jas Burn	56	557
Blankenhorn Geo			Burnside Alexr	52	412
Henry	53	32			
Bisseau James Ed			Cameron Alexr by		
ward	53	147	Executors Wm Og-		
Boone Thomas	53	437	ilvy Charles Shaw &		
Boone Thomas, Exec-			Donald Cameron	55	556

ORDER BOOK

of

John Faucheraud Grimké

August 1778 to May 1780

(Continued from the October Number)

December, 1778

Head Quarters, Sunbury. 9th. Decr 1778

Sir

You are to proceed with the Galleys under your command to Ossabaw or near Shannons Point, from thence one Galley is to be detached to take post at Warsaw so as to cover the Entrance up to Thunderbolt & another Galley to Tybee to cover the entrance into Savannah River The Orders you give to the officers commanding the Galleys at the above-mentioned places are, to keep the most vigilant lookout, that no Surprise Shall happen, at the same time that it will be their duty to attac or annoy the Enemy should they enter into the Harbour whenever they can, in case they are inferior to the Galleys in force; They are by no means to sustain an attac against odds that may make the prospect of Success improbable in that case they are to Retreat to Augustine Creek, where they are to Remain until further Orders   I am Sir &c (Signed)

Robert Howe Maj Genl

12

Head Quarters, Savannah

Parole. Huger

The Dep Quarter Master Gen is immediately to Report to Head Quarters the number & size of the boats in Public Service, & at what places they are   He is also to report tomorrow morning the exact State of the Stores of every kind in his Department   Each Officer actually in barracks is to be served with One Candle per night   The Dep Quarter Master Genl will give orders accordingly

The Dep Clothier Gen & the Commissaries of Purchases Issues are to Report to Col° Elbert as soon as possible the State of the Continental Stores & the exact Situation of their Several Departments

Surgeons of Regiments also will report the quantity of Public Medicines they have rec'd., the quantity they have on hand & likewise what they have expended.

The Com': Officer of the Continental Corps of Artillery in the State of Georgia is to Report to Col'. Elbert as immediately as possible the ordanance & other Stores in his Department.

18:    Parole, Bull

The Commanding Officer in Camp will immediately by Express transmit to Head Quarters an exact Return of every Corps under his Command particularizing therein all Absentees, also a Return of the Fixed & loose Ammunition & other Stores in Camp.

The Commanding officer of Fort Morris will immediately transmit to the Com'. Officer at Head Quarters an exact Return of all Ordanance & other Stores at Sunbury & Fort Morris.

Head Quarters, Savannah.

24:    Parole, Lincoln.

A large Detachment of Continental Troops being expected in Town tonight, the Dep: Quarter-Master General is immediately to have the Barracks prepared to receive them & wood provided for their use.

The Artillery of every Cont: Corps now acting in this State, is to be under the Command of Col'. Owen Roberts, who is to be respected & obeyed accordingly.

Complaints having been made that the Troops have suffered for want of wood, the Dep: Quarter Master Gen: will give the strictest Orders to prevent this from happening for the future & to be attentive that his Orders are Executed.

Orderly Hour at 11 oClock in the Morning
Night Orders

Any Person or Persons who coming into Town, shall upon being challenged give the word *Thunderbolt*, shall be permitted to pass the Guards & Sentinals of the Continental Troops.

25   Morning Orders

One Serg' one Corp & 6 Privates are to mount a guard at the battery the East end of the Town immediately They will Parade at Head Quarters and receive their orders from the Dep Adjutant Gen'

The Dep Quarter Master Gen will immediately Report to Head Quarters the Number of Musquet & other Cartridges ready made

Sir

I am ordered by the general to direct you to move the 200 men, now under March, into Savannah as immediately as possible & that you will order the Remainder in Camp at Medway Meeting House to proceed without delay & encamp on this side of Ogéchee River leaving the Posts which have been established at Spencers Hill, Newport River & Colonels Island standing until further Orders

The General thinks proper that a Guard of 25 or 30 men should be established upon the Hill over the Causeway on the other side of Ogéchee River   I am Sir &c   John F Grimke Dep Adj' Gen

   Col° Sam Elbert Com'
      of the Georgia Brigade

P S   The above Detachment to the Southward of the meeting House are to Retire to Sunbury, sending an Express to the Com' officer at Ogéchee, should they be compelled to Retreat

------

Sir

The arrival & anchoring of the Enemy in this Harbour makes it probable that an attack upon Savannah is intended & that the principal object of the Enemy is to possess themselves of this Town   The General therefore strongly recommends that the Inhabitants of the Town of Sunbury & of the Parish of S' Johns should not be disheartened by the Troops marching to the assistance of their fellow Citizens in Savannah & pledges himself to them that no Measure which can be with Propriety adopted for the Defence of Sunbury, shall be wanting on his part & that in case the enemy should move to the Southward & there is a probability of their relinquishing the present mode of attac & translate it to Sunbury, the General will Endeavour by his rapid movement to the Southward to convince the Inhabitants how much He has at Heart the defence & protection of that valuable Town & Spirited Parish

In the mean time He recommends that the Inhabitants of the Parish should form themselves into a Corps of Light Horse & by scouting in small Parties beyond our out-guards as far as the Alatamaha, or even beyond that River to prevent a surprise by a return of the Troops from Florida

You will be pleased to have the above published to the Inhabitants of Sunbury & of S' John's Parish.

The Com' Officer of Artillery at Sunbury will immediately have the Cannon in the Fort & the Field Pieces put in proper order for service

One Sub One Serg' One Corp & 9 Matrosses to be detached from the garrison at Sunbury with a Field-Piece to the Cause-way leading from the landing at Colonel's Island   They are to be encamped on this side of the Causeway & the Detachment at the Landing is to Retire to this body & defend the Post with the Utmost Vigor & as long as possible should they be attacked   They are to destroy the Causeway upon retiring & cut down the Trees so as to make the roads as impassable as possible still Skirmishing as they Retire   I am, Sir, &c,

John F Grimké Dep Adj' Gen'
To the Com' Officer at
      Sunbury

Parole, Walton

The necessity of Service requiring that the militia & Confederal Troops should act conjunctly in support of one Common Cause & under one Common Commander & the Command of the Militia being vested by the Executive authority of this State in the Com' officer of the Confederal Troops within this State, the General warmly recommends & earnestly Hopes that Harmony, Esteem, & Confidence may reciprocally actuate the bosom of each Corps . that no Contention may arise but what Results from the noble Emula___ __ __ ____ __ _____ _____ _____ The militia

in time of Peace are the Respectable Citizens of the State—
in War the natural and valuable Soldiers of it.   In either
view they merit the Consideration & Respect of all but particularly of the army who are ordained to protect & defend
their Persons, Property, Rights & Privilegdes.   Not compelled by necessity to the Practice of Manoevores, should
any of them happen not to be as Expert in performing as
those whose Duty it is constantly to practice them. They
merit not Derision for a Defect which nothing but want
of Habit Occasions, nor must they receive it   It calls for
the Friendly aid & delicately offered assistance of every
officer   A Contray conduct will degrade those who practice
it & as all Jest & Ridicule Amongst Corps however well
intended or Sportively begun have a strong tendency to
lessen Esteem, weaken Confidence & destroy that Union
upon which the Safety of this State depends Every thing
of this sort is absolutely forbidden & will be treated as dis-
obedience of Orders

Col" Walton commands the Militia as Col" Com' & is
to be respected & Obeyed accordingly

Col" Walton will Report immediately to Head Quarters
the number of troops under his Command & the places at
which they are posted (N B No Report ever was made)

The Comᵉ officer of the Militia Corps of Artillery will
immediately Report to Head Quarters the Strength of his
Corps, The Field Pieces, Military Stores & all other Articles
in his Department

Comᵉ officers of every Corps are to have their arms and
accounterments & all other matters in the best order possible for immediate Action

The Dep· Quarter Master Gen· & Commissary of Issues
of the Confederal Troops are to serve the Militia with
wood, Provisions, & other articles usually served to the
Confederal Troops

Exact Provision Returns are to be regularly made by
the Quartermaster of each Corps daily, previous to their
being removed

No Guns are to be fired in or about Town except on
Duty

Com" of Brigades will make an immediate Return of their respective Commands

An Orderly Serg from Col Walton's Command, from each Brigade of the Confederal Troops & from the Corps of Artillery to attend the General daily

Orderly Hour at 11 o'Clock in the Morning

The Commissary is ordered to furnish the two Detachments of Troops, which arrived this day with a gill of Rum per Man

---

26   December 1778   Head Quarters Savannah Morning Orders

Field officers of every Corps are to give in the dates of their Commissions to the Dep. Adjutant Gen immediately

One Capt 2 Sub' three Serg' & 30 Rank & File to be taken by Detachment from the Carolina & Georgia Brigades to be ready for immediate command they are to be furnished with 30 rounds of Ammunition & three days Provisions the officer commanding the Party will receive his Orders from the Dep Adj Gen

One Serg' & 15 Rank & File to be warned for fatigues immediately & are to be taken by Detachment from the Carolina & Georgia Brigades They will attend the Commissary of Slaves [? illegible]

The Dep Quartermaster Gen is immediately to Report the number of Waggons, Horses, Negroes, & boats to Head Quarters, which He has in Service at present

Piquet

1" Brigade	2ᵈ Brigade
1 Cap	1 Sub
1 Sub	1 Serg'
3 Serg"	6 R & F
39 R & F	

The Dep Quarter Master Gen will attend Head-Quarters at 10 o Clock every Morning for Orders

Parole, Georgia

Every officer of the Staff whether Civil or Military is to keep an orderly book in which they are to insert the daily orders which concern their Respective Departments

Sir / You are to proceed to Rae Hall the Plantation of
M⁵ Somerville about 6 Miles up the River, with the Detachment under your command where you will take post
& place Sentinels upon the Mount near the River Side You
are to give notice when any of the Enemys vessels or boats
shall appear off that Port by Express to the General   You
will Secure yourselves also on the Land side from being
surprised & should occasion require make a vigorous Resist-
ance either by land or water.   You will be careful to keep
your Arms & Accoutrements in the best order possible for
immediate Service   You will Examine all boats passing
your Post & those which appear to be carrying away the
goods of the Inhabitants or upon Public Service you will
permit to pass.   You will be careful to Restrain your men
from doing any injury to the Property of the Inhabitants
in general and particularly & of that Plantation, & you are
not to suffer more than one man to be absent at a time from
your command   I am Sir &c

To the officer com⁵ }
a detachment marching }   John F Grimké D A G
to Rae Hall }

---

27   Morning Orders

The Detachments of the Several Confederal Brigades
now in Town are to Parade at some convenient place near
the Barracks to day at 12 ô Clock   The Adj General will
mark out the Parade for this Purpose   All officers to attend

Parole, Houston

As the Continental Troops will probably be ordered to
form an encampment to Day, They are therefore to Prepare themselves to March immediately upon Receiving
Orders

Congress having appointed L' Col" Ternant Inspector
of the Confederal Troops in the States of South Carolina
& Georgia, He is to be respected & obeyed accordingly
He is agreeable to the Directions of Congress to train &
discipline the Troops in his Department in those Manoevres
practised in the grand army, that one Uniform diciphne
may prevail thro' the whole Army of the Ancient States

The Inspector when visiting Barracks, Tents, Messes, Guards, Piquets & Posts is to be Considered & treated as an officer of the Day

The Col°: Com'. of Militia is to make a return of the number of Troops now in Town under his Command & when other Detachments arrive, he is to immediately Report this arrival & number to the General

Sir / The General received your letter last night by Express & has been so exceedingly engaged in business that your dispatch could not be dismissed before to Day. He has sent you five pounds of Sulphur about 4 fathoms of Match rope & one ream of Cartridge Paper

By your Return the General Observes you have thirty barrels of Gun-Powder in the magazine at Sunbury which He considers as amounting to three thousand weight, a sufficient quantity in his opinion for your defence until He could support you with the Army   The Detachments of Continental Troops advanced to the Southward of your Post have orders to Retreat to Sunbury should the Enemy attempt to Penetrate the Country from the Southward & the General leaves to your discretion when you shall withdraw those Detachments from their Posts, hoping at the same time that you will inform the General by Express when the above detachments have joined, the reasons for their retreat & such other important Circumstances as may occur You will immediately have a return of Cap' Morris' Company made to Head Quarters by the first opportunity   The Governor has vested the Command of the Militia in the General & we are in a fair way of becoming so formidable by the Happy Union that we need not be apprehensive of an attac even in our present Circumstances; but should the Enemy delay their descent for only three days we shall at least double their number & be capable of a good defences both at Sunbury & at Savannah   As soon as the Troops expected up arrive you will be supported by a considerable body   The General would wish also to hear what number of Inhabitants can reinforce the Fort at Sunbury should it be attacked & if they have formed any scouting parties to the Southward   We have at present no saltpeter in Store, but as soon as any arrives which is daily Expected from

Charles-Town, you shall have some sent to you. The General hopes the flats which Capt: Melvin pressed in Sunbury have been sent round to O'géchee Ferry if not, He Requests you will Exert yourself to have this business Executed without delay.

The General has ordered the Dep: Quarter master General to send a deputation to his assistant to press whatever you may want. You will therefore apply to him. I am Sir &c. John F. Grimké D: A: G:

Major Lane or com°.
officer at Sunbury.

Signals between the Galleys & Army.
By the Galleys to the Army.

A number of armed boats approaching.   Three minute guns.

The Enemy's Fleet approaching.   Two Minute Guns & three Minutes after two more.

The whole Fleet Standing to Sea.   Five Minute Guns.

A part standing to Sea, leaving a Number behind.   One Gun & three Minutes after two more fired quick.

By the Army to the Galleys.

For a Galley to come to Savannah.   Three minute Guns.

For two Galleys.   Two Minute Guns & three minutes after two more.

For three Galleys.   Five Minute Guns.

For the Fleet.   One gun & three minutes after two more fired quick.

For a boat with an officer.   Two Minute Guns.

For Col. White.   Three Guns fired quick as possible.

A cap' of the Day is to be appointed who is to visit the Night Guards. He will attend the Parade at Retreat Beating

One Sub. three Serg' & fifty rank & file are to be immediately warned for fatigue.

The Commissary of Issues is to deliver a gill of Rum to each man who has been upon fatigue, the officer of which fatigue is to sign a Return of the same

The Piquets will Parade at Retreat Beating at Barracks

Detail of Piquet

1ᵗ Brigade	2ᵈ Brigade
1 Sub	1 Cap'
3 Serg'.	1 Sub
41 R & F.	1 Serg'
	9 R & F

For Fatigue

1 Sub	
3 Serg'.	9 R & F.
41 R & F	

28: Morning Orders

The Army is to march precisely at 9 ó Clock this Morning. the Baggage is to be immediately packed up & the Horses put to the Waggons

The Com' Officer of Artillery will give immediate orders to prepare the train of Artillery to march with the Line; if it cannot be ready in time He will follow the Line as soon as possible

The Dep Quartermaster Gen. will have the Entrenching & all other Tools for Field-Use got ready for the Service of the Army A waggon is to be immediately prepared to Receive them in which they are to be put

One Sub one Serg'. & Six Privates are to attend M' Hornly immediately to take care of the negroes impressed in the Public Service & to give all possible assistance thereto

Detail for this Duty

1st Brigade	2^d Brigade
1 Lieut	
1 Serg^t.	
4 Privates	2 Privates

Detail for Fatigue

1st Brigade	2^d Brigade
1 Cap	1 Cap:
3 Lieut	1 Lieut
3 Serg^t	1 Serg^t
70 R & F	14 R & F.

Head Quarters   Camp on Fairlawn 29 Decr 1778
Gene^l Orders by Major Genl Howe
Parole, Firmness

The first Brigade is to be immediately told off into 16 Platoons of an equal Number of Files,—the odd Files to be formed in one Platoon on the right Wing of the Brigade to act as Light Infantry according to Exigencies—

Two Field Officers to be appointed to the Command of the right & Left Wing of both Brigades.

The 2^d. Brigade is to be told off into 8 Platoons of an equal Number of Files; the odd files to be formed on the left of the Brigade, in order to act as Light Infantry, as will be directed

One Officer is to be appointed to the Command of every Platoon, composing a Brigade   Another Officer is to be placed on the left of the whole, & the rest are to fall into the rear of the Platoons as Bringers up, in order to preserve Order and regularity throughout the Lines

Col° Huger will command the *Right* Wing of the Army, composed of the 1st Brigade & Light Troops belonging to it—

Col° Elbert is to command the *Left* Wing, composed likewise of the 2^d Brigade & Light Troops belonging it—

The Artillery of both Brigades & the Park to be posted before & during the Action as shall be directed, & defend their ground until further Orders —The Artillery when ordered or forced to retreat is to fall into the road leading to the Western Defile, where Col° Roberts is to take as advantageous a post as possible to protect the retreat of the Line

The first Brigade after being told off, is to form in a close Column by platoons upon the right, & so remain until Orders to display by the Left

The 2ª Brigade is also to form in a close Column by Platoons upon the right & remain in that formation until Orders to display by the right

Both Columns are to fire by Platoons as they display, and afterwards as will be directed by the Commanding Officers They are likewise to defend this Ground by Fire & Bayonet until ordered or forced by Circumstances to retreat which will be done in the following manner The Light Infantry of the 1ª Brigade to make the Advanced Guard & protect the retreat of the Artillery

The Line is to march by the right, & the Light Infantry of the 2ª Brigade to make the rear guard with a Field piece

Colº Huger to lead the Colum of retreat to the Western Defile & Colº Elbert to bring it up, & have the Charge of the rear Guard

The 2ª Brigade will support it by Detachments in case of Necessity Ammunition Waggons are to march between the advanced Guard & Main Body—

In Case of a General Route or confused retreat the place of Rendezvous is on the other Side of the Western Defile near Mʳ McGillevray's Gate The 1ª Brigade is to draw up in Battle Array at the Entrance of the Western Defile in the rear or Flanks of the Artillery according to the Nature of the Ground in order to support the passage of the 2ª. Brigate & Artillery— The Light Infantry of both Brigades to join & make the rear Guard after the passage of the Defile The 2ª Brigade after having passed is to draw up at the Head of the Defile & take such Disposition on both sides of it as will be most likely to defend the Approaches of the Enemy on the Flanks

The Militia are to defend the Fort & when no longer tenable to spike the guns, & destroy the Ammunition & retire to the place of Rendezvous

Further Orders as Occasion requires

[Th ·   s battle which took place upon the 29th of December in which General Howe was defeated and severely criticised for the defeat a court of inquiry was held, but Howe was acquitted A full account of this battle is given by McCrady in his first volume on the Revolution in S C , and an even better account in Jones' History of Georgia, vol 2   The following letter, gives a personal experience during the battle, by John F Grimke   It is in the Ms Collections of this Society (Laurens' Papers, vol 25, No 69)—Editor.]

Endorsed

    Copy of Col Grimké's
Letter to his Father
30 December 1778

                   Ebenezer December 30th

I have but just time to inform you that the Enemy landed yesterday morning at Mr Girardeau's place about two miles from Savannah— A proper disposition was made of the Troops to engage them which accordingly began half-past 2 oClock & the Enemy having possessed themselves of an advantageous spot of ground doubled our right flank & very nearly cutt off our retreat   Col[n] Elbert's Brigade are almost all of them taken prisoners & he himself escaped only by swimming a creek   This was the case with me also & the greatest difficulties occurr'd in getting thro' the swamp   I lost my Horse, Saddle, pistols &c the horse being so fatigued with the days labour that he had not strength to get out of the swamp, I was therefore obliged to leave him & his appurtenances

We effected a retreat thro' a very heavy fire of the Enemy for near a mile, but I believe we have lost but few men kill'd I assure you it is wonderful how so many escaped as the Enemy were six times more than our number   We have been compelled to retreat to this place & are still proceeding towards Augusta the river being so high that we cannot cross ove at Zubly's ferry & we being so exceedingly weakened that it is impossible to withstand them should they approach   I have the pleasure of informing that I escaped unhurt tho' I was in the midst of the heaviest fire— If you do not send us men we shall all be made prisoners

P S· We have ab' 100 Troops to the S" ward in the fort at Sunbury which will fall of course & the men become prisoners

(To be continued)

HISTORICAL NOTES

ABSTRACTS FROM THE RECORDS OF THE COURT OF ORDINARY—
The following additional abstracts are of entries recorded
upon the last few pages of the volume (wrongly) dated on
the binding, 1687-1710, which was thought to be completed
in the issue of this Magazine for last April (vol XIII, pages
84-88) Several blank pages coming between the records
were misleading and led to the conclusion that all of the
records had been printed—Editor

Oct 26, 1703 William Chapman entered Caveat that
no Lycences should be granted for the marriage of Catherine Rowland with any person she being Servant to the said
Chapman

September 16, 1700 Robert Gibbes Esq, entered Caveat
to the estate of ———— Baynard, bricklayer deceased, as
principal creditor, and prays for letters of administration

Sept 17, 1700, Dove Williamson entered his Caveat to
the estate of ———— Baynard, bricklayer as principal
creditor, and asks for letters of administration

Sept 25, 1700 Mr. Francis Fidling enters his caveat to
the estate of Thomas Baynard bricklayer, and asks for
letters of administration

July 3ª 1703 Mr Samuel Nichols entered his caveat to
the estate of Roger Nichols his father lately deceased as
eldest son and heir at law, and prays letters of administration &c

July 3, 1704 Mr John Flavell entered caveat to the
estate of Mr Joseph Quelch deceased as principal creditor

August 26, 1704 Mr John Lawrence entered his caveat
to the estate of Mr James Braxton deceased, as principal
creditor

October 30, 1705 Mr John Filben entered his caveat
that no letters of administration be granted for the estate
of Mary Perriman deceased until he is first called, he being
principal creditor

16 April 1706 Madam Elizabeth Blake entered her caveat
that no letters of administration be granted for the estate
of John Milward deceased until she is called, she being
principal creditor

22 April 1706. Mr. Louis Pasqureau and Company enter their caveat to the estate of Thomas Barker deceased as principal creditors

17 August 1706 Mrs. Mary King widdow and relict of Thomas King deceased entered her caveat to her husbands estate that no letters of administration be granted without she is called

August 22, 1706 Mr William Gibbon entered his caveat to letters of administration to the personal estate of Daniel Trezevant late on Cooper River deceased, as principal creditor

February 3d 1706 Robert Lewis entered caveat to letters of administration to the estate of John Murrill late on Wando River, on behalf of the children of the said John Murrill by his wife Elizabeth & caveat all persons till he is heard concerning the same

July 21st 1711 John Cooper entered his caveat to letters of administration of the estate of Forthesque Tuberville Esq

July 22d 1711 Mr Thomas Farr and Elizabeth his wife entered their Caveat against proving the will of Capt John Emperor late deceased not being proved in time

THE CHARLESTON CHAMBER OF COMMERCE —The following item from the *South Carolina Gazette*, Saturday, December 13, 1773, gives the exact date of the establishment of the Chamber of Commerce

"Last Thursday there was a General Meeting of the Gentlemen in Trade of this Town, at Mrs Swallow's [a tavern] when it was proposed that a Chamber of Commerce should be formed. John Savage, Esq was chosen Chairman, and a Committee of twenty-one appointed "

In the issue of the paper for Feb 28, 1774, this further notice is found

"The late Institution of a Chamber of Commerce in this Town, it is said, has given Rise to an Idea of forming a Chamber (or House) of Counterpoise "

A WOMAN'S WARDROBE IN THE EARLY PART OF THE 18TH CENTURY An advertisement in the S. C. Gazette for November 2, 1738, gives us much more fully than most of them, an idea of the dress of the women of that day.

"Lost on the 17th of last Month, between Dorchester and Charlestown, a Linnen Bagg with sundry Things therein, viz one Womans Suit of Cloaths of Sattin strip'd with red, green and white. one Suit of all white Sattin, one Yellow Night Gown faced with red Taffety, one yellow Suit of yellow Peiling, and one blue Night Gown faced with white, a red Callimanco Night Gown faced with Brocade, one child's stiffen'd Coat of an Ash Colour'd Damask, and sundry other Womans wearing Apparel, with Head Dresses and shifting Linen, one Sampler with the Child's Name and Age and Date and Place of her abode. a piece of Work embroider'd for a Top of a Table, and two Papers of Gloves, and a Hatt Band from a Funeral, directed for Wm Linthwait and Mrs Sarah Clapp, and two Papers directed one for Mrs· Yore and Mrs Mary Baker, and sundry other Things   Any one that can give any Information to me in Dorchester or to Wm Linthwaite in Charlestown, or to the Printer so that they may be had again shall have from either 10l reward paid on sight

John Leay "

AN ORDER OF GENERAL MARION'S —The below given original autograph order of General Marion, now in my possession, was purchased by my father, the late William M Read. Esq, at a sale of autographs in New York City   It is in excellent preservation.

M Alston Read

"General Orders at Wadboo 29th. Septr 1782
"No Officer or Private of the State Legion or Militia to Leave Camp without my permission, Any Officer or Private who disobeys this Order, may expect to be called to an Account agreeable to the Articles of War and the Militia Laws of this State
[Signed]   "Fran Marion
"B. G. M "

LIST OF PUBLICATIONS

OF THE

SOUTH CAROLINA HISTORICAL SOCIETY.

COLLECTIONS.

Vol. I., 1857, $3.00, Vol. II., 1858, $3.00; Vol. III 1859, out of print. Vol IV., 1887, unbound, $3.00, bound $4.00; Vol. V., 1897, paper, $3.00.

PAMPHLETS.

Journal of a Voyage to Charlestown in So. Carolina by Pelatiah Webster in 1765. Edited by Prof. T. P. Harrison, 1898   75c.

The History of the Santee Canal. By Prof. F. A Porcher. With an Appendix by A S Salley, Jr., 1903
75c.

THE SOUTH CAROLINA HISTORICAL AND GENEALOGICAL MAGAZINE.

Volume I, 1900, Edited by A. S. Salley, Jr. Complete Volume. $10.00

Single copies of Nos. 2-4, $1.25 each.

Volume II to IX, 1901-1908, Edited by A. S. Salley, Jr.
Unbound $5.00 each.

Volume X to XIII, 1909-1912, Edited by Mabel L Webber   Unbound $5 00 each.

Members get a discount of 25 per cent on the above prices

Address: South Carolina Historical Society,
Charleston, S C

THE

SOUTH CAROLINA

HISTORICAL AND GENEALOGICAL

MAGAZINE

PUBLISHED QUARTERLY BY THE

SOUTH CAROLINA HISTORICAL SOCIETY

CHARLESTON, S. C.

VOLUME XIV., NO. 2.   APRIL 1913.

Entered at the Post-office at Charleston, S. C., as
Second-Class Matter.

PRINTED FOR THE SOCIETY BY
WALKER, EVANS & COGSWELL CO
CHARLESTON, S. C.
1913

PUBLICATION COMMITTEE.

Joseph W. Barnwell,   Henry A M. Smith,
          A. S. Salley, Jr.

EDITOR OF THE MAGAZINE.
Mabel L. Webber.

CONTENTS.

N. B.—These Magazines, with the exception of No 1 of Vol I, are $1 25 to any one other than a member of the South Carolina Historical Society. Members of the Society receive them free The Membership fee is $4.00 per annum (the fiscal year being from January to January), and members can buy back numbers or duplicates at $1 00 each In addition to receiving the Magazines, members are allowed a discount of 25 per cent. on all other publications of the Society, and have the free use of the Society's library

Any member who has not received the last number will please notify the Secretary and Treasurer,

Miss Mabel L. Webber,
South Carolina Historical Society,
Charleston, S C.

PUBLICATION COMMITTEE.

Joseph W. Barnwell,   Henry A. M. Smith,
              A. S. Salley, Jr.

EDITOR OF THE MAGAZINE.
Mabel L. Webber.

CONTENTS.

———

N. B.—These Magazines, with the exception of No. 1 of Vol. I, are $1.25 to any one other than a member of the South Carolina Historical Society. Members of the Society receive them free. The Membership fee is $4.00 per annum (the fiscal year being from January to January), and members can buy back numbers or duplicates at $1.00 each. In addition to receiving the Magazines, members are allowed a discount of 25 per cent. on all other publications of the Society, and have the free use of the Society's library.

Any member who has not received the last number will please notify the Secretary and Treasurer,

Miss Mabel L. Webber,
South Carolina Historical Society.
Charleston, S. C.

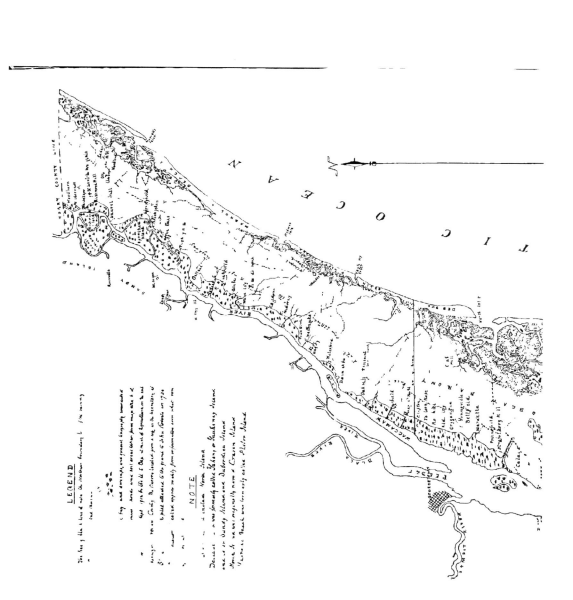

The South Carolina Historical and Genealogical Magazine.

| VOL XIV | APRIL, 1913 | No. 2 |

THE BARONIES OF SOUTH CAROLINA.

By Henry A. M. Smith.

X

HOBCAW BARONY.

The Hobcaw Barony took its name from the Indian name applied to the point of land opposite the town of Georgetown on Winyah Bay, the extreme southern terminus of the neck of land lying between the Waccamaw river and the sea The extreme point is now known as Fraser's point

The Indian name of the whole locality covering the lower end of the peninsula seems to have been "Hobcaw," and the early white settlers called the point, Hobcaw point There was another Hobcaw in South Carolina, viz. the locality on the south bank of the Wando river where that river debouches into Cooper river opposite Charleston neck. The territory between Shem or Shem-ee creek and the Wando river was known as Hobcaw neck and the point now called Remleys point was Hobcaw point

The Barony as originally run out was one of the baronies included in the ten baronies aggregating 119,000 acres laid out as early as 1711[1] and divided among the Proprietors by lot on 21 November, 1718.[2]   This barony must have been drawn by Lord Carteret, for on 5th December, 1718, a formal grant was executed granting "unto John "Lord Carteret a Barony consisting of Twelve thousand "Acres of Land English Measure situate, lying and being "upon Waccamaw River and Commonly called Hobcaw "point butting and bounding as appears by a plot or plan "thereof hereunto annexed."[3]

John Lord Carteret, Baron Carteret of Hawnes (afterwards Earl Granville) to whom the Barony was granted, was one of the Lords Proprietors of Carolina—the celebrated Lord Carteret, and "one of the first orators, purest "patriots, keenest wits, brightest classical scholars, and "most ardent convivialists of his time."

He held the barony for about twelve years and then by deeds of lease and release, dated respectively the 18th and 19th February, 1730, conveyed to "John Roberts of Dean's "Court in the County of Middlesex esq[r]" * * * * * "all that said Barony consisting of Twelve thousand acres "of Land English measure situate lying and being upon "Waccamaw River commonly called Hobcaw point"[4]

The consideration paid by John Roberts was £500 sterling   There is nothing on the record to indicate that Lord Carteret did anything towards settling up and reducing to cultivable condition any part of the barony; and the price paid would rather import that there were no improvements on the tract when sold

The General Assembly in 1731 enacted a Statute declaring that, whenever upon a resurvey it should appear that there was actually contained within the bounds of any person's plat more acres of land than was expressed in the grant then the person holding the plat should be preferred before any other person for a new grant for such overplus, at the same quit-rent as reserved in the original grant

[1]Trans Hist Soc of S C , vol 1, p 191
[2]Ibid, p   192
[3]Off Hist Commⁿ Bk "Grants 1694-1739," p 457
[4]Office Secy of State, Grant Bk B   B 1734-1737, p 571

John Roberts applied to the Crown for a resurvey of the barony to ascertain the acreage within the bounds of the plat of the barony, and on such resurvey it was found that the barony as originally surveyed and laid out contained 13,970 acres He thereupon applied under the Statute for a grant to cover the overplus and on 30 September, 1736, a formal grant was issued to him, granting him the overplus and recognizing and confirming to him the entire acreage of 13.970 acres as contained in the boundaries of the plat annexed to the original grant to Lord Carteret.[5]

From John Roberts the barony passed to Sir William Baker, Nicholas Linwood, and Brice Fisher. The record so far as the writer has been able to examine does not show exactly when or for what consideration John Roberts parted with the property, or whether or not during his ownership anything was done towards its reclamation On 21 October, 1765, Sir William Baker, Nicholas Linwood and Brice Fisher (all apparently merchants of London) appointed Paul Trapier and Francis Stuart or the survivour as their attorneys, with full power of sale of the property[6] Francis Stuart soon after died, leaving Paul Trapier as his survivour under the power Paul Trapier was the son or grandson of the ancestor of the family of that name in lower South Carolina, and was at the time apparently a merchant in Georgetown The division of the barony seems to have been made at that time, for the sale was made in parcels

The first sale according to the record was apparently to Robert Heriot, to whom Paul Trapier as attorney conveyed 2,177 acres on 5th November, 1766[7] On 12 December. 1766, he conveyed 2,412 acres to Thomas Mitchell,[8] and on 2nd January, 1767, the following transfers were made. viz:

    To Benjamin Huger, 1711 acres[9]
    To Benjamin Trapier, 1515 acres[10]
    To Peter Secare, 1061½ acres.[11]

[5] Ibid
[6] M C O Charleston, Bk T No 4. p 64
[7] Ibid
[8] Unrecorded MSS deed
[9] M C O Charleston, Bk W No 4. p 11
[10] Ibid Bk Y No 3 p 1
[11] Ibid l 1 l   p 1

On 6th January, 1767, the lower or southern end of the barony including the "point" proper and aggregating 3,303¾ acres was sold to Samuel Clegg[12]

There was another sale made to Henry James Daubuz The deed is not on record, but the conveyance to Peter Secare gives as his North boundary Henry James Daubuz Thus by the 2nd January, 1767, the entire barony had been disposed of in these parcels

Beginning from the Northern boundary line and going South, the order of the subdivisions sold was as follows:

Thomas Mitchell	2,412 acres
Robert Heriot	2,177 "
Benjamin Huger	1,711 "
Henry James Daubuz, estimated	1,789¾ "
Peter Secare	1,061½ "
Benjamin Trapier	1,515 "
Samuel Clegg	3,303¾ "
Contents of barony	13,970 "

Thomas Mitchell died apparently early in 1768 He left a will[13] whereby he devised the tract of 2,412 acres, part of Hobcaw Barony, to his son Edward He left a wife, Hester (née Esther Marion and widow of John Allston), three sons, Anthony, Thomas, and Edward, and three daughters, Mary (who married Maurice Simons), Sarah, and Elizabeth Edward (who married Mary Moore) was the father of Dr Edward Mitchell, who for many years resided on Edisto Island and was the father of the late Julian Mitchell of the City of Charleston.

Edward Mitchell, to whom the 2,412 acres had been devised, on 9th March, 1785, conveyed 1,206 acres or the northern half to William Allston,[14] sometime Captain in Marion's command and afterwards Col William Alston This tract was afterwards known by the name of "Clifton" and appears to have continued in the descendants of William Allston until a few years ago

[12]Ibid, Bk L No 3, p 61
[13]Prob Court Charleston, Bk 1761-1777, p 169
[14]M C O Charleston, Bk. Q No 5, p 446

The southern half, or 1,206 acres, was on 4th February, 1786, conveyed by Edward Mitchell to John Allston   It was subsequently known by the name of "Forlorn Hope." From John Allston the property apparently descended to his only daughter, Mary, who married (en seconde noces) Benjamin Huger (son of Major Benjamin Huger of the Revolution).   It was, or rather 793 acres of it was, under the name of "Forlorn Hope" transferred in 1835 by the executors of Benjamin Huger to William Algernon Alston [15]

To the tract of 2,177 acres conveyed to Robert Heriot he added the 1,711 acres conveyed to Major Benjamin Huger and which the latter on 15 January, 1772, conveyed to Robert Heriot [16]   Making 3,888 acres acquired and held by Heriot.

After Heriot's death his executors conveyed 1,243 acres, being the northern "slice" of the 3,888 acres to Roger Heriot, who conveyed it to M[rs]. Mary Heriot, who on 1st January, 1802, conveyed it to William Alston [17] This plantation was known as "Rose Hill" and was on 1st January, 1803, transferred by Col William Alston to his son, William Algernon Alston [18]

The next slice of this 3,888 acres forms the plantation known as "Alderley." Exactly when it was transferred from Robert Heriot or his estate the record does not show, but in 1802 it appears to have been owned by Benjamin Huger (son of Major Benjamin Huger) and in 1808 by Col. Francis Kinloch Huger, the youngest son of the same Major Benjamin Huger, who held it for many years

The remainder of the 3,888 acres, after Heriot's death, was sold off apparently in two "slices" to Thomas Young The uppermost seems to have been called "Armordale" or "Annadale" and was after Young's death sold off in separate parcels, that bounding on the river containing . . . . acres was acquired by Benjamin Allston and afterwards known as "Oryzantia," and the pineland and sea shore part containing some 460 acres was sold off to Col William

---

[15] Unrecorded MSS deed
[16] M C. O. Charleston, Bk T No 4, p 61
[17] Unrecorded MSS deed
[18] Unrecorded MSS deed

Alston 5th April, 1808." The next slice of 780 acres was purchased from Heriot's estate by Thomas Young 30 Jany., 1794," and called "Youngville." At Young's death this also was sold in separate parcels, the riceland portion, fronting on Waccamaw river was on 8th March, 1808," sold to Benjamin Allston, S[r], for 296 acres, and the pineland and sea shore part on the same day sold to William Alston, and together with the 460 acres adjoining formed Col William Alston's "Crab Hall" tract The 296 acres of Youngville, purchased by Benjamin Allston, was also subsequently transferred to Col. William Alston.

The tract bought by Henry James Daubuz seems to have been divided; 870 acres called "Bellfield" at some time passed into the hands of Thomas Young, at whose death it was sold to Col William Alston, on 8th March, 1808." The remainder of the Daubuz tract seems at some time to have become united in the lands of the holder of the tract of 1,061½ acres of Peter Secare and to have been known with the last by the name of "Marietta."

The 1,515 acres sold to Benjamin Trapier he seems to have transferred to William Burnett, for Burnett on 9th July, 1784, split it in two slices, the upper of 746½ acres subsequently known as "Friendfield" he transferred to Edward Martin," and the lower of 768½ acres, subsequently known as "Strawberry Hill" he transferred to Peter Foissin."

The 3,303¾ acres sold to Samuel Clegg was also divided into two, sometime after his purchase, by a line running north and south from the boundary of the purchase to Winyah Bay. The western part fronting on the Bay and on Waccamaw river was called "Calais," and in 1796 was owned by the Rev Hugh Fraser, the Rector of the Parish of All Saints. It was from him the point received the name of "Frasers Point," by which it is now known.

The eastern part was sold to one Michaux

[19]Unrecorded MSS deed
[20]Ibid
[21]Ibid
[22]Ibid
[23]M C O Charleston Bk F No 6 p 560
[24]Ibid, Bk Q No 5, p 200

All these lower plantations, Marietta, Friendfield, Strawberry Hill, Frasers Point or Calais, and Michaux, were in 1860 owned by the late William Algernon Alston, and thus it will be seen that the entire barony, with the single exception of "Alderley" was at one date or another owned by an Alston.

The destruction of the records of Georgetown County during the war of 1861-1865 renders it very difficult, if not impossible, to trace connectedly the devolution of the title to the Barony as subdivided to the present time

The barony became, with the rest of Waccamaw neck comprising All Saints Parish, a part of that rich, populous and productive rice planting region in Georgetown County The barony, as a part of the long narrow peninsula between the sea and Waccamaw river had no distinctive history apart from the remainder The plantations into which it was subdivided became a part of the series of plantations stretching from Winyah Bay to the Horry County line The crop—the money crop—of these plantations was rice As a rule the plantation of each owner extended in a "slice" from the river to the sea In the case of many, if not most, the rice land included in addition to a body of rice land on the peninsula proper, another body of rice land on the west side of the Waccamaw river upon the delta or swamp lying between the Waccamaw and Peedee rivers. The high land on the peninsula was the site of the dwellings of the planters and of their negro labourers Most of the planters had also a summer residence upon the sea beaches or near to them, either upon that part of the seashore attached to the plantation proper or upon some more accessible beach The high land also furnished the soil for the corn, oats and other crops, as well as the pasturage for the live stock

The reclamation of this large area of swamp growth and its reduction to a condition of arable productivity was an enormous task for the time when, and the labour with which, it was performed

Originally, from the contemporaneous descriptions, this swamp was covered with a thick forest growth of cypress and gum, intermixed with other swamp growth. It was also subject to the flux and reflux of the tides   Twice in every twenty-four hours the land was submerged by the tidal flow and no work could be performed on it until the water receded   In periods of excessive rain and the freshets thereby caused the swollen waters from the river might remain on the lands for days or weeks, the fall of the tide on such occasions being insufficient to lay bare the land To reclaim the soil under such circumstances it had first to be dyked or banked in and then the forest growth had to be removed, and then the land had to be again canalled, ditched and banked into smaller subdivisions, so as to permit the tilth of the soil and its proper drainage and irrigation   Nothing but an ocular inspection of the area can give an adequate idea of the skilful engineering and patient, intelligent supervision that went to the successful result   The only labour at the disposal of the settlers who accomplished the feat was of the most unskilled character, African savages fresh from the Guinea coast   It was an achievement no less skilful than that which excites our wonder in viewing the works of the ancient Egyptians The task of reclaiming a swamp delta such as that between the Waccamaw and Peedee rivers involved an engineering skill no less than the construction of a pyramid, yet no one knows how many decades went to the last, and the first was performed in comparatively a few years.   In both cases the labour was forced, a corvée, but in all probability the Egyptian was more skilled, better trained and under more exact discipline.

The southern planter who accomplished the result was a man who worked with his brains on an extended scale: but he gave to his task no less assiduous, continuous and patient industry than the northern farmer who worked with his hands in the field on a small scale

Most of the earlier grants to land on Waccamaw neck seem to have been made, commencing about the year 1711, when Landgrave Robert Daniell, Thomas Hepworth, Michael Brewton, Joseph Pawley, Percival Pawley and others obtained grants on the neck north of the barony   The space of this article is too limited (as really it should be confined to the barony) to give any detailed account of the successive grantees and settlers of the neck

Somewhere about 1730, as approximately as the writer can judge, the Alston or Allston family acquired lands and settled on Waccamaw.

The two first comers of the name appear to have been John and William, two of the sons of John Alston the original immigrant.[25] Exactly where they settled the writer has not been able to definitely determine. From tradition and from the fact that each of the two plantations has a private family cemetery or burying ground upon it, it is probable, as a safe surmise, that their respective settlements were at "Turkey Hill" and "The Oaks." A copy of the inscriptions over the graves at "Turkey Hill"[26] and "The Oaks"[27] have already been published in this Magazine None of the stones at either are very old: the oldest being at "Turkey Hill" dated 1780

The immigrant John Alston spelt his name with a single "l." His descendants on Waccamaw seem to have accepted and used the spelling Allston, using the double "ll". About 1792 his great grandson, Col William Alston returned to the original form and all the descendants of this last have ever since used the single "l" The other members of the family and their descendants have retained the form Allston.

Whenever and wherever the Alstons or Allstons located they in no great space of time spread out and gradually acquired a good majority of the area of the neck There are some plantations that have been always held by other names, but it is no exaggeration to say that at one time or another the great majority, say four-fifths, of the plantations on the entire neck has been owned by one of the name of Alston or Allston If the usual habit of this American country had been followed of ignoring the name given by

---

[25] S C Hist & Gen Mag , vol 6, p 116
[26] S C Hist & Gen Mag vol 10 p 181
[27] Ibid , l2, p

the aborigines and substituting the name of a settler the
peninsula might well have been called Alston land or
Alston's neck.

In June, 1777, the Marquis de la Fayette landed in South
Carolina.[28] He had sailed from Bordeau on the 26th March,
preceding under the name of Gilbert du Motier in company
with the Baron de Kalb and several other officers from the
French army, and landed near Georgetown on the 14th
June [29] Garden. in his anecdotes,[30] says they "landed on
"North Island in Winyaw Bay and were welcomed with
"the most cordial hospitality by the family of Major Huger,
"who made it their summer residence"

The late Col. Francis Kinloch Huger (son of Major
Benjamin Huger), according to his own account as related
by his daughter, the late Miss Elizabeth Huger, stated "that
"General la Fayette had first landed at my father's house
"on North Island in the harbour of Georgetown in South
"Carolina   The small vessel in which they had sailed from
"France, made the land off that part of the coast, lying as
"they knew to the north of Charleston * * * They
"sent a boat to obtain information, and observing a canoe
"fishing outside the breakers desired it might be brought
"to their vessel   The negroes in the canoe were people of
"my father's, who * * * piloted the boat * * *
"to my father's house on the island, which they reached
"about nightfall * * * These circumstances were told
"me by my mother   Their guests remained with them
"another day and night until a carriage and horses could
"be brought from the plantation and my father accompanied
"them by land to Charleston "[31]

Johnson, in his "Traditions of the American Revolution"
"states.[32] "In 1777, while residing on his rice plantation
"near Georgetown. Major Huger was called upon by two
"strangers, neither of whom could speak a word of Eng-
"lish * * * They told him that they had left France
"to visit America and had been put ashore near George-

[28]Gazette of State of S C, for June 16 1777
[29]Appleton's Ency of Biography "La Fayette"
[30]1st series, p 95
[31]"Olmutz." pp 5. 6
[32]p. ...

"town on North Island, wishing to proceed northwardly.
"One of them announced himself as the Marquis de la
"Fayette, the other as the Baron de Steuben They were
"hospitably entertained by Major Huger, introduced to his
"neighbours and friends and then conveyed in his own
"equipage to Charleston "

Johnson's account is evidently not exact He wrote
many many years later (in 1851). It was Baron de Kalb
not Steuben who came with de la Fayette Steuben arrived in America on 1st Decr, 1777, at Portsmouth, New
Hampshire[22] The rest of Johnson's account of Major
Benjamin Huger and his family is very inaccurate.

The Marquis himself states as follows. "After having
"encountered for seven weeks various perils and chances
"we arrived at Georgetown in Carolina Ascending the
"river in a canoe his foot touched at length the American
"soil and he swore that he would conquer or perish in that
"cause Landing at midnight at Major Huger's house he
"found a vessel sailing for France which appeared only
"waiting for his letters Several of the officers landed,
"others remained on board and all hastened to proceed to
"Charleston "[23]

On the 15th June, writing to his wife "at Major Hugers"
he says

"I have arrived my dearest love in perfect health at the
"home of an American Officer * * * I am going this
"evening to Charleston "[24]

And again writing to her from Charleston, on the 19th
June, he says "I first saw and judged of a country life
"at Major Huger's house "[25]

In a note to these memoirs it is stated that in 1828, Mr
Jared Sparks, preparing to publish the writings of Washington, made a voyage to France and saw and conversed
with de la Fayette, from whom he obtained much information, and it is believed that the details of de la Fayette's

[22] Ency: Brit, 11th Ed, vol. 25, p 904
[23] Memoirs, correspondence and manuscripts of General Lafayette, published by his family, London, 1837, vol 1, p 14.
[24] Ibid, p 92
[25] Ibid p 94

narrative as given by Sparks was related or written by the Marquis himself[31]

Sparks in his "Writings of Washington," vol V, p. 450, states as to de la Fayette's arrival· "It was dark before "they came so near the shore as to be able to land La "Fayette and some of the officers entered the ships boat, "which was rowed to the beach Here they debarked and "a distant light served to guide them. When they arrived "near the house whence the light proceeded the dogs "growled and barked and the people within supposed them "to be a party of marauders from the enemy's vessels   * "* * He found himself in the house of Major Huger, a "gentleman not more remarkable for his hospitality than "for his worth and highly respectable character Major "Huger provided horses to convey him and his companions "to Charleston."

It seems most plausible that after a long sea journey the travellers landed at the first avilable landing place, viz on North Island at the entrance to the harbour, and there found Major Huger at his summer residence on the seashore, the customary place for planters in the neighborhood to make their summer residence The writer of this article can state that the tradition when he was a boy among the old planters who made their summer residence on South Island, was that a large sand hill or dune on North Island, just opposite, was the first land in America trodden by de la Fayette Of late—very recent—years an impression has existed that the plantation called "Prospect Hill" on the Waccamaw, was the plantation of Major Huger visited by de la Fayette This is wholly erroneous Major Huger never owned or is known to have occupied "Prospect Hill" In 1777 "Prospect Hill" was owned by Joseph Allston who devised it to his son Thomas, who married his cousin Mary, daughter of Captain John Allston of the "Foot Rangers or Rovers,"[38] also apparently called the "Raccoon" company of riflemen,[39] who, under Col.

[31]Ibid, p 6, note
[38]Coll[ns] Hist Soc , vol 3, p 128, and S C Hist & Gen Mag , vol 9, p 116
[39]Drayton's Memoirs vol 2, pp 288 289

William Thomson, were on the 28 June, 1776, posted to resist General Clinton's expected crossing from Long Island to Sullivan's Island.[40] Capt John Allston died in 1795.[41] Thomas Allston died in 1794 and devised to his wife, Mary, "Prospect Hill" and she married Benjamin Huger, the eldest son of Major Benjamin Huger From the identity of name between father and son, and the fact that the son lived at his wife's plantation of "Prospect Hill," has no doubt arisen the supposition that de la Fayette visited his father there.

Col Francis Kinloch Huger, the youngest son of Major Benjamin Huger owned at one time the plantation called "Alderley," which was a part of the barony As Robert Heriot seems to have owned up to 1794 the part of the barony which, as near as the writer can locate, it seems to have formed the "Alderley" plantation, it was impossible to have been in 1777 owned by Major Benjamin Huger

It was this Col. Francis Kinloch Huger who made the gallant, if unsuccessful, attempt in 1794 to enable the Marquis de la Fayette to escape from the Austrian fortress or prison of Olmutz, for which Col Huger himself paid the penalty of an imprisonment for eight months awaiting trial and performing his sentence.

As de la Fayette arrived at nightfall on the 14th June, and wrote on the 15th that he was going that evening to Charlestown, he did not have much time to visit plantations any distance removed from North Island

The expression in his letter of the 19th June, that he first saw and judged of a country life at Major Huger's house must be taken as referring to his house on North Island The old post road came down Waccamaw neck to Calais or Fraser's Point and thence there was a ferry to Dover on the opposite shore of the Bay, and from Dover the road went by Lynch's ferry over the Santee to Charleston. De la Fayette was probably ferried directly across to Dover (leaving Georgetown to the West) and thence proceeded to Charleston

---

[40] Ibid
[41] S. C Hist & Gen Mag vol 12 p 40

Major Benjamin Huger had a plantation called "Richmond" on Peedee (possibly the plantation of that name just outside of Georgetown)." He had married *en seconde noces* Miss Marie Esther Kinloch, who seems to have resided with her mother at the Kensington plantation, next above Richmond, and was also interested in the "Rice Hope" plantation of her father on Santee river, very near the road to Charleston by Lynch's ferry So that if after going to Major Hugers summer residence on North Island de la Fayette also accompanied him to his plantation, it may have been any of the three last named places, but was quite certainly *not* "Prospect Hill."

The island bordering the ocean on the eastern boundary of the barony commonly known as "Debidue" island was anciently called Yahany or Yauhaney island, and the inlet to the north was Yahany inlet The island was afterwards called Sandy island and later Dubordieu island, whence the corruption "Debidue"

North of the barony line, Prospect Hill, Fairfield, Oak Hill, Bannockburn, Hagley, Weehauka, True Blue, Midway, Waverly, Turkey Hill, The Oaks, Brookgreen, Wachesaw, and Woodburn, were also at one time or another owned by an Alston or Allston The Forlorn Hope place was as stated the property of Capt: John Allston of the "Foot Rangers." The Midway plantation was at one time the plantation of the late Benjamin Faneuil Dunkin, a native of Massachusetts, who moved to South Carolina early in the last century, became a Chancellor and later Chief Justice of her courts and a most honoured and loyal citizen Hagley plantation was the property and home of Plowden Charles Jennett Weston, a gentleman of most excellent education and rare ability, and one of the first members of the Historical Society of South Carolina. Profoundly interested in the preservation of the history of the State, he printed at his own expense a volume of "Documents connected with the History of South Carolina," which he dedicated to the Society, trusting it might "be only an advanced skirmisher, "the predecessor of a long array of useful and curious "works published under the auspices of the Society"

"See case of Washington vs. Huger, 1 DeS. Rep , 360

Possessed of large affluence, when the hour of conflict and trial of this country arrived he sought no immunity therefrom, but freely and zealously devoted both his purse and his person to his country's service

"The Oaks" appears to have been an original Alston settlement. It belonged to William Allston (the son of John Alston the immigrant) from whom it passed to his son Joseph Allston, who was a gentleman of large fortune, mostly of his own acquisition, and great intelligence, who did much to settle and improve the Parish. He was the father of Captain (afterwards known as Colonel) William Alston of Marion's command, to whose son and his own grandson, Joseph Alston, he devised the Oaks.[43] This last Joseph Alston was also a man of rare talents. At an early age he was elected to the Legislature and made Speaker of the House, and in 1812 he was made Governor of the State. In 1801 he married Theodosia Burr and the home of the two was thereafter at "The Oaks."[44] It was at the Oaks or the Seashore place in the neighborhood that their son, Aaron Burr Alston, died on the 30th June, 1812, and it was from the Oaks that Theodosia Burr Alston departed to sail on the 30 December, 1812, on the pilot boat built schooner *Patriot* from Georgetown to New York. She went at the urgent solicitation of her father, who had but lately returned to this country, to meet him in New York

The "Patriot" was a schooner that had been built for a pilot boat, but which had been fitted out for and used as a privateer after the declaration of war with England. It had come into Georgetown to refit and then proceed to New York, carrying her guns dismounted and under deck. Mr Timothy Green, a friend of Colonel Burr, had at the latters request come to South Carolina to attend Mrs Alston on the voyage, so as to give her the medical attention her father conceived her state of health might require. They both sailed in the "Patriot." Governor Alston accompanied his wife to a point near Georgetown bar and there parted with her at noon, Thursday December 31st, 1812. The vessel never reached her destination.

---

[43] See "Theodosia" by Chas. Felton Pidgin. Boston, 1907, p 230
[44] Ibid, p 274

nor was it or any of her crew or passengers seen again A severe gale prevailed from the 1st January, 1813, for some days off the coast of North Carolina, and there is no reasonable doubt but that the "Patriot" was lost and all on board perished during that gale. She carried her guns as cargo or ballast under deck and if imperfectly secured they had broken loose during the storm, that casualty would have been sufficient to account for her foundering. The story of her having been captured by pirates resting on the fiction-like confessions of alleged old freebooters and supposed to be corroborated by an unidentified picture found on an abandoned vessel, as narrated by an illiterate old woman of Nags Head, North Carolina, and fanciful resemblances between the lady in the picture and cousins of Theodosia Burr in the 4th and 5th degree, involves so many inconsistencies, contradictions and improbabilities, not to say impossibilities, as to deprive it of the merit of any serious consideration

Governor Joseph Alston died 10 September, 1816, and was buried in the family cemetery at "The Oaks" by the side of his son

Brookgreen plantation was owned by Capt William Allston (also an officer in Marion's command)." He was the father of Washington Allston the artist, who is by tradition stated to have been born at Brookgreen. He was born on 5th November, 1779.

Waccamaw Neck was originally included in the Parish of Prince George's Winyaw, as that Parish was created by the Act of 10 March, 1721 By Act of Assembly, passed 23 May, 1767, all the lands lying between the sea and Waccamaw river, as far as the boundary line of North Carolina, were constituted a separate Parish under the name of the Parish of All Saints Waccamaw " By an Act passed 16 Mach, 1778," All Saints Parish was made a separate political division, electing two members of the General Assembly By the constitution of 1808 it elected one member of the House and also a Senator This con-

"Mills' Statistics of S C, p 570
"Stats of S C, vol 4, p 268
"Ibid, p 407.

tinued until 1865, when the Parish was abolished as a separate political subdivision. The Act of 1778 is almost a transcript of that of 1767, except that in that of 1778 the parish is divided off as a political electing unit from the Parish of Prince George Winyah and the Commissioners to build the Church Chapel of Ease and Parsonage named in the first Act were William Allston, Joseph Allston, Charles Lewis, William Pawley, Josias Allston, William Allston, J^r., and John Clarke, and in the second Act, Percival Pawley, Joseph Allston, and Thomas Butler

The Revd Alexander Glennie, the Rector of the Parish from 1832 to 1866, in his address at the laying of the corner stone of the new Church in All Saints Parish, on 27th December, 1843, stated:

"What was done by the above named Commissioners, "or at what period the original building which stood upon "this spot was erected cannot now be ascertained It is "well known that the Glebe was purchased & the Church "built before the Revolutionary War

"About the year 1793 Capt. John Allston of this Parish "caused the old Church then in a state of dilapidation, to "be taken down & had the building which lately stood here "erected at a cost of £100 sterling. This was repaired & "the interior fitted up with pews &c in 1813 On the 19th "of Novr. 1816, it was consecrated by the name of *the* "*Parish Church of All Saints* * * * by the R^t Rev^d "Theodore Dehon, at that time Bishop of this Diocese "

In 1838 M^{rs}. Mary Huger, daughter of Capt John Allston just mentioned, and widow of Benjamin Huger, son of Major Benjamin Huger, the host of de la Fayette, died, and by her Will directed her residuary estate to be paid to the vestry and wardens of the Upper Episcopal Church of All Saints Parish. The amount paid in 1840, under this request, was $5,441 81, and in 1843 the vestry determined to build a brick church, upon the site of the Parish church, with the proceeds of this bequest The corner stone was laid 27 Dec^r, 1843, and in April, 1844, the church was completed and the pews sold and on 8th April, 1845, the new building was consecrated by the R^t Revd Christopher E Gadsden, then Bishop of the Diocese It was much larger than the one it displaced and contained galleries on each side for the accommodation of the negroes   Col Joshua John Ward presented an organ to the church   M". Francis M Weston presented a bible, prayer book, a chancel chair, a marble font and a carpet for the chancel desk and pulpit   Plowden C J Weston, Esqr, presented all the necessary furniture and benches for the communion table

This edifice is still standing   A copy of the inscription on the corner stone was published in this Magazine in the number for July, 1912   Owing to mutilations and defacements it is given there imperfectly   The exact inscription taken from a copy in M' Glennie's papers is as follows

On the S E side

"The first edifice built of wood before the | Revolution "was taken down about A D 1793 | The second also of "wood was built about A D 1793 | by Capt John Allston "was repaired in 1813 | and was taken down in 1843 | This "third edifice will be erected chiefly | with the funds be- "queathed to this Church by | Mrs Mary Huger daughter "of the above | Capt John Allston | Building Committee: "Edward T Heriot | Francis M Weston, Joshua J Ward, "T Pinckney Alston. John H Tucker Architect and "Builder Lewis Rebb |"

On the N E side

"Corner Stone of the third Edifice | erected on this site | "under the appellation of | the Parish Church of All "Saints | Laid by the Rev⁴ Alex' Glennie A M | Rector "of the Parish | Dec' 27. 1843 | Glory be to God | The "Father Son and Holy Ghost "

A Church or Chapel of Ease was built in the lower part of the Parish about 1819, near the main highroad on the Oak Hill plantation   This was altered and enlarged in 1841 and accommodation provided for the negroes. and it was again further altered in 1851   The edifice was of wood and was destroyed by fire soon after the war of 1861-1865

A third church for the accommodation of the inhabitants of the Parish was built in the upper part of the Parish near the highroad on Wachesaw plantation   The corner stone was laid 2ᵈ. April, 1855, with the following inscriptions thereon

East side

In The Name of The Father | The Son & The Holy Ghost | Amen | The Right Revᵈ. T. F. Davis D. D | Bishop of South Carolina | Laid This As the Corner Stone of | A Building Dedicated To The Worship of | Almighty GOD | According To the Rites of the | Protestant Episcopal Church | Under The Name of | Saint John The Evange- list | On the II Day of April MDCCCLV |

North side

Rector of All Saints Parish | The Revᵈ Alexander Glen- nie A M. | Assistant Minister | The Revᵈ Lucien Charles Lance B A. | Building Committee | Francis W Heriot | Plowden C J Weston | Allard B. Flagg | Glory Be To God on High & on | Earth Peace Good Will | Towards Men |

The building was consecrated 15 April, 1859. This building has also been destroyed

In addition to the foregoing churches there were erected upon many of the plantations, chapels for the special ac- commodation of the negroes. In 1858, according to the report of the Revᵈ. Mʳ Glennie for that year there were no less than twelve plantation chapels constructed and in use

According to the census of 1790 there were in All Saints Parish 430 free whites and 1,795 slaves. Of these last, 877 were reported as owned by the six Allstons named as slave owners. Alexander Wilson the celebrated ornithol- ogist who made a trip thro' the lower part of South Caro- lina in 1809, thus describes his journey on Waccamaw.

"On arriving at the Wackamaw Peedee and Black river "I made long zigzags among the rich nabobs who live on "their rice plantations, amidst large villages of negro huts. "One of these gentlemen told me that he had 'something " 'better than six hundred head of blacks.' These excur- "sions detained me greatly The roads to the plantations "were so long, so difficult to find, and so bad, and the "hospitality of the planters was such, that I could scarcely "get away again "

In 1826 Mills in his statistics gives Georgetown County as possessing agricultural lands of the highest value in the entire State, choice spots of first quality rice lands selling for $300 per acre and averaging $100 per acre

Upon no section of the State of South Carolina has the economic and social destruction consequent upon the war of 1861-1865 fallen more heavily than on All Saints Parish Its inhabitants were land holding people who had so been for generations   Its lands were still held largely by descendants of the first settlers   Its industry was chiefly the cultivation of rice under a system that required a skilled disciplined and compulsory labour   With the loss of over a century's accumulated capital and the disappearance of that method of labour, the entire system upon which former prosperity was based was swept away.   The old were as a rule unable to meet the change, the young had not the capital

Forty-eight years after 1865 and nearly every acre of the Neck has passed from the descendants of those who held it in 1860   Practically not an acre of rice is cultivated Nearly every old plantation home has been burnt or abandoned   The home of Joseph and Theodosia Alston at the Oaks has shared the common fate.   Over the once fertile and arable rice fields, now abandoned, the tide flows daily as it did before they were reclaimed and Hobcaw Barony is but a large game preserve   Alas for Waccamaw

REGISTER OF
ST ANDREW'S PARISH, BERKELEY COUNTY, SOUTH CAROLINA

1719-1774

Copied and Edited by Mabel L. Webber.

(Continued from the January Number)

FUNERALS PR THE REV^d M^r. GUY

Richard Son of Richard Godfrey & Rebecca his wife Buried Nov^{br}. ye 20th 1745

John Penyman Schoolmaster at Thomas Drayton Esq Buried Decr ye 15th 1745

Elizabeth the wife of Thomas Wright Buried Dec^{br} ye 15th 1745.

Gabriel the Son of William Brandford and Ann his wife Buried Dec^{br} 19th 1745

Thomas Elmes Buried Dec^{br} ye 22^d 1745

Mary the wife of William Miles Senr Buried Jan^{ry}: ye 13th 1745*

Elizabeth the wife of Thomas Hudson Buried Jan^{ry} ye 11th 1745*

Ann The wife of Henry Wood Buried Jan^{ry} ye 28th 1745*

Cathrine Daught^r of John Man & Anne his wife Buried Feb^{ry}. ye 10th 1745*

Martha Daughter of William Chapman Senr Buried Feb^{ry} ye 25th 1745*

Elizabeth the wife of Joseph Williams Buried March ye 17th 1745*

Thomas Williams Buried April ye 4th 1746

Joseph Stent a Prentice to John Man Buried April 12th 1746.

Anne the wife of John Miles Buried April ye 23^d 1746

Elizabeth Boneau widow of Jacob Boneau Buried April ye 27th 1746

*1746 us ..i.

Ann the Daught^r of Thomas Mell Buried May ye 8th 1746.

James Bowman (Son of Robt. Bowman Decs^d.) Buried Sep^{tr} ye 1 1746

Margret Davis a Poor woman Buried p^r the Parish from Mr Clark's Septr. ye 30th 1746

Jacob Knape (or Ness's) a Dutch Boy a Prentice or Servt. to Mr Gordon Buried Sep^{tr} y^e: 30th 1746.

Ann Daught^r of William Chapman & Margret his wife Buried Octo^{br}. y^e: 1st. 1746

William Son of Christopher Guy & Mary his wife Buried Octo^{br} ye 7th 1746.

Mary Daugh^{tr} of Mary Wright (widow to Richard Wright Decs^d) Buried Octob^r ye 7th 1746

Jane Daught^r of William Cattell Junr Buried Octo^{br} ye 28th 1746

Richard Son of John Man & Anne his wife Buried Dec^{br} ye 2^d 1746

James Cheshire Buried Deb^r ye 3^d. 1746

Thomas Stoakes Buried De^{br} ye 30th 1746

Samuel Whitefield Buried (a youth under the Care of William Cattell Junr Esq) Buried Nov^{br} ye 27th 1746

BIRTHS

Samuel Son of Samuel Burges & Mary his wife Born——— 1745

Elizabeth Daught^r of William Godfrey & Ann his wife Born Nov^{br} ye 2^d 1745.

Sarah Daught^r. of Nathaniel Fuller & Sarah his wife Born July ye 8^{tb} 1746

Richard Son of John Mann & Ann his wife Born Octo^{br} ye 5th 1746

Rebecca Daught^r to John Rivers & Elizabeth his wife born 1746

Richard the Son of Ann Guy widow Alias Fickling Born Dec^{br}. ye 31st 1746

Sarah Daught^r of Petter Cattell & Mary his wife Born August ye 16th 1746

Mary-Ann Daught^r of Henry Wood & Elizabeth his wife was Born Feb^{ry} ye 11th 1746

George, Son of Edmond 2ᵈ Landgrave Bellinger & Eliza⁺ᵇ. his Wife Born August 1ˢᵗ. 1724 [sic]

Mary-Bellinger the Daughter of the sᵈ Edmond 2ᵈ, Landgrave Bellinger & Eliz⁺ᵇ his wife born September the 27ᵗʰ. 1726

John, Son of Thomas Radcliff & Eliz⁺ᵇᵗʰ his wife, Born Jan⁺ʸ. yᵉ 18ᵗʰ 1747

{ John, Son of Thomas Holman & Mary his wife was Born March yᵉ 16ᵗʰ. 1746: at 3 oClock in the Morning (John first born)

William the Son of ibid Born March yᵉ 16ᵗʰ at 2 oClock in yᵉ afternoon 1746. (Sons, twins) }

Sarah Daught⁺ of Benjamin Parrott & Ann his wife born May yᵉ 7ᵗʰ. 1747.

Mary Daught⁺ of Joseph Williams & Anne his wife born July yᵉ 2ᵈ 1747

Rebecca Daught⁺ of Christopher Guy & Mary his wife Born ――― 1747

William Son of John Godfrey & Mary his wife Born ――― 1747

Charles the Son of George Bodinton and Sarah his wife Born Sep⁺ʳ yᵉ 23ᵈ. 1747

Robert the Son of John Man & Anne his wife Born Nov⁺ᵇʳ. yᵉ 26ᵗʰ 1747

CHRISTININGS PR Yᵉ REVᵈ Wᵐ. GUY

Elizabeth Daugh⁺ʳ of William Godfrey & Ann his wife Bap⁺ᵗᵈ. July yᵉ 8ᵗʰ 1746

Sarah Daugh⁺ʳ. of Nathaniel Fuller & Sarah his wife Bap⁺ᵗᵈ July yᵉ 30ᵗʰ: 1746

Samuel Son of Cornelus Vangelder & Elizabeth his wife Bapt⁺ᵈ Sept⁺ yᵉ 29ᵗʰ 1746 Prv⁺ Bapt⁺ᵐ

Mary-Ann Daugh⁺ʳ of George Wage: man and Sibila his wife Bapt⁺ᵈ Octob⁺ yᵉ 5 1746 Serv⁺ˢ to Thomas Drayton

Richard Son of John Man & Anne his wife Bap⁺ᵗᵈ. Octo⁺ᵇʳ yᵉ 6ᵗʰ. 1746

Rebeca Daught⁺ of John Rivers & Elizabeth his wife Baptizᵈ Octob⁺ yᵉ 7ᵗʰ 1746

Richard Son of Anne Guy widow Alis Fickling Bapt^{zd}
   Feb^{ry} ye 8th. 1746.*

Sarah Daught^r of Petter Cattell & Mary his wife Bap^{tzd}
   Feb^{ry} ye 16th 1746*

Mary-kathrine Daught^r. of Petter Areheart (Swis) &
   Mary his wife Bapt^{izd} Feb^{ry} ye 16th 1746

Mary-Ann Daugh^{tr} of Henry Wood & Elizabeth his wife
   Bapt^{zd}, March ye 3^d 1746 *

Thos the Son of Thos. Heyward & Anne his wife Bap^d
   March 31st. 1747

George Son of Edmond 2^d Landgrave Bellinger & Elizth
   his Wife, Daughter of Shem Butler Esqr, an Adult,
   Bap^d. May 15, 1747

Mary Bellinger, Daughter to the s^d. Edmond the 2^d Landgrave Bellinger, & Elizth his wife Daughter of Shem
   Butler Esqr, an Adult, Bap^d May 15th 1747

John Son of Thomas Radcliff & Eliz^{bth} his wife Bap^{tzd},
   June ye 8th 1747

{ John Son of Thomas Holman & Mary his wife Bapt^{zd}.
   July ye 5th 1747
  William Son of ibid Bapt^{zd} July 5th 1747.

Sarah Daught^r of Benjamin Parrott & Anne his wife
   Bap^{tzd}. Pri^t Bap^{tm} August ye 2^d 1747

Mary Daught^r. of Joseph Williams & Anne his wife
   Bapt^{zd}. August ye 21st. 1747

Rebecca Daugh^{tr}. of Christopher Guy & Mary his wife
   Bapt^{zd} Septr ye 1st. 1747

William Son of John Godfrey & Mary his wife Bapt^{zd}
   Sep^{tr}. ye 3^d 1747.

BURIALS P^r Y^e REV^d M^r GUY

Janu^{ry} ye 26th 1746/7 Then was Buried ———— Robertson
   (the widow of John Robertson who died aBord the
   Malborough Privatteer of Rhode Island Cap^{tn} Benjamin Car Commander) Buried from M^r. Roger Sanders's
Ebsworth Darvil Buried Jan^{ry} ye 29th 1746.* James Island

*1747, new style.

Sarah Daugh[r] of Petter Cattell & Mary his wife Buried Feb[ry]. y[e]. 20th: 1746 *

Thomas Son of Thomas Butler Sen[r]. Decs[d]. & Elizabeth his wife Buried March 6th 1746*

William Wells Buried at S[t] Georges p[r] the Rev[d] Samuel Quinsey April y[e] 19th 1747

James Son of Doc[tr] John Lining & Sarah his wife Buried April y[e] 26th 1747 p[r] y[e] Rev[d] Samuel Quinsey Mins[tr] of S[t]. Georges

James Scarlet Buried August y[e] 15th 1747

Anne Hipworth widow Buried Sept[r]. y[e] 2[d]. 1747 at M[r]. Josheur Toomers p[r] Rev M[r] Guy

Anne the wife of Thomas Hayward Buried 1747 Inter[d] without a minister.

William Son of John Godfrey & Mary his wife Buried Sept[r]. y[e] 6th 1747

Elizabeth the wife of Cornelus Vangelder Buried Sep[tr] y[e] 13th 1747

Sarah Daught[r] of William Chapman Jun[r] & Mary his Wife Buried Sept[r]. y[e] 25th 1747.

Elizabeth Daughter of Thomas Wright (Buried at M[r]. George Bellingers) Oct[r] y[e] 1 1747

Martha Lepord Buried Octo[br] y[e] 9th 1747.

Thomas Saunders Buried Nov[br]. y[e] 15th 1747.

Margret the wife of William Chapman Buried Feb[ry] y[e] 2[d] 1747*

Anne the wife of John Man Buried March y[e] 12th 1747*

Sarah Daugh[r] of Thomas Butler Sen[r] Decd & Elizabeth his wife Buried March y[e] 9th 1747 † (Inter[d] without a minister)

Anne-Booth the wife of William Ross Bur[d]. March y[e] 27th 1748

Stephen Fitch Buried April y[e] 4th 1748.

Doct[r] Robert De Arques Buried May y[e] 2[d] 1748

Elizabeth Rose wd Buried April 17th. 1748

*1747, new style
†1748, new style

BIRTHS

James Son of Frances Ladson Jun[r] & Elizabeth his wife
    Born 1747

Sarah-Evelin Daughter of Daniel Pepper & Mary his wife
    Born Octob[r] y[e] 13th 1747

Angelica Daught[r] of Samuel Maverick & Katherine his
    wife Born [no date given]

John Son of John Whitter Jun[r] & Hannah his wife Born
    Sep[r] 6 1746 [sic]

William Son of Richard Godfrey and Rebecca his wife
    Born Feb[ry]: y[e] 8th 1747.

William-Carlile Son of George Welsh & Anne his wife
    Born —— 1747

Elizabeth Daughter of Nathaniel Fuller & Sarah his wife
    Born Octob[r]. y[e] 24th 1747

William Son of William Ross & Anne-Booth his wife
    Born March y[e] 17th 1747/8

Thomas Son of Richard Lake & Mary his wife Born Decb[r]
    y[e] 19th. 1747

Ann Daughter of William Brandford Jun[r]. & Mary his
    wife Born July y[e] 1st 1748

Margaret Daughter of George Wage· man & Sibilia his
    wife Born y[e] 14th of August 1748

Ann-Dell y[e] Daught[r] of William Rivers & Mary his wife
    Born July y[e]· 13th: 1748

Henry Son of Thomas Drayton & Elizabeth his wife Born
    —— 1748

William Son of William Chapman Jun[r]. & Mary his wife
    Born —— 174— [sic]

Jehu Son of James Boswood & Martha his wife Born
    Dec[br] y[e] 24th 1747

Robert-Cooper Son of the Rev[d]. William Guy & Elizabeth
    his wife Born Dec[br]. 26th 1748

Elizabeth Daught[r] of Benj[m] Heep & Mary his wife Born
    Decb[r]. y[e] 20th 1747.

Elizabeth Daugh[tr] of William Miles Sen[r]. & Martha his
    wife Born Jan[ry] y[e] 17th 1748

Mary Daught[r] of Thomas Hayward & Anne his wife Born
    Decb[r] y[e] 20th 1748

Jane Daugh'' of Archibald Scot & Aggnes his wife Born
Oct'. y' 6ᵗʰ 1748

Charlott Dagh'' of Daniel Pepper & Mary his wife Born
Novᵇʳ y' 17ᵗʰ 1748.

Peggy Daught' of Ibid Born Novᵇʳ. 17ᵗʰ 1748.

CHRISTININGS Pʳ THE REVᵈ Mʳ GUY

Charles the Son of George Bodington and Sarah his wife
Baptᵗᵈ: Octoᵇʳ y' 27ᵗʰ 1747

Robert the Son of John Man & Anne his wife Baptᵗᵈ.Novᵇʳ.
y' 29ᵗʰ 1747 (Prv' Bp'ᵗᵐ) Receᵈ March y' 23ᵈ. 1748
into the Congregation.

James Son of Frances Ladson Jun' & Elizabeth his wife
Baptᵗᵈ Decbʳ: y' 27ᵗʰ 1747

Sarah-Evelin Daught'. of Daniel Pepper & Mary his wife
Baptᵗᵈ. Jan'ʸ. y' 10ᵗʰ 1747* Prv' Bp'ᵗᵐ.

Angelica Daught' of Samuel Maverick & Katherine his
wife Bapᵗ'. Febʸ y' 7ᵗʰ. 1747*

William Son of Richard Godfrey and Rebecca his wife
Baptᵗᵈ Febʸ· y' 15ᵗʰ 1747 *

William-Carlile Son of George Welsh & Anne his wife
Bapᵗ'ᵈ March y' 12ᵗʰ 1747 *

William Son of William Ross & Ann-Booth his wife
Baptᵗᵈ. March y' 21ᵗ 1747*

Sarah Cattell an Adult the widow of Andrew Cattell
Baptᵗᵈ. March y' 29ᵗʰ 1748

Elizabeth Daughter of Nathaniel Fuller & Sarah Bapᵗᵗᵈ.
March 23ᵈ 1748

Sarah Daugh'' Recd into the Congregation† [sic]

Thomas Son of Richard Lake & Mary his wife Baptzd.
July y' 2ᵈ. 1748.

Ann Daughter of William Brandford Jun'. & Mary his
wife Baptᵗᵈ. July y' 9ᵗʰ 1748 Prv' Btsᵐ

Margaret Daught' of George Wage man & Sibilia his wife
Bapᵗᵗᵈ Septᵇʳ· y' 11ᵗʰ 1748

Ann-Dell Daught' of William Rivers and Mary his wife
Bapᵗᵗᵈ· Octoᵇʳ y' 16ᵗʰ 1748

---

*1748, new style

†Thi i 'v p i 1d .. ~ i , ' N ' i 1
and Sar ' '·lh , ' , i (' j¯'t.

Henry Son of Thomas Drayton and Elizabeth his wife
  Bap^t^d. Nov^br. ye 28th 1748

William Son of William Chapman Junr. & Mary his wife
  Bapt^zd: Dec^br ye 1st: 1748.

Jehu Son of James Boswood & Martha his wife Bapt^zd:
  Dec^br ye 11th 1748

Robert Cooper Son of the Rev^d. William Guy & Elizabeth
  his wife Bapt^zd. Jan^ry. ye 2^d: 1748‡ Prv^t. Bapt^zm

Elizabeth Daught^r of Benja^in Heep & Mary his wife Bapt^zd.
  Jan^ry. ye 7th 1748 Pr^v. Bapt^zm

Elizabeth Daught^r of William Miles Sn^r, & Martha his
  wife Bapt^zd Jan^ry. 21st 1748 ‡

MARRIAGES 1747/8 P^r. THE REV^d WILLIAM GUY

Thomas Jucks & Violets Crawford Sp^r. married March y^e
  10th 1747°

James Hoskins & Elizabeth Streater Sp^r married March
  ye 22^d 1747°

William Boneau & Hanah-Rebecca Heap Sp^r married April
  ye 10th 1748.

Dct^r Robert De Arques & Elizabeth Butler widow married
  April ye 10th 1748

William Miles S^nr & Martha Godfrey wdo married May
  ye 19th 1748

John Man & Martha Fairchild widow married Feb^ry. y^e
  9th 1748

Joseph Wells & Margaret Wood Sp^r. married March y^e
  9th 1748.

Stephen Elliott & Elizabeth Butler Sp^r. married April y^e
  23 1749

Thomas Miles & Mary Fairchild Spinst^r married May y^e
  3^d 1749

Henry Wood & Mary Brown Sp^r married July ye 8th 1749

William Sterland & Elizabeth Camplin Sp^r. Married Nov^br:
  ye 26th 1749

Joseph Williams & Elizabeth Turner married Jan^ry y^e
  10th 1749*

---

‡1749, new style
°1748

William Chapman & Elizab^th Brown Spn Married Feb^ry
ye 14th 1749*

Benjamin Elliott & Mary Odingsells of Edisto Island Married p^r the Revd William Guy Feb 22^d 1749/50

Abraham Bosomworth & Susannah Seabrook Sp^r. Married
Nov^br ye 3^d. 1749.

John Ansley & Mary Childs Spr married Jan^ry ye 18th
1749

Benjamin Cater & Mary Bedon Sp^r. married June ye 11th
1750

Robt Yonge & Elizabeth D'Arques wd^ow Married June
ye 19th 1750

Thomas Miles (Son of Thomas Miles) & Mary McTeer
Sp^r. Married Nov^br. ye 19th 1750—of St Paull's Parish

John Miles & Sophia Sarah Guy Sp^r mar^d p^r. Rev^d
Mr Keeth March 7th 1750/51

Christopher Guy & Jane Chapman married p^r Rev^d M^r
Keeth June 6th 1751.

BURIALS

Charles Ransom Buried at Mr Henry Woods (he belonged
to the Fowey Man of War) Bur^d August ye 7th 1748

Elizabeth Daught^r of Nathaniel Fuller & Sarah his wife
Buried Septr ye 3^d 1748

Mary Daughter of Charles Cattell & Kathrine his wife
Buried Septr. ye 7th. 1748 p^r the Rev^d. M^r. Coot† of S^t.
Georges

Elizabeth Daughter of Isaac Ladson & Rachel his wife
Buried Septr ye 19th 1748

Richard Butler Buried Sep^tr 27th 1748 (intr^d without minister)

Elizabeth Daughter of John Clark & Elizabeth his wife
Buried Octo^br ye 2^d 1748

Ann Waight widow Buried Dec^br. ye 18th 1748

Henry Heep Buried Jan^ry: ye 13th 1748 * (Inter^d. without
a minister)

---

*1750

†Rev William Cotes minister at St Georges, Dorchester, from
1746 until his death in 1752. (Dalcho page 349.)

Abraham Ladson Son of Frances Ladson Sn.ʳ Buried
Jan.ʳʸ. y.ᵉ 19ᵗʰ 1748* Inter.ᵈ without a minister

Benjamin Heep Buried Jan.ʳʸ. y.ᵉ 20ᵗʰ 1748* Inter.ᵈ. without
a minister

{ Martha the wife of William Miles Sn.ʳ. Buried Jan.ʳʸ y.ᵉ
22.ᵈ 1748*

Elizabeth Daught.ʳ to William Miles Sn.ʳ & Martha his
Wife Buried Jan.ʳʸ y.ᵉ 22.ᵈ 1748*

Joseph Heep Buried Feb.ʳʸ y.ᵉ 8ᵗʰ 1748*

John McCarley Buried 17ᵗʰ Feb.ʳʸ 1748*

Elizabeth Godwin Widow Buried April y.ᵉ 13ᵗʰ 1749

Mathew Petit Buried from Doct.ʳ. Howzendorff May y.ᵉ 3.ᵈ
1749

Sarah the wife of Zacheus Ladson Buried May y.ᵉ 17ᵗʰ
1749

Richard Fuller Buried May y.ᵉ 19ᵗʰ 1749

Henry Son of Thomas Drayton & Elizabeth his wife
Buried June y.ᵉ 1ˢᵗ 1749

Robert the Son of Henry Yaw & Hannah his wife Buried
August y.ᵉ 29ᵗʰ 1749

Hanah y.ᵉ wife of Henry Yaw Buried Sep.ʳ y.ᵉ 9ᵗʰ. 1749.

Martha Thompson widow Buried August y.ᵉ 30ᵗʰ 1749

Elizabeth Daughter of Richard Lake and Mary his Wife
Buried Sept.ʳ ye 22.ᵈ 1749

Elenor ———— a young Wooman who Died at M.ʳ Claypool buried Sep.ʳ y.ᵉ 22.ᵈ. 1749 Int.ʳᵈ without a Minister.

BIRTHS

Thomas Son of Samuel Jones & Mary his wife Born [no
date given]

Elizabeth Daughter of Ibid Born Nov.ᵇʳ: y.ᵉ ——— 1747

{ Sarah the Daught.ʳ of Zackeus Ladson & Sarah his wife
Born April y.ᵉ 13ᵗʰ 1747

Abishag y.ᵉ Daught.ʳ of Ibid Born April y.ᵉ 5ᵗʰ 1749

Nathaniel Son of Nathaniel Fuller & Sarah his wife Born
——— 1748

Richard Son of Frances Rose & Mary-Anne his wife Born
July y.ᵉ 8ᵗʰ 1748

*1750

Elizabeth Daughter of Richard Lake & Mary his wife Born August y° 26th 1749

Joseph Son of William Milford & Susanah his wife Born Septr 1749

Mary y° Daughter of John Rivers & Elizabeth his wife Born —— 1749

Elizabeth Daughter (of Sarah Fuller wd. of Nathaniel Fuller Decd.) Born March y° 3d. 1749/50

Thomas Son of Benjamin Parrott & Anne his wife Born August y° 2d. 1749.

John Son of Samuel Maverick & Catherine his wife Born 1749

Christopher Son of William Chapman & Mary his wife Born March y° 7th 1749

Richard Son of John Godfrey & Mary his Wife Born July y° 1st 1749

Thomas Son of Petter Cattell & Mary his Wife Born August y° 8 1749

John Son of Richard Godfrey & Rebecca his wife Born [no date given]

Elizabeth the Daughtr of William Walter & Mary his wife Born Jan'y 11th. 1747/8

Sarah Daughtr of Christopher Guy & Mary his wife Born March y° 29th 1750

Charles Son of Edmund Bellinger & Mary-Lucy his wife Born April y° 16th 1750

Joseph Son of Katherine Chapman Born Decbr y° 27th 1749

Mary Daughtr of John Swiney & Mary his wife Born March y° 4th 1749

William-Michall Son of Michall Hats & Mary his wife Born March —— 1749 Servt to William Backshell

CHRISTININGS Pr Y° REVd Mr GUY 1748/9

Mary Daughtr of Thomas Hayword & Anne his wife Baptd Febry. y° 19th 1748

Jane Daughter of Archibald Scot & Agnes his wife Baptd Febry y° 26 1748/9

{ Charlotte Daughtʳ of Daniel Pepper & Mary his wife
   Bapᵗᶻᵈ. Febʳʸ. yᵉ 26 1748
  Peggy Daughtʳ of Ibid Bapᵗᶻᵈ. Febʳʸ. 26. 1748

Nathaniel Son of Nathaniel Fuller & Sarah his wife Baptᶻᵈ
   April yᵉ 13ᵗʰ 1749

{ Thomas Son of Samuel Jones & Mary his wife Baptᶻᵈ
   prvᵗ. Baptᶦᵐ May yᵉ 3d 1749
  Elizabeth Daughtʳ Ibid Baptᶻᵈ. May yᵉ 3ᵈ 1749

Sarah Daughtʳ of Zackeus Ladson Baptᶻᵈ. May yᵉ 17ᵗʰ
   1749

Abishag Daughtʳ of Ibid Baptʳᵈ May yᵉ 17ᵗʰ 1749

Richard Son of Frances Rose & Mary Anne his wife
   Baptᶻᵈ June yᵉ 18ᵗʰ 1749 (Prvᵗ Baptᵉᵐ)

Richard Son of John Godfrey & Mary his wife Baptᶻᵈ:
   July 1 1749

Thomas Son of Petter Cattell & Mary his wife Baptᶻᵈ
   August yʳ 8ᵗʰ 1749

John Son of Richard Godfrey & Rebecca his wife Baptᶻᵈ.
   Septʳ 7ᵗʰ 1749

Elizabeth Daughter of Richard Lake & Mary his wife
   Baptᶻᵈ Prvᵗ Bapᵗᵉᵐ Sepᵗʳ yᵉ. 7ᵗʰ 1749

Joseph Son of William Milford & Susanah his wife Baptᶻᵈ.
   Novᵇʳ yᵉ 26ᵗʰ 1749 (James Island)

Mary Daughter of John Rivers & Elizabeth his wife
   Baptᶻᵈ Decbʳ yᵉ 24ᵗʰ 1749.

Elizabeth Daughter (of Sarah Fuller widʳ Nathᵉˡ Fuller)
   Baptᶻᵈ March yᵉ 4ᵗʰ 1749 Entʳᵈ after his death [sic]

Charles Willᵐ Frederick son of Frederick Holzendroff and
   Anna Rosanna his wife Baptᶻᵈ March yᵉ 18ᵗʰ 1749

Thomas Son of Benjamin Parrott & Anne his wife Baptʳᵈ
   March yᵉ 25ᵗʰ 1750

John Son of Samuel Maverick and Katherine his wife
   Baptᶻᵈ March yᵉ 25 1750

Christopher Son of William Chapman & Mary his wife
   Bapᵗᵉᵈ: March yᵉ 25 1750

Sarah Daughter of Christopher Guy & Mary his wife
   Baptᶻᵈ. March yᵉ 29ᵗʰ 1750

Elizabeth Daughtᵗ. of William Walter & Mary his wife
   Baptᶻᵈ. April yᵉ 5ᵗʰ 1750

Charles Son of Edmund Bellinger & Lucy his wife Bapt^d.
April ye 22^d 1750

Joseph Son of Katherine Chapman Bapt^d. April ye 22^d
1750

Mary Daught^r of John Swiney & Mary his wife Bapt^{ed}
April 29th 1750

William-Michall Son of Michall Hats & ——— his wife
Bapt^{ed} April 29 1750 Serv^{tt} to Mr Backshell

BURIALS P^r THE REV^d M^r GUY

Robert Mc ham Buried oversear to William Miles Senr
Buried Oct^{br} 28 1729

Anne the wife of Joseph Williams Buried Nov^{br}. ye 6th
1749

Elizabeth the wife of Jacob Ladson Sn^r Buried Nov^{br} y^e
18th 1749 (Intr^d without a minister)

Nathaniel Fuller Buried Dec^{br}. ye 26th 1749

Petter the Son of Cornelus Vangelder & ——— Buried
Jan^{ry}. ye 14th 1749*

Jonathan Miller Buried Jan^{ry} 16th 1749*

Jane the wife of William George Freeman Esqr Buried
Feb^{ry}. ye 27th 1749*

Jacob Ladson Sn^r. Buried March ye 2^d. 1749*

Mary Fuller widow Buried March ye 2^d 1749*

Elizabeth Perry wd^o Buried March ye 18th 1749*

Mary ye wife of Christopher Guy Buried April y^e ———
1750

Corbet Son of William George Freeman & Jane his wife
Buried May ye 3^d 1750

Mary the wife of William Branford Junr Buried May y^e
18th 1750.

Charles Son of Edmund Bellinger & Mary Lucy his wife
Buried April ye 27th 1750

Sarah Daught^r of John Champneys & Sarah his wife
Buried July ye 5th 1750

Mary the wife of Elisha Butler Buried July ye 18th 1750

Daught^r. of William Cattell Junr & Ann his wife Buried
August ye 18th 1750 Intr^d without a Minister

*1750

Christoph' Savage a poor Man Bur^d at M' Benjn Cattell's
    August ye 20   1750.

John Clark Buried August ye 21st 1750.

Elizabeth Daughter of Sarah Fuller wd^ow. Buried August
    ye 23^d. 1750

Rob'. Gordon Buried Broth' to John Gorden Bur^d August
    ye 28th 1750

Mary Anne Daught'. of Henry Wood Bur^d Sept'. ye 16th
    1750

James Manning Buried Octob'. 14th 1750

Rebeca Daught'. of Joseph Claypool & ———— his wife
    Buried Oct' ye 26th 1750.

William Chapman Sn' James Island Buried October y^e ·
    27th 1750 (Inter^d without a minister)

BIRTHS

Edmund the Son of Landgr^ve. Edmond Bellinger & Mary-
    Lucia his wife Born August ye 1 1743

John Son of Ibid Born Nov^br ye 28th 1745

Lucia Daught' of Ibid D° Feb^ry 11th 1747

Charles Son of Ibid Do April ye 16th 1750

Elizabeth Daught' of John Man & Martha his wife Born
    Sept' ye 5th 1750

{ William Son of William Bee & Elizab^th his wife Born
    Nov^br ye 10th 1744
{ Joseph Son of Ib^d Born May 3^d 1748

Anne Daught' of John Harris & Elenor his wife Born
    Sept' 27th 1750

Mary Daught' of James Ladson & Sarah his wife Born
    July ye 12th 1750 of St Pauls Parish

John Son of Thomas Heyward & Anne his wife Born
    Decem^br 11th 1750

William Son of Thomas Miles & Mary his wife Born
    Nov^br. ye 21st 1750.

John Son of Hannah Whitter widow of John Whitter
    Jun' Decs^d Born Dec^br. 9th 1751.

{ Benjamin Ladson Son of Capt Isaac Ladson & Rachel
    his wife was Born Dec^br. ye 27th 1745
{ Abraham Son of Ibid Born August ye 25th 1750.

Sarah-Anne Daught' of Thomas Rivers & Sarah his [sic] Born Oct'. —— 1750.

Susanah y' Daughter of Benjamin Perry & Susanah his wife Born March y' 6ᵗʰ 1747

Richard Son of Ibid born April y' 6ᵗʰ: 1750 in St Pauls Parish

Dorothy Daughter of Colcheith Golightley & Mary his wife Born March y' 29ᵗʰ 1747

Mary Daught' of Ibid born June 14ᵗʰ 1749

William Son of Henry Wood & Mary his wife born Sept' y' 30ᵗʰ 1751

Benjamin Son of William Cattell Jun'. & Anne his wife born July y' 13ᵗʰ 1751

Elizabeth Daugh'' of Frances Rose & Mary-Ann his wife born June 15ᵗʰ, 1751.

Ann Daught' of Philip Culp & Christian his wife Born Octᵇʳ y' 27ᵗʰ 1751.

Mary y' Daught' of Matthias Smith & Mary his wife Born Decb' y' 20ᵗʰ 1751

Anne The Daughter of Benjamin Parrott & Anne his wife Born Jan'' y' 31'' 1752

Elizabeth Daught' of Benjamin Perry & Susanah his wife Born July 20ᵗʰ 1754 in St Pauls Parish

CHRISTININGS P' THE REVᵈ Wᵐ. GUY

{ William Son of William Bee & Elizabᵗʰ his wife Baptᵗᵈ: August y' 11ᵗʰ 1750

{ Joseph Son of Ibid Bapᵗᵗᵈ D° 11ᵗʰ 1750

Abraham Son of Isaac Ladson & Rachel his Wife Baptᵗᵈ prv' Baptᵗᵐ Sep'' y' 13ᵗʰ 1750

Elizabeth Daught' of John Man & Martha his wife Baptᵗᵈ. Sept': y' 19ᵗʰ 1750

Anne Daught'. of John Harris & Elenor his wife Baptᵗᵈ Oct' y' 15 1750

John Son of Hannah Whitter widow of John Whitter Deces'd on Jam's Island Baptᵗᵈ Novᵇʳ y' 3ᵈ 1750

Isebela Daught' of Honorah Campbel a poor woman Stranger Baptᵗᵈ. Novᵇʳ. y' 7ᵗʰ 1750

Mary Daughter of James Ladson & Sarah his wife Bapt^d
 Nov^br ye 9th 1750 of St Pauls Parish

John Son of Patrick Molholland & Mary his wife Bapt^d.
 Nov^br 18th 1750 St Paul's Parish

Elizabeth Daughter (of William Miles Junr at Aishypoo)
 Bapt^d. March 31st 1751 p^r ye Revd Mr Rowan*

Sarah-Anne Daught^r: of Thomas Rivers Bapt^d. June y^e
 23^d 1751 Bapt^zd by ye Rev^d. Mr. Rowan

William Son of Henry Wood & Mary his wife Bap^tzd:
 Octo^br. ye 27th 1751 p^r ye Rev^d. M^r. Rowan

Benjamin Son of William Cattell Junr Dec^c. & Anne his
 wife Bapt^zd. Octr. 27th 1751 p^r the Rev^d. Mr Rowan

Elizabeth Daught^r of Frances Rose & Mary-Anne his wife
 Bapt^zd. Nov^br. 7th. 1751 p^r ye Rev^d. M^r. Rowan

Ann Daught^r of Philip Culp & Christian his wife Bapt^zd.
 Feb^ry· ye 2^d 1752

Mary Daught^r of Matthias Smith & Mary his wife Bapt^zd
 Feb^ry ye 2^d· 1751. [1752]

Anne ye Daughter of Benjamin Parrott & Anne his wife
 Bap^tzd. March ye 1st 1752

Elizabeth Daught^r of Edmund Bellinger & Mary-Luci his
 wife Bapt^zd March ye 22^d· 1752. Bapt^zd p^r the Rev^d
 Mr Chas Martyn †

MARRIAGES 1751/2

George Bellinger & Elizabeth Elliott widow Married p^r
 ye Revd Mr Rowan Nov^br ye 7th 1751

Henry Richmond & Elizabeth Manning Sp^r. Married p^r
 ye Rev^d Mr Coots Deb^r ye 3^d 1751

MARRIAGES P^r THE REV^d. Mr CHARLES MARTYN

William Webb & Sarah Miles Sp^r Married p the Rev^d M^r
 Martyn April ye 30th 1752

Thomas Godfrey alis Garnear & Elizabeth Chapman Sp^r
 Married July 9th 1752

---

*Rev John Rowan of St Paul's Parish   (Dalcho, page 340)
Revd Wm Guy buried Dec 11, 1750
 †Rev Charles Martyn succeeded Mr Guy as rector, arriving
from England early in 1752. (Dalcho, page 340)

William Boneau & Mary Anger Sp^r. Married March ye 5th 1753

Samuell Bowman & Keziah Ladson Sp^r Married July 18th 1753.

Philip Smith & Mary Snipes of S^t. Pauls Married July 7th 1753

John Miles & Anne Fitch Sp^r Marr^d. Septr. ye 9th 1753.

Henery Smith & Anne Philbin Sp^r. Married Sept^r: y^e· 20th 1753.

Doct^r. William Scott & Elizabeth Clark Married Nov^{br}. ye 24th. 1753.

Richard Baley & Rachel Ladson Sp^r. Married p^r ye Revd Mr Baron Octob^r ye 17th 1754

Arnold Cannon & Sarah Anger Mr^d p^r the Rev^d. Mr Baron† Octr ye 31st 1754

William Mell & Elizabeth Richmond Married wd^o [?] p^r the Rev^d M^r. Martyn Feb^{ry} 3^d 1755

Cornetys Vangelder & ———— Bateman widow Married p^r M^r. Martyn April —— 1755.

---

†Rev Alexander Baron of St Paul's Parish

(To be continued)

ORDER BOOK

of

John Faucheraud Grimké.

August 1778 to May 1780.

(Continued from the January Number)

January 1779   Head Quarters, Purisburgh.

3:    Orders by Major General Lincoln.

Parole, Athol.   Countersigns { Anson
Andrews.

The Troops will immediately after dinner remove to the height near the River at the lower end of the Town where they will take possession of the Camp marked out by the Dep: Quarter Master General.

after orders

The Waggons belonging to each Regiment are daily to supply this respective Corps with wood under the Direction of the Reg': Quarter Masters.

It is expected that officers will use every means in their Power to Prevent the Soldiers from destroying the fences or wantonly injuring the Inhabitants in any respect whatever.

Upon an alarm the Regt⁴: are immediately to Parade in front of their respective Encampments, & there continue under arms, until Orders are given to the Contrary.

Officers Com⁸: Corps will order Vaults to be dug & Privies built around them at convenient distances in the rear of the Encampment

The adjutants of the different Regiments will attend for orders every day at 12 ô Clock, until the Troops are Brigaded.

4:    Parole, Countersigns.

5:    Regimental Orders by Col°: O. Roberts.

The Quarter Master of the Artillery will daily & as early as possible issue Provisions to the Officers & Men of that Corps The Coll° & his Servant only excepted; & as soon as conveniently afterwards Forage for the Artillery & Waggon Horses

Com°. officers of Companies &c to make Morning Reports daily to the adjutant by 9 ôClock precisely, or be answerable to a Court-Martial for their Neglect

G . O Parole, Carolina;

Countersigns $\begin{cases} \text{Chatham} \\ \text{Camden} \end{cases}$

One Serg' One Corp & 12 Privates from Gen' Rutherfords Brigade to Relieve the Guard of the Hospital, & to take their Order from the [illegible] general:—— The Steward of the Hospital is to apply to the Dep: Commissary of the Army for Provisions.

The General has observed a constant firing round the Camp & is concerned to find a custom so unmilitary prevail; it may be productive of the worst Consequences He therefore forbids the practise in the most positive terms, & officers are desired to use the uttermost vigilance to detect & bring to Punishment every Person offending against this order

A general Court Martial consisting of one Field officer Six Cap' & Six Sub': to sit immediately for the tryal of Cap' Scott of the Georgia Light Dragoons Pres'· Col°· Huger Judge Advocate, Cap' Lining

---

6 G O·

Parole, Dittingham; Countersigns $\begin{cases} \text{Dartmouth} \\ \text{Dunkirk} \end{cases}$

One Captain Two Subalterns, three Sergeants, three Corporals, and 45 Privates from the Second Brigade to Relieve the Guard at Zubly's Ferry this Morning, & to be visited by a Field Officer from that Brigade, who will make his Report at Head Quarters daily.

A Return is immediately to be made of the Field officers of the two Brigades with the Dates of their Commissions

Officers of the Day are expected to dine at Head-Quarters in future without a particular Invitation

All expert Rifle-Men belonging to Gen'. Rutherford's Brigad who are provided with Rifles are to be brought 1 into three Companies, & Commanded by such officers as Gen¹. Rutherford shall appoint from the Line.

The Court-Martial now sitting are authorized to Try all Prisoners that may be brought before them.

7:   R. O. by Col°. Roberts.

A Waggon to be got ready immediately to carry Powder from the Schooner Charlestown Packet to the Magazine

G: O:

Parole, Edenton; Countersign $\begin{cases} \text{Elbert} \\ \text{Edgecombe} \end{cases}$

The Regimental Waggons are to be appropriated entirely to the use of the respective Battalions, & not to be employed by the D: Q: M: G: in the common use of the Army.

Officers coming off Duty will Report to the Field-officer of the Day the strength of their respective guards, & Picquets. A copy of which being returned to the Commissary, he will supply to each Non-Commissioned Officer & Soldier one Gill of Rum.

All Parties returning from Command and Fatigue are to Receive a like distribution of Rum, a Report being signed by the officer commanding the Party, or (if a Non. Commissioned officer) by the officer of the Day

The Dep: Quartermaster General will make out the encampment of the 1ˢᵗ. Brigade (agreable to the Plan of the Inspector) in one line the right supported by the River. As soon as the ground is marked out. the Troops will take possession of it.

Cap¹. Clement Nash is appointed assistant to the Dep: Quarter Master Gen: & is to be obeyed as such.

The Discharge of Three Pieces from the Park of Artillery is to be the Signal of Alarm; when all officers and soldiers will, without relay. repair to their respective Posts.

8:   R: O: Col°: Roberts.

Mʳ Alexander is appointed to act as Waggon Master to the Corps of Artillery: All Drivers & Waggoners of the Service are to respect & Obey him as such. When the whole of the artillery move, it must be in the following order; by the right Two guns & an ammunition Waggon.

then one gun & another waggon alternately; Capt: Du—
[illegible] in the rear.

G: O: Parole Fortune.   ⎰France
                  Countersigns⎱Friendship

The Detachments sent to assist the vessels up the River
are ordered to Return to their respective Regiments.

The Gen: Court Martial for the tryal of Capt: Scott of
the Georgia Light Dragoons charged with altering his Captains Commission to that of Major Commandant of the
said Corps have found him guilty & sentence him to be
reprimanded in presence of the Officers of the Army. But
when the General reflects on the nature of the Crime, (upon which He avoids any observation at present) He is
constrained to disapprove the Sentence as inadequate to
the offence & directs the Court to meet tomorrow Morning
at 9 óClock to review the matter.

Francis Kinloch Esq: now acting as a Volunteer in the
Army is to be considered as a Confidential officer attend-
ant on Gen: Moultrie: & all orders from the General conveyed thro' him are to be Obeyed & He respected accordingly.

9:    Parole, Countersigns

10:    Parole, Howe, Countersigns ⎰Henderson
                        ⎱Hampton

G: O: No officer is to make use of the Waggon Horses
or send them out of Camp on any pretence whatever, without leave of his Brigadier General.

The Dep: Quarter Master Gen: is to have all the Public
Horses branded immediately.

The Waggon Horses are to be constantly fed at the
Waggons & kept in geers During the Night.

The General is sorry to find that the Order relative to
the burning of fences has not been so strictly attended to
as it ought to have been. He once more expressly forbids
it; & any Person found sitting by a fire made of rails shall
be answerable for the same & punished as the offender.

Waggoners are positively forbid riding their Waggon
Horses on any pretence whatever.

The Inspector will review the Continental Troops this Day by Regiments; the two on the right wing at Noon, those on the left & the Georgia Troops at 4 in the afternoon.

After orders

The Sick from Gen: Rutherfords Brigade are to be sent to the fixed Hospital at M^r: Heywards Plantation where proper care will be taken of them: The Sick from Gen: Moultries Brigade will be sent to the flying Hospital in Purisburgh, where the Regimental Surgeons will Obtain the form of making out Certificates.

11: G: O:

Parole, Integrity.   Countersign $\begin{cases} \text{John} \\ \text{James} \end{cases}$

The North Carolina Brigade is to be paraded for review at 4 ôClock this afternoon.

Col: Sumner's Reg^t: is to encamp on the left of the 1st: Brigade under the direction of the Inspector.

A Return is to be immediately made of the number of Tents in the different Regiments.

General Returns of the two Brigades to be made to the Dep: Adjutant Gen: tomorrow at orderly time.

The Commissary is to serve out flour to the Troops every other Day when it can be procured.

After orders

A guard from the 2^d: Brigade consisting of One Capt: 2 Sub^s & 40 Privates to Parade tomorrow at 9 ôClock. They are to receive their orders from the Dep: Adjutant Gen: to march to the Euhaws, ten miles from Purisburgh & to be relieved in a week. The whole army to be in readiness to march tomorrow at 8 ôClock, at which time the Waggons will be loaded & the Quarter Master & Commissary Depm^t. Waggons will be loaded & the Quarter Master & Commissary Departments be ready to move.

12: G. O:

Parole, Kimbolton.   Countersigns $\begin{cases} \text{Kilkenny} \\ \text{Kildare} \end{cases}$

Com^r: officers of Corps are immediately to Complement

their quantity of Ammunition to fifty rounds of Cartridges. [illegible] may be obtained of the Dep: Quarter-Master Gen: [illegible] at the Park of Artillery.

13:    R: O: by Col⁰: Roberts.

The Quartermaster of the Artillery will deliver to the Quarter Master of each Regiment requiring it One Pound of twine.

The Men of the Artillery to Receive this Day One gill of Rum per man of the Commissary for which the Quartermaster will make a return: as much is to be delivered to Waggoners & Drivers of the same Corps.

G: O: Parole, Lancaster: Countersigns { Little / Locke

No Waggons now in Public Service are to be purchased by any individual, nor any Waggons discharged from the service without leave of the general.

The Two Companies of Light Infantry draughted from the North Carolina Militia are immediately to be removed to Purysburgh & to encamp with the Company under the Command of Lt. Col: Lydell on the left of Col: Sumners Regiment.

14:    R: O: by Col⁰: Roberts

The men of the Carolina Artillery are to be equally divided between Capt: Mitchell & Davis: the former with Lt: Budd to take charge of the Two Guns on the Right of the Park; Capt: Davis with Lt: Tate are to command the other Two Carolina Pieces. When they move each Division is to have an Ammunition waggon with it.

G: O.

Parole, Manchester.   Countersigns { Melvin / Morris

The Gen: Court Martial (whereof Col: Huger is President) now sitting for the tryal of all Prisoners that may be brought before them Report Benjamin Fatherie of the 3d. Regiment, charged with insolence & abusive Language to the adjutant found guilty & sentenced to be reduced to the Ranks & Receive 50 lashes on the bare back with the Cat of Nine Tails. The General approves the Sentence.

but Remits the Stripes. ——Paul Garrison of the 3ᵈ. Regiment found guilty of Desertion Only & Sentenced to Receive fifty lashes with Switches, the Court in Consideration of his having been punished in the 3ᵈ. Regiment for Desertion & of the manner of Capᵗ. Jarvey's inlisting him, recommend him to mercy; The General approves the Sentence & for the Reasons which induced the court to recommend to Mercy; He remits the Punishment.—— Lewis Dominique Lottinger, John Devechier, & Peter Geoffrey all of the 1ˢᵗ: Regᵗ: charged with Desertion, found guilty, & sentenced to receive 100 lashes on the bare back with switches.

The General approves the Sentence & Orders They may be Executed tomorrow at Guard Mounting.

Wᵐ. Fickling of the 5ᵗʰ. Regᵗ. Charged with Desertion found Guilty, & sentenced to be Shot to Death. The General approves the Sentence.

15:   R: O. by Colᵒ. Roberts.

The Quartermaster will issue Rum this Day in proportion and agreeable to the Order of the 13ᵗʰ Instant.

G: O: Parole, Otway.   Countersigns { Obey
                                       Observe

The Sentence of Gen: Court Martial on Wᵐ. Fickling of the 5ᵗʰ. South Carolina Regiment is to be put in Execution on Tuesday Next at 11 ôClock in the forenoon.

The Gen: Court Martial (whereof Colᵒ. Huger is Presᵗ.) now setting for the tryal of all Prisoners that may be brought before them have sentenced Benjamin Geeso of the 1ˢᵗ. South Carolina Battalion (charged with Desertion to which He pleaded guilty) to receive 100 lashes on the bare back with switches

The General approves the Sentence & orders it to be put in Execution next Monday at Guard Mounting.

16.   G: O.
      Parole, Countersigns

17:   G. O.

Parole, Philadelphia, Countersigns { Packer
                                     { Pinckney

The Gen: Court Martial whereof Col": Huger is now President, Sitting for the tryal of all Prisoners that shall be brought before them have sentenced Boswell Brown of the 3ª: Continental Regiment of South Carolina (charged with Stealing £179, 15S. Sterling & found guilty to run the Gauntlope twice thro' the Brigades—which Sentence the General is obliged to disapprove, because it directs a Punishment vague & Uncertain & which may greatly exceed 100 Stripes, the highest Corporal Punishment allowed by the Rules & Articles for the Better Government of the Army. He is exceedingly sorry that the Court after Reconsidering the matter has reduced him to the altarnative of approving a Sentence which He supposes He could not Justify or to suffer the guilty to pass Unpunished (for he cannot mitigate until he first approves) The latter therefore He is constrained to do & orders the Prisoner to Return to his duty. The Gen: Court Martial whereof Col": Huger is President is dissolved.

All the loaded arms which cannot be drawn are to be discharged this afternoon at Retreat Beating.

18.   G: O.

Parole, Quibble Town. Countersigns { Quin
                                    { Quibble

The Dep: Quartermaster Gen: is to appoint a convenient landing to which all Boats are to be removed & made fast & a Sentry from the Main Guard to be put over them with orders to suffer No Person to Remove either Boats or Oars without an Order from Head Quarters, from the Dep: Quarter Master Gen: or from the Field Officer of the Day.

19.   R: O. by Col". Roberts.

When the Waggoners or Drivers of the Artillery have any Harness or Guns out of Order or Wanting Repair they are to Apply to the Quarter Master and he to the Quarter Master General who will give proper Orders for mending the same or for the supply of such articles as from time to time may be wanted.

G . O . Parole, Richmond

Countersigns $\left\{\begin{array}{l}\text{Rapid}\\\text{Report}\end{array}\right.$

All deserters from the enemy immediately on their arrival in Camp are to be carried to the Field officer of the Day to be examined, who will Report to the General & if there be any thing material in their Examination, He will bring them to Head Quarters.

The Dep· Quarter Master Gen is to furnish the different Regiments with Tools which are to be returned as soon as the ditches are dug to carry off the Water from the Encampment

The Dep Quarter Master Gen . is to make a Return as soon as possible of the Waggons including regimental Waggons, which will be particularly Expressed, & Stores of every kind belonging to the Department

The Execution of Wm Fickling is postponed until 11 ôClock tomorrow Morning

Three Companies of Expert Riflemen of fifty each with a proper number of Officers to be immediately draughted from Genl Richardson's Brigade, to act as light Infantry: He will appoint an officer to take the Command of them They will tomorrow Morning encamp on the ground where the Light Infantry from North Carolina are now encamped.

From Gen Richardsons Brigade for Fatigue One Serg^t One Corp & 12 Privates to Parade at the Quarter Master Genl Store at 9 ôClock tomorrow

A Gen Court Martial to sit tomorrow morning for the tryal of Capt Lewis & Lt Lyttle of the N^o Carolina Brigade· President Col^o· Pinckney 3 Cap· & 3 Sub^s from the South Carolina & 3 Cap^s: & 3 Sub^s. from Col^o. Sumners Brigade

---

20   R O by Col^o Roberts

The Quarter Master will this Day issue Rum as directed by an Order of the 13th Inst.

The Artillery Quarter Guard to be placed about 40 paces in the front of the Park where a Tent must be pitched for that purpose which be delivered by the Com^r: Officer

G: O. Parole, Sullivan. Countersigns { Sinclair
{ Spencer

The General Court Martial now sitting are to try L.
Charles Alexander of Col: Sumners Regiment.

The General has thought proper to pardon W^m. Fickling
now under Sentence of Death & who was to have been this
day Executed: He relies on it that no Encouragement
will be taken from this Lenity, or that any in future will
transgress from an Expectation that they shall pass with
impunity.

The officers of the Main Guard are desired to dine at
Head Quarters the day they are relieved.

21: Parole, Thompson. Countersigns { Telfair
{ Taylor

The Gen: Court Martial now sitting are to try all Prisoners that May be brought before them.

Two of the Light Horse are to attend daily at Head
Quarters.

The Taptoo [sic] in future will be beat in Camp at 9
ôClock until further Orders, at which time the roll must
be called & after that no Soldiers suffered to be absent on
any pretence whatever.

23. R. O. by Col: Roberts.

A Captain from the Artillery is to be appointed for the
Day who will visit the Guard & Sentinels at least thrice
each night at proper Hours & make a Verbal Report every
Morning to the Com. Officer.

Capt. Dufau is to join the Georgia Brigade now under
Marching Orders, with his Company & one Field Piece &
Receive his orders from L: Col: Roberts Commanding
officer of that Brigade: what ammunition & Store He may
want will be delivered him by the Quarter Master, He giving a receipt for the same.

G: O. Parole. Countersigns {

24: R. O. by Col. Roberts.

A gill of Rum to be delivered by the Quarter Master to

each Man, Waggoner, & Driver of the Regiment & Train of Artillery.

Capᵗ. Mitchell must look on himself as Comᵍ. his Company only in Camp, & all Orders delivered by the adjutant must be strictly obeyed by officers as They will answer for the Contrary to a Court Martial.

G: O. Parole.   Countersigns

All Non-Commissioned officers & Soldiers are forbid being absent from Camp after retreat Beating & any one transgressing this Order will assuredly be punished at the Discretion of a Court Martial.

A Gen: Court Martial to Sit immediately for the Tryal of all Militia Prisoners of the State of South Carolina: Colᵒ: Richardson President. Six Capt: & Six Sub: from the same Corps Members. All Evidence to attend. Doctor Charlton is desired to act as Judge Advocate.

---

25.   G: O. Parole. Countersigns.

All loaded Arms that cannot be' drawn are to be discharged this Evening at Retreat Beating.

---

26.   G: O. Parole. Countersigns

The General having been informed that different methods of going & Receiving the rounds are practised, for the sake of Uniformity directs the following mode to be adopted. —— The Field officer of the Day going the Grand Rounds is to be Escorted by a Party of Two Light Horse Men who are to be paraded at Guard Mounting & receive their Orders from him. When he comes within 20 paces of the Sentry is to Challenge & being answered *Rounds* is to Say *Stand Rounds, Sergeant turn out the Guard.* No round is to advance after the Sentry has Challenged & Ordered to Stand. When the Sentry Calls, the Sergeant is to turn out the Guard with Shouldered Arms & the officer is to put himself at the Head of it: He will then Order the Sentry with a party of Men to advance towards the rounds & Challenge; when the Sergᵗ of the Guard comes within Six Paces of the Escort, He is to challenge briskly, the Escort answering *Grand Rounds,* He replies *advance One with the Countersign.* Then One of the Escort advancing alone gives the Serg'. the Countersign in his Ear, He then Returns leaving the men He brought with him & informs his officer of the Countersign He received, & if it be right the officer orders the Serg': to Return & bid the officer of the Rounds *Advance & give the Parole* The Serg' of the Guard then Orders his Men to wheel from the Centre & form a Lane with rested Arms, through which the officer of the rounds advances (his Escort remaining) & whispers the Parole to the officer Com': the Guard. The Rounds are to be received with rested arms.

27   G: O   Parole   Countersigns

No officer is to carry a Fusil when on Guard   At ½ past 8 òClock in the Morning the Drummers Call is to be beat on the Right of each Brigade, which will be answered on the Left and alternately to the Center, when the Drum Major observes the Beat has gone thro' the Brigade, he will order one tap of the Drum on the Right which will be answered in like manner from the Right to the Left— then two taps, then three   Immediately after which the Drummers of each Regiment will give three Ruffles & begin the Troop—The same order will be observed at Retreat & Taptoo—beating   As soon as the Troop beats the Adjutants will have the Guards immediately turned out on their Regimental Parades properly Armed & [illegible]—They will then March them to the grand Parade where The Dep: Adj' Gen'. or Brigade-Major of the Day will tell them off and distribute them to the different officers, giving the Commissioned officers Commanding Guards the Parole, and Countersigns & the non Commissioned officers Commanding Guards the Countersign sealed up

The Field Officer of the day is to be relieved in the Grand parade before the Guards March off

The officers of the different Guards are to Salute The Field officer of the day as they pass him when marching of the Parade by dropping the point of the Sword

Corporals are to be attentive in marching their reliefs to prevent their men from straggling or carrying their arms in an unsoldier like manner.

The relief to march with fix'd Bayonets.

R: O: by Col°: Roberts.

All officers are to attend roll calling both morning & evening to this the officer of the Day will attend & Report all neglects

A Drum-head Court Martial to sit immediately for the tryal of Matthew Sullivan confined for Theft by Lieut Jackson. Cap'. Mitchell Pres': L': Budd & Tate Members.

The Quarter Master will deliver Rum to the officers at the Rate of 1 gill p'. Day since their arrival

Officer of the Day tomorrow Cap': L': Elliott.

28. G: O. Parole. Countersigns.

The Field officer of the Day is to Visit the Guard at Zubly's, the Piquet on the River above & the Piquet at the Cross Roads.

A Captain of the Day will be appointed who will be relieved on the Parade at Guard Mounting & Visit such Sub'. & Serg': Guards as the Field officers of the Day shall direct.

When the Captain of the Day visits alone, He is to go as Visiting Rounds, but to be received in the same Manner as Grand Rounds.

A Return to be immediately made to the Dep: Adjutant Gen of the Number of Cartridges & loose ball in each Brigade & a Weekly Return of the same to be Made every Monday Morning.

All the lead not Moulded into Bullets which is in possession of the different Regiments is to be returned to the Quarter-Master Gen: to be cast & Receipts to be taken for the quantity delivered.

R: O. by Col". Roberts.

Com°. officers of Companies are to make Returns of the Mens names who have Blankets & particularize those who have not as soon as possible to the Com°: Officer

Officer of the Day tomorrow Cap'. Mitchell.

29.   G: O. Parole, Countersigns.
       R: O by Col⁻: Roberts.

The Quarter Master is to take a fatigue Party & Remove the artillery Guns & Timbers about three feet furthere to the front, where they now stand, & be particularly nice in ranging them on a line

Officer of the Day tomorrow Cap'. Davis

---

30.   G: O. Parole. Countersigns

Officers of Companies are strictly enjoined to have the arms & ammunition of their Men examined [illegible] at Retreat Beating & to make them accountable for every Cartridge delivered them.

The General is Sorry to observe the great neglect of Orders which too generally prevails in Camp & from which if persisted in the most fatal Consequences will probably ensue: the exsessive waste of ammunition & the neglect of making due returns are Instances among many which Justify the Observation. He therefore call for the Exertion of every officer to enforce that Discipline & Obedience to Orders without which no Military operation be conducted with any prospect of success

       R: O. officer of the Day tomorrow Cap: L'. Elliott.

---

31.   G: O. Parole. Countersigns
       R: O. Officer of the Day tomorrow Cap'. Mitchell

(To be continued)

HISTORICAL NOTES

INSCRIPTIONS FROM POMPION HILL CHAPEL.—The church at Pompion Hill was erected in 1703 on the east side of the Eastern branch of the Cooper River. It was built of cypress. The funds were contributed by private subscription, Sir Nathaniel Johnson liberally assisting The Cemetery was 400 feet square on the original map This was the first Church of England church built outside of Charleston, and was used later as the Chapel of Ease for the Parish of St Thomas and St. Denis The first church having become ruinous, a new chapel was built at Pompion Hill, of brick; it was begun in 1763, and is still in existence, being one of the very few colonial chapels remaining as built The floor is tiled, the seats face the aisle, the pulpit with sounding board and prayer chancel are at the vestry end, and the communion chancel at the opposite end of the aisle The river has claimed part of the graveyard Fuller accounts of this church may be found in Dalcho and the "Annals and Registers of St Thomas and St Denis"

We are indebted to Mr. Joseph Ioor Waring for the copies of such inscriptions as remain

Beneath this Stone | Lies sacredly deposited | the Remains of | Benjamin Simons | who departed this Life | on the 7th September 1789 | in the 53rd year of his age, | Together with six children | and | Catharine Simons | his Consort | who at the age of 79 years & 9 months | died, Beloved and regretted | 8th November 1820, | and to whose Memories | this monument is erected | in affectionate remembrance by | Jonathan Lucas | "Lo! Soft remembrance, | Drops a pious tear | And holy friendship | Sits a mourner here " |

Inscribed | to the Memory of | Elizabeth Harleston | wife of Wm Harleston | and Daughter of | Roger and Frances Susanna Pinckney | who was born 9th January 1772 | married 9th December 1789 | and died | the 26th September 1790 | aged 18 years and 8 months |

Beneath this spot | were buried the Remains of | Ann Simons | Wife of | Benjamin Simons | and Daughter of | Edward and Mary Keating | who died the 20th April | 1754 | Aged 36 years | and | Benjamin Simons | her Husband | who died 30th April 1770 | Aged 59 years. |

The Mortal Remains of | Mrs Lydia Bryan | Repose beneath this Stone | She was the Wife of | John Bryan of Camp Vere | And Daughter of | Elias and Lydia Ball | of Kensington | Aged 86 years and 16 Days | Having filled the relative duties | of Daughte, Sister, Wife, Parent | Friend and Mistress | In a manner becoming an | eminently pious and steadfastly devoted | and tryly humble Christian | who adorned the Doctrine of God | her Saviour in all things |

Sacred to the Memory of | John Bryan | of Camp Vere in this Parish | whose Remains are deposited | beneath this Stone | He was the Son of | Michael Bryan and Elizabeth Wood | Born a Newcastle England | and died on 10th day November 1805 | Aged 51 years and 11 months, | having been a resident of this | Parish for 28 years. |

In Memory of | John Bryan of Camp Vere in this Parish | Son of John and Lydia Bryan | He was born 18th July 1791 | Married 28th November 1810 | to Eliza Catharine Legare | and died on 14th April 1848 | Near this spot are also interred | the remains of three infant children | In evidence of their affectionate | regard for his Memory this Monument | is erected by his 13 surviving children |

To the Memory of | Thomas Karnow Esq | A native of this Parish | Who died on 15th July | 1820 | Aged 76 years | And for upwards of 50 years | a Resident of this Parish |

Sacred to the Memory of | John Hasell Quash | who departed this Life | 9th November 1846 | Aged 60 years and 4 months | In the same grave are deposited | the mortal remains of | Robert Harleston Ingraham | Infant son of W[m] Postell and | H. Harlesto Ingraham | 20th July 1848 |

In Memory of | Hannah Harleston Ingraham | Wife of | Wm Postell Ingraham | who was born 28th July 1809 | Died 20th February 1869 |

William Postell Ingraham | Born 10th December 1848 | Died 12th March 1875. |

CORRECTIONS —Referring to the article in our January number on "The Tattnall and Fenwick Families in South Carolina" we are indebted to D^r J G B. Bullock of Washington, D C, for the information that Dr George Jones had no issue by his marriage to Mrs Macartan Campbell, but that Noble Wymberley Jones, his son by a previous marriage, married a daughter of Macartan Campbell and Sarah Fenwick, thus carrying a Fenwick descent into the Jones family.

LIST OF PUBLICATIONS

OF THE

SOUTH CAROLINA HISTORICAL SOCIETY.

COLLECTIONS.

Vol. I., 1857, $3.00; Vol. II., 1858, $3.00; Vol. III., 1859, out of print. Vol IV., 1887, unbound, $3.00, bound, $4.00; Vol. V., 1897, paper, $3.00.

PAMPHLETS.

Journal of a Voyage to Charlestown in So. Carolina by Pelatiah Webster in 1765. Edited by Prof. T. P. Harrison, 1898.   75c.

The History of the Santee Canal. By Prof. F. A. Porcher. With an Appendix by A. S. Salley, Jr., 1903.
                                                          75c.

THE SOUTH CAROLINA HISTORICAL AND GENEALOGICAL MAGAZINE.

Volume I, 1900, Edited by A. S. Salley, Jr. Complete Volume. $10.00

Single copies of Nos. 2-4, $1.25 each.

Volume II to IX, 1901-1908, Edited by A. S. Salley, Jr.
                                        Unbound $5.00 each.

Volume X to XIII, 1909-1912, Edited by Mabel L. Webber.   Unbound $5.00 each.

Members get a discount of 25 per cent. on the above prices.

Address: South Carolina Historical Society,
                                        Charleston, S. C.

THE

SOUTH CAROLINA

HISTORICAL AND GENEALOGICAL

MAGAZINE

PUBLISHED QUARTERLY BY THE

SOUTH CAROLINA HISTORICAL SOCIETY

CHARLESTON, S. C.

VOLUME XIV., NO. 3.   JULY 1913.

Entered at the Post-office at Charleston, S. C., as
Second-Class Matter.

PRINTED FOR THE SOCIETY BY
WALKER, EVANS & COGSWELL CO
CHARLESTON, S. C
1913

PUBLICATION COMMITTEE.

Joseph W. Barnwell,   Henry A. M. Smith,
              A. S. Salley, Jr

EDITOR OF THE MAGAZINE.
Mabel L Webber

CONTENTS.

N. B.—These Magazines, with the exception of No. 1 of Vol I, are $1 25 to any one other than a member of the South Carolina Historical Society   Members of the Society receive them free.   The Membership fee is $4 00 per annum (the fiscal year being from January to January), and members can buy back numbers or duplicates at $1 00 each   In addition to receiving the Magazines, members are allowed a discount of 25 per cent on all other publications of the Society, and have the free use of the Society's library.

Any member who has not received the last number will please notify the Secretary and Treasurer,

Miss Mabel L Webber,
South Carolina Historical Society,
Charleston, S. C.

DABIT · OTIA · DEUS

Brisbane of Barnhill.

The South Carolina Historical and Genealogical Magazine.

VOL. XIV. JULY, 1913. No 3

THE BRISBANES

Compiled by E. Haviland Hillman, F. S. G

FIRST PART

ORIGIN OF THE NAME[1] AND ARMORIAL BEARINGS

There is every reason to believe that the name "Brisbane" is derived from the village of Brespan, in the commune of Limerzel, arrondissement of Vannes, department of Morbihan in Brittany, not far from the original home of the Stewarts at Dol, with whom the Brisbanes were early associated There are numerous variations in the spelling, nine being found in the list of interments at Greyfriars in Edinburgh, viz   Brisbane, Birsbane, Bisben, Bisbine, Bisbing, Brasbein, Bresben, Brisbin and Brisbon, and in other documents, Brisbain, Brisbaine, Brisben, and even Brushbene In former times spelling in England and Scotland was phonetic and the change from Brespan to Brisbane is but slight The name is spelt Brisbon in 1314 and 1348 (Ireland)[2] and Brisebone for Sir Nicholas Brisebone of

---

[1] For the theory as to the origin of the name, the compiler is indebted to the Rev Charles E Butler, great grandson of Rear Admiral Sir Charles Brisbane, K C B

[2] In Ireland, between 1707 and 1793, the following variations are found Brisben, Brisbin, Brisbeane, Brisbane, Bresbane Birsban, Birsba

Montgomeryshire in 1283.   There is absolutely no ground for assuming a Saxon origin for the family, while there is every reason for believing a Breton or Norman one   That the name was originally territorial may be fairly assumed from the fact of the "de" prefixed in early instances, as e g with "Allanus de Brysbane" who obtained a grant of the lands of Macherach in Stirlingshire, to which Malcolm, Earl of Wigton (created in 1334) is witness

ARMORIAL BEARINGS

"The family wore as their ancient armorial bearings a Field Sable that is Black, a chiveron cheque or and Gules, betwixt three Cushions of the Second"   There was in existence in 1748 "a charter granted by John Brisbane of Bishopton in the year 1546 which had the chiveron cheque with two Cushions in chief and a hunting horn or bugle, stringed proper in Base"   This Bugle may have "been occasioned by their frequent alliances and intermarriages with the noble family of Simple" (Sempil)' "but for more regularity the Lairds of Bishopton take the three Cushions as more adapted to the bearings of a Principal Family." "They wore for crest, a Stork's Head holding in her Beak a Serpent waved and proper, and for Motto of old 'Certamine Summo' and of late 'Dabit Otia Deus'"   From the register of Lyon Court it appears that "the ancient family of Bishopton used to Carry for Supporters two Ramp Hounds Proper'"   There were never any visitations in Scotland and the Register of Scottish Arms is based upon and dates from an Act of the Scottish Parliment in 1672 which required everyone to enter his arms, and between 1672 and 1677, we find the Arms of Brisbane of Bishopton

---

'Sempil Arms —Arg a chev chequey gu and of the 1st between three hunting horns sa, garnished of the 2nd

'"A Memorial of the Ancient and Honourable family of Brisbanes of Bishopton, etc" by George Crawford, 1748

entered as follows, viz   "Sa., a chevron chequy or and gu between three cushions of the second "[5]

PART II

SOME EARLY BRISBANES AND THE BISHOPTON LINE

The family of Brisbane is of great antiquity and reputation. "They were originally settled in Montgomeryshire and Shropshire in England early in the XII Century." Members of the family "appear to have accompanied Walter Fitzalan (the first of the Stewarts) from Shropshire, England, to Scotland in the county of Renfrewshire, during the reign of David I(1124-1153) and under his auspices obtained lands in the west of Scotland " "This is instructed by the connection of the Brisbanes with the Priory of Wenlock, in Shropshire, from which the monks, who assisted Fitzalan in the foundation of the Abbey of Paisley, and his other retainers and followers came; and by assumption of part of the Stewart Arms" "on those of the Brisbanes " Occasional notices occur of members of the family, between the date of their settlement in Renfrewshire and "John Brisbane of Bishopton, in Renfrewshire, about the middle of the Fourteenth Century," the earliest of the

[5]The arms used by James Brisbane, of Charleston, South Carolina, eldest son of William Brisbane, the Emigrant, were Sa , a chevron chequy or. and gu between in chief two cushions of the second, and in base a garb (or sheaf of wheat) of the last   The compiler believes that James Brisbane introduced the 'garb or" owing to the fact that his mother Margaret Stewart may have belonged to a family of Stewart in Scotland, whose arms were "Az three garhs or (2nd and 3rd quarters) all within a bordure argent " As, however, without their having been registered at Lyon Court, he had heraldically no right to introduce the garb, the compiler has used for the purpose of this Genealogy, the arms recorded by his first cousin, Robert Brisbane of Milton, of the cadet branch of the Brisbanes of Barnhill, (paternally descended from the Brisbanes of Bishopton) to which branch James Brisbane belonged, and to which arms he had a right   The compiler is sustained in his belief by Sir James Balfour Paul, Lyon King of Arms. Court of the Lord Lyon. H M Register House, Edinburgh, who writes   "I have no idea where the South Carolina Brisbanes got their wheat sheaf, possibly it was from some coat of a female ancestor " James Brisbane, chose for his motto "Dabit Otia Deus", one of the two used by the Brisbanes

name from whom a connected line can now be authentically deduced "[6]

SOME EARLY BRISBANES

(a) King Robert the First (1274-1329) granted the lands of Little Rothy, Aberdeen, to Thomas Brisbane

(b) King Robert III (1340-1406) granted the lands of Balincard, Perth, to Duncan Brisbane

(c) In 1361 Thomas and Alexander Brisbane, brothers, witnessed a charter by the Earl of Mar.

(d) Among the MSS, at Colzium House, Kilzyth, N. B., belonging to Sir Archibald Edmonstone, Bart of Dunteath, there is a charter by Donald, Earl of Lennox (1373) granting the lands of Macherach, Stirlingshire and Holme of Dalmartyne to Allanus de Brysbane son of Guglielmo de Brysbane   The deed is without date but it must have been drawn up within or soon after the year 1343, Malcolm Flemming, Earl of Wigton, who was that year raised to that honor, being a witness to the grantee   It is probable that this William (who, as noted by Lord Hailes in his "Annals of Scotland" "held the office of Chancellor of the Kingdom of Scotland" in 1332) was the immediate ancestor of John Brisbane of Bishopton in Renfrewshire, in the middle of the XIV century, hence, no doubt, the three cushions in the shield of the Brisbanes, the cushions being distinctive of his office. The compiler has seen at Brisbane House, Largs, Co Ayrshire, where the present representative of the family resides, the oak chair on which the chancellor sat   The date 1357 is carved on it, as are also the arms.

THE BISHOPTON LINE

I John Brisbane of Bishopton, in Renfrewshire, in the middle of the XIV century.

II John Brisbane, succeeded his father, obtaining (1st Sept, 1407) a charter for infefting him as heir to his father in the lands of Bishopton

III. John Brisbane of Bishopton

[*] From "A Genealogical Table of the Families of Brisbane of Bishopton, etc" by William Frazer

IV. John Brisbane of Bishopton. He married Mary, daughter of Sir William Sempil of Eliotston, by Agnes, daughter of Alexander, second Lord Montgomery.

V Matthew Brisbane of Bishopton, who falling at the Battle of Flodden, 9th September, 1513, and leaving no issue, was succeeded by his brother,

V John, whose retour of service in the lands of Killincraig, holding of the crown, relates the circumstances of his brother's death at Flodden, and whose charter of the estate of Bishopton, dated 4th July, 1514, is granted by John, Lord Erskine, son of Lord Robert, who also fell at Flodden field He was succeeded by his son,

VI. John Brisbane of Bishopton, who, as heir of his father, obtained a charter, dated 12th August, 1523, from John, third Earl of Lennox, of the lands of Ballincleirach, in the district of Campsie and county of Stirling From a sasine, dated in 1523, it appears that his wife was Elizabeth, daughter of Sir William Lindsay of Dunrod He fell at the battle of Pin Kie, 10th September 1547, and was succeeded by his eldest son, John, who was served heir to his father in the lands of Killincraig, 21st May, 1549, and the continuator of the Bishopton Line There were undoubtedly at least two other sons, William Brisbane of Barnhill, progenitor of the Barnhill branch, and Simon Brisbane, whose son Simon, was the progenitor of the Brisbanes of Selvieland

PART III

BRISBANES OF BARNHILL

VII William Brisbane of Barnhill
"There came of the family of Bishopton, many Cadets that were younger Brothers of the House of Brisbane, as the Brisbanes of Barnhill and Selvieland, Shire of Renfrew '"

'From an original MS entitled "A Memorial of the Ancient and Honorable family of the Brisbanes of Bishopton, etc" by George Crawfurd, Esq, Historiographer and Antiquarian Drawn up at Glasgow, the 16th August, 1748, now in the possession of Mrs George A Hickox of Washington Depot, Conn

The earliest record, that the compiler has seen of William Brisbane of Barnhill, in the Parish of Inchinnan, Renfrewshire, the progenitor of the Barnhill branch of the Brisbanes, to which the South Carolina family belongs, is found in the Exchequer Rolls of Scotland, Vol XX, in the year 1573, in reference to a payment to him of £40   He is designated as a "Servitor" to the late (d 1572) Regent of Scotland. John, Earl of Mar, Lord of Erskine   In 1587, he was already married to Isobel Maxwell, who may have been a daughter of William Maxwell, generally designated of Carmaderick, d 13th July, 1542, (fourth son of Sir John Maxwell of Pollock) and Janet Cathcart his wife   These certainly had a daughter Isobel,' who was a contemporary of William, and living in the vicinity of Bishopton, and as one of William Brisbane's daughters is named Janet, she may have been so named for her, if Isobel her mother, was Janet Cathcart's daughter   William Brisbane of Barnhill, died 11th January, 1591, as appears from his Testament Dative and Inventory,' leaving by his wife Isobel

Children   7 (Brisbane) 3 sons and 4 daughters, all born before 1591

    i   John.
    ii   James
    iii   William
    iv   Janet
    v   Elizabeth
    vi   Isobel.
    vii   Sibbilla

VIII William, b before 1591, (or possibly John or James)

The only positive later record of William, that the compiler has found, appears in the "Privy Council Records" dated 1609, relating to a feud between Lords Eglintoun and Glencairn, which includes the names of "John, William

'Sir William Frazer's "Memoirs of the Maxwells of Pollock," Vol I, p 456
'Edinburgh Commissariot Testaments, Vol 29

and James Brisbane, sons of the late William Brisbane of Barnhill."[10]

IX James Brisbane, was the son of William (or possibly John or James) and undoubtedly the grandson of William Brisbane of Barnhill Unfortunately, no Parish records in Renfrewshire, outside of Glasgow, commence earlier than 1705, so there is no way of proving which of the sons of William Brisbane of Barnhill, was his father. From the fact that he names his eldest son, William, it is fairly safe to assume, that it was the third son, William On 2nd May, 1700, he was admitted a Burgess and Guildbrother of Glasgow, by right of his father.[11] He married first Jean Mitchell, d. February 1669; secondly in 1669, Anna Knox, the daughter of William Knox

Children[11] by second marriage · 9 (Brisbane) 4 sons and 5 daughters

    i William, b 20th Oct, 1670; who succeeded
        Witnesses William Knox and Francis Brisbane [12]
    ii John, b 21st Nov, 1674; d before Oct, 1687.
        Witnesses· John Bhisban of Bishoptoune, John Birsbane of Barnhill
    iii Elizabeth, b 3rd June, 1677
        Witnesses William Birsban, John Birsban
    iv Grissel, b 12th Dec, 1680
        Witnesses. Thomas Blackwell and James Davidson
    v Anna, b 21 Jan, 1683
        Witnesses· Mr Matthew Birsban, Doctor of Physic, and Thomas Blackwell

[10]It is very likely, however, that he may be identified with a William, whose retour of service, dated 6th Sept, 1655, describes him as "Servitor to Umquhile Hew Lord Sempill" It also mentions his wife, Margaret Sempill, and "nearest and lawful heir, Francis Brisbane" A Retour of Service (or inquisition) does not necessarily always give the names of all the children of the deceased

[11]M S Register of Burgesses, which in no instance gives any particulars beyond dates and names

[12]From Glasgow Registry of Births

[13]The Francis Brisbane, mentioned in Note (10) and probably brother of James, to the birth of whose son he is witness

vi Matthew, b 18th Jan., 1685
    Witnesses: Mr Matthew Brisben and Francis
    Brisben
vii John, b 11th Oct , 1687
viii Anna, b 7th Jan., 1690
ix. Janet, b 17th July, 1692.
    Witnesses: Mr William and James Birsbanes.

X William Brisbane, born 20th Oct , 1670; succeeded
his father Was probably the individual of the name who
was at Glasgow University in 1687 (Mun Alum Univ.
III, p 145) On 27th Oct., 1691, he was appointed one
of the "Doctors" or masters in the Grammar School of
Glasgow. (Glasgow Records, 1691-1717, p 40) He was
admitted a Burgess and Guildbrother of Glasgow, 14th
Jan , 1703, (M S Register of Burgesses) and in December, 1715, demitted his office in the Grammar School He
received a similar appointment, August, 1721, in the Grammar School of Hamilton, and remained there until 1726
After this, Mr Brisbane settled in Glasgow and the "houses
and gardens at the head of the closs thereof belonging to
Mr William Brisbane, late Rector of the Grammar School
of Hamilton" are described by Mr McUre, whose "History
of Glasgow" was first published in 1736, "as being situated
on the north side of the Trougate." (History of Glasgow,
1830 edition, p 129) "Mr William Brisbane, teacher of
grammar" was buried in the High (Cathedral) Churchyard of Glasgow, on September 6th, 1733 (M S Records of Mortality) He married before 1701, Catherine
Paterson, daughter of Walter Paterson of Craigton, and
Jean Freeland, his wife
    Children· 9 (Brisbane) 7 sons and 2 daughters
      i Jean," b 24th Aug , 1701; d ... .
      ii. James, b 8th Nov , 1702, d before 1711
      iii. Ann," b 18th April, 1704; d . ...

"One of these daughters married William Paterson, and it is
likely that she emigrated with her husband to S C at the same
time as Robert and William Brisbane Robert Brisbane in his
Will, dated 26th Aug , 1774, mentions his nephews, James and
Matthew Paterson, and a niece, Margaret, all of whom were in
South Carolina A James Paterson, who may be the above, married in Charleston, 7th May, 1796, Miss Martha Wilks, daughter
of Capt Hugh Will ("Marri e Notices" etc by A S Salley,
Jun... M ...t Peter ... ... l wi... nd had
a ...u William Lowry)

ɪv Walter, b 3rd March, 1706; "discipulus quintae
classis," University of Glasgow in 1720   Burgess and Guildbrother of Glasgow in 1731
Succeeded his father in 1733.   He married Margaret, daughter of John Paterson of Craigton, by
whom he had,

  1 Robert, who recorded his arms in the Lyon
Court, 12th Feb , 1793   The entry is as follows; "Robert Brisbane, Esq , of Milton, of
the family of Barnhill, which family is paternally descended from the ancient family of
Bishopton. Arms Sa a chevron chequy or
and gu between three cushions of the second,
within a bordure of the last   Crest   A
stork's head erazed, in his beak a serpent
nowed, both proper   Motto· "Certamine
Summo"   Robert died unmarried and in-
sane at the Manse of Strathblain, 9th Sept ,
1807

  2 Mary, b 19th March, 1766; who married 6th
Jan , 1794, Dr James Jeffrey, and d 13th
June 1806, leaving an only daughter, Mar-
garet Anne,[16] b .... 1801, who succeeded
to the estate of Milton, as heiress of her
Uncle, Robert Brisbane

v Robert, b 1707; was a "discipulus quintae classis"
of the University of Glasgow in 1723; emigrated
to South Carolina about 1733; was one of the
founders of the Charleston Library Society in
1748; joined the St Andrew's Society between
1740 and 1748; Secretary of the Right Worthy
& Amicable Order of U B I Q U A R I A.
N S in 1746; Assistant Justice (Layman) in
1764; in 1774, J P for Charleston District   He
died unmarried in December, 1781, "in the 75th
year of his age "

[16]Margaret Anne Jeffrey, married 6th Sept , 1818, John Aytoun,
of Inchdairney, Scotland, and left two sons, Roger and James, and
one daughter, Elizabeth Anne, all of whom died within the last
generation without issue

    vi. William, b abt 1710, of whom later.
    vii James, b 16th December, 1711; d. before 1733
    viii John, b. 6th March, 1717; buried 3 Feb., 1720,
          in the High (Cathedral) Churchyard, Glasgow.
    ix Matthew, b ......; d. unmarried, probably be-
          fore 1733

PART IV [16]

DR WILLIAM BRISBANE [17] OF CHARLESTON, S C, AND SOME OF HIS DESCENDANTS.

(1) William[1] Brisbane, surgeon, the progenitor of the Brisbanes of South Carolina, was the third son of William and Catherine (Paterson) Brisbane, and was born in Glasgow or vicinity about the year 1710 He was a "discipulus quintae classis" in the University of Glasgow[18] in 1726

---

[16]For data in the preparation of Part IV of the Genealogy, the compiler is indebted to Mrs Harriet Ruth Tracy, of Torquay, Eng, Mrs George A Hickox, of Washington Depot, Conn, Mrs G B Reed, of Benson, Omaha, Miss Emma P Arthur, of Selma, Ala, Mrs N A Shannon, of Camden, S C, and others Most especially is he indebted to Miss Mabel L Webber, Secretary of the South Carolina Historical Society, without whose invaluable assistance the work could not have been undertaken

[17]For the connecting link between Dr. William Brisbane, of Charleston, South Carolina, and his ancestors in Scotland, the compiler is indebted to Mrs George A Hickox (Mary Catherine, daughter of William Brisbane, of Charleston, S C), of Washington Depot, Conn, who furnished him with a copy, (in the handwriting of Mrs Abbott Hall Brisbane) of a claim made by William Brisbane, eldest son of James Brisbane (and grandson of the above William, the Emigrant) to succession, Title and Estates in Scotland This claim was lost in favour of Margaret Ann Jeffrey (b 1801) daughter of Dr James Jeffrey and Mary Brisbane, this latter, the daughter of Walter Brisbane brother of the above William The claim runs as follows "Wm Brisbane at his decease left four sons and one daughter vizt Walter, Robert, Wm, and Matthew, and Mrs Paterson Robert and Matthew died single Walter at his decease left a son and a daughter, and devised by Will his Estate as follows To his son Robert a house or houses in Glasgow" etc.. "and to his daughter Mary a certain legacy when of age," etc "Mary came of age and married" (Dr James Jeffrey) "and is since dead" (d 13th June, 1806) "leaving an infant daughter," etc
"Walter's brother, Wm Brisbane, married and left children, his (Wm's) eldest son, James, also married and is since dead, his (James') eldest son, William, is married, and at present living Walter's only (surviving) sister married Wm Paterson, and died leaving two sons" (Wm and Matthew Paterson) "who are now living," etc The document is signed at Queen St (Edinburgh), on 18th Oct, 1806, by Adam Rolland, who was a Writer to the Signet

    ... ... by the
... ...

He emigrated to South Carolina between 1731 and 1733
In 1736 he was living in the "House that lately belonged
to John Brand, over against the Quaker's Meeting," which
was "outside the wall, near to the present King Street,"
and "had a Town Lott at Strawberry, with a Dwelling
house, kitchen and stable "[19] Before 1740 he was in partnership with Messrs Mowbray & Chalmers.[20] It is not
known where he received his degree—he did not qualify
at any of the Scotch Universities, but may, like his kinsman "the learned Dr Matthew Brisbane, physician in
Glasgow" have done so, in Holland, and if not there, then
possibly in one of the French Universities That he practised in Charleston is evident, from the fact that he styles
himself, "Surgeon," and in a Release dated 1st Oct, 1741,
he is described as "William Brisbane of Charles Town,
Practitioner of Physick" Though brought up in the Church
of Scotland, as were all his forebearers, he became a Baptist
and was a Corporator of the First Baptist Church of
Charleston in 1745[21] In 1748 he had a plantation "pleasantly situated on Ashley River, with delightful Prospect
to ten or a dozen plantations and in sight of the Ferry "[22]

Dr Brisbane visited his native land several times, and
being in failing health made his last voyage in May or June
of the year 1771, hoping to derive some benefit by the
change He died in Scotland two days after his arrival [23]

[19]So Ca Gazette June 5th, 1736
[20]So Ca Gazette Feb 23rd, 1740
[21]Manley's "History of the first Baptist Church of Charleston,
S C"
[22]So Ca Gazette Dec 26th 1748
[23](Died) "William Brisbane, Esq, two days after his arrival in
Scotland, where he went for the recovery of his health," So Ca
and Am Gazette, 30th Sept, 1771
Col Hayne's Record, Vol X, p 167, of this Magazine, gives
June as the month he died in
Dr William Brisbane's Will is dated 11th May, 1771 His son,
William Alexander Brisbane, qualifying as Executor 1st Nov,
1771, and Adam Fowler Brisbane the 17th Feb, 1773 He gives
to his "son William Alexander Brisbane that Tract or Tracts of
Land containing in the whole eleven hundred acres partly bounded
in Deas Creek" which he "bought at the sale of Hugh Brian's
Estate" To "loving wife Eunice Brisbane in three months after
my death £7,000 current money of this province" Mentions six
childrent, vizt. William Alexander, Catherine Elliott, Adam Fowler, Margaret, Hannah, Robert "and the young child if any should
be born after my decease within the space of nine months"
William
younger
tion his
undoubt

He married, first, at Charleston, Oct 18th, 1733, Margaret Stewart,[24] of Beaufort, born about 1719; died in Charleston 14th April, 1760, aged 41 [25] She was the daughter of Adam Stewart[26] and .... Fowler [27] He married, secondly, shortly before October, 1760, Hannah Staples,

[24]"St Philips Register "Oct. ( ) 1733. Then was married William Bresben and Margaret Stewart "

[25]First Baptist Church Yard. Charleston, S C, inscription on tombstone In Memory of | Mrs Margaret Brisbane | late Wife of William Brisbane, Esqr | to whom she was married near 27 years | in which Time she bore him 14 children | was a native of this Place | of a lively Spirit | enjoyed a great share of health | considering she was of a weakly Constitution | her life she endeavoured to conform | to the strictest Rules | of Virtue and Religion | For many years before her death | she spent a great part of her Time | in carrying on | a Religious Correspondence with her Christian friends | She was a good Wife | a tender and affectionate Mother | a kind Mistress | a sincere friend | and a real Christian | beloved while living and died in the Small Pox | lamented by all who knew her | on the 14th April | 1760 | and in the 41st Year of her age | (illegible) Following of them who through Faith | and Patience inherit the Promise

[26]Adam Stewart's Will, dated 14th Aug, 1764, proved 1st Sept, 1767, mentions "son-in-law Doctor William Brisbane" "grandchildren James Brisbane, William Brisbane, Adam Fowler Brisbane and Catherine Elliott, the wife of Joseph Elliott " The following interesting obituary notice of Adam Stewart appeared in the "So Ca Gaz and Country Journal," for 1st Sept, 1767 Died, "Mr Adam Stewart in the 79th year of his age, a native of Ireland, who came from thence in the early part of his life to this Province He was one of those who took Major Bonnet, and the other Pirates that were executed here about Fifty years ago He afterwards carried his Majesty's Act of Grace to the Pirates then in the Bahama Islands, who thereupon submitted themselves "

[27]It seems safe to assume that the first wife of Adam Stewart, mother of Margaret Stewart, was a sister of James Fowler James Fowler or "Vowler" as the name is written in the Parish Register, of North Tamerton, Cornwall, was born there the 5th Aug 1695, the son of James and Joan Vowler, the grandson of James Vowler and Phillipa Facy
The Will of James Fowler, of Charleston, Merchant, dated 27th April, 1753, proved 20th July, 1753 mentions "nephew, James Brisbane, son of Dr William Brisbane, William Brisbane and Catherine his sister " James Fowler's widow, whose maiden name was Martha Widdicomb, and who later married Benjamin d' Harriette, in her Will dated 27th May, 1758, proved 28th March, 1760, leaves to "niece, Margaret Brisbane, wife of Dr William Brisbane" her "Silver tea Kettle with Lamp" her "picture, Chinaware on the Buffet and Rest of furniture in the red parlour" "use of" her "gold watch and its appurtenances &" her "diamond hoop ring for life & at her death sd ring & watch to her dau, Catherine Brisbane" also "£3,000 of this Province "
The fact that one of Dr William Brisbane's sons by Margaret Stewart was named "Adam Fowler" leads us to infer that he was named "Adam" for his grandfather and "Fowler" for the surname of his grandmother, the wife of Adam Stewart

born March 1740/41;[28] died in Charleston, 18th Oct , 1764, "in the 25th year of her age "[29] She was the daughter of Abraham Staples and Sarah Monalin He married, lastly, 3rd April, 1768, Eunice Stevens,[30] daughter of the Rev. John Stevens After Dr. Brisbane's death his widow married, 18th July, 1778, Alexander Hogg of Charleston, S. C

Children by first marriage 4 (Brisbane) 3 sons and 1 daughter

(2) i. James (2), b ...., 1735

ii William Alexander (2), b ...., 1740, joined the St. Andrew's Society in 1772; was J P for Beaufort District in 1774,[31] Member of the Second Provincial Congress, from St. Peter's, in 1775,[32] and from the same parish to the General Assembly in March ..... April, 1776[33] He was staying at New River in 1777 and was evidently acting at the time as agent for Henry Laurens, while the latter was in Congress The Hon William Brisbane died, unmarried, the first days of December, 1778[34] His obituary notice states "He was an early and steady asserter of his country's rights, a sincere friend and an honest man " He left the 1,100 acres conveyed and confirmed to him in his father's Will, to his brother, Adam Fowler Brisbane

---

[28] Prince Frederick's Parish Register

[29] First Baptist Church Yard, Charleston, S C, inscription on tombstone 'In Memory of | Mrs Hannah Brisbane | Late wife of | William Brisbane Esqr, | To whom she was married above four years | In which Time | She bore him three children | She was | A Native of this place | a sincere Christian a good Wife | Tender and affectionate Mother a Kind | Mistress | She was sickley for above a year before her | Death | But resigned to the Will of God | was quite composed in her last | Moments | and died October 18, 1764 | In the 25th Year of her age | and lies interred with her youngest child | underneath this stone

[30] Married, Dr William Brisbane to Miss Stevens (Tuesday, April 12, 1768) from "Marriage Notices in the So Ca Gaz and Country Journals, 1765-1775," etc , by A S Salley, Jr

[31] Well's Register and Almanack for 1774

[32] From 'List of Members of Second Provincial Congress of So Ca" in "Extracts from Journals of the Provincial Congress of So Ca," etc, Charles Town Printed by Peter Timothy M D C C L X X V I

[33] "Journal of the General Assembly Mar - Ap 1776" Printed by the ʃ

[34] "So ·

    iii   Catherine (2), b ...., 1744, m. first[35] 24th
        March, 1763, Joseph Elliott, b 1735, d 1767 (his
        second wife), son of Joseph Elliott and Edith
        Whitmarsh.   She m secondly,[36] 19th June, 1773,
        Andrew Hewatt
        Child by first marriage. 1 (Elliott) son.
        1   James (3), b 12th Feb, 1764;[37] he was living
          in Camden District in 1786

(3) iv   Adam Fowler (2), b in Charleston, ..., 1754

Children by second marriage; 3 (Brisbane) 2 daughters,
and 1, sex unknown.

    v   Margaret (2), b about 1761, m first,[38] in Charles-
        ton, 18th Aug, 1781, John Smith, by whom she
        appears to have had one daughter, name unknown,
        deceased before 3rd Feb, 1802, who m Henry D
        Ward* and had a son, Henry Dana Artemas
        Ward[39]   She m secondly, after 1788,[40] Dr Isaac

[35]"On Thursday last was married Joseph Elliott, Esqr of St.
Andrew's Parish, to Miss Catharine Brisbane, daughter of William
Brisbane, Esq" (Saturday, March 26, 1763)   From 'Marriage
Notices in the So Ca Gaz," etc, by A S Salley, Jr

[36]"The same day" (Saturday) 'Mr Andrew Hewatt was married
to Mrs Katharine Elliott, widow of Joseph Elliott, Esqr." From
"Marriage Notices," etc

[37]See Vol XI, this Magazine, p. 100, note 14

[38]St Philip's Parish Register (M S) "Aug 18, 1781   John
Smith and Margaret Brisbane were married per Licence."

*Henry Dana Ward, youngest son of Gen Artemas Ward, of
Mass, was born Feb 6, 1768, died at Middleton, Conn, Aug 23,
1817, graduate of Harvard University, 1791, married (1st) July
17, 1798, Eliza Ann Smith, daughter of John & Margaret Smith
of Camden, S C   She died 1802   Mr Ward was an Attorney &
Counsellor at Law   Issue by 1st marriage·
    Henry Dana Artemas Ward, of Middleton, Conn, born
May 31, 1800 d April 4, 1827, at Columbia, S C   Graduated
at Yale, 1819   Married Nov 9, 1820, Eliza Ann Tracy, born
Apr. 27, 1799, dau of Dr Ebeneza & Maria (Ward) Tracy, of
Middleton, Conn   Issue
    1   Henry Dana Artemas, Detroit, Mich, b Nov 27, 1821,
       d Dec 17, 1895   Graduated at Yale   Was an Attor-
       ney at Law
    2   Eliza Maria, b Ap 18, 1823, d Dec 23, 1823
    3   Franklin Samuel, b Ap 6, 1825, d Aug 30, 1826
From data furnished by Mr Artemas Ward and Rev Geo K
Ward, both of N Y—Editor

[39]Margaret (Brisbane) Alexander's Will by right of deed of
trust dated 3rd Feb, 1802, proved 13th June, 1806   "To Grandson
Henry Dana Artemas Ward—3 slaves when 21" "husband to have
use of the house where I live, called the Blue House, on Broad
.. .. be sold
.. .. 12 .. .. .. he is 21
.. .. Henry .. W .. .. ..

Alexander (his second wife), son of Abraham
Alexander, a leading magistrate in Mecklenburg
County [a]

vi Hannah (2), b. about 1762, no further data Probably died young.

vii Child (2), buried with her

Child by third marriage i (Brisbane) son

viii Robert (2),† b ...., 1770; no further data
Probably died young

James (2) Brisbane, (William[1]) Planter, b ....., 1734;
joined the St Andrew's Society in 1764 and was its Secretary in 1774 [b] In this latter year he was Justice of the
Peace for Charleston District [c] Unlike his two brothers,
William Alexander and Adam Fowler, he early, in 1775,
evinced his attachment to the British cause, maintaining
"that Carolina was subject to the British Act of Parliment"
and firmly believed at the time that Great Britain would
eventually triumph, as witnessed by his Memorial to the
British Government [d] He had considerable property, (as
proved by the inventory of his goods, accompanying the
Memorial, amounting in all to over £20,000 sterling), and
leaving the country at that time, with a small family of
children growing up, and no means of support, except his
Plantations, meant his "Total ruin" He was banished
from Charleston in October or November, 1775, and went

[a]M C O Y 5, p 543 On 15th Aug , 1788, Adam Fowler
Brisbane, of Camden, Planter, and Mary his wife—convey to
Margaret *Smith*, one town lot in Camden

[b]According to "Historic Camden," she had by Dr Isaac
Alexander, a daughter, Amelia, who married 23rd Oct , 1800,
William Adamson This seems to be an error If Margaret was
a widow on 15th August, 1788, as appears from above note, she
could not have had a marriageable daughter by Dr Isaac Alexander in 1800 Amelia Alexander was undoubtedly Dr Isaac
Alexander's daughter by his first wife

†The following notice from the Charleston Times, July 3, 1804,
may refer to this Robert
"Died at Savannah on the 23 ult Mr Robert Brisbane, of
South Carolina, aged 37 years   "

[c]Charleston Year Book, 1894, p 286 James Brisbane, Clk of
St Andrew's Society, of Charleston, S C , in 1774

[d]Well's Register and Almanack for 1774

[e]Mem..... .. James Br.b... .. .h. B.t.h G.........'.
Hon Bo.. ?   . .   .   ..   '   . .   .   . . .
sustained   . .   . .
of Inder   . .   .

to Savannah, Georgia, but not being allowed to remain
there returned to his Plantation at New River During
the year 1775 he invented a Rice Machine [45] In Jan., 1776,
he was ordered to depart in twenty-four hours, from his
Plantation, and his second wife, Sally Stanyarne, "being
taken in labour the same day, Died the next morning in
consequence of their almost unexampled Persecutions." In
February he was advised by Henry Laurens to go to his
place on John's Island, which he did, and remained there
till the 4th June, 1776, "when his elegant House at White
Point, just finished, was erased to the ground by order of
Gov. Rutledge" He was harrassed and persecuted from
one province to another for several years until May, 1780,
when Charleston having surrendered to the British, he was
then appointed to the Department of the Post Office, also
Conservator of Peace and later Sheriff and Officer of the
Board of Police in that city By means of this he was
"enabled to support his Family" On Charleston being
retaken by the Americans he was banished by an Act of the
General Assembly, passed 26th Feb, 1782, and left with
two of his sons at the Evacuation of Charleston, on 14th
December, 1782 He arrived in England "In Feb" (1783)
"with two sons, one 17 and the other 11," whom he "sent
to Scotland, leaving a wife" (Margaret) "and five children
in Charleston reduced from affluent circumstances and without means of future support for himself or them"

The Memorial is dated 25th May, 1783, at No 40, Mon-
ument Yard, London He later lived at 81 Cannon Street
It is more than likely that he visited his cousin, Robert
Brisbane, of Milton, County Renfrewshire, in Scotland,
with whom he may have left his two sons, while he was
attending to his claim in London He remained in Great
Britain until June, 1787, and very soon after sailed for the
Bahamas, and settled in Nassau, New Providence, where
his wife, Margaret, and a part of his family joined him.
He was in partnership in that place until December, 1789,
with Alexander Spiers, (the firm being "Brisbane & Spiers")
when the partnership was dissolved In Dec, 1788, he was
granted 800 acres of land on Andros Island (one of the

[45]Letters to Henry Laurens See Vol IV this Magazine, p 11

Bahamas) In the "Muster Roll of the Volunteer Nassau Artillery Company" of 13th Nov, 1793, under Commissioned Officers, his name appears as "Captain Lieutenant "[46]

"In consequence of the services to America of his brother, Col Adam Fowler Brisbane, and of his son, William Brisbane, who, against his father, espoused while a boy the American Cause, some portion at least of the confiscated property was restored to the family "[47]

He died at Nassau on 26th Feb, 1794, after having held with credit several official posts [48]

James Brisbane married first, before 1759,[49] Rebecca, daughter of Richard Baker and Mary Bohun. She died in Jan., 1772 [50] He married, secondly, 24th May, 1772,[51] Sally, daughter of John Stanyarne of John's Island She died .... Jan, 1776 [52] He married lastly, before December, 1782, Margaret .... [53]

[46]A lieutenant with the rank and duties of captain but with a lieutenant's pay—as in the first Company of an English regiment

[47]Copied from a record found in an old Bible, and preserved by Miss Gertrude Brisbane, daughter of Benjamin Lawton Brisbane

[48]"Bahama Gazette" of Friday the 28th of February, 1794 "On Wednesday Evening died here James Brisbane, Esq He was a Valuable and useful Member of Society and filled Several respectable official Situations with Credit to himself and advantage to the Community

[49]She was unmarried in 1752, when her father, Richard Baker, made his Will, and was James Brisbane's wife in 1759, when a deed of partition was filed in the Court of Common Pleas of Charleston, by her brother, Richard Bohun Baker, the property in question being 440 acres of land left by their Uncle, Josiah Baker

[50]Col Hayne's Record Deaths, 1772 "January Rebecca (James) Brisbane" This Magazine, Vol X, p 167

[51]"As was James Brisbane, Esq, to Miss Sally Stanyarne, one of the daughters of the late Mr John Stanyarne, of John's Island From "Marriage Notices in the So Ca. Gaz." etc, by A S Salley, Jr

[52]Letter to Henry Laurens See this Magazine, Vol IV, p 10 Also referred to in his Memorial

[53]Probate Court, Charleston, 1793 p 293, Will of James Brisbane "and whereas a great part of what I possess or have any pretensions unto, either as compensation for loss in the late unfortunate American War, or restoration of confiscated property, came thro my late wives, I think I should in justice pay the proper attention to my children by them '—"My present wife Margaret, £100 Bahama Currency" "property to be divided into 10 shares"— Wife 1 share for life—Son William 1/3 of 8 shares & gold seal with Emblem of Hope & 1/4 of Books" "Son Robert 1/3 of Est that is 8/10, with gold seal of Appolo's head, 1/4 of Books"—

Children by first marriage. 4 (Brisbane) sons

1 William (3) [James (2), William (1)], b 25th Nov 1759 A member of the South Carolina, St Andrew's, and Charleston Library Societies. In 1790 he owned a plantation in St John's Parish, Colleton Co., Charleston District He married 22nd Jan, 1795,[54] Mary Deveaux, daughter of Andrew Deveaux and Catherine Barnwell "In the year 1801, he sold his plantation and with his wife began an extended tour of travel His various journeyings, chiefly by private coach, reached during the five following years over our Eastern States, Great Britain, Ireland, Switzerland, Holland and France," covering in all 20,294 miles While in Scotland, he made a claim to the property of his father's first cousin, Robert Brisbane of Milton. (See Note 17, p 124)

Shortly after his return to Charleston, he acquired as his country seat, Milton Lodge, on Ashley River As he had no children of his own he adopted, in 1812, the youngest son of each of his two half-brothers, John Stanyarne Brisbane and Adam Fowler Brisbane, viz William and William Henry, to whom he left the greater part of his fortune.[55]

"Son John Stanyarne Brisbane 1/3 of Estate and gold watch with seal with my arms, 1/4 of books & such furniture as is in the possession of my sister-in-law and his Aunt, Susannah Stanyarne."

Son Adam Brisbane 1/10 of Est 1/4 of Books, his mother's share at her death, small seal with arms, etc Executors, friends Thomas Forbes, William Burly Hall and sons William and John Brisbane Dated 17th Jan, 1794, and proved before John, Earl of Dunmore, Ordinary of the Bahama Islands, New Providence, July 29, 1794 On 13th May 1796, William Brisbane qualified as Executor

[54]"Married In St Paul's Parish, on Thursday, the 22nd instant, William Brisbane, Esq, to Miss Mary Devaux" From "Marriage Notices," etc, by A S Salley, Jr

[55]William Brisbane's Will dated 25th Oct, 1821, proved 9th Jan, 1822, mentions "nephew and adopted son William Henry Brisbane, when 25 (subject to use of my wife for life) Milton Lodge on Ashley River, books, furniture, cattle, etc & 22 negroes, watch seal with family coat of arms etc also house & lot No 39 Meeting St, pew 9 in St Paul's Church" -

"To nephew and adopted son William Brisbane when 25 (subject to use of wife) lot & house 15 Meeting St, with contents, horse & servants (9) gold Repeater watch etc pew No 92 in St
[illegible] [illegible] ($12,000) s equiv-
[illegible] Milton Lodge."

He died 9th Dec , 1821,[55] and was buried in his family vault in the Churchyard of St Paul's, Charleston, two days later, on 11th Dec., 1821 Mrs. Brisbane survived her husband twenty-four years, dying in 1845.

The white Italian marble Baptismal font, in the Chancel of St. Paul's in Charleston, was the gift of Mr. Brisbane and has the following inscription, "Presented by Wm. Brisbane to St. Paul's Church, Radcliffeborough, 1817."

ii. Robert (3), born about 1761; joined the St Andrew's Society in 1780. Probably died unm in 1794, before his father's will was proved [57]

iii (A son (3), name unknown, born about 1776; in Scotland in 1783 while his father was in England. Probably died before 1794 Not mentioned in his father's will

iv. (Son) (3), name unknown, b about 1772; in Scotland in 1783 Probably died before 1794. Not mentioned in his father's will

Child by second marriage: 1 (Brisbane) son.
(4) v John Stanyarne (3), b about 1773

Child by third marriage· 1 (Brisbane) son
(5) vi Adam Fowler (3), b 3rd Sept , 1783.

Other children[58] (not known by which marriage).
vii. ....
viii ... .

---

[55]"Died on the evening of the 9th inst in the 62nd year of his age, William Brisbane Esq" Charleston Courier, 14th Dec , 1821

[57]This appears from an Inventory of two Bonds given to above Robert Brisbane during his lifetime which after his decease became the property of James Brisbane and returned as his, in an inventory of his effects lodged in the Office of the Ordinary of Charleston Dist Had Robert left issue these two bonds would not have been included in the inventory of James Brisbane's effects

[58]James Brisbane, had, besides those named, two other children living with his wife Margaret, in Charleston in 1783, names not known, as proved by his Memorial

(To be continued)

SOME FORGOTTEN TOWNS
IN LOWER SOUTH CAROLINA

By Henry A M. Smith

SOMERTON

The Rev· William Screven stated to have been the first
Baptist minister to come to the province of South Carolina
is said to have located himself with some of his congregation "on Cooper River a few miles above Charles Town"
which settlement he called "Somerton" from his English
home in Somersetshire. This is the statement as made by
M[rs] Poyas (the octogenarian lady who published her book
in 1855[1]).

She also places the date of his arrival in October, 1682,
but the reasons for concluding this to be erroneous and for
fixing the date as not earlier than 1698 have been given
already in this Magazine.[2] The same account of Screven's
arrival is given in an historical sketch of the first Baptist
Church published in the Charleston Year Book for 1881
presumably derived from the work of M[rs] Poyas   D[r]
Ramsay in his History of South Carolina (vol 2, p 27),
states that M[r] Screven was the first Baptist minister and
began his ministerial labours in the province about 1683,
but does not mention Somerton, nor does D[r]. Shecut in his
sketch of the City of Charleston, published in 1819, in
which he merely repeats Ramsay. This "settlement" as
denominated by M[rs] Poyas has been supposed to indicate
a town or small village formed by the Rev M[r] Screven
and his congregation, and its exact locality as being the
site of the first Baptist settlement in South Carolina is a
matter of interest

On 11 January, 1711, there was made a grant to William
Screven of 260 acres.[3] The tract so granted was on Charles
Town Neck about seven miles from Charles Town and
about one mile from Cooper river—between what is now

[1]Olden Time of Carolina, pp 28 and 112
[2]S. C Hist & Gen Mag , vol IX, pp 87 and 230
[3]Off Sec... of State Grant Bk ... p ...

SOME FORGOTTEN TOWNS
IN LOWER SOUTH CAROLINA

By Henry A M. Smith

SOMERTON

The Rev William Screven stated to have been the first Baptist minister to come to the province of South Carolina is said to have located himself with some of his congregation "on Cooper River a few miles above Charles Town" which settlement he called "Somerton" from his English home in Somersetshire This is the statement as made by Mʳˢ Poyas (the octogenarian lady who published her book in 1855[1])

She also places the date of his arrival in October, 1682, but the reasons for concluding this to be erroneous and for fixing the date as not earlier than 1698 have been given already in this Magazine[2] The same account of Screven's arrival is given in an historical sketch of the first Baptist Church published in the Charleston Year Book for 1881: presumably derived from the work of Mʳˢ. Poyas Dʳ Ramsay in his History of South Carolina (vol 2, p 27), states that Mʳ Screven was the first Baptist minister and began his ministerial labours in the province about 1683, but does not mention Somerton, nor does Dʳ. Shecut in his sketch of the City of Charleston, published in 1819, in which he merely repeats Ramsay This "settlement" as denominated by Mʳˢ Poyas has been supposed to indicate a town or small village formed by the Rev. Mʳ Screven and his congregation, and its exact locality as being the site of the first Baptist settlement in South Carolina is a matter of interest

On 11 January, 1711, there was made a grant to William Screven of 260 acres[3] The tract so granted was on Charles Town Neck about seven miles from Charles Town and about one mile from Cooper river—between what is now

[1]Olden Time of Carolina, pp 28 and 112
[2]S C Hist & Gen Mag, vol IX, pp 87 and 230
[3]Off Secy of State Grant Bk 38 p 391

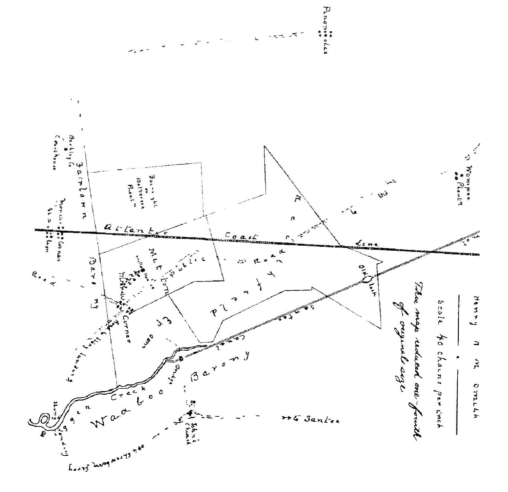

Henry A. M. Smith

Scale 40 chains per inch

This map reduced one-fourth
of original size

the U S Navy Yard reservation and the main public road up the Neck William Screven does not appear to have long retained it, nor is there any evidence that there was ever any settlement in the form of a village or town upon it, or that it was ever known as Somerton

On 23 January, 1698, William Screven acquired from John Stewart a tract of 804 acres[4] which had been granted to Stewart 14th October, 1696.[5] It was situated near a locality known as "Wampee" on the west side of Pooshee or Biggin Swamp, one of the headwaters of the Cooper River and some 40 miles or more from Charleston.

On 11 January, 1700, there was granted to William Screven 300 acres at Wampee[6] adjoining to the East on the 804 acre tract. These two tracts, aggregating 1,104 acres, William Screven and his wife Bridget, on 15th October, 1708, conveyed to René Ravenel. In the conveyance no name is given to the plantation, but it remained in the Ravenel family for near a century and a half, always known by the name of Somerton, which name it still bears

In a nuncupative will made by Robert Wetherick on 5 September, 1700, he styles himself as "late of New England "then of Somerton in y[e] County aforesaid" (Berkeley)[7] On 17 May, 1701, a grant was made to Elizabeth Wetherick of 325 acres at Wampee[8] which also bounded on the 804 acre tract and which she conveyed on 26 March, 1728, to Paul Ravenel,[9] who seems to have incorporated it into the Somerton plantation A tract of 1,000 acres near Wampee was, on 6 Nov'r, 1704, granted to Champernoun Elliott;[10] and Permanow Screven (a son of the Rev· William Screven) at the same time owned an adjoining tract,[11] as also Humphrey Axtell.[12] The Wethericks, Elliott, and Axtell, seem all to have been Baptists, and the Wethericks and Elliott were either related to or in some sort of connection

---

[4]M C O Charleston, Bk P N° 6, p 309
[5]Ibid, p 308
[6]Off Secy of State, Grant Bk 38, p 401
[7]Prob Ct Charleston, Bk 1671-1727, p 72
[8]Off Secy of State, vol 38, p 392
[9]M C O Charleston, Bk P N° 6, p 318
[10]Off Secy of State, vol 38, p 475
[11]Ibid
[12]M C O Charleston, Bk P N° 6, p 310

with William Screven * From all which it would appear that the Somerton at which William Screven settled was the plantation of that name on Biggin swamp where he settled on his arrival in the province about the year 1698, and that it was never a town or village

According to an old map seen by the writer, all the Somerton settlement and plantation buildings were upon the 300 acres granted to William Screven

BERMUDA TOWN

The earliest mention (known to the writer) of Bermuda Town, is in a deed dated 3 October, 1699,[13] from James Allen. J[r], to Thomas Fry, of a parcel of land containing 25 acres or thereabouts, bounding "Northward upon the "Broad Path or Common High Road that leads from "Sewee to Bermuda Town" That it was laid out as a town with provision for a school appears from the minutes of a meeting of the vestry recorded in the Register Book of Christ Church Parish, wherein it is recorded, that at a meeting of the vestry, held 8th October, 1716, it was agreed "that Col Logan procure a Warrant to run out the Land "belonging to the School House in Bermuda Town for the "use of the Parish."

In a deed dated 20 July, 1726, from James Fitzgerald to Maurice Harvey there is conveyed "seventy acres situate "on a part of Hobcaw Neck commonly called Bermudoes "Town being part of a quantity or parcell of Land con- "taining Two hundred and ten acres" bounding "to the "Southward on Cornbow Creek "[14]

---

*Mrs Elizabeth Wetherick was the daughter of Robert and Mary Cutt, of Barbadoes and Kittery, Maine, she was a sister of Bridget Cutt, who married the Rev Wm Screven, (See *New England Historical and Genealogical Register*, vol 27, page 146 and vol 44, p 112 Also will of Francis Champernoun, *York County* (Me) *Probate Records*, vol 1, pp 54-55) Elizabeth Cutts married first, about 1685, Humphrey Elliot, of Kittery, Me, and second, Robert Wetherick, of New England and So Ca, by Humphrey Elliott, she had two sons, Champernoun Elliott and Robert Elliott, they both came to Carolina with her (as did her mother, Mrs Champernoun) and died here, leaving descendants in female lines only —Editor

[13]Off Hist Com[a]., Grant Bk 1696-1703, p 157

[14] ...

Cornbow or Combow Creek was the same as Wackendaw or Wackendau Creek.[15]

On 15 April, 1734, Henry Gignilliat vintner and Hester his wife mortgage to Joseph Wragg a tract of 50 acres "in Bermuda Town," bounding "West on a creek that goes "into Wandoe river."[16]

Wackendaw creek is the first creek of any size that flows into the Wando river on its Southeast bank next above the junction of the Wando and Cooper rivers The low grounds at the head of Wackendaw Creek approach quite nearly the low grounds at the head of Shem or Shem-ee creek and the body of land bounded by these two creeks on the North and East, Wando river on the West, and Cooper river on the South is known as Hobcaw Neck On the U S. Coast survey map Wackendaw creek is called Hobcaw creek, and on Mills Atlas of Charleston District it is called Wacanoaw.

How or when the name Bermuda Town was given does not appear on the record From the boundaries given to the lands described in the deeds it would appear to have been situated on the Northern or Eastern side of Wackendaw creek and not strictly on Hobcaw Neck The "Town" seems to have been never much more than a name, but the name "Bermuda" continued as the name of a plantation, which in the early part of the nineteenth century was owned by Nicholas Venning, J'. On p 277 of the Christ Church Parish Register appears "Mortimer Williams Ven-"ning born at Bermuda Plantation Christ Church Parish "Sept 22 1816 son of Nicholas Venning J' and Martha "his wife who was the daughter of Thomas Allan of Eng-"land "

The plantation of that name as now known contains 265 acres and bounds directly on Wando river and not upon Wackendaw creek[17] as was the case with Bermuda Town A part of the plantation called "Belle View" lies between Bermuda and the creek. This, however, may be only a shifting of names during the long successive ownerships of

---

[15]Off Secy of State, Grant Bk. 38, p 436 Grant to John White 18 Sept, 1703
[16]M C O Charleston, Bk M, p 78
[17]M C O Charleston, Bk V N° 16, p 201

near two centuries, and the present Bermuda plantation, in all probability, represents approximately the site of Bermuda Town.

MONCKS CORNER.

The town of Moncks Corner was situated on a tract of 1,500 acres granted to Landgrave Joseph West, 15th November, 1680.[1] This tract lay adjoining and just to the North of Sir Peter Colleton's Fairlawn Barony. Landgrave West on 7 December, 1686, conveyed the entire 1,500 acres to James Le Bas[2]

This was the James Le Bas to whom the Lords Proprietors, on 26th September, 1685, agreed to grant 3,000 acres of land[3] and for which 3,000 acres a warrant was by the Governor and Deputies in the Province issued to the Surveyor General of the Province, 6 May, 1686[4]

In the list known as the "St. Julien" list of the French protestant immigrants seeking naturalization there is mentioned "Mr Jacques Le Bas né a Can, fils de Jean Le Bas "et Anne Samborne, Pierre Le Bas son fils né à Can"

On the death of the James Le Bas who acquired the 1,500 acres his land descended to his son and heir, Paul Peter Le Bas, on whose death, 8th February, 1724, the land descended to his son and heir, another James Le Bas[5]

This last on 29th June, 1729, conveyed 400 acres to John Vicaridge[6] which Vicaridge subsequently (prior to 1733) transferred to Peter Colleton, second son of the then Sir John Colleton, and by whom apparently the 400 acre tract was named Epsom On 22 April, 1735, James Le Bas conveyed 1,000 acres to Thomas Monck[7] The residue, about 100 acres, Le Bas seems to have retained The writer has not been able to ascertain who this Thomas Monck was as respects his connection with any others of the name. In all his signatures to deeds, as appearing now on the

[1] Off Secy of State, Grant Bk 38, p 35
[2] Off Hist Comn Memo Bk 3, p 420
[3] Trans Hist Soc of S C, vol 1, pp 115 & 123
[4] Warrants for lands in S C, 1680-1692, p 190
[5] M C O Charleston. Bk N, p 302
[6] Off Secy of State, Memorial Bk 4, p 262
[7] M C O Charleston. Bk N, p 302

record, he spells his name Monck with a "c." There was another family in South Carolina who appear to have spelled the name Monk, without the "c"

On 19 July, 1682, the Lords Proprietors write to the Duke of Albemarle that they are informed that he has granted to "M[r] John Monke of Kingsclere 1000 acres of "land together with expenses to carry him and his family "and servants" to Carolina* The then Duke of Albemarle was Christopher Monk son of George Monk the first Duke and one of the original Proprietors and grantees under the Charter of South Carolina The abstract of the same communication as given in the English publication[9] is that the grant was to "M[r] John Monk of Knightsbere" evidently a mistake of the copyer for there is (according to the 10th Ed. of the Encyclopaedia Brit) a Kingsclere in Hampshire, but no Knightsbere in either England or Scotland

On 28 July, 1682, the Duke of Albemarle writes that he has granted to "M[r] John Monke of Kingsclere Draper and "his heirs" 1,000 acres and £50 for the transmission of his family to the Province

On the following 22 February, 1682, the Lords Proprietors by letters patent of that date and on motion of the Duke of Albemarle created "John Monk" a Cassique of Carolina,[10] and on February 15, 1683, commissioned "John "Monk Esq'." Muster master of all forces raised in the Province of Carolina[11]

This John Monk arrived in the Province about 8th September, 1683, with his wife, seven children, and two servants[12]

On 1st January, 1683 O S (1684 N S), a warrant was issued to lay out to the "Hon[ble] Cassique John Monke" 490 acres, that being the acreage to which he was entitled under the proposals of the Lords Proprietors for at that time bringing so many settlers into the Province[13]

[8]Collections Hist Soc of S C, vol 1, p 106
[9]Cal of State Papers, A & W I 1681-1685, p 268
[10]Collections Hist Soc S C, vol 1, p 107, for copy of the patent see Off Hist Com[n] S C, bk 1694, 1739, p 54 from back
[11]Coll Hist Soc S C, vol 1, p 107
[12]Warrants for Lands in S C, 1680-1692, p 116
[13]Ibid

This 490 acres he subsequently transferred to Robert Hull [14]

On 10 April, 1684, a warrant is issued to lay out to the "Hon[ble] John Moncke one of y[e] Cassiques of this Province" 1,000 acres granted him by the Lords Proprietors [15] On an old plat in the possession of the writer it is stated that this 1,000 acres was laid out to him on the North side of Goose Creek and that he subsequently transferred 800 acres to Robert How.

What became of all his seven children the writer has not been able to ascertain

On 5 May, 1704, a grant of 120 acres is made to "Thomas Monck" [16] which from its boundaries appears to have been located in what became the Parish of St Thomas next adjoining Thomas Akins· and according to the Register of St Thomas Parish a Thomas Monck was married on 11 March, 1708, to Martha Aiken, had a daughter Sarah, baptised 1 March, 1712-13, and was himself buried 4 March, 1713 [17] An Edward Monck, late of South Carolina, Bachelor, died, and administration on his estate was issued in England to his mother, Joane Monck, widow, 22 July, 1713 [18]

A Stephen Monk of Goose creek declaring himself to be the son and heir of John Monk, one of the Cassiques of the Province, makes the following conveyances·

640 acres in Berkley County to George Peterson 24 March, [19] 1723

180 acres in Colleton County to W[m] Holmes 19 May, [20] 1729

100 acres in St Georges Parish to W[m] Glaze 9 January, [21] 1728.

165 acres in Colleton County to James Basford 13 May, [22] 1729

---

[14]Ibid, p 147
[15]Ibid, p. 146
[16]Off Secy of State, Grant Bk 38, p 452
[17]Register of St Thomas and St. Denis, pp 25, 75, 108
[18]S C Hist & Gen Mag, vol V, p 101
[19]M C O Charleston, Bk D. p 80
[20]Ibid, Bk K, p 55
[21]Ibid Bk H p 3
[22] [ ] [ ] 571

In all these deeds it is declared that the land transferred
is part of the 24,000 acres to which his father was entitled
as a Cassique   On 8 February, 1734, he mortgages to
Samuel Prioleau a negro slave, his cattle, riding horse,
coopers tools, &c."

The deeds are all signed with a mark "S M " in lieu of
a full signature.   A Thomas Monk of St Stephens, who
dies in 1764, leaves a Will dated 26 Sept'., 1763, leaving
his property to his brothers, John and Stephen Monk "
On 24 October, 1755, a George Monk transfers a negro
slave to his wife, Martha "

It may be all these "Monks" were the descendants of John
Monk the Cassique, but there is no sufficient indication that
Thomas Monck of Moncks Corner was so, or that he had
any connection with the "Monks."   He may have been a
son of the Thomas Monck of St Thomas who married
Martha Aiken, but the dates make it improbable

Prior to the purchase of the 1,000 acres from Le Bas
Thomas Monck had, on 6th January, 1732, married Miss
Joanna Broughton, daughter of Col Thomas Broughton,
President of his Majesty's Council in the Province, a large
landholder, a man of fortune and one of the most prominent men in the Province, and the bride was according to
the notice in the Gazette "a young lady of merit and
fortune "²⁶

To advance his son-in-law Col Broughton turned over
to him slaves and other property to the value of £3,000.
(in provincial currency; about £428 sterling) for which
Thomas Monck gave his bond by way of marriage settlement to his brothers in law "Nathaniel Broughton of Mul-
"berry and Andrew Broughton of Seaton" for the use of
Monck and his wife during their lives and after their
deaths to the children of the marriage

It is probable that he purchased the property so as to be
in the same neighbourhood with his wife's family, for both
Mulberry and Seaton are within a few miles of Moncks
Corner   On 23 March, 1738, to secure this marriage bond

---

²³Ibid, Bk. R, p 161
²⁴Prob Ct Charleston, Bk 1760-1767, p 317
²⁵Ibid, B̄ 1 ̄ ̄ ̄ ̄ ̄
²⁶Salt ̄ ̄ ̄ ̄ ̄

he mortgaged 600 acres, the Southern part of the 1,000 acres, which 1,000 acres he describes as commonly called "Mitton."[27]

When the place was so named does not appear As Monck so soon after his acquisition speaks of it as "Commonly" called "Mitton" it is probable that it was so named during the ownership by the Le Bas family. Landgrave Wests' ownership was very short, only about 6 years At the present date the pronunciation is "Mitton," but it is sometimes spelt in the old deeds "Milton " The marriage settlement as recorded spells it "Mitton " The Will of Thomas Monck as recorded spells it "Milton," perhaps an error of the copyer

The town probably did not exist when Monck purchased the property From the name "Moncks Corner" the presumption would seem that the town came into existence during his ownership The name of the town arose from the following circumstance

The main high road from Charleston forked on the Mitten plantation. The road to the right ran across Biggin and Wadboo creeks, and to the settlements on the Eastern branch of the Cooper river, and to those on the Santee from English Santee to the sea, and across the Santee river to Georgetown, and generally the Northeastern part of the country The road to the left of the fork was known as the road to the Congarees and led to the settlements in St. Stephens Parish and to French Santee, and across the Santee at Nelson's Ferry into the Northwestern interior A road from the fork also ran Southeasterly to the landing on Biggin creek called Stony Landing, situate on a part of the Fairlawn Barony[28] which was at the head of navigation on Cooper River In place of the long land route over the bad road of the period from Charleston to this point, some 35 miles, freight was transported by water up the Cooper river to Stony Landing and thence by pack animals or bearers into the interior by either of the roads mentioned.

---

[27] M C O Charleston, Bk T, p 456
[28] S C Hist & Gen Mag vol XI, p 193

The "fork" was the "corner" and being on Monck's land was called "Moncks Corner"

Unlike most of the small towns attempted to be created at that time in lower South Carolina, Moncks Corner seems to have grown by virtue of its position and never to have been laid out on any regular town plan. The taverns and stores constituting the so-called town being built on both sides of the roads at the fork.

His first wife having died, Thomas Monck, on 11 July, 1745, married Mary de St Julien, the widow of Paul de St Julien and daughter of Theodore Verdity, also described in the Gazette as "a lady of very great merit with a good "fortune"[29] He died in June, 1747, leaving only one child, a daughter by his first wife named Joanna Broughton Monck To this daughter he devised the 600 acres mortgaged to secure the marriage settlement bond, and to his wife, Mary, he devised the other 400 acres of the 1,000 acres purchased from James Le Bas[30] This 400 acres Mary Monck conveyed on 30 June, 1752,[31] to William Keith, who had previously, on 15 August, 1749, acquired from Ann Le Bas and Thomas Sabb, Executrix and Executor of James Le Bas, 91 acres of the 100 acres not sold by Le Bas[32] These two last tracts were attached to the "Keithfield" plantation, and the name "Mitton" seems afterwards to have been borne by the 600 acres of Joanna Broughton Monck

On 9th October, 1760, Joanna Broughton Monck married John Dawson.[33]*

[29]Salley, So Ca Marriages. p 11
[30]Probate Ct Charleston, Will Bk 1747-1752. p. 17.
[31]M C O Charleston, Bk M M. p 144
[32]Ibid, p 148
[33]Dawson Family Records, p 345.

*Mitton, near Monck's Corner, John Dawson, Has imported per Capts Strachn, Mitchell & Curling, in the fleet from London, A Large and compleat assortment of dry goods (which were put on board a schooner as they came out of the vessels to prevent any infection of the Small-pox), which, with rum, wine, sugar, bar iron, and salt, &c, he will sell at the above place at the Charles-Town prices, and allow the height of the market for deer-skins, butter, flour, tallow, &c

N B The above store will be removed to the corner as soon as the new house can be fitted, where a good assortment will always be kept" (Advertisement in The South Carolina Gazette Saturda

The record in South Carolina does not show much about John Dawson previous to this date. The "Dawson Family Records" states that he emigrated to Charlestown previous to 1759, a somewhat safe inference, taking the date of his marriage as proved. He is stated by the late Fred[k] A. Porcher to have been a merchant at Moncks Corner[34] He died in Charleston, 7 May, 1812, leaving a large family of sons and daughters, and his descendants are very numerous By his Will he devised to his son, Lawrence Monck Dawson, the plantation called "Mitton,"[35] the title to which he may have acquired from his wife by marriage settlement, or releases for the purpose.

Lawrence Monck Dawson, after his acquisition of Mitton purchased an adjoining plantation called "Battersea,"[36] formerly the "Fairsight" plantation of Major Charles Colleton, and to the entire tract of 1,120 acres the name Mitton was applied.

On 20 February, 1829, after the death of Lawrence Monck Dawson the entire tract was, by the Court, on application of his minor heirs, sold off[37]

As an evidence of the continuity of land holding in lower South Carolina prior to 1860, it will be seen that from 1686 to 1829, some 143 years, the "Mitton" plantation had been in the hands of two families, Le Bas and Monck

Moncks Corner never attained any size The only account of any length regarding it the writer has been able to find is that of the late M[r]. Samuel Du Bose, in his reminiscenses of St Stephens Parish There he says

"Before the revolution Moncks Corner was a place of "some commercial importance. There were three or four "well kept taverns and five or six excellent stores These "were generally branches of larger establishments in "Charleston and as they sold goods at Charleston prices "they commanded a fair business. The usual practice of "the Santee planter was to take his crop to Monck's Corner,

[34]Trans Huguenot Society of S C, N° 13, p 33
[35]Prob Ct. Charleston, Will Bk E, p 264
[36]M C O Charleston, Bk N 9, p. 117
[37]Ibid, Bk J N°. 16, p 187

"sell it there, receiving cash or goods in exchange, dine,
"and return home in the afternoon "

Mr Fred^k. A Porcher, in his Article already referred to,
says ·

"I have never known Monck's Corner without at least
"one house and I remember when four or five remained as
"relics of this old commercial mart   *   *   *

"The principal merchants of Monck's Corner were also
"Charleston Merchants   The last of them were Mr John
"Dawson and M^r. Simeon Theus   I cannot say when it
"ceased to be a commercial port but probably about the
"commencement of the century, as the first named of these
"gentlemen lived several years in Charleston after he had
"retired from Monck's Corner "

The position of Moncks Corner which gave it commercial importance, during the revolutionary war also gave it
military importance   It commanded the two roads mentioned, the main direct road to Charleston, and access to
the navigation of Cooper river   To secure this last an
earthen redoubt was constructed by the British on the
Fairlawn Barony near Stony Landing

During the siege of Charles Town Gen' Isaac Huger,
in command of the American cavalry, took post near
Monck's Corner   There they were attacked by the British
under Lieut· Col· Tarleton, and having been surprised
suffered a total defeat.   Huger, himself, Col William
Washington and other officers escaped on foot to the
swamp, but the entire American force was captured or
dispersed with the loss of nearly all their horses.

So important was Monck's Corner in position that the
British established a post there and fortified the Colleton
Mansion at Fairlawn in the immediate vicinity of the Cor-
ner.

It was to Monck's Corner that Lord Rawdon fell back
after he abandoned Camden and from whence he advanced
to relieve the siege of Ninety Six

Lt Col. Coates was posted at Monck's Corner in July,
1781, when threatened by Sumter's advance, and from
Monck's Corner he retreated to Biggin Church and thence
down the East side of the Cooper river with the Americans

in hot pursuit   General Stewart, in command of the British Army fell back on Monck's Corner, after the battle of
Eutaw Springs, and with the retreat from Monck's Corner
to Charleston in November, 1781, the British occupation
of the State, outside of Charleston and its environs, termi-
nated

After the revolutionary war Monck's Corner seems to
have rapidly decayed   The opening up of the back country,
the Santee Canal and other routes of trade destroyed any
commercial position it had. With the construction of the
Northeastern railroad (now the Atlantic Coast Line),
which passed within a mile or so of it, it ceased entirely to
exist   A railroad station was constituted on the railroad
on part of the old Fairlawn Barony, to which the name of
Monck's Corner was transferred and which is now the
County seat of Berkeley County   All that remains of the
original Monck's Corner is a few crumbling piles of broken
bricks and some shade trees on either side of the road   The
road to Stony Landing is now obliterated and the site of
the old village has not even a name

REGISTER OF
ST. ANDREW'S PARISH, BERKELEY COUNTY, SOUTH CAROLINA.

1719-1774.

Copied and Edited by MABEL L. WEBBER.

(Continued from the April Number)

BURIALS P^r Y^e REV^d WILL^m. GUY.

Martha Ladson widow Buried Nov^{br}. y 7th 1750.

Mary the wife of John Godfrey Buried Nov^{br}. ye 8th. 1750

William Ladson Buried Nov^{br}: y^e: 13th: 1750.

{ Mary La,frong [?] w^{dn} Buried Nov^{br}: 14th 1750. Lived
{ with Doc^{tr} Holzendroft.

Sarah the wife of Thomas Rivers Buried Nov^{br}. ye 15th
1750

The Rev^d. William Guy* Buried p^r the Rev^d. M^r. Orr.
Decb^r ye 11th 1750.

Sarah Daughter of Sarah Fuller widow to Nathaniel Fuller
Decsd. Buried Deb^r: ye 27th 1750 Intrd. without a
minister.

Zackeus Ladson Buried Dec^{br}. ye 29th 1750 Intrd. without
a minister.

Anne Cattell widow Buried p^r the Rev^d. M^r. Keeth Jan^{ry}:
ye 4th 1750/1.

Elizabeth Rixem wid^{ow} Buried Jan^{ry}: ye 5th 1750/1. Inter^d.
without a minister at Mrs Quinseys.

Benjamin Fuller Buried p^r the Rev^d. M^r. Coots Recct^r of
St Georges Buried Feb^{ry}. ye 24th 1750/1.

Benjamin Stanyarn Buried April ye 20th 1751 Inter^d without a Minister

---

*Yesterday departed this Life, aged 62 years, very much lamented, particularly by his Parishioners, and by every one who had the Pleasure of an acquaintance with him, the Revd. Mr. William Guy, Rector of St. Andrews parish for upwards of 30 years past. Of whom it may be truly said, He lived the life of the Just, and died the Death of the Righteous.—South Carolina Gazette, Dec 10 1750.

Samuell Jones Buried May ye 11th 1750   Inter^d. without
    a Minister

John Godfrey Alias Garnear Buried June ye 29th 1751
    Intr^d without a Minister.

William Cattell Junr Esqr Buried p^r the Rev^d M^r. Coats
    Minister of St Georges August ye 4th 1751

Frances Ladson Sn^r Buried p^r ye Rev^d. Mr Coots August
    ye 4th 1751

William Branford Sn^r Buried August 26th 1751 p^r the
    Revd Mr Keith

Doct^r Charles Hill Buried Septr ye 1st 1751.   Inter^d with-
    out a minister

Mary Hull wd^o. Buried ye 31st Octr 1751 Aged About 90
    years Intr^d. without a Minister

Elizabeth the wife of Thomas Drayton Esqr Buried p^r y^e
    Revd Mr Coots Novr. ye 6th 1751

Thomas Goering Buried Nov^{br} 30th 1751 Intrd. without a
    Minister.

Robert Yonge Esqr Buried at Too Goodoo plant^n. in S^t
    Pauls Parish p^r the Revd Mr Rowan Decr ye 4th 1751

Thomas Mullens Buried at Mr Edmund Bellingers Janry
    ye 25th 1752   Inter^d without a minister

Mary-Bellinger the Wife of Thomas Elliott Junr of S^t
    Pauls. Buried p^r ye Rev^d M^r. Rowan Minister of the
    S^d Parish Jan^{ry}: ye 31st 1752

Sophia-Sarah the wife of John Miles Buried Feb^{ry}· ye 2^d
    1752 P^r. ye Revd Mr Keith.

Ann Daught^r of Daniel Peper & Mary his wife Buried p^r
    ye Revd Mr Charles Martyn June ye 22^d: 1752

Amelia Daught^r of Mary the wife of William Hats Buried
    July ye 19th 1752. p^r Rev^d M^r. Martyn

William Miles Sn^r Buried p^r ye Revd Mr Martyn August
    ye 10th 1752

William Cattell Sn^r. Buried August 19th 1752 p^r ye Rev^d
    Mr Martyn

Sarah Ann Daugh^{tr} of Thomas Rivers Buried Octr y^e
    19th 1752: Intrd without a minister

Sarah Daught^r of Mary Jones w^{do} Buried Deb^r 24th 1752
    p^r M^r. Martyn

John Mickleborrough A poor man Buried June ye 8th 1753 M^r. Martyn.

Mary the wife of William Walter Esq Buried p^r ye Rev^d. Mr Martyn Septr 3^d 1753

Sarah Anne Daughter of Doct^r Thomas Honour & Rebecca his wife Buried p^r Revd Mr Martyn Septr. 4th 1753

Charl^s. Son of Benj^m. Elliott & Mary his wife Buried p^r Revd Mr Martyn Septr 4th. 1753

Hugh Ohair Buried Decb^r 1753 p^r Mr Martyn

BIRTHS

Margarett Daugh^r of Thomas Heyward & Anne his wife born March ye 31st 1753

Daniel Son of Daniel Pepper & Ann his wife Born May ye 14th 1733 [sic] at Dorchester.

Gilbert Son of Daniel Pepper & Mary [sic] his wife Born April 19th 1736 at Dorchester

Samuel Son of Daniel Peper & Mary his wife Born Nov^{br} 23^d, 1750 at James Island

Elizabeth Daughter of Landgrave Edmund Bellinger & Mary Luci his wife Born Nov^{br} ye 8th 1751

Sarah Daught^r of Mary Jones widow born [no date given]

Ann Daughter of Thomas Fuller & Lydia his wife born Nov^{br}. 15th 1750

Anne Daughter of Daniel Pepper & Mary his wife born ―― 1752

Martha Daught^r of Archibald Scot & Agnes his wife born Feb^{ry} ye 10th 1752

Richard Son of Thomas Fuller & Lydia his Wife Born 23^d April 1749

Henery Son of Henery Richmond & Elizabeth his wife born Nov^{br} ye 6th 1751

John-Alleyne Son of William Walter & Mary his wife Born August ye 12th; 1752.

Richard Son of Richard Lake & Mary his wife Born January ye 7th 1752

William-Charles Son of Richard Lake & Mary his wife Born January ye 9th 1753

Elizabeth Daughter of Isaac Ladson & Rachel his wife, Born Jan^{ry} 28th 1753

Thomas Son of John Harriss & Elenor his wife Born Oct[r] 1752

Beaulah the Daughter of John Man & Martha his wife Born June 14th 1752

Sarah Anne Daught[r] of Doct[r]. Thomas Honour & Rebeccah his wife Born April 30th 1753

Sarah Daught[r]. of Francis Rose & Mary Anne his wife Born April 30th 1753

John Son of Henry Wood & Mary his wife Born Decb[r] 14th 1753

Joseph Son of Thomas Fuller & Lydia his wife Born June y[e] 6th 1753

CHRISTININGS P[r] THE REV[d] M[r] MARTYN

Sarah Daughter of Mary Jones widow Bapt[zd] April y[e]: 30th 1752

Anne Daughter of Daniel Pepper & Mary his wife Bapt[zd]: May y[e] 3[d]. 1752

Martha Daughter of Archibald Scott & Agnes his wife Bapt[zd] May y[e] 3[d] 1752

Mary Anger an Adult Bapt[zd] May y[e] 24th 1752. Age Regs[rd] page y[e] 2[d] *

Ephraim Son of Ambrose Jackson & Amey his wife Bapt[zd] Oct[r] y[e] 15th 1752

Richard Son of Thomas Fuller & Lyda his wife Bapt[zd]: Nov[br] y[e] 21, 1752

Henery Son of Henery Richmond & Elizabeth his wife Bap[tzd] Jan[ry] 21, 1753

John-Alleyne Son of William Walter & Mary his wife Bapt[zd] March y[e] 9th 1753

{ Richard Son of Richard Lake and Mary his wife Bapt[zd] March y[e]. 15th 1753
William-Charles Son of Ibid Bap[tzd] 15th Ma[ch] 1753

Glen Son of John Drayton Esq[r] & Margaret his wife Bapt[zd]: 25 March 1752   [sic]

Elizabeth Daught[r] of Isaac Ladson & Rachel his wife Bap[tzd] March y[e] 30th 1753

Abraham Son of Ibid Reced[d]: into y[e] Congre[tion] Prv[tly]. Bapt[zd] Before 30 March

_____

*S. C. H. M. XII, page 176

Thomas Son of John Harriss & Elenor his wife Bapt^d
April y^e 1st 1753

Joseph a Malata Child of M^r. John Gordon Bapt^d June
y^e—1753

Beulah the Daught^r of John Man & Martha his wife Bapt^d
June y^e 17th 1753.

Edmund the Son of Langr^tt Edmund Bellinger & Mary-
Luci his wife Bapt^d June ye 24th 1753

Sarah Anne Daught^r of Doct^r Tho' Honour & Rebeckah
his wife Bapt^d August 1753

Sarah Daught^r of Francis Rose & Mary-Anne his Wife
Bapt^d 1753

John Son of Henry Wood & Mary his Wife Bapt^d. Jan^ry:
ye 13th 1754

Joseph Son of Thomas Fuller & Lydia his wife Bapt^d
March ye 14th 1754

BIRTHS

Philip Son of Philip Culp and Christian his wife Born
Feb^ry. 14th 1754

{ Billey Son of Petter Earhart & Margaret his wife Born
Nov^br 1, 1754 Serv^tt to Thos Drayton

{ William Son of William Johnson a free negro Born May
ye 18th 1739
Sarah Daught^r to D^o born March 21st. 1741

Isabella Daughter of Benjn Elliott & Mary his wife Born
Octo^br 8th 1753

Mary Daught^r of Richard Lake & Mary his wife Born
Decb^r ye 2^d 1754

David Son of Archibald Scot & Agnes his wife Born
Octo^br. 18th 1753

John Son of Daniel Pepper & Mary his wife Born July y^e
31st 1753 James Island

Elizabeth Daught^r of Samuel Bowman & Keziah his wife
Born Nov^br ye 28th 1754

Samuel Son of John Harris & Elenor his wife born Feb^ry
13th. 1755

Christian Daught^r of Jacob Hinckele & Hannah his wife
born 1754

Jacob Son of Michal Hats & Cathrine his wife born ——
    1752

Mary Ann Daught' to Ib^d born 1753

John Fitch Son of John Miles & Anne his wife Born
    Feb^ry. 5th 1755

Elizabeth Daught' of Doct' Thomas Honour & Rebecka
    his wife Born Janu^ry. ye 14th: 1755.

Robart Son of Mallory Rivers & Mary his wife born
    March 8th: 1755

David Son of David Taylor & Jane-Baynes his wife born
    Sept' 14th 1753

Sarah Daught' of Thomas Godfrey alis Garnear & Eliza-
    beth his wife born August ye 25th 1753

Twins {
    Joseph-Thomas Son of Thomas Holman & Mary his
        wife Born Nov^br: 2^d 1754 oldest
    Walter Son of Thomas Holman & Mary his wife Born
        Nov^br 2^d. 1754 ye Youngest about 10 min^ts Diff-
        erence
}

CHRISTININGS P^r REV^d Mr MARTYN

Philip Son of Philip Culp & Christian his wife Bapti^zd
    April ye 7th 1754

Billey Son of Petter Earhart & Margaret his wife Bapt^zd
    April. 7th: 1754 Serv^tt to Thos Drayton

William Son of William Johnson a free negro Bapt^zd April
    12th 1754

Sarah Daught' to D° Bapt^zd April 12th 1754

Benja^mn Elliott Bapt^zd May 18th 1754

Isabella Daught' of Benjn: Elliott & Mary his wife Bapt^zd
    May ye 19th 1754

George Son of Edmund Bellinger & Mary Luci his wife
    Bapt^zd 1754

David Son of Archibald Scot & Agnes his wife Bapt^zd——
    1753 [sic]

Elizabeth Daughter of Benjamin Perry & Susanah his wife
    Bapt^zd Priv^t & Recev^d: in the congreg^ton Sep' ye 1 at
    Chappel in St Pauls 1754

Elizabeth Daught' of Saml Bowman & Keziah his wife
    Bapt^zd p^r Revd Mr Martyn Feb^ry ye 12th 1755

Samuel Son of John Harriss & Elenor his wife Baptrd March 1st · 1755

Christian Daught^r to Jacob Hinckele & Hannah hs wife Bapt^{td} March 26 1755

Jacob Son to Michal Hats & Mary his wife Bapt^{td} March 26 - 1755.

Mary Ann Daught^r to Ib^d Bapt^{td} March 26 1755

Robert Son of Mallery Rivers & Mary his wife Bapt^{td} April 18th 1755 p^r Mr Bell ye Dissenting Minest^r James' Island

John Fitch Son of John Miles & Anne his wife Bapt^{td} April ye 27th 1755

Elizabeth Daught^r of Doct^r Thomas Honour & Rebecka his wife Bapt^{td} May ye 25th 1755

David Son of David Taylor & Jane-Baynes his wife bapt^{td} June ye 1st 1755

Sarah Daught^r of Thomas Godfrey Garnear & Elizabeth his wife Bapt^{td} June ye 1st 1755

{ Joseph-Thomas Son of Thomas Holman & Mary his wife Bapt^{td} Septr ye 29th 1755

{ Walter Son of Thomas Holman & Mary his wife Bapt^{td} Septr ye 29th 1755

Thomas Son of Thomas Hayward & Anne his wife Bapt^{td} Septr. ye 21 1755

Frederick Son of John Paul Trout & Catherine his wife Bapt^{td} Septr 1755

MARRIAGES P^r REV^d Mr MARTYN.

The Revd Charles Martyn and Sarah Fuller Married p^r ye Rev^d. Alexander Barron Married April ye 13th 1755 In May registered.

Jeremiah Savage & Sarah Brown widow Mard July ye 5th 1755

James Smith & Sarah Ladson Sp^r Married Nov^{br} ye 27th 1755.

Thomas Scott & Mary Whitter Sp^r Married Feb^{ry} 11th 1756

Benjamin Parrott & Hannah Witter wd^o Married May ye 27th 1756

William Simson Esqr & Elizabeth Bull Sp^r Married April 12th 1756

Patrick Hews & Rebeccah Anger Sp^r. Married July ye 5th 1756

William Fanen & Elizabeth Obryan Married July 17th 1756

David Conoley & Sarah Mortimore Married March ye 23^d 1757

Jehu Elliott & Mary West Sp^r Married May ye 3^d 1757

Thomas Smith & Elizabeth Holmes widow Married May 8th 1757

William Finley & Hester Taylor Sp^r Married June ye 18th 1757

Thomas Ferguson & Kathrine Elliott widow Married Octob^r ye 30th 1757

Richard-Park Stobo & Mary Harvey Sp^r Married Novb^r 24th : 1757

Jonathan Rivers & Frances Stone Sp^r Married Decb^r ye 6th 1757.

John Cattell (Son Benj^m.) and Mary Levingston Sp^r Married Jan^{ry} ye 19th 1758

Coll^o Robert Rivers & Elizabeth Ston [sic] widow Married Sep^t 14 1758

William Chapman Sn^r [?] & Elenor Harris widow Married Octo^{br}. 19th 1758

John Croskeys & Jemima Manning Sp^r Married Octr 19th 1758

BURIALS P^r Y^e REV^d M^r. MARTYN

Mrs Mary Sereau Buried Octr. ye 9th 1755

William Carr Buried Octob^r 12th 1755

———— ye wife of Cornelus Vangelder Bur^d Interr^d without a Minister Octr. 13th 1755

Anne Simms a poor woman died at William Johnson free negro Buried Nov^{br}. 2^d 1755

Isabelah Daughter of Benjamin Elliott Buried Nov^{br} ye 4th 1755

Francis Son of ffrancis Rose Buried Nov^{br} ye 5th 1755

Peter ———— a Dutch servant man of Thos Draytons Esq 1755

Thomas Son of Benjamin Parrott Buried Nov^{br} 2^d 1755 Interr^d without a Minister.

William Holman Buried Nov^br. ye 29th 1755 of St Barthol^m^e Parish Int^rd without Minister

William Reed Buried Jan^ry 7th 1756

Mary Anne ye wife of ffrancis Rose Buried March ye 4th 1756

William Son of Dr James Reed & Martha his wife buried March 5th 1756

Mr Joseph Fuller Buried April ye 27th 1756

Thomas Rivers Buried May ye 20th 1756

Jacob Grapue [?] Buried July 21st 1756

Adam Beher ye Orginist Buried August 4th 1756 inter^d. without a Minister.

Stephen Rusel Sn^r Buried Augs^t 27th 1756

Elizabeth the wife of ffrances Ladson Buried Augus^t 27th 1756 inter^d without a minister

William Son of Thomas Melachamp & Eliza^bth his wife Buried Sep^tr 15th 1756.

Richard Reverstock Buried Septr. ye 30th 1756 Died at M^r. Thos Draytons.

James Shaw Buried a poor man. Died at Mr Linthwites Burd Oct ——[Missing]

BIRTHS

Thomas Son of Thomas Hayward & Anne his wife Born August ye 18th 1755.

Elizabeth Daughter of Thomas Fuller & Lydia his wife Born Feb^ry 24th, 1755

Francis Son of Francis Rose & Maryann his wife born —— 1755

Charles the Son of Henry Wood & Mary his wife born April ye 3^d 1756

Daniel Son of Daniel Pepper & Mary his wife Born May ye 24th 1755

John Son of Josiah Claypool & Sarah his wife Born [no date given.]

John Son of Archibald Scot & Agnes his wife Born Dec^hr. ye 4th 1756

Anthony Son of William Boneau [sic] & Mary his wife born Dec^br 23^d 1756.

Jean Daught^r of William Chapman & Mary his wife born
    June ye 5th 1755
Sarah Daught^r of John Taylor & Barbrey his wife born
    August ye 26th 1756.
Sarah Daught^r of Thomas Fuller and Lyda his wife Born
    Octob^r 3^d 1758 [sic]
Elizabeth Daught^r of John Johnson & Nancy his wife born
    May the 30th 1755.
William Son of William Mell & Elizabeth his wife Born
    ye 17th Febry· 1757
John Son of Michal Hatts & Catherine his wife Born ——
    1756.
Anne Daught^r of Thomas Godfrey (alis Grenier) & Eliza-
    beth his wife Born March ye 20th 1757
Mary Daught^r of Philip Culp & Christian his wife born
    Jan^{ry} 27th 1757
Betsy the Daught^r of Jacob Hinckle & Hannah his wife
    born Sep^{tr} ye 1756
James Son of Henry Wood jun^r & —— his wife Born
    May 12th 1756

CHRISTININGS P^r Y^e REV^d Mr MARTYN

Charles the Son of Henry Wood & Mary his wife Baptrd
    May ye 9th 1756
Daniel Son of Daniel Pepper & Mary his wife Bapt^{zd} June
    ye 27th 1756
George Yeomans Son of Mary Yeomans wid^o Recev^d in
    the Congregation (Privatly Bap^{tzd} p^r ye Rev^d M^r M^c-
    Gilkrist in Charles Town Before) Rec^d July ye 4th 1756
John son of Joshua Claypool and Sarah his wife Bap^d Sept^r
    15th 1756
Sarah Daught^r of John Taylor & Barbrey his wife Bapt^d
    Septr 12, 1756 Jam^s Island.
John Anger An Adult Baptrd Septr ye 30th 1756
Anthony Son of William Boneau & Mary his wife Baptrd.
    Sep^{tr} 30th 1756
Elizabeth Daught^r of John Johnson & Nancy his wife
    Baptrd Deb^r 1756
John son of Archibald Scot and Agnes his wife. Baptrd
    Dec^{br} ye 19th· 1756

Elizabeth the Daught^r of Thomas Fuller & Lyda his wife Bapt^{zd} Dec^{br} 17th 1756

Sarah Daught^r of Ibid Dec^{br}. 1756

Herculus-Peter-Clark an Adult negro Man belonging to Mr William Greenland in Cha Town Bapt^{zd} Feb^{ry} ye 27th 1757

William Son of William Mell & Elizabeth his wife Bapt^{zd} Feb^{ry}. ye 27 1757

John Son of Michal Hatts & Catherine his wife Bapt^{zd} March 20th 1757

Anne Daught^r of Thomas Godfrey (alis Granier) & Elizabeth his wife Bapt^{zd} March 28 1757

Mary Daught^r of Philip Culp & Christian his wife Bapt^{zd} April 3^d 1757

Betsey Daughter of Jacob Hinckle & Hanah his wife Bapt^{zd} April ye 3^d 1757.

James Son of Henry Wood jun^r & —— his wife Bapt^{zd} May ye 1st. 1757

John Son of Doct^r. Thomas Honour & Rebecca his wife Bapt^{zd} May · 15th 1757

BURIALS P^r THE REV^d Mr MARTYN

Stephen Russel Buried Octo^{br} 14th 1756 at James Island

John Anger Buried Octob^r. ye 14th 1756

John Son of Josiah Claypool & Sarah his wife Buried Oct^r: ye 16th 1756

Benjaman Son of Capt Frances Ladson Buried p^r ye Revd Mr Cope Octo^{br} 22^d 1756

Capt Thomas L Elliott of St Pauls Parish Buried Dec^{br} ye 10th 1756 p^r Rev^d M^r. Alex Baron

Martha the wife of Doct^r James Reed Buried Octr 24th 1756

Jane-Baynes the wife David Taylor Buried Nov^{br}. ye 9th 1756

James Lowry Buried Dece^{mbr} 6th 1756.

Mark Cremer Buried June 25th 1757

Sarah the Daught^r of Thomas Fuller & Lyda his wife Buried August ye 5th 1757

Jane a Free Musto woman Buried at Mrs Yonges July 1757

John Garrott Buried Inter^d. without a Minister August ye 30th 1757

Benjamin Son of Benjamin Elliott & Mary his wife Buried August 31 — 1757

Elizabeth the wife of William Chapman Buried Octo^{br}. ye 24th 1757

Thomas Son of Josiah Claypool Decs^d. & Sarah his wife Buried Octr 23^d 1757 Inter^d without a minister

Benja^a Stone Buried Jam^s Island Intr^d without a Minister Septr 1757

Francis Ladson Buried Nov^{br} ye 11th 1757 inter^d without a Minister

Mary the wife of Thomas Scott Buried Nov^{br}. ye 16th 1757 James Island

Elizabeth juks widow a poor wooman Buried Octob^r y^e — 1757

Edward Mathews Buried at Mrs Yonges 1757

John Harriss Buried Nov^{br} ye 20th 1757.

Hesther Hayward widow at James Island Buried Novr ye 25 1757. Interd without minister

Archibald Scott Buried Decb^r ye 19th 1757 inter^d. without a Minister

Elizabeth Fuller widow Buried January ye 1st 1757.

Benjamin Parrott Buried Jan^{ry} ye 9th 1757

John Son of Doct^r Thomas Honour & Rebecca his wife Buried Jan^{ry}: ye 27th: 1758

Cheseman Son of Richd Lake & Mary his wife Buried Feb ye 23^d 1758

Anne the Daught^r of John Harriss Dec^d. and Elenor his wife Buried March ye 8th 1758

Anne the wife of Col^o Robert Rivers Buried March ye 19th 1758

BIRTHS

John Son of Doct^r. Thomas Honour & Rebecca his wife Born   1757

Parke the Son of Daniel Pepper & Mary his wife Born March ye 24th 1757

Edward Son of John Miles & Anne his wife Born April —— 1757

William Son of William Royal & Mary his Wife born April y* 6. 1757

James Son of Benjamin Stone & Elizabeth his Wife born May y* 19th 1757

Benjamin Son of Benjamin Elliott & Mary his Wife Born July 28 1757

Thomas-Odingsell Son of Benjamin Elliott & Mary his Wife Born March y* 16th 1757

Thomas Son of Thomas Scott & Mary his wife Born August the 1st 1757

Cheseman Son of Richard Lake & Mary his Wife Born August y* 1st 1756

Martha Daught^r of Isaac Ladson and Rachel his Wife born Octo^{br}. y* 2. 1757

Anne the Daught^r of John Harriss & Elenor his wife born Nov^{br} y* 16th 1757

Elizabeth Rebekah Daught^r of Edward Legge & Elizabeth his wife born Octo^{br} y* 6 1757

George the Son of Landgrave Edmund Bellinger & Mary-Lucia his wife born March y* 16th 1754

{ Burnaby Bull Son of Ibid born August y* 19th 1756
{ Mary Daught^r of Ibid Born Octo^{br} y* 4th 1757

Anne Daught^r of Thomas Hayward and Anne his wife born July y* 8th 1757

Mary the Daught^r of John Baxter & Anne his wife Born Septr y* 24th 1757

Martha Daughter of James Smith & Sarah his wife Born January y* 23^d 1758

Thomas Son of Thomas Godfrey & Elizabeth his wife Born April y* 5th 1758.

Thomas Son of John Drayton Esq & Margaret his wife Born Octo^{br} y* 5 1758

(*To be continued*)

ORDER BOOK

of

John Faucheraud Grimké.

August 1778 to May 1780.

(Continued from the April Number)

February 1779.   Head-Quarters, Purysburg.

1 :   G : O.   Parole, Countersigns {

The Brigade now Brig.: Gen: Moultrie is to be Commanded by Col°: Huger as Col°: Com¹: & the detachment of N°: Carolina Troops & Levies now under Col°. Sumner & Col¹: Armstrong are to be in one Brigade, under the Command of Col°: Sumner as Col°: Com¹:; The Two Brigades to compose a Division under the Command of Brigadier General Moultrie.

The North Carolina Militia who arrived with Gen¹: Rutherford are to be in one Brigade & commanded by him & those with Gen¹: Ash in one Brigade & to be commanded by Gen¹: Bryant. The two Brigades to form a Division under the Command of Major Gen: Ash.

R : O: by Col¹. Roberts

A gill of Rum to be delivered by the Quarter Master to each Man, Waggoner & Driver of the Regiment & Train of Artillery.

Officer of the Day tomorrow Captⁿ Davis

---

2 :   G : O.   Parole,   Countersigns
R. O. by Col°: Roberts.

The Corps of Artillery in Camp having no Drum of their own, are to be Governed in the Ordinary part of Duty, by the Drums of the line such as Roll-calling, Guard Mounting, issuing of orders &c.

Officer of the Day tomorrow, Cap¹. L¹: Elliott.

---

3 :   R : O. by Col°: Roberts.
Officer of the Day tomorrow Cap¹. Mitchell.

The Quartermaster will take particular care that all the

Waggoners & Drivers of the Artillery have all their Geers
& Harnesses in proper order for immediate use; Should
anything be wanting, He is to apply for it directly to the
Quarter Master Gen: whose business it is to furnish him
with such Articles.

 G: O

 Parole, Countersigns

Capt. Robt: Rayford of the 6th N^o: Car Battalion is
appointed Brig · Maj to Col^o Sumner & is to be respected
& obeyed accordingly

The Inspector of this Department is immediately to introduce into this army the same Exercises, Maneuvers &
Discipline which are at present practised in the Main Army,
conformable to the regulations approved of by the General
for that Purpose. Accordingly the Majors of Regiments
& Brigade Majors will meet tomorrow Morning at 10
ô Clock at the Inspectors Quarters in order to take Copies
of the Regulations & receive such other Instructions and
orders relative to the Exercise of the Troops as may be
necessary.

Copies of the Regulations are to be delivered to the
Brigadiers by the Brigade Majors & to the Com^{ts}: of Reg^{ts}:
by the Majors or adjutants

The Cap^s. & Sub^s. will meet at the Majors Tent to re-
ceive the regulations & other orders relative to the Exercise;
They will take Copies of them & read & explain to the
Soldiers such parts as they think necessary

The Troops will in future exercise every mor^g. from
½ past 6 to ½ past 8 ô Clock & every evening from 4 to
6 ô Clock, agreable to the Directions of the Inspector all
officers in Camp without Distinction are to give Regular
& punctual attendance at the time of Exercise—

As we do not know how soon we may be called into
Action the General Hopes that the Gentlemen of the Army
will be sensible of the necessity of having the same Maneuvers performed by the whole army & will Chearfully
exert themselves upon the occasion

The Inspector will take care by frequent visits, to the
Guards, Posts Tents &c · that the regulations are strictly

adhered to & that no innovation or modification of them whatever take place.

An orderly Serg'. is to attend at the Inspectors Quarters & to be relieved daily.

The Inspector when visiting Posts, Piquets, Guards, Tents, or attending the Grand Parade, is to be considered & treated as an officer of the Day.

The Brigadier General or Officer Com': Brigades will Report to Head Quarters a Major to act as Brigade Inspector.

4:   R: O. Officer of the day tomorrow Cap: Davis

G: O: Parole. Countersigns {

5:   R: O: by Col'. Roberts

The Mor⁶: Reports of the Artillery are to be made to the Com⁶: officer at 10 ôClock until further Orders.

Officer of the Day Cap': L': Elliott

G: O: Parole   Countersigns {

The Gen: Court Martial (whereof Col': Pinckney is President) now sitting for the Tryal of all Prisoners that may be brought before them, report, L'. Charles Alexander charged with leaving his post & being absent from his Guard when a flag from the Enemy arrived & with not reporting agreable to his Duty one of his Guard deserted to the Enemy, found guilty of a breach of the 4ᵗʰ. Act. of the 13 Sect: of the articles of war, by leaving his Guard & Sentence him to be repremanded in the Presence of the Nᵒ. Car: Brig: The General approves the Sentence & directs the Field officer of the Day to reprimand L': Alexander agreable to the Sentence of the Court tomorrow Morᵉ: at 12 ôClock.

Cap': Macjah Williams charged with beating a Waggoner, acquitted by the Court.

L': James M'Kenna Ass'. Dep: Quarter Master charged with taking fifteen Dollars each from Patterson & Fisher Waggoners in the Public Service to pay their Accounts; with confining John Graham Waggoner without appoint-

ing somebody to take Charge of his team & with offering
to discharge the said said Grahams Waggon for a sum of
money, Found Guilty on the first Charge of behaving in a
scandalous Manner, unbecoming the Character of a Gentleman & Sentenced in pursuance of the 21" & 22ᵈ Articles
of the 14 Section of the Articles of War, to be discharged
the Public Service & his Crime, name, place of Abode &
Punishment to be published in the Gazettes of this State,
in & about Camp & to pay the Money He Recᵈ of Patterson & Fisher into the Hands of Gen Rutherford who is
requested to remit it to them.   The General approves the
Sentence & directs the Publication to be immediately made

Major Henry Dixon is appointed Brigade Inspector to
Colᵒ Sumners Brigade & to be respected & Obeyed as
such

    After G . O
The Gen   Court Martial of which Colᵒ: Pinckney is
President is dissolved.

    A Gen: Court Martial is to sit to morrow Morning for
the Tryal of all Prisoners that may be brought before
them.   President, Colᵒ. Armstrong, Members 3 Capˢ &
3 Subˢ from Colⁿ· Hugers & 3 Capˢ. & 3 Subˢ. from Colᵒ
Sumners Brigade · All Witnesses to attend

    The Light Troops on the left of Colⁿ Sumners brigade
are to join Colᵒ: Kershaws Corps immediately & to be
encamped under his Direction

6.   R: O Officer of the day tomorrow Capˢ. Mitchell
        G: O: Parole,   Countersigns

    The Gen: Court Martial of which Colᵒ. Pinckney was
Presᵗ have further reported Benj Webster of the 2ᵈ Sⁿ
Car: regᵗ: charged with Desertion, found guilty & Sentenced to receive 100 lashes, but on Consideration of the
Prisoners having been constantly employed in the Service
of the United States, during his absence from his regiment
& also of his general good Character recommend him as an
Object of Mercy   The General approves the Sentence &
remits the Punishment agreable to the recommendation of
the Court

    John Bailey of the 6ᵗʰ Sᵒ: Car: regᵗ· charged with neglect of Duty found guilty & sentenced to be reprimanded. The General approves the Sentence & directs the Brigade Major to reprimand him in presence of the Brigade this Afternoon at Retreat Beating.

Major Gresham private in the 6th. S[o]: Car: reg[t]: charged with Desertion. found guilty of deserting from the N[o]: Car: New Levies & sentenced to Serve in one of the N[o]: Carolina Batt: during the War, agreable to a Stipulation made by an Act of Assembly of that State with the New Levies at the Time of their Enlistment & that 30 Dollars be deducted out of the remainder of his Bounty or pay due him by the State of S[o]: Car: and the Court recommend it to the Com[g]: Officer of the reg[t]: to which He shall be turned over to endeavours to procure a compensation from the State of N[o]: Carolina for the Clothing advanced him by the State of S[o]: Car: & pay it & the bounty into the Hands of the Com[g]: off: of the 6th S[o]: Car: Reg[t]: The Gen: approves the Sentence.

7:   G: O.   Parole   Countersigns {

R: O: by Col: Roberts

Officer of the Day tomorrow Cap[t]: Davis.

The Quartermaster will immediately have 150 flannel Cartridges for Field-Pieces charged with Powder; 22 O[z]. in each.   Two men & an officer from each Company are to attend this Business at the Magazine & See that it be properly done.

8:   R: O: Officer of the Day tomorrow, Capt: L[t]. Elliott
     G: O: Parole, Countersigns

Lt. George Petrie is appointed a Sec[d]. Lieutenant in the first S[o]: Car: Reg[t]: & is to be obeyed & respected accordingly.

9:   R: O.   Officer of the Day tomorrow Cap: Mitchell
The Quarter Master will immediately deliver Rum as Usual to the men of the Artillery & Train.

The fixt Ammunition now in the Lockers both round & Case Shot must be well aired & put in their proper chests instead of which the Quarter Master will deliver 15 flannel Cartridges charged to be placed in the Lockers of each Gun.

G: O.

Parole. Countersigns {

10: R: O. Officer of the Day tomorrow
Parole, Rutledge. Countersign, Augusta

11: Camp 5 miles to the westward of Purisburg. 11ᵗʰ Febᵞ: 1779
G: O.

Parole, Ninety Six, Countersign, Brave.

Untill an increase of Officers & Men render it necessary to make a new Disposition, the following one is to take place, & be observed until further orders.

Twenty eight Files are to be draughted out of the Sᵗ. Carolina Brigade to act as Light Infantry with that of the Nᵗ. Carolina Brigade under the Command of one of the Field-Officers of the former: they are to be formed & Officered agreeable to the Rules given for the formation of Troops. the remainder of the Brigade is to be told off & formed into three equal Battalions of eight Platoons each, Organized & officered as directed in the formation of Troops. the Command to be rotted [sic] by the Brigadier according to Sinrority & reported at H. Q.

The North Carolina Brigade is to be told off & formed into two Battalions of 16 Platoons each the officers & Non-Commissioned officers are to be equally divided & placed into two Battalions according to former Instructions.

The Corps of Pioneers belonging to that Brigade are to be included in the Line of it & told off with the rest.

The first Battalion is to be on the Left of the Brigade [and] is to be commanded by Colᵗ. Armstrong & a Major & the 2ᵈ. Batl. by Lᵗ. Colᵗ. Thackson & a Major.

The Light Infantry of both Brigades are to encamp, & draw up on the Right & Left of the Division so as to cover most effectually the flanks of the order of Battle &

Encampment in the position that Gen'. Moultrie will think best from the Nature of the ground

The Army will March every Morning by the Right untill further Orders, the Troops will Wheel by Platoons or Sections of 4 files according to the Difficulties of the Road, & when those Difficulties are of such a Nature as to render their last march impracticable, the sections will open from the Center branching out to the Right & Left & March on both sides of the Road untill they can form again into Platoons, which must be done as often as possible in order to Guard beforehand against the Dangers of a loose march in presence of an Enemy

The Officers are to take a particular Care to keep their men in their respective Platoons & to preserve as much as possible to necessary Distance for forming

The New Guard will parade every Morning the Wing of the Army to March by & make the Advanced-Guard They are to be told off and formed into 2 or 4 Platoons according to the Gen' formation of Troops & to march in Front of the Army at such a Distance as to corrispond with the Troops next them, The officer of the Day will order a Section of 5 or 6 files with a Serj' & Corp' to March at the distance of 100 paces in front of the advanced Guard & 3 flankers to advance by files on the same line with that Section at 100 Paces from both Flanks

The Advanced Guards are to be immediately followed by a Field-Piece Men & Ammunition belonging to it— The light-Infantry of the S° Carolina Brigade is to March after this Artillery & cover it in case of necessity

The S° Carolina-Brigade comes next, & at the center of the Division the Park with the Troops & Ammunition belonging to it & the Ammunition of both Brigades

The N° Carolina Brigade follows immediately with a Field Piece in their rear supported by the light Infantry of that Brigade which comes next   The commanding Officer of that Brigade will bring up the whole Line   The Hospital, Baggage, & Provision Waggons, are to march immediately under the direction of the Waggon-Master & the Line not to be altered on any pretence whatever with-
... ... they will be fol-

lowed by the Old Guards, who will form the rear Guard
of the Army & have the particular charge of that chain
of Waggons. They are to be formed & marched regularly
as the Troops of the Line with a Section of five or six
Files at a 100 Paces in their Rear & flankers on both sides
of that Section, as directed for the advanced Guard

Both Brigades will furnish flankers in the proportion of
1 file p 100 Men, to march at the Distance mentioned before from the flanks opposite to the Interval of the 2ª.
Brigade.

The flankers are to be very attentive particularly on the
Left & to receive proper instructions from the Brigadier.

They are to be relieved every Hour or ½ hour according to the Difficulties of the March

The officer of the Day will head the Line of March,
direct the Pioneers ahead, examine & report the considerable Defiles & narrow Passes he meets with, to the Commanding officer of the Division & take instructions accordingly   He is likewise to preserve order and regularity
throughout the Line from the advanced Guard to the
Chain of Waggons   When a Carrage [sic] breaks in the
Line it is to be taken aside & mended as soon as possible
without interrupting the march

The officer of the Day before, will bring up the whole
Army, collect all Stragglers, keep the police & preserve
order & regularity throughout the Line of Waggons, taking a particular care that the Waggons are not unneces-
sarily halted & that the soldiers do not Ride or put their
Packs therein Without his permission

The Artificers with their Tools will march at the Head
of the line of Waggons & be alert in doing what they are
ordered

The Drums & Fifes of a Brigade are to be divided
into two equal parts to march in front & rear of the Brigade & encamp in that manner without beating or playing
at any time of the Day or Night without Orders from the
officer of the Day or Brigadier

As the Troops in the rear of the line of March are very
often distressed by the Head of the Column moving too
slow or

will be the signal to be given by the rear & to be answered along the Line for the Head of the Column to move slower, & two ruffles without flams to move quicker.

The Artillery will encamp in the following manner, One Field Piece &c: on the right of the S^o: Ca: Brig: between that Brig: & the Light Infantry belonging to it: Another Field-Piece on the Left of the N^o: Car: Brig: between that Brigade & their Light Infantry & the Park at the Center of the Division not above 12 paces in front of the Line. The proper interval will be left between the two Brigades for the artillery.

The Gen: Court Martial of which Col^o: Armstrong was President, have reported W^m. Whitehead of the 3^d: Georgia Battalion charged with Desertion found guilty & Sentenced to receive 100 lashes on his bare back, but reflecting on his good Character do recommend him as an Object of Mercy: The General approves the Sentence & remits the Punishment Agreable to the recommendation of the Court.

W^m. Ginine [?] of the 5th S^o Car: Batl: Charged with Desertion, found Guilty & Sentenced to receive 100 lashes with switches on his bare back: The General approves the Sentence & directs it to be put in Execution tomorrow Morning at Guard Mounting

Truman Magalan of the 6th: N^o: Car: Battalion charged with Desertion, found Guilty & Sentenced to receive 100 lashes on the bare back, but some circumstances appearing on the Tryal they recommend him as an object of Mercy. The General approve the Sentence, but for the reasons assigned by the Court remits the Punishment.

12: Camp 5 Miles from Purisburgh.
February 12, 1779.
R: O. Officer of the Day tomorrow Capt. L^t: Elliott
G: O. Parole Philadelphia Countersign, forty five

13: R: O. Officer of the Day tomorrow Capt: Mitchell
G: O. Parole, Washington; Countersign, Two.

The Court Martial whereof Col^o: Armstrong was President have reported Rowland William of the first S^o: Car: Reg^t: charged with Desertion, found Guilty, & Sentenced to Receive 100 lashes on the bare back with Switches. The General approves the Sentence & directs it to be put in Execution to morrow morning at Guard Mounting.

  After Orders

The Troops are to hold themselves in readiness to march tomorrow Morning at 8 ô Clock.

14: R: O.   Officer of the Day tomorrow Capt. Davis
  G: O.   Camp at Purisburgh.

  Parole, Princestown: Countersigns Purisburgh, Philadelphia.

15: R: O. Officer of the Day tomorrow Cap: L: Elliott
  The Quarter Master will have a Soap ration return made out tomorrow morning for the Artillery Corps for the Time They have been doing Duty at this Post.

  G: O: Parole Rochester. Countersigns Ross Rye.

---

16.   Head Quarters Purisburgh.
  R. O. Officer of the Day tomorrow, Capt. Mitchell.

  G: O. Parole. Superior. Countersigns Swift Sure

A Gen: Court Martial is to sit immediately for the tryal of all Prisoners that shall be brought before them: Pres: L: Col: M'Intosh; Members 4 Cap. & 3 Sub from Col: Hugers Brigade; 2 Cap: & 3 Sub: from Col: Sumners Brigade. All witnesses to attend.

17: R: O. Officer of the Day tomorrow Cap. Davis

  G: O. Parole Temperance. Countersigns Times Truth

Capt Oliphant is appointed one of the Generals Aids de Camp, & is to be obeyed & respected accordingly.

A: O. The Light Infantry of Col. Sumners Brigade are to encamp this Evening on the bank of the River to the northward of Purisburgh.

18: R. O.   Officer of the Day tomorrow Capt. Wm. Mitchell

The Quarter Guard of the Artillery is to consist of One Serjeant, One Corporal & twelve Men.

All Artillery Men off Duty are to hold themselves in readiness for Fatigue under the Serj'. Major. He is to receive his Orders from the Commanding Officer   The Quarter Master is to have the Stores brought with Cap'. De Treville's Party put to Rights immediately allowing to the Small Gun as many Rounds in its Lockers as the Rest. The Case Shot to be returned into the proper Chest   What loose Powder there may be in the Waggon, must be sent to the Magazine.   The Quarter Master will have a Sponge & Rammer made for a twelve Pounder, and a traversing Hands pipe for the two Pounder Field-Piece

G   O   Parole, Vigilance

Countersigns $\begin{cases} \text{Vigour} \\ \text{Victory} \end{cases}$

All Carcasses & Filth in & about Camp are to be thrown in to the River below the Encampment or buried: the Dep: Quarter Master Gen: will be Careful that the Regimental Quarter Masters & others in his Department carry this order punctually into Execution

Af   Or   A Return of the Names & Dates of the Commissions of all officers present of the Two Brigades is to be made to the Adjutant General tomorrow Morning at Orderly Time

---

(To be continued)

HISTORICAL NOTES

A PLAY-BILL IN 1764 —Seilhamer, in his *History of the American Theatre*, vol. 1. page 161, states that the *Orphan of China*, by Arthur Murphy, was produced for the first time in America by the American Company of Comedians, at the Southwark Theatre in Philadelphia in 1766; he also states that the name "American Company" was first used at the opening of this theatre 21st November, 1766. He was evidently unaware of a notice in the *S. C. Gazette*, Nov 5, 1763, stating that a "Company of Comedians arrived here last Monday from Virginia called the American Company "* It is unfortunate that Mr. Seilhamer's useful work should be so absolutely at fault in regard to the history of the theatre in South Carolina. He gives the date of the opening of the first theatre in Charleston as 22 Dec, 1773 As a matter of fact, Charleston apparently had the first theatre in America; at any rate one was built here in 1735. (McCrady, vol. 2, page 256)

The following advertisement shows that the American Company of Comedians gave the *Orphan of China* as a benefit performance in Charleston in 1764, two years earlier than the claimed date for its first appearance in America The cast of the play as given here in 1764, is very different from the cast that gave the play at the *Southwark* in 1766, only Mr Allyn, Mr. Douglass, Mr. Morris and Mrs Douglass appearing on both lists

The *Orphan of China* was written in 1755, and first acted in 1759 The farce, *The Anatomist or the Sham Doctor*, was written by Edward Ravenscroft, and first printed and played about 1697; it was reprinted in 1722, then revised and compressed into two acts about 1743; in this shape it was repeatedly reproduced down to as late as 1801 (*Dic of Nat. Biog.*)—Editor

*See Article in the Nation, Vol XCVI, No 2487 (Feb 27, 1913) page 201, by Robert Adger Law

'By Permission of His Excellency For the Benefit of Mr Morris, On Monday the 26th of March, will be performed At the New Theatre in Queen Street, By the American Company of Comedians, A Tragedy Called the

Orphan of China

Timurkan			Mr Allyn
Octar			Mr Emmet
Zamti			Mr Douglass
Etan			Mr Hallam
Hamit	By		Mr A Hallam
Morat			Mr Morris
Orasming			Mr Furell
Zimventi			Mr Barry
Nirvan			Mr Morris

Mandure by Mrs Douglas

The Prologue to be spoken by Mr Hallam, and the Epilogue by Mrs Douglass

After the Play. *The White Cliffs of Albion,* sung by Mr Furell. To which will be added, a Farce called

The Anatomist, or the Sham Doctor

Old Gerrald			Mr Morris
Young Gerrald			Mr Douglass
Mons Le Med'cine	By		Mr Allyn
Martin			Mr A Hallam
Crispin			Mr Hallam
Simon			Mr Furell
Doctors Wife			Mrs Crane
Angelica	By		Mrs Morris
Beatrice			Mrs Douglas
Waiting Woman			Mrs Allyn

After the Farce, *The Padlock of the Mind* sung by Mr Barry, and a song called *The Broom.* by Mrs Morris

To begin exactly at Half past six o'Clock

Tickets, without which no Persons can be admitted to be had of Mr Cannon. of whom Places for the Boxes may be taken

Boxes, 40s Pit. 30s Gallery, 20s "

(*South Carolina Gazette,* March 17. 1764)

TOMBSTONE INSCRIPTIONS FROM "RICHMOND" AND "HYDE PARK" PLANTATIONS —Richmond plantation, on the Eastern bank of the Cooper River, according to Dr Irving (*Day on Cooper River*) was for a long time the seat of Col John Harleston

Mr Harleston purchased a large tract of land from Dr Martine, which comprised the two plantations of "Richmond" and "Farmfield " In the subsequent division of the property "Richmond" fell to Col Harleston's daughter, Jane, who married Mr Edward Rutledge, and "Farmfield" to his daughter, Eliza, who married Thomas Corbett

"Hyde Park," also on the Eastern Branch of the Cooper

River, was part of the estate of Isaac Ball The inscriptions were copied recently by Mr Joseph Ioor Waring

"RICHMOND" PLANTATION

Beneath this Marble | are deposited the Remains of | Col John Harleston | and | Elizabeth Harleston | his Wife | Who departed this Life | He on the 14th September 1793 | Aet, 54 years | She the 4th January 1805 | Aet, 55 years |

Sacred to the Memory of | Thomas Corbett | Who died 28th July 1800 | Aged 5 years and 19 Days

Sacred to the Memory of | Elizabeth Harleston Corbett | Died 22nd January 1804 | Aged 11 months |

Beneath this Tablet | are deposited the Remains of | Mrs Mary W Read | Wife of John Harleston Read | Who departed this Life | 9th day of May 1817 | At "Rice Hope" Plantation | Aet 27 | Here lieth also the Body of | Sarah Annabell Withers | Their daughter who | died on 13th September 1817 | in Charleston | A tender victim to the | then prevailing fever | Age 5 years 4 months and 9 days |

Sacred to the Memory of | J Withers Read | Late a Lieutenant of the | U S N | Born 18th March 1817 | Died 28th June 1851 |

James Corbett | Obit 24th September 1817 | Aet 1 year and 7 months |

In Memory of | Mrs Jane Rutledge who departed this Life | 11th November 1835 | Aet 62 years |
[Long inscription]

Here lie the Remains of | Rev Edward Rutledge | Who died on the | 15th of March 1832 | Aged 33 years and 4 months |

Sacred to the Memory of | Nichalas Harleston Rutledge | Who died November 7th A D 1835 | Aged 26 years and 23 days | In testimony of her affection | this Tablet is erected by his afflicted Widow |

INSCRIPTIONS AT "HYDE PARK" PLANTATION.

Sacred | To the Memory of | John Wilson | Who departed this Life | August 13th 1790. | Aged 40 years | This Memorial of her affection | was caused to be erected by | his Widow |

Sacred to the Memory of | John Coming Ball | who died at Hyde Park | 20th October 1764 | Aged 50 years and 2 months | And of his two Wives | Catharine Ball | who died at H Park | the 25th of September 17— | Aged 32 years | and | Judith Ball | who died at H Park | the 2nd August 1772. | Aged 47 years. | As also of several of their children | and grandchildren | This tribute of respect to their | memory is erected in 1821 by | Isaac Ball | Grandson of John Coming | and Judith Ball |

To the Memory of | David Franklin | who died on this Plantation | the 19th December 1797 | Having resided thereon 11 years and | 3 months as Overseer for | John Ball who caused this stone | to be put up in testimony of | his regard for Honest Franklin | "A Wits a feather, a Chiefs a rod | An Honest man, the noblest work of God " | His Wife and two of their | children are interred South of him |

LIST OF PUBLICATIONS

OF THE

SOUTH CAROLINA HISTORICAL SOCIETY.

COLLECTIONS.

Vol. I., 1857, $3.00; Vol. II., 1858, $3.00; Vol. III. 1859, out of print. Vol IV., 1887, unbound, $3.00, bound $4.00; Vol. V., 1897, paper, $3.00.

PAMPHLETS.

Journal of a Voyage to Charlestown in So. Carolina by Pelatiah Webster in 1765. Edited by Prof. T. P. Harrison, 1898. 75c.

The History of the Santee Canal. By Prof. F. A. Porcher. With an Appendix by A. S. Salley, Jr., 1903. 75c.

THE SOUTH CAROLINA HISTORICAL AND GENEALOGICAL MAGAZINE.

Volume I, 1900, Edited by A. S. Salley, Jr. Complete Volume. $10.00

Single copies of Nos. 2-4, $1.25 each.

Volume II to IX, 1901-1908, Edited by A. S. Salley, Jr. Unbound $5.00 each.

Volume X to XIII, 1909-1912, Edited by Mabel L. Webber. Unbound $5.00 each.

Members get a discount of 25 per cent. on the above prices.

Address: South Carolina Historical Society, Charleston, S. C.

THE

SOUTH CAROLINA

HISTORICAL AND GENEALOGICAL

MAGAZINE

PUBLISHED QUARTERLY. BY THE

SOUTH CAROLINA HISTORICAL SOCIETY

CHARLESTON, S. C.

VOLUME XIV., NO. 4,   OCTOBER 1913.

PRINTED FOR THE SOCIETY BY
WALKER, EVANS & COGSWELL CO
CHARLESTON, S. C.
1913

PUBLICATION COMMITTEE.

Joseph W. Barnwell,   Henry A. M. Smith,
                    A. S. Salley, Jr.

EDITOR OF THE MAGAZINE.
Mabel L. Webber.

CONTENTS.

N. B.—These Magazines, with the exception of No. 1 of Vol. I, are $1.25 to any one other than a member of the South Carolina Historical Society. Members of the Society receive them free. The Membership fee is $4.00 per annum (the fiscal year being from January to January), and members can buy back numbers or duplicates at $1.00 each. In addition to receiving the Magazines, members are allowed a discount of 25 per cent. on all other publications of the Society, and have the free use of the Society's library.

Any member who has not received the last number will please notify the Secretary and Treasurer,

Miss Mabel L. Webber,
South Carolina Historical Society,
Charleston, S. C.

The South Carolina Historical and Genealogical Magazine.

VOL XIV   OCTOBER, 1913   No 4

THE BRISBANES

Compiled by E Haviland Hillman, F. S G

(Continued from the July Number)

John Stanyarne (3) Brisbane, [James (2), William (1)] b ...., 1773; when his father, James Brisbane, was banished from Charleston in 1782, he intended taking John with him, but at the last moment, as the vessel was about to sail, he got into one of the small boats on which passengers had come on board, hid under a seat and returned on shore, where he remained with an old aunt, probably Susannah Stanyarne

He married 19th March, 1795.[59] Maria Hall, b ..... , d. 8th April 1831, the daughter of the Hon George Abbott Hall and Lois Mathews[60] From 1801 to 1804 he owned the plantation on Goose Creek called Otranto where the Otranto Hunting Club now is, and later had his country seat at Malona, Ashley River   He died about 1850

Children   6 (Brisbane) 3 sons and 3 daughters

---

[59]"Married   On Thursday evening last William [an error, should be John] S Brisbane Esq of John's Island, to Miss Maria Hall, daughter of the late George Abbott Hall, Esq" (Monday, March 23, 1795) From "Marriage Notices" etc, by A S Salley, Jr

[60]Through this alliance the descendants of this marriage can claim as ancestors, Gov Robert Gibbes of S C, Dr Henry Woodward, and Hon the Col John Godfrey, Lois Mathews being the daughter of John Mathews and Sarah Gibbes   See this Magazine, Vol XII, p   .

(6) i. Sarah Harriet (4), b   ..., 1797
(7) ii. John Wilson (4), b   ..., 1801.
      iii Maria (4), b. about 1802; d unm 1864
(8) iv Abbott Hall (4), b 4th Dec. 1804
      v. Elizabeth (4), b ... ., 1807; d unm between May
          13th and July 18th, 1867
(9) vi William (4), b 22nd July, 1809

6

Sarah Harriet (4) Brisbane [John S (3), James (2),
Wm (1)], b ...., 1797, married at St Michael's Church,
Charleston, S C., 17th Dec, 1816, Alexander Gillon, son
of Commodore Alexander Gillon and Ann Purcell   She
died in Islington, suburb of Charleston, 14th Aug. 1828 and
was interred at Malona, on Ashley River, the country seat
of her father, John Stanyarne Brisbane   Her husband was
afterwards, on 12th July, 1832, killed, in a duel with John
Wilson, at Eddings Bay, Edisto Island, S C, aged 37
years.
      Children.   4 (Gillon), 2 of which survived
(10) i Anna Maria (5), b 25th Nov 1817
      ii. Alexander (5), b in Charleston 23rd Aug 1821
          m Mlle. Elize Bart of Port Au Prince, Hayti.
          He died there 25th Feb 1874   His widow and
          a daughter survived him, and later returned to
          France, since which time all trace of them has
          been lost

10

Anna Maria (5) Gillon, [Sarah H (4) Brisbane, John
S (3), James (2), Wm (1)], b 25th Nov 1817; m. first,
28th May 1838, John Benjamin of Stratford Conn, at
which place they resided until his death on Sept 22nd,
1846   She then returned to Charleston. S. C., and married
secondly, ..., Dec 1851, Thomas Nathaniel Farr, of
Summerville, S C   She died 26th March, 1910, and was
interred in St Paul's Churchyard, Summerville, S C
      Children by first marriage· 6 (Benjamin) 3 sons and
3 daughters

    ı. Alexander Gillon (6), b 2nd Jan 1839, d 1840

    ıı. Elvıra Nıcoll (6), b. 27th Nov 1840; drowned near Sullıvan's Island, S C., 14th Aug., 1884, while savıng the life of a child. A beautiful memorial window has been erected to the memory of her heroıc deed ın the little Chapel of the Holy Cross, Sullivan's Island. She was burıed at St Paul's, Summervılle, S. C

    ııı. Alfred Alston (6), b 2nd Jan , 1841, d. 1858.

    iv Anna Elizabeth (6), b. 3rd Jan , 1844; m George W. Scott of Brooklın, N Y ; d 1910, leavıng 2 daughters,

        1 Annıe Gıllon (7), m to Theodore D Armour
        2. Nellie Benjamın (7), unm

(11) v. Johanna (6), b. 17th Sept., 1846

  Children by second marrıage: 1 (Farr) survıvıng
    vı Thomas Nathaniel (6), b ....; m 1898, Ethel Lıbbey

      Children· 5 (Farr) daughters
      1 Annıe Gıllon (7), b July, 1899
      2 Bessıe Brısbane (7), b
      3 Katherıne (7), b. ......
      4 Elınor (7), b. .. ..
      5 Abbey (7), b ....

11

Johanna (6) Benjamın [Anna M (5) Gıllon, Sarah H (4) Brısbane, John S. (3), James (2), Wm (1)], b 17th Sept , 1846; m. first, ... Wıllıam Henry Fishburne He died 1st Feb , 1891 She married secondly, 12th June, 1893, Samuel Gourdın Pınkney, of Charleston, S. C He died 26th March, 1902 His wıdow now resides wıth her daughter, Mrs W Lorıng Lee, at Sumter, S. C

  Children, all by first marriage: 5 (Fishburne) 3 sons and 2 daughters

    1 Elizabeth Brısbane (7), b 3rd Dec , 1869; m 13th Feb 1890 Theodore Dehon Ravenel She died

4th Oct 1898 Since his wife's death, Mr Ravenel has remarried twice

Children: 3 (Ravenel) sons.
1 Theodore DuBose (8), b 30th Nov, 1890
2 William Fishburne (8), b 17th Nov, 1895.
3 Samuel Fitz Simons (8), b. 28th Sept 1898.

11 Harriet Chalmers (7), b 26th Feb, 1873; m 17th Aug., 1904, Washington Loring Lee, of Sumter, S. C.

Children 3 (Lee) 2 sons and 1 daughter
1 William Fishburne (8), b. 23rd July, 1905; d. 12th Sept, 1906
2 Pauline Loring (8), b 3rd Feb, 1907.
3. Washington Loring (8), b 30th Sept., 1908

111. Charles Cochran (7), b 25th May, 1876; m 14th Sept., 1898, Virginia Alma Ingram

Children. 7 (Fishburne), 4 sons and 3 daughters
1 Alma Ingram (8), b 7th July, 1899, d Feb, 1904
2 May Ingram (8), b 7th March, 1901
3 Charles Cochran (8), b 7th Nov, 1902
4 Harriet Ingram (8), b 5th May, 1905
5 William Henry (8), b 1st Dec, 1906
6 George (8), b 26th Jan, 1909
7. Robert Purdy (8), b. 23rd Jan., 1911

iv John Benjamin (7), b 8th Feb., 1878; m. 7th Nov. 1901, Jeannie Bently Gibson.

Children: 3 (Fishburne), 1 son and 2 daughters
1 Anna Benjamin (8), b 4th Nov, 1902.
2. Mary Tennant (8), b 12th Dec, 1904
3. John Benjamin (8), b 17th Dec., 1908

v. Alexander Gillon (7), b 22nd Jan, 1883 m 16th Feb, 1911, Jane Hutchinson Owen.

Child· 1 (Fishburne) son
1 Alexander Gillon (8), b 23rd May, 1912

7

John Wilson (4) Brisbane [John S. (3), James (2), Wm (1)], b. 1801, m 22nd March, 1827," Mary Susannah. the daughter of Commodore Alexander Gillon, and Ann Purcell. He was killed by being thrown from his horse while hunting, 28th Aug., 1833."

Children. 2 (Brisbane) daughters
    i. Mary Susannah (5), b. 11th June, 1828, m. 3rd June, 1847, at Litchfield, Conn, Gideon H Hollister He was a prominent lawyer, State Senator, U S Minister to Hayti, and also the author of a "History of Connecticut" and other works. He died 24th March, 1881   Mrs. Hollister lives at Litchfield, Conn

        Children   3 (Hollister) 2 sons and 1 daughter.
        1. Gertrude (6), d. an infant
        2 Abbott Brisbane (6), b   .. , d 1859
        3 Robert (6), b. ... ...; d 1866

    ii Maria Hall (5), b 11th June, 1831; m at Litchfield, Conn , F O Beeman   She died 17th Jan , 1863

        Child 1 (Beeman) son
        1 Allen Everett (6), b ... ...; a clergyman in the Epicopal Church.

8.

Abbott Hall (4) Brisbane, [John S. (3), James (2), Wm. (1)], b 4th Dec , 1804; graduated at the U S Military Academy in 1825   Served in the Florida War against the Seminole Indians in 1835-6, as Colonel of the South Carolina Volunteers, and was engaged in the skirmish of Tomoka, 10th March, 1836, where he so distin-

---

"Record from old Gillon Bible "March the 22—1827. John W Brisbane married to Mary Susannah Gillon at Goose Creek in the Parish of St James—Goose Creek, by the Rev Mr Hankill, Rector of St Paul's Church, Charleston"
"Ibid "Died August 28—1833, aged 32 years, John W Brisbane of Charleston, S C , buried at Malona, Ashley River, Maria Brisbane'- plant.tion "

guished himself for his bravery that he was called the
South Carolina Hotspur   On his return to Charleston he
was made Brigadier General of Militia of S. C.   Soon
after he was appointed Constructing Engineer of the projected "Charleston and Cincinnati Railroad" in which
position he served for four years   In 1847-8 he was
Superintending Engineer of an Artesian Well for the supply of water to the city of Charleston, and at the same time
elected, Professor of History, Belles Lettres and Ethics at
the Citadel Academy, which position he held until 1853,
after which he retired to his plantation, Accabee, near
Charleston   He was the author of a political romance
"Ralphton or the Young Carolinian."

He married in . ..., Adeline E. White, daughter
of the distinguished painter John Blake White, and died in
Summerville, S. C., 28th Sept., 1861, leaving no issue
Mrs. Brisbane, who with her husband, became a member
of the Roman Catholic Church, joined, after her husband's
death, the Ursuline Convent of Columbia, S. C.

9

William (4) Brisbane, [John S. (3), James (2), Wm
(1)], b. 22nd July, 1809; was adopted by his uncle, William
Brisbane, in 1812; educated at Coates School, and that of
Mr. Partridge in Middleton, Conn., finishing his education
by European travel.

He married first, 3rd March, 1831, Julia Hall Lowndes,
the daughter of James Lowndes and Catharine Osborne,
the celebrated beauty   Born in 1811, she died 4th Dec.,
1847   He married secondly, in New York City, 2nd Oct.,
1857, Sarah Hogan, the daughter of Judge William Hogan,
of Hogansburgh, N. Y.   Mr. Brisbane died at Hogansburgh, 30th Aug., 1860.

Children by first marriage: 9 (Brisbane) 3 sons and 6
daughters

> 1. Mary Catherine (5), b in Charleston, S. C., 12th
> Jan., 1832; married at Wiltown, S. C., 22nd
> April, 1856, the Hon. George A. Hickox, b 11th
> June, 1830, a distinguished member of the Litch-

field, Conn County Bar He edited for twenty-
five years "The Litchfield Enquirer," and his
editorials were well known all over the United
States, as models of thought and expression He
passed away at his ancestral home in Washington, Conn, 7th June, 1903, "leaving many
mourning friends but not one enemy " He was
a descendant of John Elliott. (The Apostle to
the Indians) Mrs Hickox resides with her family at Washington, Conn. [She died in June,
1913]

Children 2 (Hickox) 1 son and 1 daughter,
    both born at Litchfield, Conn.
1 William Brisbane (6), b 18th March, 1863;
    m 8th Oct , 1890, Zaydee Bancroft Keese,
    b 6th April, 1866; d 6th Aug , 1902

    Child 1 (Hickox) daughter.
    1 Zillah Keese (7), b 13th April, 1892

2 Frances Elliott (6), b 1st April, 1864; unm

(12) ii Julia Lowndes (5), b 31st May, 1833
(13) iii. Harriet Ruth (5), b 6th Dec , 1834
(14) iv. Catharine Osborne (5), b. 3rd Aug., 1836
    v Amarinthia (5), b 22nd Feb , 1838, unm.
    vi William (5), b 14th July, 1839, served in C S.
        A., d unm at Litchfield, Conn., 5th July. 1881
    vii Maria Hall (5), called "Nina," b. 15th Feb.,
        1841; unm
    viii James Lowndes (5), b 9th Dec , 1844; served
        in C. S. A , d unm 7th April, 1899
    ix Lewis Morris (5), b 27th July, 1846; served in
        C S A , and acted as courier to Gen James
        Chestnut, Junr ; d unm 6th March, 1905.

    Children by second marriage· 2 (Brisbane) daughters
    x Jane C. (5), b 13th Aug., 1858; married 15th
        Oct., 1878, Frank Schlesinger. Both deceased

        Child 1 (Schlesinger) daughter surviving
        1 Bertha Margaret (6), b 6th June, 1881,

xı Margaret L (5), b. 26th April, 1860; m. 18th July, 1882, George M Ransom, M D

>Children· 2 (Ransom) sons.
>>1 Frank Brisbane (6), b 25th June, 1883
>>2 Henry Morgan (6), b 22nd April, 1885; m. 23rd Nov., 1908, Catherine Byer Issue

12

Julia Lowndes (5) Brisbane, [Wm (4), John S (3), James (2), Wm (1)], b 31st May, 1833; m. at Wiltown, S C, 10th April, 1855, Roland Smith Rhett. He died.....
Children   10 (Rhett) 7 sons and 3 daughters
>1. Julia Lowndes (6), b 20th March, 1856, unm
>ıı. Roland Smith (6), b. 28th April, 1858; m 22nd Dec, 1891, Mary Clapp Sibley.
>ııı Abbott Brisbane (6), b. 11th Jan, 1860, m 6th June, 1899, Eleonor Orr Lee   Issue
>ıv Thomas Grimke (6), b 14th Jan, 1862; m ....
>v William Brisbane (6), b 16th Dec, 1863; m 16th Dec, 1899, Elizabeth Virginia Tyler. Issue
>vı Mariana Parker (6), b. 18th March, 1866, Thos Gordon Coleman
>vıı Charlotte Haskell (6), b. 31st May, 1869; unm
>vııı James Smith (6), b 8th April, 1872.
>ıx. Edward Lowndes (6), b. 25th March, 1874, m the Hon Frances Fairfax
>x Henry Parker (6), b 31st Jan. 1878, m Issue

13

Harriet Ruth (5) Brisbane, [Wm (4), John S. (3), James (2), Wm (1)], b in Charleston, S C, 6th Dec, 1834; m at Litchfield, Conn., 5th June, 1860, Cadwallader Colden Tracy, of New York; son of George Manning Tracy and Mary Colden Willett   From early youth Mrs Tracy evinced a decided inventive genius, possibly inherited from her great-grandfather, James Brisbane," and between

---

"James Brisbane's letter to Henry Laurens   See this Magazine. Vol IV, p 11

1889 and 1893 was granted by the U. S Gov't Patent Office, no less than eleven patents for mechanical inventions.["] The most remarkable of these was a very important departure in the improvement of sewing machines, and she was congratulated on the success she had "achieved in the practical solution of a problem which" had "been attempted by many of the ablest sewing machine experts in the world, only to be abandoned as unsolvable.'''[''] Some of these were exhibited at the World's Fair in Chicago in 1893, for which she was presented with several silver and bronze medals and a diploma from the World's Columbian Commission for her Models of Passenger Elevators

Mrs Tracy is also highly gifted as a writer of verse and prose and has often contributed to magazines and other periodicals She resides in England

Children 5 (Tracy) 1 son (d. in infancy) and 4 daughters

i Julia Lowndes (6), b on Staten Island, N Y, 10th Aug, 1865; unm

ii Adeline Brisbane (6), b at Columbia, S C, 8th April, 1869; unm.

iii Caroline Ruth Colden (6), called "Rose," b in Brooklyn, N Y, 3rd March, 1871; m on Staten Island, 18th April, 1894, Frederick William Corse

Child 1 (Corse) son
1 Cadwallader Colden (7), b 7th Feb, 1896.

iv Mary Colden Willett (6), b. in New York City, 22nd Feb., 1873; m. in London, England, 14th May, 1908, Eduardo Haviland Hillman, of Santiago, Chile, S A Reside at 13 Somers Place, Hyde Park, London, England

14

Catharine Osborne (5) Brisbane, [Wm (4), John S. (3), James (2), Wm (1)], b 3rd Aug 1836; m Sept,

["]Amongst others, safety devices for preventing the falling of elevators and the closing up of the shafts, also a folding bed

['']From a letter signed by John E. Sweet, Engineer and Inventor, Lewis E Grover, Man Colt's Firearms Co, John Thomson, Inventor, W F. Durfee, Sewing Machine Expert and F R Hutton, Professor of the Columbia School of Mines

1860, Charles Sinkler Darby, M. D, b 14th July, 1837, d 11th May, 1894.

Children· 6 (Darby) 2 sons and 4 daughters
  i   Catharine Lowndes (6), b 16th Nov 1861; unm.
  ii. Charles Sinkler (6), b 5th Nov, 1866, d 30th Aug., 1896
  iii. Julia Lowndes (6), b 18th March, 1868; unm
  iv Ruth Brisbane (6), b 11th Oct 1869; unm.
  v   William Russell (6), b 20th April, 1872, m ...... , Clara Hale

  Children: 3 (Darby) sons
  1   Joseph Hale (7), b 19th Dec, 1904
  2   Charles Sinkler (7), b 20th Feb, 1908
  3   William Russell (7), b ....

  vi Mary Preston (6), b. 30th May, 1874; unm.

5.

Adam Fowler (3) Brisbane. [James (2), Wm (1)], b in Charleston 3rd Sept, 1783, while his father was in England   Married 14th Dec, 1803, Mary Ann Mosse, b. 10th March, 1786, d. 10th May, 1854.   She was the daughter of Dr. George Mosse and Phoebe M. Norton (his second wife)   He died in Charleston, 15th June, 1830, and was buried in St Paul's Churchyard

Children. 2 (Brisbane) 1 son and 1 daughter.
(15) i. William Henry (4), b. 12th Oct., 1806
     ii Elizabeth (4), b ... ., d 29th Oct., 1839, m Alexander B. Lawton.

     Children· 3 (Lawton) daughters
     1. Mary Jane (5), b. abt. 1832; m Montague La Fitte   No issue
     2   Martha (5), b 1834; m Judge Walter Gwinn of Florida   No issue
     3. Eusepia (5), d. an infant.

15.

William Henry (4) Brisbane, [Adam Fowler (3), James (2), Wm (1)], b 12th Oct 1806; adopted at the age of six by his uncle, William Brisbane, who left him Milton Lodge on Ashley River   He died at his home in Arena, Wisconsin, 5th April, 1878   He married 28th May, 1825, his cousin, Anna Lawton, b. abt. 1806; d   17th Feb., 1888

Children: 7 (Brisbane) 4 sons and 3 daughters

    i   Anna Cornelia (5), b. 25th July, 1827; d. 26th April, 1828

    ii   Bently Hasell (5), b. 31st Aug., 1829; d. 22nd March, 1846

(16) iii   Benjamin Lawton (5), b. 8th April, 1834

(17) iv   William Henry (5), b. 20th June, 1838

    v   Phebe Adeline (5), b. 14th May, 1841; m. 10th March, 1862, Herbert Reed. He died 28th April, 1875

        Children   4 (Reed) 2 sons and 2 daughters

        i   Herbert Brisbane (6), b. 24th May, 1864; d. 9th June, 1896; m. 11th April, 1889, Mary G. Pinney Issue: 1 daughter, Erma Gladys (7)

        2   Anna Julia (6), d. in infancy

        3   Martha (6), d. in infancy

        4. George (6) Benjamin, b. 19th Nov. 1873

    vi. Mary Julia (5), b.   : d. 18th March, 1845

    vii. John Edward (5), b. 7th April, 1847; d. 2nd Feb., 1863

16

Benjamin Lawton (5) Brisbane. [Wm. H. (4), Adam F (3), James (2), Wm. (1)], b. 8th April, 1834; m. 22nd Jan., 1854, Sarah Emily Dickson   He died at Council Bluffs, Iowa, 10th Nov., 1893

Children: 5 (Brisbane) 2 sons and 3 daughters

    1   William Henry (6), b. 22nd Jan., 1855; m. in Omaha Neb., 1897.

        Children   2 (Brisbane).

        1. Winfred (7), b. .

        2   ..   .   (7)

ii   Alfred (6), b. 3rd Sept , 1861; m ..   .., Olive Miller

Children: 2 (Brisbane) sons
1 Benjamin, b ..
·2 Reuben, b   ...

iii Anna E (6), b 7th July, 1864, m .... , Charles W Johnson. Issue
iv. Julia (6), b . ..; m   ., Lloyd Robinson Issue
v Gertrude (6), b ....., m   . , Nels Miller Issue

17.

William Henry (5) Brisbane, [Wm H (4), Adam F. (3), James (2), Wm (1)], b at Lawtonville, S C, 20th June, 1838, m 20th June, 1865, Elizabeth A Sniffen   He died 12th May, 1897
Children: 9 (Brisbane) 3 sons and 6 daughters

i Henry Charles (6), b 23rd Dec, 1865; m 25th August, 1889, Dora Koester

Children 3 (Brisbane) 2 sons and 1 daughter.
1. De Tours H (7), b 18th August, 1890
2 Clarence L. (7), b 10th Feb., 1893
3. Earl L. (7), b 5th May, 1899

ii. Mary Anna (6), b. 6th Sept , 1868; d. .. . ..
iii Adeline Catherine (6), b 16th April, 1870, d .. . , 1871
iv Elizabeth Rosa (6), b 1st Feb, 1872, d in infancy.
v John Benjamin (6), b. 15th Oct , 1874; m 31st Aug , 1896, Julia Eva House

Children: 3 (Brisbane) daughters
1 Ethel (7), b 13th Oct., 1897
2 Mariem (7), b. 26th July, 1903
3. Lucille (7), b 27th March, 1907

vi Mariem (6), b 27th May, 1876; m 15th Oct , 1895, James Christian   Issue.

vii Edith Marie (6), b 4th Jan 1878, m 4th April, 1898, Arthur Braze. Issue

viii. Phebe Elenor (6), b 22nd July, 1879; d. 1882.

ix Edward Alfred (6), b 7th May, 1881; m. 20th Dec, 1906, Edith Gertrude Clements

Child: 1 (Brisbane) son.

1 William C (7), b 17th Jan, 1909

3

Adam Fowler (2) Brisbane, [Wm. (1)], third son of Dr William Brisbane and Margaret Stewart, was born in Charleston in 1754 He "settled in Camden certainly as early as 1780" as proved by the Court House Records of that place In 1784 "he was elected to the Legislature" and was a Member of the Constitutional Convention in 1790. "He was chosen first President of the Camden Orphan Society in 1787, and in 1791 was appointed one of the first Judges of Kershaw" "His residence stood on the east side of Fair Street near the corner of King" and in 1791, when General Washington visited Camden, it was placed at his disposal. "It was subsequently burned" (Brasington House now on site) It is believed by his descendants that he was an officer in the Revolutionary War, with the rank of Colonel, and that at one time he served under General Washington This was related by the late Dr Adam Brisbane Arthur, his grandson, but no record, I believe, has been found to substantiate it He married 23rd May, 1775, Mary Camber of Savannah, Georgia, daughter of Sir Thomas Camber.* He died in Richland District, 1st July, 1799 Mrs Brisbane survived her husband twenty-one years and died in Camden, S C., 10th Aug, 1820

Children 5 (Brisbane) 2 sons and 3 daughters

1 Adam Fowler (3) Junr, b 19th Dec, 1779; m ....., Margaret Irvin, in Kershaw Dist He died 3rd Jan, 1806, leaving no issue His widow

*Another daughter of Sir Thomas Camber married George Walton, Signer of the Declaration of Independence, and still another, married Major John Habersham of Georgia

married afterwards, before 1808, Thomas Sal-
mond

(18) ii   Elizabeth Dale (3), b 5th Dec, 1781

iii   William Alexander (3), b ...., 1783: d May,
1784

(19) iv   Mary Hannah Camber (3), b 26th June, 1785

Twins v   Margaret (3), b 26th June, 1785

18

Elizabeth Dale (3) Brisbane, [Adam F. (2), Wm (1)],
b 5th Dec., 1781; m. 26th July, 1802, William Ancrum
She died in Kershaw Dist 1st Sept, 1826

Children·   5 (Ancrum) sons

i   William Porcher (4), b 7th March 1808: d ....,
1810.

ii   Fowler Brisbane (4), b 23rd Jan, 1811; d ...
1830

iii   George Octavius (4), b 5th April, 1813: d. ......,
1824

(20) iv   William Alexander (4), b. 10th June. 1815

(21) v   Thomas James (4), b 17th July. 1817

20.

William Alexander (4) Ancrum, [Elizabeth D (3) Brisbane; Adam F. (2). Wm (1)], b 10th June, 1815: m
27th March, 1837, Charlotte Elizabeth, daughter of James
Kennedy Douglas, of Galoway, Scotland   He died ......
1862

Children   6 (Ancrum) 2 sons and 4 daughters

(22) i   Mary Douglas (5), b 3rd Jan, 1840

(23) ii   Thomas James (5), b 12th Sept, 1841

(24) iii   Elizabeth Brisbane (5). b. 25th April, 1843. d.
..., March, 1905

iv   James Kennedy Douglas (5), b 23rd Sept, 1844,
d in service C S A. 10th July (? Feb), 1864

(25) v   Ellen Deas (5). b 9th March. 1846

(26) vi   Margaret Douglas (5), b 6th March. 1848

22

Mary Douglas (5) Ancrum [William Alexander (4) Ancrum, Elizabeth D (3) Brisbane, Adam F. (2), Wm (1)], b. 3rd Jan 1840; m 22nd Feb, 1860, Charles J Shannon, Surgeon, C. S. A.

Children. 4 (Shannon) 1 son and 3 daughters

    i. Ellen Deas (6), b. 7th Dec, 1860; d. 22nd Feb., 1844; m William De Saussure Boykin No issue

    ii. Charles John (6), b 1st July, 1863; m 30th April, 1895, Emily Jordan Nesbit. Children· 2 (Shannon) sons.

        1 Ralph Nesbit (7), b 18th Feb, 1896
        2 Charles John (7), b 29th July, 1907

    iii. Leila Martha (6), b. 2nd April, 1867
    iv. Charlotte Douglas (6). b 23rd July, 1869

23

Thomas James (5) Ancrum, [Wm Alexander (4) Ancrum, Elizabeth D. (3) Brisbane, Adam F. (2), Wm (1)], b 12th Sept 1841; d. 29th May, 1900; m 29th March, 1870, Mary Cantey.

Children 2 (Ancrum) daughters

    i Elizabeth Hamilton Boykin (6). b 25th June, 1876, m 25th April, 1900, Caleb Clark Moore

    Children: 3 (Moore) 2 sons and 1 daughter
        1 Thomas Ancrum (7), b 10th Feb, 1901
        2 Albertus Adair (7), b 6th Sept, 1904
        3 Camilla Agnes (7), b 24th Sept, 1906

    ii. Camilla Cantey (6), b 15th Aug, 1877; m 15th Aug 1900, William Hamilton Haile She died 12th Sept., 1905

    Children 3 (Haile) daughters
        1 Minnie Cantey (7), b 30th March, 1901
        2 Susan Hamilton (7), b. 27th July, 1902
        3 Elizabeth Ancrum (7), b 13th Nov., 1904

Elizabeth Brisbane (5) Ancrum, [Wm Alexander (4) Ancrum, Elizabeth D (3) Brisbane, Adam F (2), Wm

24

(1)], b 25th April, 1843, d 18th March, 1905; m 17th
Dec., 1867, Samuel Boykin, C. S. A.

Children. 9 (Boykin) 4 sons and 5 daughters

   1 Mary Hopkins (6), b 29th April, 1869; m first
      11th Dec, 1888, Charles H Green, M D, who d.
      21st March, 1900, m secondly Dec, 1906, E F.
      Bell

      Children by first marriage   3 (Green) 2 sons and
         1 daughter
      1 Charles H (7), b. 17th June, 1890, d 28th
         Sept 1905.
      2 Samuel B (7), b 25th June, 1894; d 28th
         March, 1905.
      3 Elizabeth B (7), b 30th Dec, 1896.

   11 Charlotte Ancrum (6), b. 16th Feb, 1871; m. 11th
      Feb, 1902, Thomas Davis Porcher

      Child 1 (Porcher) son
      1 .John Stoney (7), b 29th March, 1910

   111. Samuel Burwell (6), b. 23rd May, 1873, d 2nd
      July, 1885
   iv Leila Brisbane (6), b 4th June, 1876
   v. William Ancrum (6), b 2nd Aug 1878; m 17th
      July, 1901, Florence Harlee Coachman

      Children: 3 (Boykin) 1 son and 2 daughters
      1. Helen Mortimer (7), b. 21st July, 1902.
      2 Florence Harlee (7), b 26th Sept, 1903.
      3 William Ancrum (7), b 2nd Feb, 1907

   vi Lemuel Whitaker (6), b. 4th Jan, 1880
   vii Ellen Lee (6), b 29th Aug 1882, m 18th Oct,
      1911, Thomas Frederick Bell
   viii Meta Deas (6), b 2nd Nov, 1883; m 26th Dec,
      1907, John Gibbes Barnwell
      Child 1 (Barnwell) son
      1 John Gibbes (7), b 26th Jan., 1911
   ix Samuel (6), b 6th July, 1886; d 26th June, 1887

25

Ellen Deas (5) Ancrum, [Wm Alexander (4) Ancrum, Elizabeth D (3) Brisbane, Adam F (2), Wm (1)], b 9th March, 1846, m. 22nd June, 1863, Major Francis Dickinson Lee, C S A

Children. 5 (Lee) 3 sons and 2 daughters.

    i. Ellen Deas (6), b. 21st Oct , 1866, m. . ...., George Hoffman

        Child 1 (Hoffman) daughter
        1. Ellen Lee (7), b . . . .

    ii. Francis Dickinson (6), b 21st Jan , 1870; m . . . Adine Tyrrel

    iii Mary Elizabeth (6), b 5th April, 1873.

    iv. Douglas Ancrum (6), b. 12th Oct , 1876.

    v Lynch Deas (6), b . . . Sept., 1879; d . . . ...1911.

26

Margaret Douglas (5) Ancrum, [Wm Alexander (4) Ancrum, Elizabeth D. (3) Brisbane, Adam F (2), Wm. (1)], b 6th March, 1848; d 8th April, 1883; m 9th Nov , 1869, Samuel Francis Boykin.

Children: 7 (Boykin) 5 sons and 2 daughters

    i Douglas Ancrum (6), b 15th Jan , 1871; m 9th Nov , 1897, Mary Elizabeth Boykin

        Child 1 (Boykin) daughter
        1 Ellen Douglas (7), b 20th Nov , 1898.

    ii William Whitaker (6), b 5th Sept , 1872, d in infancy

    iii Samuel Francis (6), b 15th June, 1874, m 11th April, 1899, Anne Llewellyn Alexander.

        Children· 2 (Boykin) 1 son and 1 daughter.
        1 Martha Chambers (7), b. 31st Jan , 1900
        2. Francis Hart (7), b. . . . .. June, 1912.

    iv. Martha Rives (6), b 22nd Sept , 1875, d 12th Sept., 1911, m 14th April, 1903, John J Workman.

Children   4 (Workman) 2 sons and 2 daughters
1   Elizabeth Brisbane (7), b 18th June, 1904
2. Martha Boykin (7), b. 19th July, 1905
3   John James (7), d in infancy
4   William Gatewood (7), b 22nd May, 1910

v. William Ancrum (6), b 5th Oct, 1877; m 1st June, 1905, Anne Beecher Smith

Child   1 (Boykin) son
1   William A. (7), b. ...., 1907

vi   Lynch Deas (6), b 31st Oct., 1878; d in infancy.
vii   Ellen Deas (6), b   ..., 1881; d in infancy

21

Thomas James (4) Ancrum, [Elizabeth D (3) Brisbane, Adam F (2), Wm. (1)], b 17th July, 1817, served in the C S. A ; d in 1887; m in ...., 1840, Margaret Douglas.
Children   10 (Ancrum) 3 sons and 7 daughters
(27)   1. William Alexander (5), b ...... , 1843
          11   Mary Camber (5), b   , 1845, d in infancy
          iii. Charlotte Douglas (5), b   , 1847, d. 1909, m in 1870, James Cantey   No issue
          iv   Thomas Brisbane (5), b ...... , 1850, d unm in 1911
(28)   v   Elizabeth Brisbane (5), b ......, 1852
(29)   vi   Margaret Frances (5), b   ..., 1856
          vii   James Douglas (5), b   , 1858; d 1861
          viii   Catherine Porcher (5), b ...., 1860, d.   . 1861
          ix   Mary Catherine (5), b   , 1862, m   .   . 1880, Douglas Blanding De Saussure   No issue
          x. Jessie Douglas (5), b   ...., 1865; m   ... 1893, Clarendon Rivern Spencer

Children   4 (Spencer) sons
1   Clarendon R (6), b ...... , 1894
2   Douglas Ancrum (6), b   . . 1896
3. Charles Holmes (6), b   .   . 1898
4   Thomas Ancrum (6), b   , 1900.

27

William Alexander (5) Ancrum, [Thomas James (4) Ancrum, Elizabeth D (3) Brisbane, Adam F. (2), Wm. (1)], b ....., 1843; served in C S A., m in ...., 1877, Anna Calhoun.

Children: 7 (Ancrum) 5 sons and 2 daughters.
 i. Anna Aurelia (6), b. ... ., 1878; m ...., 1901, John Miller.

  Children 2 (Miller) daughters
  1 Betty Calhoun (7), b ...., 1905
  2 Marjorie Dodd (7), b ...., 1907

 ii William (6), b ...., 1881; Lieutenant in the U. S Army; m ...., 1909, Cora Carrison

  Children 2 (Ancrum) 1 son and 1 daughter
  1 William (7), b ... ..., 1910
  2 Margaret Carrison (7), b .. .. , 1912

 iii Sarah Calhoun (6), b ...., 1882; m ...., 1906, Edward Eve.

  Children. 4 (Eve) 2 sons and 2 daughters.
  1 Anna Calhoun (7), b . .., 1907.
  2. Edward Armstrong (7), b . ..., 1908
  3 Sarah Norwood (7), b. ...., 1910.
  4 Christopher Fitzsimmons (7), b. 1912

 iv Calhoun (6), b ... ., 1883; m ...., 1910, Dixie Quarles

  Child: 1 (Ancrum) daughter
  1 Dixie (7), b. ....., 1911

 v Andrew Simonds (6), b ... ..., 1885 Unm
 vi Thomas (6), b. . .., 1886. Unm
 vii James Norwood (6), b. ... . 1891 Unm.

28.

Elizabeth Brisbane (5) Ancrum [Thomas J (4) Ancrum, Elizabeth D. (3) Brisbane, Adam F (2), Wm (1)], b ....., 1852; m ..... 1882. John Boykin.

Children: 3 (Boykin) 2 sons and 1 daughter.
  i Edward Mortimer (6), b . .., 1882; m   ,
      1909, Elizabeth Lowndes   No issue
  ii Thomas Ancrum (6), b ...., 1884
  iii. Frances Johnson (6), b. . . . . ., 1886.

29

Margaret Frances (5) Ancrum, [Thomas J. (4) Ancrum,
Elizabeth D. (3) Brisbane, Adam F (2), Wm. (1)], b.
...., 1856, m . . .., 1877, Robert C Johnson
Children. 6 (Johnson) 2 sons and 4 daughters
  i. William E. (6), b . ..., 1877.
  ii Charlotte Cantey (6), b . ., 1879, m   ,
      1900, Matthew R Singleton

      Children   3 (Singleton) 2 sons and 1 daughter
      1. Richard (7), b ...., 1901
      2. Robert Johnson (7), b. ... ., 1904, d in in-
          fancy.
      3. Martha Rutledge (7), b .. , 1908

  iii. Margaret Ancrum (6), b .. .. .., 1881; m   . . ,
      1909, Alexander G. Clarkson

      Children: 2 (Clarkson) sons
      1. Alexander Garden (7), b. .   , 1910
      2 Robert Johnson (7), b .. ..., 1912

  iv. Annie Cunningham (6), b .. . , 1886; m ... ,
      1907, Henry D Boykin

      Children: 2 (Boykin) daughters
      1 Frances Ancrum (7), b ...., 1908
      2. Ellen Deas (7), b. ...., 1910.

  v Mary Douglas (6), b. .... , 1888, m . . .. , 1912,
      Daniel M Jones.
  vi Robert Cunningham (6), b .   1890.

19

Mary Hannah Camber (3) Brisbane, [Adam F. (2),
Wm (1)], b 26th June, 1785; m at Camden, S. C., 28th

Nov., 1805, Reuben Arthur, b in Lexington Dist., S. C,
4th April, 1774, d in Sumpter Co, 11th March, 1833
Mrs. Arthur died 20th Nov, 1857.

Children 9 (Arthur), 5 sons and 4 daughters. All born
at Camden

    1 Mary (4), b 12th Jan. 1807; d. 6th Nov 1809.
    ii. William Henry (4), b 8th June, 1808, d. in La-
        fayette Co, Arkansas 26th Sept 1840
    iii Thomas Brown (4), b 21st March, 1810; d 14th
        Jan, 1833
    iv John Singleton (4), b.   Jan, 1813; d. 19th
        May, 1813
(30) v. Adam Brisbane (4), b 26th May, 1814
(31) vi Elizabeth (4), b 25th Sept, 1816
(32) vii Mary Margaret (4), b 21st March, 1819
    viii (Capt.) John Camber (4), b 19th Dec, 1821;
        m 27th Feb, 1843, Mary C. Gray

        Children 3 (Arthur) 2 sons and 1 daughter.
        1 Mary Gray (5), b . , 1847; m . Dec.
          1864, Charles English
        2 Reuben (5), b 1850
        3. Edmund (5), b 1852

    ix. Martha Anna (4), b 27th Nov., 1827; d   ..,
        April, 1904; m ...., 1845, Judge George R.
        Evans of N. C.

        Children: 3 (Evans) 1 son and 2 daughters
        1. Mary A. (5), b ...., April, 1846; unm
        2 Katherine (5), b ...., May, 1847; unm.
        3 Benjamin (5), d in infancy

30.

Dr. Adam Brisbane (4) Arthur, [Mary H C (3) Brisbane, Adam F. (2), Wm. (1)], b 26th May, 1814; m first
2nd March, 1837, Mary Rebecca Atkinson, b. ...... April,
1821, d . .. October, 1843 He married secondly, 1845,
America Robinson, b ... . 1824, d , 1885 Dr Arthur
d . . . Nov., 1872.

Children by first marriage: 5 (Arthur) 2 sons and 3 daughters.

    i. Elizabeth (5), b. 22nd Nov , 1837 , m 22nd August, 1859, Dr. Edward M Vasser, d Feb., 1879 Mrs Vasser is living at Selma, Ala.

    ii. Mary Ann (5), b 10th Aug., 1839; d 12th May, 1864; m. 16th Nov , 1856, Dr A. Bowie

    iii. Thomas (5), b. 18th Oct., 1840; d. in infancy.

    iv Emma Polk (5), b 9th Nov , 1841; living at Selma, Ala

    v. William Henry (5), b. .... April, 1843; d. in infancy

Children by second marriage .   9 (Arthur) 1 son and 8 daughters.

    vi Coralie (5), b. 20th Feb 1846; m ...., R E. Webster

    vii. Sarah (5), b. . .. . April, 1847; d. 14th Feb., 1896; m ..... April, 1874, John Deusler.

    viii. Mary Anna (5), b. .... Dec , 1849; m. .. .., 1889, William Price

    ix. Louise Salmond (5), b .... March, 1852; d. .... March, 1878

    x. Carolina (5), b. . ..... Feb., 1855; d ...... Jan , 1862

    xi Evelyn (5), b .... Oct , 1856; m abt 1893, P. Welborn

    xii Florence (5), b. .... May, 1858; m .... ., Joseph Shough.

    xiii. Ada (5), b. .... Sept , 1861 ; d. 1900; m. .... , William Merkel

    xiv. William Ancrum (5), b 16th Jan , 1864; m. 24th March, 1899, Adele Fowler

    Children   4 (Arthur) daughters.

    1 Adele (6), b 24th March, 1900

    2 Dorothy (6), b. 29th Sept , 1902; d 3rd Aug., 1904

    3 Anna Brisbane (6), b 26th Jan., 1904.

    4 Elizabeth (6), b 3rd Aug , 1907

31

Elizabeth Dale Ancrum (4) Arthur, [Mary H C (3) Brisbane, Adam F (2), Wm (1)], b. 25th Sept , 1816; m 5th May, 1836, near Claiborne, Ala , James Barnes Diggs   She died 7th Sept , 1839.

Children   3 (Diggs) 1 son and 2 daughters

    i James Shepard (5), b 24th Jan , 1838; d 1st Jan , 1893

    ii Elizabeth Arthur (5), b 22nd Aug , 1839; m 1st S D Hays, of Ohio, Nov , 1856; he died June, 1860   Issue, 2 children, George J., died young, and Anna D , who died 1887. Md 2d Feb , 1864, John Edwards of Hillsboro. Ohio. 3 children, Edward D , Robert J , and Mary L , all living

    iii Mary Anna (5), (twin to Elizabeth Arthur), b 22nd Aug , 1839; d 18th Sept , 1909

32

Mary Margaret (4) Arthur, [Mary H C (3) Brisbane, Adam F. (2), Wm (1)], b 21st March, 1819; d _ _ ; m at Claiborne, Ala , 29th Nov , 1836, Dr John A English

Children   5 (English) 3 sons and 2 daughters

    i Richard Henry (6), b   . Dec , 1837; d _ _ . 1881 ;m .. . May, 1866, Hattie Stringfellow

        Children   4 (English) 3 sons and 1 daughter

        1 William Henry (7), b

        2. Thomas Portis (7), b   .

        3 Emma (7), b   ..

        4 John Quinlan (7), b

    ii Elizabeth Dale (6), b 12th Nov , 1839, d   _ _ . 1870; m Dr Lawrence

    iii. Mary Anna (6), b   . , 1840; d in infancy

    iv Charles Edward (6), b 6th March, 1842 , d   _ _ . 1878

    v John A. (6), b   _ _ . 1846

SOME FORGOTTEN TOWNS
IN LOWER SOUTH CAROLINA

By Henry A. M Smith

CHILDSBERRY OR CHILDSBURY

On 14th July, 1698, a tract of 1,200 acres was granted to one James Child[1] The land granted was on the Eastern bank of the Western branch of the Cooper river, at a point designated in the later documents referring to it as "The Strawberry" or "Strawberry " It probably or possibly had that name before the grant to Childs, but the writer of this article has never been able to positively assure himself of that fact by any anterior evidence. From an early period in the eighteenth century it was so known and it has retained the name of "Strawberry" to the present day The grant bounded to the South on the lands of M[rs] Aphra Coming, afterwards known as "Comings T" or "Comingtee" and to the North on the estate called "Mepkin" which had been granted to the three Colleton brothers, Sir Peter, James, and Thomas. and which finally vested in James as the last survivour of the three[2]

From a clause in the will of James Child he would appear to have come from Coleshill in the Parish of Augmondi, County of Hertford, England. At any rate he owned a house and lands there

To the tract of 1,200 acres James Child added the following grants, either contiguous to or in the near vicinity of the 1,200 acres, viz:

> 800 acres granted 1st June, 1709[3]
> 100 acres granted 8 Sept , 1711[4]
> 100 acres granted 21 March, 1715/16[5]
> 500 acres granted 19 October, 1716[6]

[1] Off Secy. State Grants. vol 38, p 364
[2] S C Hist. & Gen Mag , vol 1, p 330
[3] Memo Bk , vol 4, p 118
[4] Ibid
[5] Grant Book, vol 39, p 189
[6] Ibid

SOME FORGOTTEN TOWNS
IN LOWER SOUTH CAROLINA

By Henry A. M. Smith

CHILDSBERRY OR CHILDSBURY

On 14th July, 1698, a tract of 1,200 acres was granted to one James Child[1] The land granted was on the Eastern bank of the Western branch of the Cooper river, at a point designated in the later documents referring to it as "The Strawberry" or "Strawberry" It probably or possibly had that name before the grant to Childs, but the writer of this article has never been able to positively assure himself of that fact by any anterior evidence From an early period in the eighteenth century it was so known and it has retained the name of "Strawberry" to the present day. The grant bounded to the South on the lands of M[rs]. Aphra Coming, afterwards known as "Comings T" or "Comingtee" and to the North on the estate called "Mepkin" which had been granted to the three Colleton brothers, Sir Peter, James, and Thomas, and which finally vested in James as the last survivour of the three.[2]

From a clause in the will of James Child he would appear to have come from Coleshill in the Parish of Augmondi, County of Hertford, England At any rate he owned a house and lands there

To the tract of 1,200 acres James Child added the following grants, either contiguous to or in the near vicinity of the 1,200 acres, viz:

> 800 acres granted 1st June, 1709[3]
> 100 acres granted 8 Sept , 1711[4]
> 100 acres granted 21 March, 1715/16[5]
> 500 acres granted 19 October. 1716[6]

[1]Off Secy State Grants vol 38, p 364
[2]S C Hist. & Gen Mag , vol 1, p 330
[3]Memo Bk , vol. 4, p 118
[4]Ibid
[5]Grant Book, vol 39, p 189
[6]Ibid

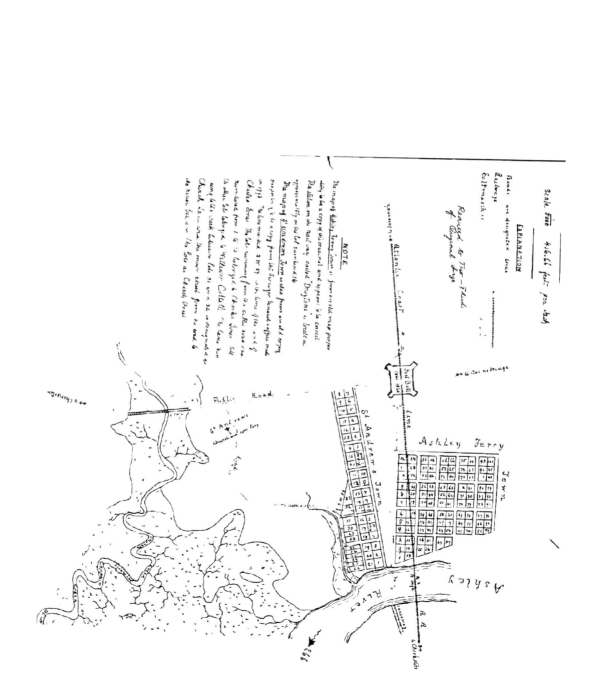

Exactly when James Child laid out the Town there appears to be nothing to show.   There is no plan of it in existence that the writer has ever seen.   It was located at the bluff on the river, called the Strawberry Bluff, and must have been laid out at or prior to the 25th September, 1714, for in the deed from "James Child of Childsbury Town "Yeoman" to "Stephen Sarrasin Merchant" he sells some seven town lots which "appear by the Towne Platt dated "25 September, 1714'"   By this deed James Child conveyed seven lots, each containing an half acre, viz. three front lots, numbers 8, 9, and 10, and four other lots, numbers 20, 21, 28, and 29.   The streets named on which these lots bound are Craven street, Mulberry street, and Church street, and some lots must have been already sold as these lots also bounded on the lots of John Moore and Marks Holmes.   The proviso is added that if two houses are not built on the lots within one year, then the lots would revert to James Child.

James Child died about August 29, 1720, (the date when his will was probated).   By his will, which was dated 29 October, 1718[1] he describes himself "of Childsbury Town "on Western Branch of Cooper river."   By his will he gave an acre and a half in the town for a Church or Chapel and a burying place for the inhabitants of Childsbury Town, a square in the middle of the town as shown on the plat for a market place; and lot number 16 to trustees for a free school, with a house for the schoolmaster, the trustees to employ a learned schoolmaster to keep a grammar school to teach Latin to boys and children until prepared for a college or university, and to teach English to children, and "to learn them to write and keep "accts by Arithmetic" the children of all the inhabitants of the western and eastern branches of Cooper River who contributed to the ferry and causeway to have the benefits of the school provided the parents should send firewood for their children in winter, or pay two shillings and sixpence Carolina currency per annum to the schoolmaster.   He further gave " a square of land upon north-

[1] M. C. O. Charleston, Bk O, p. 287.
[1] Prob. Ct. Ch. lk. I. Pl. 1671-1727 F. 127-142

"westernly of the ferry street" "with two acres and a halfe "of land Butting on the River Bay," and the marsh land between the Bay and the river as shown on the town platt, to trustees for a college or university, when any pious and charitable persons should think to put it to that use   He also gave all the rents of his Luckins plantation whereon he then dwelled, commencing from September, 1718, and also £100 with which to build a school house, and also £500 as security for a salary for the schoolmaster, the interest to be paid every six months in Carolina currency   To the inhabitants of Childsberry Town he gave the commoning and pasturage of 600 acres of land provided each lot owner put in only two cows, with power to the lot owners to elect a hayward; and gave the hill by the tanhouse and the river bay, containing one hundred acres, to build upon in time of war, a citadel for the defence of the town

The town must have assumed some position during the life of James Child or shortly after his death, for on 15 February, 1723, an Act was passed[9] which recited that James Child had by his will given 500 acres for a common adjoining "the town commonly called Childsberry" and also £600 to be placed at interest for the support of a free school, and also a place for a market in the town, and that "the inhabitants of the said town are very much "incommoded as well for want of certain market days in "each week to be appointed for Childsberry town" as for want of public fairs to be held there at least twice a year &c

The Act then provided that public open markets should be kept in Childsberry every Tuesday and Saturday in the week without payment of any toll for three years, and that two fairs should be kept annually in May and October

On 9th December, 1725, an Act was passed[10] "for estab-"lishing a Parochial Chappel of Ease at Childsberry to the "Parish Church in St John's Parish"   This Act recited "that James Child, deceased, and several others of the said "parishioners have voluntarily and generously subscribed "to the building a Chappel of Ease to St John's Parish, at "a place commonly called Childsberry, and have accordingly

---

[9] Stats at Large of S C, vol 3, p 204
[10] Ibid p 252

"built the said Chappel at their own charge," and further provided that the chapel so built should be taken as a Chapel of Ease to the Parish Church, and that the rector of the Parish should celebrate service therein every fourth Sunday during the year

The Chapel so built was of brick, the parishioners having subscribed "a considerable sum"" and the same building stands to-day near Strawberry Ferry, on the ground originally given by James Child

In March, 1731, according to the Council Journal of the day, a petition was made by the "Trustees of the free "school at Childsbury Ferry praying that the Several Leg- "acies left the said School may be united and Consolidated" and on 9 June, 1733, an Act was passed" reciting the gifts made by James Child in his will of £500 current money for a free grammar school at Childsbury and £100 in like money and a lot for the school, and that several gentlemen in the Province had raised £2,200 in like money to be added to M^r. Child's legacy, and the Act then declared the following trustees of the school and fund, viz   Hon Thomas Broughton, Lieut Governor, Rev^d M^r. Thomas Hasell and Anthony Bonneau, John Harleston, Nathaniel Broughton, Thomas Cordes and Francis Lejau Esq^{rs}

The trustees were to meet at least once every three months at Childsbury and to fill any vacancies among themselves   No one could be a trustee who had not subscribed £100.

With all this the town seems nevertheless to have soon practically disappeared as such

During the lifetime of James Child a part of the 1,200 acres granted him seems to have gone by the name of "Luckens" or "Luckins" plantation or farm and by his will he gave this 'Luckin's Farm" to his grandson, Robert Dix, with a proviso that if he died in infancy then the plantation was to go to the testator's grandson, William Child, son of Isaac Child

Robert Dix did die in infancy, without issue, and Isaac Child, the father of William Child, by his memorial

---

^{1}Dalcho, p 267.
^{2}Stats at Lar   d   p 3

on 16 Febry., 1732, claims as the property of his son and himself 500 acres called "Luckens plantation" part of the "Strawberry land," 477 acres known as the 'Strawberry bluff" adjoining the river, 123 acres called "Oak Grove" part of the "Strawberry Land" and 100 acres called the "Parsonage" also part of the "Strawberry plantation" which tracts together, making 1,200 acres, were granted to James Child on 14 July, 1698, and are "well known by the name of the 'Strawberry plantation'"[13] In the same memorial he claims also for his son William the 600 acres (part of the 800 acre grant) devised by James Child for a commons, and in the memorial of William Child himself made 9 Sept'., 1737,[14] he claims the 1,200 acres or "Lucken's Farm" and the 600 acres called the "Commons"

In 1736, William Child advertises in the Gazette, requiring all persons to whom M' James Child, of Childsberry Town, had sold lots, to produce their titles

From all which it appears that the Town had decayed and the lot owners had abandoned their lots; and that there being no one to use the commons, occupy the lots, or walk the streets, the devisees or heirs of James Child had retaken the property The "college or university" died with the drying of the ink on the parchment (or paper) of the will. The testators' zeal for education was also evidenced by his bequest of all his books and surveying instruments to that son of his son Isaac who should become a Latin scholar, and if none of his sons should so succeed, then they were to go to begin a library in the school house

The name of Childsbury also disappeared and the town site became a part of a plantation The earlier name of Strawberry reasserted itself and has continued

In 1748 the ferry is granted and called as Strawberry ferry and has ever since been so known. The Chapel has always been called, as it still is, Strawberry Chapel Of all that James Child sought to devote to the public use there seems to have taken effect and continued, only the acre and a half for a chapel and burying ground, and for a time

---

[13]Off Hist Comm Memo Bk. 4, p. 18
[14]Ibid, Bk 3, p 189

at least the school house lot, and to neither even of these has his name continued to be attached.

The burial ground around the Chapel is still in use.

"Beneath the giant oaks that shade with their majestic "wings the Strawberry burial ground repose the ancestors of many of those who own property in the Parish."[15] The property so held by James Child subsequently covered four plantations on the river, viz Rice Hope, Strawberry Ferry, Clermont and Elwood D' Irving in his "Day on Cooper River" states that it was at Childsbury that the British forces in the Keowe expedition were landed from their transports and marched under Governor Littleton : and that at the same place Col Wade Hampton took fifty prisoners and burned four vessels laden with valuable stores for the British Army quartered near Biggin Church."[16]

At Strawberry Ferry—i. e the plantation of that name —says the same writer, the "Strawberry Jockey Club" used to hold its annual meetings. The club having been dissolved in 1822, the race course was ploughed up and converted into a corn-field

The exact location of the town and its position with regard to the river cannot be given, for so far as the writer knows there is no plan now in existence From the description of lots in the deeds and other references, it appears to have been on "Strawberry Bluff" on the river on part of the 1,200 acre grant The name is spelt differently in the documents and the printed Statutes The correct form was probably Childsbury, altho' pronounced and more frequently spelt Childsberry

ASHLEY FERRY TOWN

Sometimes called Butler Town and Shem Town

At a very early date a ferry was established over the Ashley River at the point later known as Bee's ferry and where the present railroad bridge of the Atlantic Coast Line Railway crosses the river

In 1711[17] an Act was passed establishing the ferry and

[15]Irving's "Day on Cooper River," (1842), p 10
[16]Ibid. p 23
[17]Statu

laying out a road through the land of M[r] Shem Butler, on the South side of the river to be the road and landing place for the ferry. On the North side of the river the road and landing place were on the plantation of Landgrave Edmund Bellinger (the second Landgrave of the name) then or afterwards called "Stony Point" or "Rocky Point" from the outcrop of the marl near the surface of the land on the river bank

Several grants had been made to Shem Butler of land at that locality, viz

    15 July, 1703,[18] .   .   ..418 acres
    16 July, 1703,[19] .... 1,332 acres
    5 May, 1704,[20] ----------------------------------700 acres

Exactly upon which of these grants the Town was laid out cannot well be ascertained   The existing copy of the "Model" or plan simply says it is on land previously granted to Shem Butler, deceased   The same map states also that the map was made in September, 1724, by the desire of Shem Butler, but apparently after his death   Shem Butler left a will, dated 9 October, 1718, which was probated 9 May, 1723, about which date was the date of his death[21]

By his will, Shem Butler directed all his property to be equally divided between his children and his wife, and apparently the division as made among them was after the Town was laid out, as after that date the lots are found as owned by different distributees.

On 12 July, 1732, his widow, Esther Elliott (who had married since Butler's death, William Elliott) conveyed to Daniel Cartwright twelve of the Town lots at Ashley River Ferry[22]   On 14 June, 1745, Joseph Butler, one of the sons and devisees of Shem Butler, conveys to Benjamin Whitaker eleven lots in "Butler's Town" on the South side of Ashley river.

Daniel Cartwright, on 27 Nov, 1738[23] conveys to John Steel, vintner, lot No 90 at Ashley River bounding on

[18]Off Secy State Grant Bk 38, p 431
[19]Ibid, p 432
[20]Ibid, p 450
[21]Prob Ct Charleston Bk 1722-1724, p 168
[22]M C O Charleston, Bk T, p 453
[23]Ibid, Bk S, p 325

Broad street "the said lot is bluff to the river," and on 26 Novr, 1739,[24] conveys to John Lee, Chairmaker, lot 81 at Ashley River Ferry

In the release from Joseph Butler to Charles Crubin 4 April, 1732,[25] it is "Ashley River Ferry Town (called by the name of Butlers Town)" and so also in the release from Joseph Butler to John Biggs, Blacksmith, 26 April, 1732[26] In the Release from Elizabeth Bellinger to Charles Pinckney, 4 Jany, 1743,[27] the lot is styled as situate in "Shem Town, als Butler Town, at the ferry on Ashley river On the copy of the map of the town in the possession of the writer it is styled "Shem Town"

On 15 Febry, 1723, an Act was passed entitled "An Act "for settling a Fair and Markets in Ashley River Ferry "Town in Berkley County for the better improvement of "the said Ferry, it being a principal Ferry leading to "Charleston"

This Act provided that public and open markets should be held in Ashley River Ferry Town every Wednesday and Saturday without toll for three years, and that two fairs should be held annually on the first Tuesday in May and last Tuesday in September, and that a majority of the inhabitants and residents should purchase and establish a public market place in the town[28]

By an Act passed 22 Septr 1733[29] a grant was made to Edmund Bellinger of the right to maintain the ferry called "Ashley Ferry" from Stony Point, he having for several years maintained a causeway leading to the ferry

To what extent the town grew it is now impossible to say There were transfers of lots between parties and as late as 1751 William Cattell in his will dated 8 August 1751[30] devises a "House at Ashley Ferry." Probably there was always there the usual tavern, inn, or rest house for travellers over the ferry with a blacksmith shop, and general store,

[24]Ibid, Bk V, p. 424
[25]Ibid, Bk K, p 32
[26]Ibid, p 47
[27]Ibid, Bk A A, p 71
[28]Statutes S C, vol 3, p 217
[29]Ibid vol 9 p 82
[30]Prob Ct Charleston Bk 1752-1756 p 15

the usual accompaniment of such places, but the place is not mentioned as a town in any of the descriptions of the province at or near that time and seems to have soon lost all claim to being a town In December, 1821,[n] the ferry was granted to Joseph F Bee, and for many years prior and subsequent to 1860 was generally known as "Bee's ferry" in contradistinction to the ferry over the Ashley River from the City of Charleston, where the bridge now stands

The map annexed to this article is from an old copy of the map of the Town

It was at this ferry that occurred the incident related in James's Life of Marion, where Col Benjamin Thompson of the British Army (afterwards Count Rumford) with a view of crossing the river for the purpose of surprising and capturing General Greene, who was at his headquarters a few miles higher up the river, ordered his cavalry to swim across The tide was at ebb and the banks on each side miry Upon the protest of his next in command Major Fraser, that it was impossible, the attempt was directed to be made by a sergeant, the best trooper and swimmer in the corps, but in the attempt the horse was drowned and the sergeant himself barely saved, and the attempt to cross abandoned

ST ANDREWS TOWN

This was a small projected town laid out contiguous to the Parish Church of St Andrews and not far from Ashley River Ferry Town, on the south side of Ashley River

On 12 October, 1701, a grant of 38 acres of land had been made to Francis Fidling This 38 acres, Francis Fidling, on 24 February, 1701, transferred to Thomas Rose and by several mesne conveyances this 38 acres, together with a house and lot at Ashley River ferry, commonly called Ashley Ferry store, adjoining the 38 acres, with two or three acres of marsh land adjacent, became vested in Thomas Dymes, under whose will his executors sold the whole on 22 May, 1734, to William Cattell[n] Thereafter

[n]Statutes at Large, vol 9, p 510
[n]M C O Charleston, Bk O, p 128

William Cattell laid out the Town on part of the 38 acres under the name of St Andrews Town.[32]

It was very near Ashley River Ferry Town or Butler's Town, being separated from it only by the road to the ferry landing place and a comparatively narrow strip of land, part of the landed property of Shem Butler, which went to his eldest daughter, Elizabeth Butler, who married the second Landgrave, Edmund Bellinger, and after his death Thomas Elliott.

The town, although laid out by William Cattell, was not all on his 38 acres. A part of it was on a tract of 140 acres granted to Francis Fidling, 14 August, 1701, and which had become vested in Abraham Waight, who on 22 July, 1703, conveyed it to Charles Jones.[34] So that a certain number of the lots in the projected town belonged to William Cattell and a certain number to Charles Jones.

Cattell on 6th May, 1735,[35] conveyed to John Haydon, Cordwainer, lot No. 30, and on 15 March, 1736,[36] to Jane Monger lot No. 2 in St. Andrews Town, the deed in each case stating there was a building on the lot conveyed. Charles Jones, on 11 June, 1748,[37] conveys to Elizabeth Fuller three acres in St Andrews Town, bounding West on High Street and South on the King's High Road, and on 6th March, 1755,[38] Charles Jones (to whom the land had come from his father, Charles Jones, deceased) conveyed to Elizabeth Fuller 25 acres immediately adjoining. In 1739 William Cattell conveys to Elizabeth Fuller a lot in St Andrews Town[39] and a little earlier Charles Jones conveys to her lots 1, 14, and 15, in the same town.[40]

Beyond the model of the Town and the record of transfers of lots on it, and the evidence from some of the deeds that there were houses on some of the lots, nothing appears upon the record concerning the Town. It is doubtful if its existence ever went much beyond its plan. Any reason

[32]Ibid. and Book V, p 207
[34]M C O Charleston, Book P. P 448
[35]Ibid, Bk O, p 128
[36]Ibid, Bk V, p 207
[37]Ibid, Bk D D, p 149
[38]Ibid, Bk P P, p 448.
[39]Ibid, Bk X, p 136
[40]Ibid, i 12.

for a town at that point would have applied more strongly to the adjacent Ashley River Ferry Town, immediately at the ferry, and there was not sufficient demand for a town to support one at the latter point

The map is taken from an old copy in the possession of the writer, which recites that the original was made 22 May, 1734

ADDENDA —The following extracts from the *South Carolina Gazette,* August 9 and 16, 1760, show "Shem Town," to have been at that date, a place at least large enough to accommodate the General Assembly, at that time small-pox was an epidemic in Charles Town, and the Cherokee Indians had renewed hostilities

So Ca Gazette, August 9, 1760

' On Wednesday last his honour the lieut governor was pleased to adjourn the general assembly till Wednesday next (the 13th instant), then to meet at *Shem-Town Ashley-Ferry,* in order that all our representatives (many of whom have been prevented from attending by the Small-pox) may assist in deliberating on affairs of the greatest weight and importance to this province at this crisis, which require as well the fullest house as dispatch"

S C Gazette, Aug. 16, 1760

We hear from Shem-Town Ashley-ferry, that a bill has been brought into the commons house of assembly there, and had two readings for forthwith raising a regiment of 1000 men to act against the Cherokees * * *—EDITOR

REGISTER OF
ST ANDREW'S PARISH, BERKELEY COUNTY, SOUTH CAROLINA.

1719-1774

Copied and Edited by Mabel L. Webber.

(Continued from the July Number)

CHRISTNINGS P^r REV^d. Mr MARTYN

Edward Son of John Miles & Anne his wife bapt^d June ye 12th 1757.

William Son of William Royal & Mary his wife Bapt^{zd} June ye 19th 1757

James Son of Benjamin Stone & Elizabeth his wife Baptz^d June ye 19th 1757

Parke Son of Daniel Pepper and Mary his wife Bapt^{zd}. June ye 20th 1757

Benjⁿ Son of Benjamin Elliott & Mary his wife Bapt^{zd} June ye 23^d 1757

Thomas Odingsell Son of Ibid D^o 23^d 1757

Thomas Son of Thomas Scott & Mary his wife Bapt^{zd} Augt 14th, 1757

Cheseman Son of Richard Lake & Mary his wife Baptz^d Octr ye 22^d 1757

Martha Daught^r of Isaac Ladson and Rachel his wife Bapt^{zd} Octr ye 22 1757

Mary Daught^r of Landgrave Bellinger and Mary Luci his wife Bapt^{zd} Novb^r ye 14th 1757

Anne the Daught^r of Thomas Hayward & Anne his wife Bapt^{zd} Nov^{br}. 16th 1757

Anne Daught^r of John Harriss & Elenor his wife Bapt^{zd} Nov^{br} ye 20th 1757

Elizabeth-Rebecca Daught^r. of Edward Legge & Elizabeth his wife Bapt^{zd} Janry ye 15th 1757

William An Adult Negro Man belonging to the Rev^d. Mr Martyn Bapt^{zd} Ja^{ry} 15th 1757

Mary the Daught^r of John Baxter & Anne his wife Bapt^{zd}
March ye 12th 1758

Martha Daught^r of James Smith & Sarah his wife Bapt^{zd}
June ye 18th 1758

Thomas Son of Thomas Godfrey & Elizabeth his wife
Bapt^{zd} June ye 28th 1758

William Son of Samuel Bowman & Keziah his wife Bapt^{zd}
Sep^{tr}. 3^d 1758

Henry Son of Richard Lake & Mary his wife Bapt^{zd} Octo^{br}
ye 3^d or thra^{bt} 1758

BURIALS PR THE REV^d Mr MARTYN

Henry Wood Sn^r Buried April 6th 1758 Interrd without a
Minister

Charles Cattell Buried April ye 9th 1758 p^r ye Rev^d M^r
Martyn

Richard Godfrey Buried April 24th 1758, inter^d. without a
minister

Edward Pickrin at James Island Buried April ye 10th 1758
intr^d without a Minister.

Wilowbey West Buried May ye 4th 1758 inter^d without a
minister

John Cattell Son of Benjn Buried May ye 14th 1758

Elizabeth Yonge widow Buried Septr 9th 1758

Elizabeth Mock a Dutch Girl that Lived at Capt Thomas
Fullers Buried Septr 18th 1758 inter^d without a minister

A young Infant Son of Doct^r Thomas Honour & Rebecca
his wife Buried Octo^{br} 26, 1758

Mary Carr widow Buried 1758

Sarah Butler widow Buried March ye 5th 1759.

Isaac Nicholas of St Pauls Parrish Buried March ye 9th
1759 p^r Rev^d M^r. Martyn

William Miles Buried May ye 6th 1759 p^r ye Rev^d M^r
Smith.

Susanah Barlow widow Buried Septr ye 1st 1759

Mary ye wife of Jehu Elliott of St. Pauls Parish Buried
p^r ye Revd Mr Martyn May 1759

Cathrine the wife of Thomas Ferguson Buried Feb^{ry} y^e
11th 1760 p^r the Anabaptist Minister Mr Wheeler

Edward Mortimore Buried at M' John Harveys April 17th 1760

Philip Son of Jacob Stone & Barbrey his wife Buried May y' 4th 1760 Inter^d without a minister

Grace Hitchinson (a poor woman) Lived with Mrs Gordon Intrd. without a Minister June y' 4th 1760.

Hanah Anger widow Buried July y' · 18th 1760

Elizabeth Williamson wdow of St. Paul's Parish Buried at M'. Ferguson's p' the Anabaptis Minister M'. Wheeler August y' 31st 1760.

Elizabeth the Daughter of Thomas Godfrey & Elizabeth his wife Buried Sept'. y'. 7th. 1760 Inter^d. without a minister

Frances Daughtr of John Miles & Anne his wife Buried Sept' y' 15th 1760

George Son of George Tray & Christian his wife Buried Sept' 22^d 1760

BIRTHS

John Son of David Conoly & Sarah his wife Born Feber' y' 11th 1758

William Son of Samuel Bowman & Keziah his wife born April y' 15th 1758

Henry Son of Richard Lake & Mary his wife born Octo^{br} y' 3^d 1758.

James Son of Samuel West & Mary his Wife Born Octo^{br}. y' 22^d 1758

Hanah Daught' of George Tray and Christian his wife born Decb'. 20th 1758

Jennet Daugh^{tr} of Mary Wood widow to Henry Wood Deces^d. Born August 9th 1758

Frances Daughter of John Miles & Anne his wife born March y' 27th 1759

Binkey the Daughter of William Elliott and Sabinah his wife born March y' 4th 1758.

Sarah Daughter of Patrick Hughs & Rebecca his wife born [no date given]

Mary Daughter of Ibid born [no date]

Elizabeth Daughter of Michal Hoates & Catherine his wife . born [no date]

Philip Sone of Jacob Stone & barbrey his wife born May
  y° 20ᵗʰ 1759

Love y° Daughtʳ of Collᵒ Robᵗ Rivers & Elizabeth his
  wife born July y° 4ᵗʰ 1759

Elizabeth Daughter of Johnathan Rivers & Francis his
  wife born Augsᵗ y° 28ᵗʰ 1759

Mary Daughᵗ of William Chapman & Eloner his wife born
  y° 19ᵗʰ. Septʳ 1759

Charles Fuller the Son of the Revᵈ Charles Martyn &
  Sarah his wife was Born Novᵇʳ y° 10ᵗʰ 1758

Hester the Daughter of Thomas Hayward & Anne his wife
  Born Octoᵇʳ y° 25ᵗʰ 1759

James Son of John Ekerman & Mary his wife Born Jamᵉ
  Island 1759

Anne the Daughter of John Baxter & Anne his wife born
  June y° 9ᵗʰ 1758

James Son of William Mell & Elizabeth his wife born Janʳʳ
  23ᵈ. 1760

Thomas Son of Thomas Drayton Esqʳ & Lady Mary his
  wife born Octoᵇʳ y° 1ˢᵗ 1759

Rebecah Daughᵗ of Benjamin Perry & Susanah his wife
  born in Sᵗ Pauls Parrish Born Febrʸ y° 19ᵗʰ 1758—
  Baptᶻᵈ pʳ Revᵈ Mʳ Barron

Joseph Son of Ibid born Octobʳ y° 27ᵗʰ 1759 Baptᶻᵈ pʳ Revᵈ
  Mʳ Tonng [Tonge]

Benjamin-Smith Son of Edward Legge & Elizᵇᵗᵇ his wife
  Born July· 18ᵗʰ 1759

Ann-Barnett Daughᵗ. of William Elliott & Sabina his wife
  born April the 8ᵗʰ 1760

William Son of William Elliott and Sabina his wife born
  Decmᵇʳ 26ᵗʰ 1764

CHRISTININGS Pʳ THE REVᵈ Mʳ MARTYN.

James Son of Samˡˡ West & Mary his Wife Baptᶻᵈ Novᵇʳ.
  y° 12ᵗʰ 1758 pʳ Revᵈ Mʳ Martyn

Hanah Daughter of George Tray & Christian his wife
  Baptᶻᵈ. Febʳʳ y° 25ᵗʰ 1759

Jennet Daughᵗ of Mary Wood widow to Henry Wood
  Baptᶻᵈ Septʳ 6ᵗʰ 1759

Frances Daughter of John Miles & Anne his wife Bapt^d April ye 4th 1759 P^rr. B^rrm

Joseph Anger an adult Bapt^d April 22^d 1759

Rebecah the wife of Patrick Hughs Bapt^d. June ye 16th 1759

{ Sarah the Daughter of Patrick Hughs & Rebeccah his wife Bapt^d June 16 1759

{ Mary Daught^r of Ibid Bapt^d 16th June 1759

Elizabeth the Daughter of Michal Hoates & Catherine his wife Bapt^d. June ye 17th 1759

Philip Son of Jacob Stone & Barbrey his wife Bapt^d June ye 17th 1759

Love the Daught^r of Coll^o Robt Rivers and Eliz^bth Bapt^d August 5th 1759

Elizabeth Daught^r of Johnathan Rivers & Eliz^bth his wife Bapt^d Septr 30th. 1759

Mary Daught^r of William Chapman & Eloner his wife Bapt^d. Nov^br. 18th 1759

Charles the Son of the Revd Charles Martyn & Sarah his wife Bapt^d Nov^br 18th 1759

Hester the Daughter of Thomas Hayward & Anne his wife Bapt^d Decb^r ye 23^d 1759

Thomas Son of John Drayton Esqr & Margaret his wife Bapt^d August ye 31st 1759.

James Son of John Ekerman & Mary his wife Bapt^d Janu^ry. ye 20th 1760

Anne the Daughter of John Baxter & Anne his wife Bapt^d Feb^ry ye 12th 1760

Thomas Son of Thomas Drayton Esqr & Lady Mary his wife, Bapt^d Jan^ry ye 1st 1760

James Son of William Mell & Elizabeth his wife Bapt^d Feb^ry. ye 1st 1760

Benj^mn Smith Son of Edward Legge & Elizabeth his wife Recev^d into the Congregation Privatly Bapt^d before July ye 27th 1760

Elizabeth Daught^r of Thomas Godfrey and Elizabeth his wife Bapt^d p^r ye Rev^d. Mr Copp, Septr ye 5th 1760

MARRIAGES.

George Purkis & Mary Jones Widow Married p[r] the Rev[d]. M[r] Martyn Octo[br] y[e] 30th 1758

Doctor Colmondley Dearing & Elizabeth Bellinger widow Married Octob[r]. y[e] 31st. 1758 p[r] the Rev[d] M[r] Smith Assistant in Cha Town

William Hoster & Angelica Marit Married p[r] the Rev[d]. M[r]. Martyn Nov[br] 19th 1758

Abraham Remington & Anne Cattell Sp[r] Married January y[e] 26th 1759

Francis Rose & Sarah Balentine Sp[r]. Married p[r] the Rev[d]. [Blank] Feb[ry] 23[d] 1759

Aurthur Deloney & Sarah Bodington widow Married Feb[ry] y[e] 19th 1759

Coll[o] Henry Hyrne & Mary Golightley wd[ow] Married p[r] y[e] Rev[d] M[r] Martyn June 26th 1759

William Drayton & Mary Motte Spr of Charles Town Married p[r] y[e] Rev[d] M[r]. Cooper of Prince Williams Parish Octob[r]. 4th 1759

Edward Miles & Elizabeth Melachamp sp[r]. Married April y[e] 17th 1760

Benjamin Stone & Ruth Rivers Sp[r] Married May y[e] 22[d]. 1760

John Perry & Mary Wood widow married July y[e] 7th 1760

Samuel Huey & Gennet Brown Sp[r] Married July y[e] 7th 1760

Petter Legear & Elizabeth Hague Sp[r] Married Nov[br]. y[e] 16th 1760

Samuel Boone & Keziah Rivers Sp[r] Married Feb 20th 1761

Thomas Slan & Mary Cattell widow married p[r] Rev[d] M[r]. Sergint[1] April 30th 1761

Whitmarsh Fuller & Judith Simpson Sp[r]. Married p[r]. Rev[d]. M[r] Copp[2] July y[e] 2[d] 1761

Jan[ry] 11 1762 John Franks & Catherine Hoats wd[o] Married p[r] Dutch Minister[3]

---

[1]Rev Winwood Serjeant, of St George's, Dorchester (Dalcho, page 349)
[2]Rev Jonathan Copp of St John's, Colleton (Ibid, 361)
[3]Probably the Rev H G B Wordmann, of St John's Lutheran Church, Charles Town

Matthew Smallwood & Judith Grace Spʳ. Married pʳ yᵉ
Revᵈ. Mʳ Searjent at Sᵗ George Dorchester Januʳʸ. yᵉ
25ᵗʰ 1762

John Beale & Mary Ross Spʳ Married pʳ the Revᵈ. Mʳ.
Searjent March yᵉ 18ᵗʰ 1762

John Godfrey & Elizabeth Cha:pell wid°ʷ. Married pʳ yᵉ
Revᵈ. Mʳ Smith Octʳ. 1762.

George Tew & Mary Lambright Spʳ married Septʰʳ 23ᵈ.
1760 pʳ. yᵉ Revᵈ. Mʳ. Martyn.

BIRTHS

Elizabeth Daughtʳ: of Thomas Godfrey & Elizabeth his
wife Born Septʳ 8ᵗʰ. 1759.

George Son of George Tray & Christian his wife Born
Septʳ. 7ᵗʰ: 1760

Gilbert the Son of Joseph Elliott & Sarah his wife Born
1756.

James-Mathews Son of Henry Cannon and Susanah his
wife Born—1760

John Son of George Rusel & Sarah his Wife Born Septʳ.
yᵉ 8ᵗʰ 1760   James Island.

George Son of Jacob Hinkle & Hanah his wife born—1760

Sarah Daughtʳ of John Samways & Mary his Wife born
Decbʳ. yᵉ 24ᵗʰ 1760.

John Son of Thomas Godfrey & Elizabeth his wife born—
1760

Samuel Son of Samuell Bowman & Keziah his wife Born
May yᵉ 3ᵈ 1761

Elizabeth yᵉ Daughter of Edward Miles & Elizabeth his
wife born—1761

Anne-Elizabeth Daughter of John Baxter & Anne his Wife
Born Febʳʸ yᵉ 4ᵗʰ 1761

Martin Son of Roger Palmor & —— his —— [sic]

Roger Son of Ibid Born—1758

Thomas Son of Thomas Fuller & Lyda his wife born
March yᵉ 11ᵗʰ 1760

Sarah Daughtʳ of Edward Legge & Elizabeth his wife born
yᵉ 28ᵗʰ July 1761

Anne the Daughter of William Chapman & Elenor his Wife
Born August yᵉ 1ᵗʰ 1761

Susanah Daught^r of John Miles & Anne his wife born
Dec^{br}. y. 16th: 1761

Martha Daught^r of William Fuller & Sarah his wife Born
Feb^{ry} 3^d 1761

Thomas Son of William Mell & Anne his wife Born Octo^{br}
24th 1761

Martha Daught^r of Benjamin Marion and Margret his wife
born Septr ye 4th 1761

Elizabeth Daught^r. of Benjamin Marion & Margret his
wife Born Octo^{br}. 4th, 1759.

BURIALS P^r Y^e REV^d Mr MARTYN

Dr John Linning Buried Septr ye 16th 1760

Elizabeth the Daught^r. of Capt. Isaac Ladson & Rachel his
wife Buried Septr ye 23^d 1760

William Son of John Miles & Anne his Wife Buried Sept^r
ye 25th 1760

Maria Weaver wdo^w Buried Septr ye 30th 1760

Sarah the Daughter of Patrick Hughs and Rebecca his
wife Buried Octo^{br} 2^d 1760 interr'd without a minister

Elizabeth the Daught^r of Michael Hoates & Catherine his
wife Buried Oct^r · 2^d. 1760 interr'd without a Minister

Gilbert Son of Joseph Elliott and Sarah his wife Buried
Octob^r. ye 22^d 1760

Elizabeth the Wife of Capt Francis Lander Buried Octob^r
ye 30th 1760

Mary-Booth the Daught^r of Thomas Ferguson & Catherine
his wife Buried Octr 30th 1760

Mary the Wife of Benjamin Elliott Buried Novb^r ye 5th
1760

Thomas Drayton Buried Nov^{br} ye 13th 1760

Martha the Daughter of James Smith Buried p^r the Rev^d.
Mr Serjin of St Georges Nov^{br} ye 13th 1760.

Bridget the wife of John Gordon of Chas Town Buri^d p^r
ye Revd Mr Tonge Nov^{br} 26 1760

John Guerin Son of Mathewrⁿ Guerin &——his wife Buried
p^r Mr Wheler the Bapts' Teacher Decr. 4, 1760

Thomas Elliott Sn^r of St Pauls Parish Buried Dec^{br} 25th
1760   Buried p^r Rev^d M^r. Tong

Benjamin Cattell Buried Janu^{ry} y^{e}· 17th: 1761

Mary ye wife of John Smith Buried Janu^{ry} 25th: 1761

Elizabeth the wife of Thomas Melachamp Buried p^{r} the
    Anabap^{ist}. Teacher Mr Wheler Jan^{ry} 22^{d}. 1761

Thomas Godfrey alis Gearnear Buried Feb. ye 20th 1761
    interred without a Minister.

Michal Hoates Buried p^{r} Rev^{d} M^{r}. Martyn May 10th 1761

CHRISTININGS

George Son of George Tray & Christian his wife Bapt^{td}
    Septr 18th 1760

Gillbert the Son of Joseph Elliott & Sarah his wife Bapt^{td}.
    Octo^{br}. y^{e}. 10th 1760

James-Mathews Son of Henry Cannon & Susanah his wife
    Bapt^{td} Decb^{r} 28th 1760

John Son of George Rusel & Sarah his wife Bapt^{td} Janu^{ry}
    ye 18th 1761

George Son of Jacob Hinkle & Hanah his wife Bapt^{td}.
    Feb^{ry} 1st 1761

Sarah Daughter of John Samways & Mary his wife Bapt^{td}.
    April ye 14th 1761

John Son of Thomas Godfrey Des^{cd}. and Elizabeth his wife
    Bap^{tzd}. April ye 18th 1761

Samuel Son of Samuel Bowman & Keziah his Wife Bapt^{td}
    May 26th 1761

Elizabeth Daughter of Edward Miles & Elizabeth his Wife
    Bapt^{td} May 30th. 1761

Anne-Elizabeth Daughter of John Baxter & Anne his wife
    Bapt^{td}. June ye 2^{d}. 1761

Martin Son of Roger Palmor & —— Bapt^{zd} June ye 2^{d}
    1761

Roger Son of Ibid Bapt^{zd} June 2^{d} 1761

Thomas Son of Thomas Fuller & Lyda his wife Bapt^{td}
    April y^{e} —— 1761

Anne ye Daught^{r} of William Chapman & Elenor his wife
    Bapt^{td} Nov^{br}. 22^{d}. 1761

Sarah Daught^{r} of Edward Legg & Elizabeth his wife
    Bapt^{td} p^{r}. Revd Mr Serjeant Augs^{t}. 28 priv^{t} Bap^{tizm}
    1761

Thomas Son of William Mell & Anne his wife Bapt^{ed}. p^r
  ye Revd Mr Peirce Jany 17th 1762
Martha Daugh^r. of William Fuller & Sarah his wife Bapt^{ed}.
  p^r Revd Mr Peirce January ye 17th 1762.
Elizabeth the Daught^r of Benjamin Marion & Margaret his
  Wife Bapt^{ed}. Nov^{hr} ye 20th 1762
Martha Daugh^{tt}. of Ibid Bapt^{ed} 20 Nov^{br} 1762

(To be continued)

ORDER BOOK

of

John Faucheraud Grimké.

August 1778 to May 1780.

(Continued from the July Number)

Head Quarters, Purisburgh.

February 19, 1779

L^t: Moore is to proceed to Fort Johnson & join Capt Mitchells Company in which He is to do Duty until further orders. They are to have a Cart to Convey their Baggage, which the Quarter Master is to furnish them with.

G: O. Parole, Upright. Countersigns } Unity Use

The Night Piquets are not to be withdrawn until after sunrise.

20: R. O. by Coll^o. Roberts.

Officer of the Day tomorrow Capt. Lieut. Weaver.

Ordered that the Quarter Master issue a **gill of Rum** to the Men of the Corps of Artillery as Usual.

G: O: Morn^g. Parole, Wisdom.

Countersigns } Worth Wealth

1 Capt: 2 L^{ts}: 2 Serg^t & 40 Rank & File to Relieve the Guard at Zubly's to march immediately.

O: by Col^o: Huger Com^t:

1 Serg^t: 1 Corp: & 12 Privates from the 1st & 2^d. Brigades to Parade immediately before the Camp with 18 rounds each & there to receive their orders.

21: R: O. by Col^o: Roberts

Officer of the Day tomorrow Capt. Mitchell

Two carpenters are to be sent to assist the Workmen employed by the Dep: Quartermaster Gen:

A Rammer & Sponge Staff to be got immediately for the small Field-Piece.

O. by Col^o: Huger.

Parole. Lincoln Countersigns } Brave Virtue

The Revieller to beat every morning at break of Day at which Time all officers & Soldiers of each Corps are to Parade with their Baggage & Accountrements Compleat, & the Horses geered, this to be continued every Morning 'till further Orders.

When the waggon Horses are turned out, the Waggoners are to attend their Teams.

22: R: O. by Col.° Roberts.

Officer of the Day tomorrow Cap.ᵗ. Davis

    O. by Col.° Huger

    Parole, Moultrie

                Countersigns } Acton / Worthy

23ᵈ. R: O. by Col.°: Roberts,

Officer of the Day tomorrow Cap.ᵗ. L.ᵗ. Donnom.

Parole, Rutledge. Countersigns } Liberty / Protect

24ᵗʰ. R: O. by Col.°. Roberts.

Officer of the Day to-morrow Cap.ᵗ. Weaver.

    G: O:

The General Court Martial of which Lieut. Col.°. M°Intosh is President, now Sitting for the Tryal of such Prisoners as might be brought before them have Reported W.ᵐ. Dunning of the 6ᵗʰ N.°: Carolina Battalion charged with Desertion who pleaded Guilty Sentenced to receive 100 lashes on his bare Back.

The General approves the Sentence & Orders it to be Executed tomorrow morning at Troop beating.

Jos: Grimes a Serjt. in the Light Infantry charged with dressing himself like a Girl & being out of Camp after Retreat & Reprimanded at the Head of the Brigade to which he belonges.

The General approves the Sentence & orders it to be put in execution tomorrow Morning at Troop beating.

John Conway Ladson Serj.ᵗ. in the 1.ˢᵗ. S.°. Carolina Regiment, charged with threatening to kill Lieut. Lewis, acquitted.

The General Court Martial of which Lieut'. Col'. McIntosh is President is Dissolved.

The Deputy Barrack Master is ordered to supply the Officers & Soldiers with Wood & Candles in the following proportions.

A Brigadier General ½ a Cord of wood & 2 pounds of Candles per week.

Field Officers & Captains ¼ of a Cord of Wood & 1 pound of Candles per Week. Subalterns of each Company ¼ of a Cord of Wood and one Pound of Candles per Week.

Non Commissioned officers & Privates, not more than ten or less than six in a Mess, ¼ of a Cord of Wood & ¼ of a Pound of Candles per Week.

The Guards & and Sick to receive Double the Allowance.

25ᵗʰ. R : O. by Col'. Roberts.

Officer of the Day to-morrow Capt. Lt. Weaver.

G : O :   Parole, Antrim ; Countersigns ⎱ Andrew ⎰ Archer

All Punishments whether General or Regimental are to be inflicted at Guard-mounting in the Morning.

Six Light Horsemen from Col': Horry's Corps & Two from St. Gambles will Parade every morning with the Guards : Four of them to attend the Field officer of the Day as an Escort, Two at Head-Quarters & Two to march with the Guard to Zubly's Ferry.

---

26 :   R : O : Col': Roberts

Officer of the Day to morrow.

G : O. Parol.   Countersigns

The Troops will in future Exercise from 6 to 8 öClock in the Morning & from ½ past 4 to ½ past 6 öClock in the Evenings. The Com: officer on the Right will direct the Signal for turning out—which will be the Long Roll followed immediately by three Ruffles.

A Court Martial is to sit tomorrow for the tryal of all Prisoners Witnesses to attend. President of the Court Martial Lt: Col: Harkston Members 4 Cap'. & 3 Sub'.

from Col: Huger's, 2 Cop[ts]. & 2 Sub[s]: from Col°: Summers Brigade.

27th. R: O: by Col Roberts

Ordered that Rum be delivered as usual to Corps of Artillery this Afternoon.

A Court Martial to sit immediately for the tryal of Michael Kenleven.

President

Capt. Davis

Capt. Lieut Elliott }
Lieu[t]. Field } Members.

G: O: Parole, Circumspection

Countersigns } Caution
} Close

The Army will hold themselves in readiness to March at a Moment's warning. after orders by Col°. Roberts [space blank]

28: In Consequence of the above orders the Detachment marched off the ground at 9 oClock next morning & reached M[r]. Williamsons Plantation (the Magazine) about 5 in the Evening 16 miles distant from Purisburgh & Proceeded next Morning at 5 ôClock to Capt: Staffords, a march of 10 Miles. This being the last Post where any Provision was laid up for the Men & Horses the remainder of the Day was employed in Distributing the Ammunition & Baggage equally between the waggons, in Sending for Provisions for the Horses & having it divided amongts the Teams that the load might be more easily carried.

This Precaution was exceedingly fortunate, as no fodder could be obtained at M[rs]. Neyles where the Detachment encamped on the Evening of the 2[d]. March after a disagreable & Tedious March of 12 Miles thro a rotten deep Pine barron, in which the Waggons were frequently stalled. At 12 ôClock in the Subsequent Day the Detachment arrived at Matthews Bluff 10 Miles distant from their last encampment, Where they immediately pitched their Tents & refreshed themselves. Capt. Mitchell was dispatched to Gen: Ash to receive orders for the further Conduct of this

Detachment & this Interval was employed in putting all the ammunition & the Field Pieces into the Boat ready to cross the River, which was completed before the return of the Express   Cap' Mitchell arrived at 5 oClock precisely & had scarce communicated the orders before a firing was heard Application was immediately made to General Rutherford for 100 of his men to cross the River with the Artillery to assist in remounting the Pieces & Cover them should occasion require   This request was immediately complied with   The Troops crossed, had landed & fixed one of the Field Pieces ready for Service when the arrival of Gen · Ashe rendered this attempt to Succour his Troops Useless   The Artillery was immediately rebarked by his orders & again Crossed the River   The Militia under Gen. Rutherford assisted most chearfully in landing & remounting the Pieces which they were disposed off to cover the Flight of our Defeated Troops & their passing over the River.   It Appears that Our Camp at Bryar Creek was surprised, that the Enemy had crossed about 8 Miles higher up the River than where we were posted & had attacked Us in the rear, that our Troops had no Cartridges delivered out to them previous to the Engagement & that the Enemy's Movement was so rapid that the firing begun before Our troops had formed.   A Total Rout ensued & had not the Cont Geo · Brigade & Col° Parker's Regiment of North Carolinians bravely supported the fire of the Enemy almost every Man would have been taken Prisoner   The Troops fled precipitately & saved themselves by Swimming Bryar Creek & the River Savannah in which attempt many were drowned   Gen Elbert was taken Prisoner, having remained too long on the Field with his handful of Troops. Our loss is supposed not to amount to more than 200 killed, wounded, & taken; five Waggon loads fixed Ammunition for the Infantry, & One brass four Pounder with Two Small Iron Pieces fell into the Enemy's hands   At 10 ôClock of the same Evening Gen · Rutherford's Brigade & one Piece of Artillery were ordered by Gen. Ashe to Return & by forced Marches (having made but two halts before they reached the Sisters) arrived about 5 ôClock in the afternoon of the subsequent Day   A March of 32 miles in 19 Hours the artillery however was ordered to Proceed to Mr Wilhamsons Plantation, where they lay on their Arms until one ôClock & then renewed their March by Express Orders of Gen Ashe, to Mr Porcher's plantation 6 miles further. The Men of this Small Detachment were carried in the Waggons during this last march, being so fatigued that they could no longer travel on foot On the Morning of the 5th Gen: Ashe called in and visited the Detachment of Artillery, acquainted the Com^r officer that He was going to Purisburgh & would obtain immediate Orders for the Detachment This assurance being given an Express to Gen Lincoln was Stopped, but no Orders were rec^d ; in consequence of this Lt Rudd was sent with Dispatches to Gen · Lincoln on the 6th & at one ôClock orders were rec^d for the Detachment to March to the Sisters, where they arrived about 6 oClock in the afternoon & found the other Field Piece which had been detained at Mathewes' bluff until 10 ôClock in Morning of the 4th. The Consequences of Gen Ashes Surprise has filled our Troops with Consternation, disarmed at least one Thousand Men. put the Enemy in possession of Augusta once more, & Exposed the Frontiers of S^o Carolina from the Sisters upwards to the inroads of the Enemy's light Horse. & left them an open Communication with the Back Country Tories This action as well as the one at Savannah, with the Continual Usage of the Enemy proves, that the Militia ought to be well supported by Continental Troops, when brought to action The Stores at the Magazine are ordered to be removed to Pocotaligo at the Church near Sheldon The Troops are forming an abbatis round the Encampment at the Sisters.

(To be continued)

INDEX

LIST OF PUBLICATIONS

OF THE

SOUTH CAROLINA HISTORICAL SOCIETY.

COLLECTIONS.

Vol. I., 1857, $3.00; Vol. II., 1858, $3.00; Vol. III., 1859, out of print. Vol IV., 1887, unbound, $3.00, bound, $4.00; Vol. V., 1897, paper, $3.00.

PAMPHLETS.

Journal of a Voyage to Charlestown in So. Carolina by Pelatiah Webster in 1765. Edited by Prof. T. P. Harrison, 1898. 75c.

The History of the Santee Canal. By Prof. F. A. Porcher. With an Appendix by A. S. Salley, Jr., 1903. 75c.

THE SOUTH CAROLINA HISTORICAL AND GENEALOGICAL MAGAZINE.

Volume I, 1900, Edited by A. S. Salley, Jr. Complete Volume. $10.00

Single copies of Nos. 2-4, $1.25 each.

Volume II to IX, 1901-1908, Edited by A. S. Salley, Jr. Unbound $5 00 each.

Volume X to XIII, 1909-1912, Edited by Mabel L. Webber. Unbound $5.00 each.

Members get a discount of 25 per cent. on the above prices.

Address: South Carolina Historical Society,
Charleston, S. C.